TOM DRIBERG

HIS LIFE AND INDISCRETIONS

Francis Wheen

Pan Books
in association with Chatto & Windus

First published in 1990 by Chatto & Windus Ltd
This edition published in 1992 by Pan Books Ltd,
Cavaye Place, London SW10 9PG
in association with Chatto & Windus Ltd

9 8 7 6 5 4 3 2 1

© Francis Wheen 1990

Previously unpublished material by Tom Driberg © Bruce Hunter 1990

ISBN 0 330 31897 7

Printed in England by Clays Ltd, St Ives plc

for Joan Smith
and Beatrice, Sidney,
Bertie and Lettice

CONTENTS

LIST OF ILLUSTRATIONS

INTRODUCTION

On the morning of Thursday 12 August 1976, as Britain sweltered through the hottest summer anyone could remember, an elderly gentleman alighted stiffly from the Oxford train on to the *terra firma* of Paddington station. A couple of minutes later he hailed a taxi. His destination was the Barbican, on the other side of London.

He was a tall, burly figure, but his slight stoop and squint gave him the air of one peering down at a congregant who was about to receive Holy Communion. He looked, as his friends never tired of remarking, like a bishop. The voice, too, was episcopal: rich and round and sonorous, though fading slightly with age; a voice you might expect to find issuing from the pulpit of some vast, echoing cathedral. He carried a walking-stick.

In Bayswater, only a mile or so from Paddington, the cab-driver was alarmed to notice his passenger slumped at an awkward angle in the seat. Shouts from the front failed to rouse him. The cabbie turned up towards Praed Street and drove at high speed to St Mary's Hospital, but it was too late. By the time he arrived the passenger was already dead. The cause of death was given as heart failure. The deceased was identified as a peer of the realm, the Lord Bradwell of Bradwell-juxta-Mare in the county of Essex. The title had been conferred only a few months earlier. For the other seventy of his seventy-one years, he had been known as Tom Driberg.

The next morning *The Times*'s obituary column drew itself up to its full height and pronounced:

Tom Driberg, who worked for some years under the name of William Hickey and died under the name of Lord Bradwell, was a journalist, an intellectual, a drinking man, a gossip, a high churchman, a liturgist, a homosexual, a friend of Lord Beaverbrook, an enemy of Lord Beaverbrook, an employee and biographer of Lord Beaverbrook, a politician of the left, a member of Parliament, a member of the Labour Party National Executive, a stylist, an unreliable man of undoubted distinction. He looked and talked like a bishop, not least in the bohemian clubs which he frequented. He was the admiration and despair of his friends and acquaintances.

Until the 1980s, it should be remembered, *The Times* was still regarded as a paper of quality; not least by Tom himself, who once described it as 'an almost perfect newspaper'.[1] He was inordinately proud of the fact that in 1970 he had been a finalist – won the bronze medal, as he preferred to put it – in *The Times*'s first National Crossword Championship.

How did such an obituary come to be printed? At an editorial conference on the day of Tom's death the deputy editor, Louis Heren, asked how the paper intended to mark the passing of Lord Bradwell; he was shown a yellowing proof that had been on the stocks for years, dull and respectful, little more than an extended *Who's Who* entry. Both Heren and William Rees-Mogg, the editor, thought this inadequate. The two of them sat down in Rees-Mogg's office and jointly composed the opening paragraph quoted above. Thus it was that Tom became the first figure in public life to be exposed as a homosexual in his own *Times* obituary. He might not have minded, but some readers were startled. The editor of *New Society*, Paul Barker, who did not know Tom, recalled later the jolt of astonishment he felt when he reached the words 'a homosexual'; the obituary 'has stayed in my mind ever since'.[2]

Other Fleet Street farewells were more circumspect. 'Driberg: conscience of the Left' was the *Guardian*'s front-page assessment. The obituary in the same paper described him as 'one of the last of the well-rounded men'. The *Daily Mirror* reported his death under an eccentric headline – 'Driberg the diary king dies at 71' – which made him sound like a tycoon who had cleaned up in year-planners. It was actually a reference to the William Hickey column, which he had written in the *Daily Express* forty years earlier.

A man who toils on the backbenches of the House of Commons

for almost thirty years without achieving even the lowliest ministerial office, and who wins a mild celebrity for his evanescent work
as a newspaper columnist, can usually expect a few obituaries
followed by a long and untroubled rest in the quiet earth. But it was
soon apparent that Tom Driberg would not enjoy such gentle
oblivion.

Most of Fleet Street knew that Tom had been writing his
memoirs. Only a few friends had actually seen the work-in-
progress, and some of them had been deeply alarmed by the whole
project. Their hints and mutters had fuelled a runaway train of
rumour which Tom did nothing to discourage. He teasingly let it be
known that the book would be called *Ruling Passions*.[3] He promised to be indiscreet, and there was no reason to doubt him: having
been a tireless and salacious gossip for decades, he certainly had
plenty of indiscretions to commit. 'Drinking with him for an
evening,' according to his old parliamentary colleague John
Freeman, 'was like listening to a sort of underworld Arabian
nights.'[4] If Tom had set down in writing the scandalous anecdotes
with which he had for so long regaled acquaintances – well, a few
minds would boggle, to say the least. A few reputations might have
to be urgently reconsidered, too. If he had included the Nye Bevan
story, for instance . . .

It was irresistibly reminiscent of the panic provoked by the
memoirs of the Hon. Galahad Threepwood. As readers of P. G.
Wodehouse's *Summer Lightning* will know, ever since Threepwood
had announced that he was writing the book

all over England, among the more elderly of the nobility and gentry,
something like a panic had been raging . . . whole droves of respectable
men who in their younger days had been rash enough to chum with the
Hon. Galahad were recalling past follies committed in his company and
speculating agitatedly as to how good the old pest's memory was.
For Galahad in his day had been a notable lad about town.[5]

So, most assuredly, had Tom; and no one doubted how good
the old pest's memory was. But how much of it had he put on
paper? The Londoner's Diary in the *Evening Standard* reported, on
the morning after Tom's death, that 'the fireworks which Lord

Bradwell promised in his forthright autobiography may never explode in the literary and political world.' The manuscript was hopelessly incomplete and 'there was considerable speculation about whether it would be published at all'. Several friends sighed with relief.

Not for long. Two days later a *Sunday Times* headline yelled: 'Driberg's time-bomb: 70,000 saucy words'.

The story hardly lived up to its billing. For it seemed that although there were indeed more than 70,000 words in typescript, Tom had not got beyond his entry into Parliament in 1942. 'Sadly, the author took the saucier secrets of the Palace of Westminster to the grave with him,' the *Sunday Times* concluded. No Nye Bevan story after all. More sighs of relief in certain quarters.

Other public figures may have escaped, but he had certainly not spared himself. In the chapters already written he revealed that he was a man of voracious promiscuity who had spent much of his life 'cottaging' – hanging around public lavatories in search of pick-ups. He had omitted some of his more outrageous sexual stories: no mention, for instance, of the evening he met a uniformed London policeman walking across Hungerford Bridge and without a word, after the merest glance of consent, knelt down and fellated him. But there was still more than enough to cause a scandal.

Behind the scenes a bitter squabble then began, which has continued to this day. Would Tom have wanted *Ruling Passions* to be published in its unfinished state? Some friends – notably his former secretary Rosemary Say – insisted that he would not. Once he had finished writing the book he would have seen the folly of uninhibited confession and would have revised the earlier sections, cutting out most of the cottaging episodes. Besides, the thing was unbalanced: scarcely a word about his long political career, his chairmanship of the Labour Party, his good works, his beloved house at Bradwell. Readers might get the idea that Tom Driberg's only interest in life was sucking men's cocks.

For the people who were in a position to decide the typescript's fate, however, there were stronger imperatives in favour of publication. The publishing house Jonathan Cape had paid Tom advances totalling £5,000 for the book and now hoped, understandably, to see some return on its investment. The only man who might have been able to prevent them from going ahead was Tom's literary agent David Higham, who had been appointed Special Trustee responsible for dealing with the memoirs. But his attitude was that he had a bargain with Cape; he would honour it.

And so, at a time when the name of Tom Driberg might otherwise have been slipping forever out of public consciousness, it was thrust forward again, garish with posthumous notoriety. Jonathan Cape announced that *Ruling Passions* would be published on 23 June 1977. In spite of the promise that Tom had defamed nobody but himself, some former colleagues were still queasily anxious about 'Driberg's time-bomb'. Humphry Berkeley recalled: 'As the publication date drew near, one septuagenarian took to his sick-bed. "Tell him I think it's all right," I was able to say on the telephone to his young male companion, "his name is not in the index." I was relieved to hear that he felt well enough to take some vegetable broth for his evening meal.'[6]

The weekend before publication, the *Sunday Telegraph*'s political correspondent, Ian Waller, reported that Labour MPs were 'uneasily awaiting . . . one of the most sensational and scandalous political memoirs ever to have been published. They fear it may provoke a damaging backlash.'

On the day itself, *Ruling Passions* was a news story as well as a book to be reviewed. 'The much-touted-in-advance revelations of sex in high places, with Anglican bishops and members of the Cabinet threatened with exposure, do not occur,' the *Daily Telegraph* reported, adding that *Ruling Passions* was nevertheless 'probably the most embarrassing book ever written by a Member of Parliament'. Walter Terry, the political editor of the *Sun*, agreed: 'It is a devastating, stomach-turning document. Probably the biggest outpouring of literary dung a public figure has ever flung into print.' In the London *Evening News* Lord George-Brown denounced it as 'beastly'. The *Economist* headed its review 'Pederast's Progress', even though Tom was well known to like young men, not boys.

On the weekend after publication an editorial in the *Sunday Telegraph* condemned Tom's 'vicious life'. It conceded that 'immorality in high places' was nothing new. 'But the late Tom

Driberg's autobiography surely sets a new low, which is unlikely to pass unnoticed in the rest of the world.' The same day's *Observer* carried a long, holier-than-thou review by Malcolm Muggeridge. 'There is no indication that he was in any way troubled by the Apostle Paul's strictures on homosexual practices,' Muggeridge mocked, 'or that he made any serious attempt to relate his behaviour to the teaching of the New Testament.'

Most of the attacks went unanswered. But Muggeridge's review provoked a letter from Elisabeth Russell Taylor which was printed in the next issue of the *Observer*:

Malcolm Muggeridge's review of *Ruling Passions* was peculiarly offensive. Whatever the habits of Tom Driberg (and it seems they did not include corruption of the innocent) it is clear that Mr Muggeridge can count among his that of 'humbuggery'. He is quick to accuse Tom Driberg in his role of Anglo-Catholic of ignoring the apostle Paul's strictures on homosexual practices, yet I see no evidence that Mr Muggeridge observes Jesus's exhortation for, and examples of, compassion.

The sneer never illuminates the subject at which it is aimed.

Something more raucous than a sneer bellowed from the *Daily Telegraph*'s 'Saturday Column' the following week. Its author was Paul Johnson, who by 1977 had already more or less completed his remarkable pilgrimage of political faith: ten years earlier he had sat in the editor's chair at the *New Statesman*; now he sat at the feet of Mrs Thatcher. In the *Telegraph* he revealed that Tom was on his list of prayers for the dead – but this should not, he hastened to add, be misunderstood. The homosexuals who had Johnson's sympathy were 'those pathetic figures, like the late E. M. Forster, for whom homosexuality was a lifelong burden and shame, and who agonised about its moral consequences'.

This ridiculous misrepresentation of Forster was introduced merely to allow Johnson to point a contrast with Tom:

From first to last, Driberg was a homosexual philanderer of a most pertinacious and indefatigable kind, wholly shameless, without the smallest scruple or remorse, utterly regardless of the feelings of or consequences to his partners, determined on the crudest and most frequent form of carnal satisfaction to the exclusion of any other consideration whatever: a Queers' Casanova.

Tom's critics had, of course, plenty of reasons to dislike him. In Muggeridge's case, it was a religious grudge: Tom's left-wing, 'permissive' Anglo-Catholicism stuck in his gullet. His last meeting with Tom had been at a World Council of Churches conference in the Swedish town of Uppsala. 'The setting was exactly right, Scandinavian ultra-permissiveness providing the background to a meandering discussion in which expressions like "life-style", "identity" and "third world" occurred with great profusion,' Muggeridge recalled with a shudder.

Paul Johnson, Lord George-Brown and Walter Terry were all, to a greater or lesser degree, choleric, red-faced political apostates. In their youth they had embraced socialism (almost literally in Terry's case: he had fathered the two children of Marcia Williams, Harold Wilson's secretary); but, like the tycoon who ditches his childhood-sweetheart bride once he makes his pile, when they prospered they went off in search of something classier. They were all now well to the right of the Labour Party. It was only natural for them to feel uncomfortable with Tom Driberg, whose political opinions had remained pretty consistent throughout his life, regardless of his circumstances. But for that very reason they, of all people, could hardly denounce his politics. The revelation of his sexual *nostalgie de la boue* therefore came as a welcome gift, which they seized gratefully.

They can scarcely have guessed that there might soon be an opportunity to drag down Tom's reputation still further. Only one reviewer anticipated it. 'He would seem,' George Gale remarked, almost parenthetically, in the *Daily Express*, 'to have been a most suitable recruit for the Russian secret service.'

This promising idea was pushed a little further the following year in Chapman Pincher's book *Inside Story*. The felicitously-named Pincher had retired after more than thirty years as the *Daily Express*'s correspondent on defence, security and intelligence. His most common target had always been the Labour Party and, as he revealed in *Inside Story*, his regular sources of information included some of the most senior figures in Whitehall and Westminster. The historian E. P. Thompson aptly described Pincher as 'a kind of official urinal in which, side by side, high officials of MI5 and MI6, Sea Lords, Permanent Under-Secretaries, Lord George-Brown, Chiefs of the Air Staff, nuclear scientists, Lord Wigg, and others, stand patiently leaking in the public interest'. A typical Pincher 'scoop' would reveal that the security services were deeply alarmed by left-wing infiltration of the Labour Party.

He revived many old favourites of that sort in his book. 'The Labour Party leadership has been fully aware for many years of the infiltration by dedicated Communists posing as Socialists and has done little that is effective to counter it,' he insisted.[7] Who were the suspect MPs? Regrettably, he explained, the fear of libel writs prevented him from naming names. But there was one politician who had died and could therefore be vilified with impunity – the late Tom Driberg. Pincher claimed that while Tom was a Labour MP 'he remained a Kremlin agent of sympathy, sponsoring various Communist-front organisations, urging the withdrawal of troops from Northern Ireland, and there were deep suspicions inside MI5 that he was an active agent of the KGB'.

Pincher's zealous friends in MI5 did not seem to have much evidence for their 'deep suspicions'. If they had found anything, on past form they would have passed it on without delay to Pincher, who in turn would have been only too pleased to publish it. The best he could manage was a smear which was pretty feeble even by his standards. To disapprove of the British military presence in Ulster might be a dreadful treason according to the Pincher view of the world, but it hardly proved that Tom was an active KGB man.

There was one more element in the smear, inspired by *Ruling Passions*:

The fact that this man, who was widely known to be a homosexual pouncer of a bestial kind, haunting public lavatories to find quick conquests, as he described in his memoirs, could have become Chairman of the Labour Party, illustrates the extent to which blatant behaviour, political or private, is no bar to progress in that organisation.

The logic here is even more imaginative. Tom was a 'homosexual pouncer', yet he became Chairman of the Labour Party; therefore the Labour Party was an organisation in which people who indulge in 'blatant behaviour' (whatever that may be) could flourish; therefore Tom Driberg was a KGB agent.

Little notice was taken of the attack on Tom in *Inside Story*, but Pincher would not let matters rest there. All he needed was some help. In 1980 it arrived: he was contacted by Lord Rothschild, another member of the Great and the Good who found himself caught short and wanted to use Pincher's public convenience.

Since Anthony Blunt had been revealed as a Soviet agent the previous year, Britain had succumbed to spy mania. No weekend was complete without the Sunday papers naming yet more figures from the British Establishment who had been secretly working for the Comintern all along. Obscure academics and businessmen were dragged out of retirement to confess their sins. 'Background' pieces on Cambridge in the Thirties proliferated, their theme caught by the title of the book which exposed Blunt: *The Climate of Treason*. And one man who had been at Cambridge in the Thirties, and had known both Blunt and Guy Burgess, was Lord Rothschild. He was alarmed to see his name creeping into some newspapers. Not that there was any suggestion that he had been a KGB agent; but the mere juxtaposition was quite enough to make him fear guilt by association.

The precise motives which led Rothschild to introduce Pincher to the former MI5 officer Peter Wright are still unclear. Rothschild himself has refused to offer even a word of explanation. What is certain is that the introduction took place, and that Rothschild effected it. He also paid Wright's air fare from Australia.

Wright was a man with an empty wallet and a grudge against his former employers, both caused by his inadequate pension. The collaboration with Pincher would allow him to settle scores profitably. He would feed Pincher tales of MI5 skulduggery, spiced with wild conspiracy theories. It would make a sensational book. They would then split the proceeds.

Serial rights in the book, *Their Trade is Treachery*, were bought by the *Daily Mail*, much to the annoyance of Pincher's old colleagues at the *Express*. On 25 March 1981 the *Mail*'s front page was dominated by a large headline: 'LABOUR MP WAS DOUBLE

AGENT'. The report that accompanied it was under Pincher's name:

Tom Driberg, Left-wing Labour MP, ex-chairman of the Labour Party, member of the National Executive and finally life peer, was a double agent, working for the KGB and MI5.

I can reveal that Driberg, who died in 1976 aged 71, reported on the personal and political activities of his friends and colleagues in Parliament to both agencies.

He did this from the moment he first entered the House in 1942 to when he finally retired in 1974, and thereafter when he became a member of the House of Lords.

Both MI5 and the KGB had no illusions about the fact that he was working for the other side and both sought to use him for their own purposes . . .

There was plenty more where that came from, including a reminder yet again that Tom was 'a compulsive homosexual'. Pincher concluded with a flourish: after Tom's elevation to the peerage he had been known in MI5 headquarters as 'Lord of the Spies'.

Their Trade is Treachery became a best-seller. Its promotion was assisted by the Prime Minister, Margaret Thatcher, who went to the dispatch box in the House of Commons to confirm another of Pincher's allegations – that a former head of MI5, Roger Hollis, had been suspected by some of his colleagues of being a Soviet agent. (She added, however, that two thorough inquiries had cleared him.) She said nothing about the Driberg allegation. Pincher, resourceful as ever, managed to place a sinister construction on this silence. He persuaded himself that a deal had been done between Thatcher and the Leader of the Opposition, Michael Foot, who had been a friend of Tom: Thatcher would say nothing about Driberg and in return Foot would not embarrass her on the Hollis question.[8]

Foot was not the only person to disbelieve the suggestion that Tom was a spy. Lord Brockway pointed out that Tom 'was utterly indiscreet and could never keep a secret'.[9] Lord Paget said that, though no great admirer of the security services, he could 'not believe that even they were lunatic enough to recruit a man like Driberg'.[10]

Few heard these sceptical voices, which were drowned by

Pincher's noisy fanfares. Nor has the Pincher version faded with time: today it is as loud as ever. Hardly a month goes by in Britain without the appearance of yet another book about Blunt or Burgess or Philby or Maclean or MI5 or Peter Wright or the climate of treason or the meaning of treason; in almost every case, the allegations against Tom are recycled once more, almost verbatim. By sheer dint of repetition, Pincher's account has become the received wisdom – even though it depends on 'facts' which five minutes' research will show to be untrue.

And so Tom passes into mythology: Lord of the Spies, Casanova of the Queers. In 1988 he even turned up in a novel, Alan Hollinghurst's *The Swimming-Pool Library*, where a character called Lord Nantwich writes this diary entry:

September 26, 1943. My birthday . . . It's so dull being as old as the century, it makes one's progress seem so leaden & inevitable, with no scope for romantic doubts about one's age. However, a beautiful, hazy, pre-war sort of day – lunch at the Club with Driberg, who was very flattering & said he thought I only looked 42. He told me about some of his exploits, though I was perhaps a shade reticent about mine: with him one simply doesn't know where they'll end up – careless talk etc. We lamented the still frequent attacks & insults meted out to coloured servicemen, by the English though mainly of course by the Yanks. It seems all Driberg's attempts to counter the foul American laws, in Parliament & out, have been unsuccessful. Never mind, he said, he tried to make it up to them personally.[11]

At which point one begins to rub one's eyes and wonder if Tom really existed. Or was he a fictional creation all along? There is a Woody Allen film called *Zelig* in which the hero is a nobody who turns out to have been present, lurking in the shadows, at almost every event of any consequence in the twentieth century. Tom was a Zelig of sorts: on the picket lines in the General Strike, in Spain during the civil war, in America for Pearl Harbor, in Paris for the liberation, in Buchenwald just after it was relieved, in Korea with the Royal Marines, in London when it was Swinging. Can the man who in the 1920s was anointed by Aleister Crowley to succeed him as the Great Beast be the man who in the 1960s tried to persuade

Mick Jagger to become a Labour MP? It is a life that slips easily into myth. Unlike Zelig or Lord Nantwich, however, this man was real enough. In the parched summer of 1976 he was found dead in a London taxi.

It is, perversely, Chapman Pincher whom I must thank for first goading me into writing this book. One day in the summer of 1985 I travelled down to Berkshire to interview the old brute for *Tatler* magazine. In the course of our conversation I said I was surprised that no one had written a biography of Tom Driberg. Suddenly his bloodhound features were alert, ears and nose almost visibly twitching. Yes, he agreed, it was surprising. I was instantly alarmed. He seemed to be thinking that he would be just the man for the job.

Though I had met Tom Driberg. I scarcely knew him; but I did know that he deserved better than this. I was curious to learn more about him. I was – to misuse a word which Tom himself invariably misused – *intrigued*. Unlike Pincher, I came to the subject with few preconceptions. There was only one thing for it: I should write the biography myself.

It has been a fascinating, maddening, exhilarating experience. 'I expect a lot of people in high places will be rather nervous about the book,' several friends have said, as if I too had inherited the mantle of the Hon. Galahad Threepwood. True, certain elderly gents who are now happily married had sudden and convenient attacks of amnesia when asked what they got up to with Tom in their bachelor days; and Barbara Castle, a friend and parliamentary colleague of Tom's for thirty years, declined to see me because she had recently heard a story about Tom that was 'so bizarre that I realise I was always out of my depth with him'.[12]

Some of those who did agree to be interviewed startled me by their attitudes. Ian Mikardo had worked with Tom all through the Bevanite struggles of the 1950s and was, I had thought, a close comrade. Yet within moments of my arrival at Mikardo's flat he was grumbling that Tom 'hardly ever attended the Tribune Group, never did any of the bloody chores . . . he was a very, very bad constituency MP . . . I don't know anyone who liked him.' I went to Bath to see Mervyn Stockwood, the former Bishop of Southwark, who had been an intimate political and religious ally of Tom's since the early 1940s, and who had preached at Tom's funeral. He poured me a glass of sherry. Suddenly his voice boomed across the room: 'I would never have preached at his funeral if I'd known then what I know now – that he betrayed his country and sent people to their deaths.' I nearly choked on my sherry. What people, what deaths? 'You mustn't press me,' he growled mysteriously. I later discovered that Stockwood had, some years earlier, been told the 'truth' about Tom by none other than Chapman Pincher.

Getting at the truth about Tom has not been an easy task. On countless occasions I have longed to sit him down and interrogate him severely: did you *really* do this? But he is, regrettably, dead; and in any case he isn't always a reliable source. How, then, is one to assess the truth of – let us say – the famous Nye Bevan story? As told by Tom to several friends, it runs like this. Sometime in the late 1950s, during the period when he was out of Parliament, Tom lunched with his friend Nye Bevan one day. Mildly drunk, they returned afterwards to Bevan's office at the House. Tom was seized by a sudden curiosity: he fell to his knees, opened Nye's flies and began to fellate him. He had somehow had an instinct that Bevan would not mind, and he was right. All the hero of the Left did, as he lay pleasurably slumped on the sofa, was to shout 'Tell me a story, Tom! Tell me a story!' Tom was in no position to do so. He said later that he could disprove the rumour that Nye Bevan was a eunuch. The great man's penis was, apparently, long but a trifle thin.

Did anything of the sort happen? The only two first-hand witnesses are both dead, and there is, obviously, no other way of verifying the tale. Ultimately it depends on whom you believe. The same is true, in some cases, even when witnesses are still alive. To stay with the theme of Labour grandees and their genitalia, let us consider the strange case of Jim Callaghan's penis.

This is an anecdote that first appeared in Woodrow Wyatt's memoirs, *Confessions of an Optimist*, published in 1985:

One day in the Commons [Callaghan] said to me, 'I have had a very odd experience. I was driving back to London at night with Tom after a meeting we'd been to. We stopped to have a pee on the verge. While I was peeing Tom came up to me and took hold of my penis. "You've got a very pretty one there," he said. I got away as quick as I could. What do you make of that?'

What could I make of that? Rather him than me.

Trivial fare, perhaps, but the idea of the solid, doughty former Prime Minister having 'a very pretty one' was irresistible. I wrote to Lord Callaghan (as he now is) asking if he could remember any more details of the roadside grope – when and where it happened, for instance. He replied stiffly that no such incident ever took place. Oddly, he also forbade me to quote directly from his letter of denial. I then turned to Lord Wyatt of Weeford (as *he* now is). His veracity had been called into question, I suggested. Presumably he would not want it to be thought that he had simply invented this story? Wyatt's reply was even less friendly than Callaghan's. He was very sorry to hear that I was writing a life of Tom Driberg, he told me, and he would not assist me in any way.

So where does this leave us? There is a limited number of possible verdicts. It could be that the event occurred as Wyatt said and Lord Callaghan is lying; or, rather, it couldn't, since Lord Callaghan is not a liar. Nor, indeed, is Lord Wyatt. Another explanation that comes to mind is that Tom did grab Callaghan's penis and the encounter has for some reason slipped from the former Prime Minister's memory. Maybe readers can solve the mystery for themselves; I hope so. Meanwhile you may also care to ponder on the position of Woodrow Wyatt, a man who makes his living by denouncing the Left's irresponsibility and carelessness with the truth and yet himself includes a passage in his autobiography which he is not prepared to justify when challenged.

No thanks at all, then, to the cowardly Lord Wyatt of Weeford. But he is a rare exception. Almost everyone else whom I approached was more generous than I had dared hope. The following people spoke to me, corresponded with me, guided me through unfamiliar territory or allowed me to use copyright material, and without them this book would never have been written. I thank them all: Sir Richard Acland; Sir Harold Acton; Rosemary Say; Michael Jackson; Peter and Joan Berger; Valerie Eliot; Joan Littlewood; Paul Foot; Michael Foot; Gore Vidal; the Rt Revd Mervyn Stockwood;

Cleo Sylvestre; John Rayner; John Freeman; Ian Mikardo; Peter Rankin; Michael Duffy; Lord Bernstein; Lady Elwyn-Jones (Polly Binder); Richard Ingrams; Richard Boston; Anthony Howard; Steve Mann; Angela Pitts; Alan Watkins; Christopher Hitchens; Martin Walker; June Wells; John Underwood; the Revd Gerard Irvine; Julian Symons; Jo Richardson; the Revd Kenneth Leech; the Revd Donald Reeves; the Revd Richard Kirker; Dr Anthony Storr; Humphry Berkeley; Mary Martin; Dr David Cargill; Lord Paget; Donald Rumbelow; Michael Horovitz; Anna Lovell; Allen Ginsberg; Trevor Kempson; Michael O'Brien; Martin Nesbit; Victor Spinetti; Terence Lancaster; Louis Heren; David Kogan; Bruce Palling; Ian Irvine; Lewis Chester; Roy Dean. I am especially indebted to Kay Brand for her advice. I thank also my agent, Pat Kavanagh, and the various editors at Chatto and Windus who have followed the progress of this book from conception to forceps delivery – Jan Dalley, Andrew Motion, Jeremy Lewis, Jonathan Burnham and Carmen Callil. A grand salute is due to Tom's literary executor, Bruce Hunter of David Higham Associates, who has been generous and helpful from first to last and has kindly given me permission to quote Tom's copyright material.

I am grateful to the libraries and public institutions which have allowed me to consult material in their possession: the National Sound Archive; the London Library; the City University Library (for the New Statesman archive); the LSE Library; the British Newspaper Library at Colindale; the House of Lords Record Office (Beaverbrook papers); the BBC Written Archive at Caversham, particularly Gwyniver Jones; the Library of the Oxford Union; the Canadian High Commission.

Above all, I owe a huge debt of gratitude for the enthusiasm and helpfulness of all the staff of the Library at Christ Church, Oxford, where Tom's papers are kept, and especially to Jennie Bradshaw and John Wing, whose patience and hospitality have been a joy. Many thanks, too, to the college archivist, June Wells; and to Jennie's husband, Raymond Bradshaw (known to all as Brad), who has spent the past year or two compiling an exhaustive index to Tom's files for the benefit of future burrowers. Anyone who trawls through Tom's filing cabinets ought to be warned to expect the occasional shock. One day I found a brown envelope containing a small leather knife-pouch. Attached to it was a report from the forensic pathologist Sir Bernard Spilsbury confirming Tom's suspicion that the pouch, which had been brought back from Buchenwald, was made of human skin. I dropped it with a yelp.

CHAPTER ONE

A BOY'S OWN STORY

Thomas Edward Neil Driberg was born on 22 May 1905 in Crowborough, Sussex, a town he later came to hate more than anywhere else on earth. His mother was thirty-nine; his father was sixty-five and had already retired after a modestly distinguished career in the Indian civil service which had included spells as superintendent of census for Assam, superintendent of emigration from Assam, inspector-general of prisons in Assam and, finally, inspector of the Assam police.

Seventy years later Tom felt a thrill of recognition when he discovered Philip Larkin's poem 'This Be The Verse':

> They fuck you up, your mum and dad.
>   They may not mean to, but they do.
> They fill you with the faults they had
>   And add some extra, just for you.[1]

Tom believed that Amy Mary Irving Bell and John James Street Driberg fucked him up in countless ways, great and small. One of the most unforgivable fuck-ups was their decision, after a lifetime serving the *raj*, to retire to Crowborough. Tom had a taste for both the seedy and the splendid; Crowborough was neither. It was dull. Worse, it was *bourgeois* – a town of stockbrokers and retired majors, afternoon bridge parties and gins-and-tonic. The Dribergs' 'desirable residence', Uckfield Lodge, was furnished in mid-Victorian style, embellished with Indian souvenirs such as a brass *jardinière* from Benares and a pair of cobra candlesticks. There were few paintings on the walls but plenty of antlers. The bookcases were stuffed with *Uphill Road in India, Indian Jottings, With the Flag to Pretoria, Tibet the Mysterious, British Battles, Bonnie Scotland* and other lively yarns. There were no fewer than thirty-one volumes of *British Rainfall*: Tom's father was a dogged amateur meteorologist who spent much of each morning studying his barometer and the various measuring instruments he had set up in the garden; over lunch he would then report his findings, at length, to the assembled family.

In these circumstances it was hardly surprising that, as Tom wrote, 'I became conscious, fairly early on, of a considerable sense of *ennui*.'[2]

Crowborough offered few playmates. Tom's two brothers, Jack and Jim, were seventeen and fifteen respectively when he was born and, at least during his childhood, seemed more like absentee uncles. When he was about five years old a local girl named Dorothy Osborne came to call sometimes, but that arrangement ended abruptly one afternoon after Tom and Dorothy had been playing in the nursery. 'Suddenly she stood still in the middle of the room, began to cry, and pissed on the floor. As the rippling pool spread over the linoleum, she ran out of the room, and out of my life; for I, also in tears – tears of shocked horror – swore that I hated her, and I think my parents felt that she was not, after all, a suitable companion.'[3] Tom described the incident as 'traumatic – perhaps lastingly so': it was his first conscious discovery of his disgust for women's bodies. The feeling never abated. More than sixty years later, a young man declined an invitation to dine with Tom, explaining that he had promised to visit his girlfriend in hospital instead. 'Yes,' Tom replied vaguely, unable to conceal the contempt behind his pretended sympathy, 'there's so much to go wrong with them, isn't there? I do hope it's not her clitoris or anything like that.'

His lust for the male body was present from an early age, too; indeed if his own accounts are to be believed he was an infant prodigy in this department. At the age of two or three, crawling between the legs of his brother Jack, he looked up and noticed a small hole in the crotch of his flannel trousers. He inserted a finger through the gap (his brother appeared not to notice) and, though he did not touch flesh, experienced 'the first authentic sexual thrill of my life'. He also formed a passionate attachment to a picture of a young man on a tin of Mackintosh's toffees, 'kissing the shiny surface as one sees Indian peasants in Mexico kissing the glass that covers the relics of some saint'. The Dribergs' gardener was once stopped by the five-year-old Tom with the imperious request: 'Hemsley, will you please take down your trousers?' Hemsley refused.

Bored and friendless, Tom spent much of his time with only his parents for company. His father was distant and formal, his mother cloyingly fond; Tom resented both attitudes. 'I am sometimes disposed to think,' he wrote, 'that it might have been better if I had been dumped anonymously on the doorstep of a prosperous, child-less widower.'

Disappointment may have been one reason for his father's aloof-ness. John Driberg had yearned for a daughter, and in the weeks before Tom's birth had already named the imminent baby Jill.[4] ('You were meant to be a little girl,' Tom's mother once blurted out.) But Tom believed that this made no difference, and that the paternal coolness was instead another sign of his parents' attach-ment to an absurdly outdated code of behaviour. Even by the standards of that time and that place, according to Tom, his mother and father were 'distinctly old-fashioned'. This is something of an exaggeration. Consider one example of a supposedly antique habit cited in *Ruling Passions*:

I doubt whether many other households kept up, as we did (until my father became more or less permanently bed-ridden), the Victorian cus-tom of family prayers. These took place before breakfast, at or just before eight o'clock, in the smoking-room: the sons of the house, what-ever our ages, were expected to attend, the maids rustled in demurely, my father officiated.

In fact, the same morning ritual took place in many upper middle-class households of the time. Richard Crossman, who was born two years after Tom and was later a colleague of his on the Labour benches in Parliament, endured an almost identical ceremony:

My first memory of my father is at the assembly of the household at 7.55 precisely for morning prayers. He sat at one end of the breakfast table and my mother at the other, while the children were ranged on their special little chairs in front of the fire; then the bell was rung and the maids and nurses filed in to their places with their backs to the window.[5]

Family prayers in the Driberg household were, as Tom wrote, eventually abandoned because of his father's poor health. A photograph of Mr Driberg taken in about 1906 shows an apparently robust, Kiplingesque figure with a walrus moustache, wearing a straw hat and smoking a pipe. But he soon began to decline; and Tom, with the cruelty of which children are capable, felt embarrassment rather than pity. Other boys' fathers, he resentfully believed, were smart, brisk naval commanders, while his own was 'senile and ill', a dodderer who dribbled down his front. Perhaps in the belief that it would conceal the dribbling, John Driberg grew a beard; it quickly became matted with saliva. His monocle was continually falling out, often into his soup. He also had a glass eye. Tom later claimed to have only a 'shadowy, two-dimensional' recollection of his father: 'I remember not one word that he ever spoke to me.'

The problem with his mother was quite the opposite: his memory was possessed by her, in spite of his attempts at exorcism. He never confided in her and always reacted coldly to her displays of affection. Yet, many years after her death, when he himself was near the grave, Tom still dreamed of his mother most nights. He admitted that this might suggest 'a somewhat obsessive filial relationship of the kind from which Freud constructed his theory of the Oedipus complex'.

His earliest memory was of being unkind to her. When he was three he would sit in the nursery before bed every evening, eating his hot bread and milk, while his mother sang him 'Once in Royal David's City'. One evening he was so bored with the monotony of hearing the same hymn day after day that he covered his ears with his hands. His mother was upset. But what was most significant about the trifling act of defiance was its effect on Tom, not on Mrs Driberg: almost half a century later he told a BBC interviewer of the 'acute and poignant remorse' it still caused him.[6]

He was tormented by his conflicting feelings towards his mother – guilt at having rebuffed her so consistently, and fear of her smothering embrace. In his dreams she looked 'small, frail and wounded', but in conversation with friends he would often paint her as a stern, domineering figure in black crinoline. Once, when driving with a friend through Sussex, Tom began to shudder violently. The friend, alarmed that he might be having some sort of seizure, asked if he were all right. 'She's down there,' Tom hissed, indicating a road-sign pointing to Crowborough. But another person who knew her, Tom's sister-in-law Pearl Binder, remembers Amy Driberg simply as 'a dear old lady, very religious, who adored him'.

They fucked him up, his mum and dad. But, as Philip Larkin continued,

> . . . they were fucked up in their turn
>   By fools in old-style hats and coats,
> Who half the time were soppy-stern
>   And half at one another's throats.

Tom agreed. 'Much as I have sometimes regretted the mess that my life has largely been – and some of this must be attributable to the circumstances of my childhood – it would not be reasonable to blame my parents for behaving according to the customs, obsolescent even then, of their age and class,' he wrote in *Ruling Passions*.

'Half at one another's throats' was true enough. All families have their eccentrics, but Tom liked to boast that his had produced 'an unusually high proportion of the vicious and/or dotty'. Although there were few relations on his father's side, this was more than compensated for by his mother's large and bellicose clan, who came from Lockerbie in Dumfriesshire. Tom's mother's mother, Margaret Irving Bell, was a curmudgeonly old monster who never approved of her daughter Amy's union with a man twenty-five years her senior – and a man with a foreign surname to boot. 'You were a good daughter before you married, but he soon altered that,' Mrs Bell wrote to Amy in 1914, more than a quarter of a century after the wedding. In 1915 she came to stay with Amy at Crowborough; after two days she stormed out and refused to speak to her for the next five years.

Mrs Bell had another of her daughters, Nora, committed to a

mental hospital on the grounds of insanity. Nora's brother Maurice died at the age of thirty-five in a brawl in a male brothel in Paris. Another of Mrs Bell's sons, Bertie, was a militant spiritualist and teetotaller who one day announced that his mother 'will never enter my house again, nor will I nor my children set foot in hers, nor have any intercourse with her, until every whisky and brandy bottle is out of her house, and she has given us a promise that she will never touch alcohol in any shape or form again.' When Amy suggested that this was rather self-righteous, Bertie turned his wrath on her, extending the ban to the Driberg family: 'I will expect,' he wrote, 'full reparation before you ever come near me or mine again ... From this day forth we cut the fetters of all relationships, which have been too long irksome – you and yours never enter our house again.'[7]

Tom concluded from all this, as well he might, that the family was 'an institution destructive of true affection, a nexus of possessiveness, vindictiveness and jealousy'. Or, as the closing stanza of Larkin's poem has it,

> Man hands on misery to man.
>   It deepens like the coastal shelf.
> Get out as early as you can,
>   And don't have any kids yourself.

Like Philip Larkin, Tom didn't get out all that early; but he obeyed the final line's instruction wholeheartedly.

Tom's formal education began in 1910, when he was sent to a Crowborough kindergarten run by two elderly sisters called Hooker. Their academic standards were minimal, and Tom's parents soon decided to supplement the worthless pedagogy of the Misses Hooker by hiring a private tutor. This person seems to have made even less of an impression. 'I remember nothing about these lessons or who gave them,' Tom wrote.

Three years later he started as a day-boy at The Grange, a reputedly 'good' local establishment which was run, like so many prep schools, by a practising sadist, a former cricketer named Frank Gresson. 'None of us,' Tom wrote, 'had any doubt at all that he enjoyed the beatings he frequently inflicted.' Gresson favoured a particularly dangerous form of corporal punishment, beating on the wrist rather than the bottom. Even more cruel and unusual was the punishment meted out for offences which were thought too grave for a mere caning. It was known as the School Mobbing, and it used to take place in the school-yard during mid-morning break: 'The buzz would go round that a certain boy had broken the rules, and as he came into the yard the [head]master would simply say "Go for him". Then everyone would mob him, kicking, tearing his clothes, anything they could think of. A ghastly business.'[8] Tom incurred a mobbing for drawing a caricature of a master on the blackboard. He returned home that evening bruised and covered with dirt but did not dare tell his parents how he came to be in such a state.

Tom remembered his five years' education at The Grange as 'a process of reciprocal torture, a daily series of battles'. The battle was occasionally won by the boys. They were merciless, for instance, in their treatment of a pathetic master called Rice,[9] who had a chronic snivelling catarrh and used to suck sweets surreptitiously behind the lid of his desk. 'What we did to him was more savage than anything recorded in school-stories,'[10] Tom boasted, without ever quite explaining what form this savagery took. All he did record was that, while Rice was busy with his clandestine sweet-sucking, 'all the little boys in the back row, hardly more surreptitiously, would bring out and compare and fondle their tiny, wriggling white worms of penises.'[11]

Boys at The Grange had their trouser pockets sewn up to prevent them from playing with themselves. It was a splendidly ineffective gesture. After lessons Tom and a boy called Derek often adjourned to the WCs to continue their sexual education; locking themselves into the cubicle and discarding their chastity-belt trousers, they would experiment with any form of kissing or touching that occurred to them. Thus began Tom's 'chronic, lifelong, love-hate relationship with lavatories'.

Tom was one of the least popular boys at The Grange. As the only day-boy in a school of boarders he was a second-class citizen anyway, and his status was lowered still further by his demeanour: he was shy, chubby, *gauche*. The outbreak of the First World War in

1914 compounded his misery, for the school consensus was that Driberg was a 'Hun name' in spite of Tom's protestations that his ancestors were probably Dutch. He became known as Kaiser Tom and 'was duly bullied in accordance with the canons of English private education'. The only pupil to suffer more than Tom was a boy with a genuine Hun name, Scholtz. The tormenting of Scholtz was led by the headmaster himself, who beat the wretched child continually. Scholtz, Tom noticed, always had weals across his wrists.

Perhaps in the vain hope of proving that he was as patriotic as the next boy, in December 1914 Tom wrote a short story called 'The German Spy' for *The Grange Magazine*. Apart from a few acrostics and riddles that he had previously contributed to the magazine, it was his first published work.

'Would you two boys like to come for a walk with me?' said Mrs Thornton to her sons, Edward and Jack. 'We will go round by Haylesbury Green,' she added.

When they had got about half-way, Mrs Thornton suddenly remembered that she had some work to do in Bainston, a large town three miles away. So she left them and they went on with their walk. Soon they could just see the sea. It was now 9 o'clock, but they went on. Suddenly they saw in the distance a flash of light. This was not uncommon, as steamers kept passing. Soon, however, they could see that a code was being used. Just then they saw, from a big house on the cliff, answering flashes. The two boys looked at each other and then at the house. It was a calm night and out at sea they saw a big ship with two funnels. At her bows a little flag was flying, but they could not see of what nationality this was. They went up to the house and looked into the lower windows, but nothing was to be seen. But up above the flashes continued. They waited a minute or two, but suddenly a tall man with a large moustache came out of the house. They darted round a corner. He looked round and assured himself that no one was about. He took out of his pocket a bundle of papers and walked down to the beach. The boys followed him and heard him whistle softly. A man came up and whispered to him. He nodded and they got into a boat. At first they thought that it would be impossible to follow them now. Then Jack thought that they could swim and cling on to the boat. They got to the ship in this manner, and found that it was a German battleship. It was lying about two miles out of Bainston. They managed to get on board, and were not noticed. They hid in a cabin till about 10.30, when they went to sleep. They were awakened by rough voices and harsh guttural exclamations. They started up and found themselves looking down the barrels of at least a dozen revolvers. They made a dash for the cabin door. Luckily for them the key was in the outside. They locked it after them and dashed on to the deck. It was practically empty, so they dropped overboard. The shore wasn't far off, so they swam to it. There was a party of soldiers just starting off, who had seen the battleship, so after changing their clothes, they went with them. When they got to the vessel they found a few men about. Then they took a lot of ammunition which was on board, and captured the officers in the cabin. Some were taken to London and searched, a lot of plans being found on them. They were shot, and the two boys were rewarded.[12]

It was a brave effort, but could not compare with the gung-ho creations which other boys at The Grange were firing into the school mag like mortar rounds ('They come! The Huns! / Their thunderous guns / With loud resounding boom . . .'; or, 'Then Johnny said with cold calm rage he'd never felt before, / "I loathe the Kaiser! I won't do the goose-step any more!"'). The bullying of Kaiser Tom did not abate.

With the younger and brighter teachers away at the war, the curricular side of the school seems to have been about on a par with the standards of the Misses Hooker. The headmaster's Latin and French lessons were 'sheer tedium'. The art mistress, Miss Greene, 'fighting gallantly for refinement and against middle age',[13] spent hours producing feeble and blobby little water-colours of autumnal hues. Mr Rice remained in hiding behind his desk. It was native wit rather than anything learned in the classrooms of The Grange that carried Tom through the entrance exam for Lancing.

Tom departed from The Grange, at the age of thirteen, with a hatred of authority. Though not a socialist – he may not even have known the word – he had already begun his journey down that road. As a loner by force of circumstance, he had had plenty of time to ponder on why he felt so estranged from his parents and their values. In the autumn of 1918 he took up his place at Lancing, and for the first time in his life was able to leave Crowborough behind.

Lancing had a reputation as a 'liberal' public school. One might as well speak of a comfortable dungeon or a palatable Liebfraumilch. Liberal it may have been by comparison with some of the more philistine and flagellomaniac institutions of the time, but it was still pretty bleak. Dudley Carew, a contemporary of Tom's, has recorded that 'we slept in stone dormitories with the windows open, a minimum of bed-clothes, and then a cold bath when we got up at 6.30.'[14] There were severe beatings, usually administered by the Head of House; according to Evelyn Waugh, who was a couple of years senior to Tom at Lancing, 'most boys during their first two years got beaten at least once a term.'[15]

For his first three weeks at school, however, a new boy was immune from punishment. While in this limbo he would be instructed by a slightly older boy in all the arcane codes and privileges which encrust public school life like so many barnacles, cajoling young boys into an acceptance of the inevitability and allure of hierarchy: Third Years could wear coloured socks, coloured ties were permissible for Sixth-Formers; First Years must never put their hands in their pockets, Second Years might do so but only 'with the jacket raised, not drawn back';[16] and so, absurdly, on. After memorising these distinctions, on the third Sunday of term the boys were formally admitted into full membership of the school – or at least to the joyless status of fag – at an initiation ritual called the 'new men's concert'. One by one, each quaking youngster had to stand on a table in the House Room and sing a song (Tom chose 'The Bay of Biscay-O'). He would then be pelted with missiles by his elders. The young Waugh thought the ceremony 'a curious relic of barbarism. I don't think anyone really enjoys it. The performers certainly do not and it is seldom really funny.'[17]

As well as the fagging and beating, there was what Tom described as 'some really rough bullying'. Once, in dread of another night's pummelling in the dormitory, he cut his wrist with a razor blade. 'This earned a bandage from the matron, but did not diminish the bullying, since it was recognised as a cowardly kind of malingering.'[18] Tom suffered more than most from the bullies' attentions, for his attitude and looks were calculated to enrage heartier boys: he was pale and thin, having shed the puppy-fat that shamed him at The Grange; he wore scholarly steel-rimmed spectacles;[19] his sense of intellectual superiority gave him an aloof air. Waugh thought him merely 'reserved', but Carew detected superciliousness. Tom's unembarrassed aestheticism aroused suspicion and contempt. As Carew put it, he was 'not generally popular'.

But he was by no means friendless. Besides Waugh and Carew, his admirers included Max Mallowan, the future husband of Agatha Christie, and Hugh Molson, later a prominent Conservative politician but at this time professing 'socialism, atheism, pacifism and hedonism'.[20] (When Molson came to Lancing he was asked if he were interested in politics. 'Preternaturally so,' he replied, thereby saddling himself with the nickname 'Preters' for the rest of his school career.) Another was Roger Fulford, who later became an author of royal histories, a colleague of Lytton Strachey and a perennially unsuccessful Liberal candidate: he regarded the boy Driberg as 'a storehouse of learning and erudition'.[21]

Fulford, Molson and Waugh founded a society called the Dilettanti, whose purpose was to indulge 'in various forms of aesthetic activity' – poetry readings, lectures on art, political debate. Tom was one of the first applicants for membership. His 'interview' took an unusual form: Waugh simply strode up to him in Great School one day and barked out 'Who's your favourite artist?' Flustered by the unblinking stare of Waugh's blue eyes, Tom suddenly forgot every artist who ever lived. Eventually, in a panic, he managed to pluck a random name from some distant recess of his brain – 'Sir John Lavery'. It was a ridiculous reply. But, to his surprise, he was elected forthwith.

The sponsor of the Dilettanti was a kindly housemaster called Dick Harris. Their true mentor, however, was J. F. Roxburgh – dandy, intellectual and (in Tom's words) 'magnetically brilliant teacher' to generations of boys, both at Lancing and later at Stowe, where he was the first headmaster. Tom adored him.

It is not too fanciful to see Roxburgh as a father substitute. Tom may later have exaggerated the emptiness of his relationship with John Driberg ('I remember not one word that he ever spoke to me'), since the letters his father sent him at Lancing are full of affectionate phrases such as 'darling Tom' and 'my dear little Tom' – though a fourteen-year-old boy might well wince with embarrassment at being addressed thus. But whatever the case, there was little time left for developing fond feelings. The long sickness was drawing to its inevitable conclusion. 'I was not very well and the Dr would not let me go out to the village,' Mr Driberg admitted to Tom in a letter on 7 July 1919. Later that month he tried to sound less gloomy. He was 'much better', he announced – but then confessed that 'I have been walking around the house with a stick on account of my legs.' It cannot have come as a great surprise to Tom when, two months later, he was called into the housemaster's study to be told that his father had died, aged seventy-nine. 'The deceased gentleman was of a retiring disposition, and unostentatiously wrought numerous acts of benevolence in the town,' an obituary in the local paper revealed. 'He was an ardent and able meteorologist, and throughout his residence at Crowborough not only contributed the meteorological reports that have appeared in the church magazine, but also to the meteorological society.' A notice in the *Lancing College Magazine* paid more attention to his career in Assam: 'He was such a good and thorough worker and organiser that they always said out there, he was invariably sent to clean the "Augean Stable", and put the district in order for other men. He was one of the best sportsmen in the province, and accounted for a large number of animals.'[22]

Tom had slightly more in common with his father than he believed at the time: fifty years later, after signing an advertisement in *The Times* proposing that cannabis should be legalised, he discovered to his surprise that in 1893 John James Street Driberg had given evidence to the opium commission in Calcutta on the beneficial qualities of the drug. Nevertheless, it is probably true that the gulf between them was unbridgeable. As Tom put it: 'When my parents came home from India, as the nineteenth century was dying, they knew nothing of the new ideas that were stirring in the arts and in politics: they brought with them the prejudices formed in my father's youth.'[23]

Roxburgh, by contrast, was a kindred spirit. He was unorthodox, didactic, witty, fastidious and homosexual. (Evelyn Waugh claimed that Tom had caught Roxburgh *in flagrante* with a boy. Tom denied it vehemently.) Waugh had a theory that Roxburgh's precise, sonorous cadences – 'a hot potato in the mouth' – could still be heard years afterwards in the voices of many of his former pupils, and that 'Driberg exemplifies it in a marked degree.'[24] Tom conceded that this 'may possibly be true'.[25] Waugh himself later repudiated Roxburgh, notably in his autobiography *A Little Learning*, but at the time even he was under the spell, as his diary entry for 26 September 1919 illustrates:

Roxburgh's French is really a joy. It is almost worth doing the wretched subject. He announced the work we were going to do in the 'four delicious hours at our disposal'. The Head made some far-fetched joke . . . Roxburgh's comment was, 'Really, the Headmaster's profound classical witticisms are getting on my nerves.'[26]

To Tom, Roxburgh was an 'incomparable educator'.[27] Through Roxburgh he discovered an appetite for poetry; the newer it was the better he liked it. Roxburgh helped him to obtain books such as the Sitwells' *Wheels* and Ronald Firbank's *Concerning the Eccentricities of Cardinal Pirelli*, by vouching for their 'educational value' and thereby allowing Tom to have them charged to his school bill. Amy Driberg, who had never heard of Firbank, thus became an unwitting sponsor of the *avant-garde*.

A fondness for modern art and literature was not the only one of Tom's distinctive tastes to be already formed by this time. His other lifelong passions – High Anglicanism, left-wing socialism, wildly promiscuous homosexuality – were all firmly embedded in his personality before he left Lancing.

The religion was another part of the reaction against Crowborough: after all that drabness he hungered for extravagant ceremonial. It also came with the school. Lancing was founded in the nineteenth century to promote the Oxford Movement and had been conspicuously 'high' ever since. Not as high as Tom would have wished, admittedly: he found the services only 'moderate', and yearned for an incense-saturated High Mass. But the school was blessed with a majestic, numinous, neo-Gothic chapel. As Dudley Carew wrote, 'the Chapel at Lancing had a beauty and an atmosphere which insisted on making themselves felt.'[28] Evelyn Waugh believed that the building could be best appreciated by lying on the grass beside it and staring upwards. (And, Carew reported, he was right: 'The stone seemed to soar into the sky and, after a time, it made us almost as giddy as though we had been on the roof looking down.') As a sacristan, Tom was able to spend many hours happily arranging candlesticks or fingering vestments, often in the company of his fellow-sacristan Evelyn Waugh. When Waugh decided that he had lost his faith, it was Tom he confided in. 'One Saturday evening,' Waugh recalled in his autobiography, 'Driberg and I were doing something in the sanctuary to prepare it for next day when I revealed to him my discovery that there was no God. In that case, he remarked, I had no business to be handling the altar cloth.'[29] It should be said that Tom's recollection of the incident was rather different.[30] According to this, Tom was fussing because the altar cloth was not hanging symmetrically. Waugh replied: 'Nonsense! If it's good enough for me it's good enough for God.' Tom thought this a shocking blasphemy, but he did not take it as a confession of atheism.

After Waugh left Lancing in 1921 to go up to Hertford College, Oxford, Tom kept in touch with him, writing long, ribald, gossipy letters about the school – 'just what an hungering OL wishes to receive,' Waugh told him. In reply, Waugh sent dirty jokes ('What wines will Princess Mary and Lascelles drink on their wedding night? She will open her 24 year old port and he will indulge in cider'), attempts at literary gossip ('There are rumours that the *Times Literary Supplement* is going to cease, that Catherine [*sic*] Mansfield is not going to die after all, that J. C. Squire has taken seriously to drink at last') and *Brideshead*-style counsel ('Do let me most seriously advise you to take to drink. There is nothing like the aesthetic pleasure of being drunk and if you do it in the right way you can avoid being ill the next day. That is the greatest thing Oxford has to teach'). After Tom had endured a miserable Officer Training Corps camp one summer, Waugh wrote to express his sympathy: 'For such as us who find small comfort in sodomy, camp has little that is charming.' At the same time he sent Tom a consolatory box of S. P. Ora's Turkish cigarettes. 'One comes to them,' he explained rather preciously, 'as an abiding comfort (as after the fierce riches of Swinburne one falls into the opiate arms of Mallory)'.

When Tom went to Oxford to sit for a scholarship, Waugh was an attentive host. 'There is no need to bring evening things,' he wrote beforehand. 'Official dinners, Union speechmakings, first nights of OUDS and dances are the only things one changes for at Oxford. I should not think you will need them. If you think you will, certainly only dinner jacket.' Not that Tom's visit was lacking in entertainment: Waugh took him to the Hypocrites' Club, where certain undergraduates – all male, most homosexual – got stupendously drunk. Tom remembered 'dancing with John F., while Evelyn and another rolled on a sofa with (as one of them said later) their "tongues licking each other's tonsils".'[31] Tom's first attempt at the scholarship ended in failure. And the Hypocrites' Club was closed down by the proctors soon afterwards.

The friendship between Tom and Evelyn Waugh would have been closer still but for one large, fixed obstacle: they loathed each other's politics. From boyhood Waugh had assumed the reactionary opinions that later made him such an ornament of White's Club. Tom was just as precocious. His socialism was, he later claimed, inspired mainly by reading the prefaces to Bernard Shaw's plays, particularly *The Doctor's Dilemma*, though the debating society and the Dilettanti played some part by forcing him to defend his position against vigorous argument. (Years later he told John Betjeman that he had 'become Left' by reading Shaw's prefaces. 'Good Lord, how clever of you,' Betjeman replied in astonishment. 'Don't tell me they're good.'[32])

By the age of fifteen he was consciously on the Left. The Labour Party of Ramsay MacDonald seemed as dull and moderate as a church without incense; so, in one of his school holidays, Tom joined the Brighton branch of the newly-formed Communist Party. Quite apart from its ideological merits, it was 'part of the revolt against Crowborough';[33] like his sexuality and religious fetishism, his Communism was a way of *épatant les bourgeois* – though in this case the *épat* was somewhat diluted by the fact that he concealed his party membership from his mother, the very person against whom he was revolting. Indeed the only person in Crowborough who seems to have known of Tom's CP affiliation was Father Gurdon, the priest, who found it 'mildly amusing'.

Membership brought with it an incidental bonus: through the Party 'I was at last able to meet on terms of equality – better still, inferiority, since they had been in the Party longer than I – males of the working class.' Unfortunately, he lamented, 'those I happened to get to know best were unattractively plain.'[34] So his sexual encounters with working-class men were limited to anonymous couplings in the public lavatories of Tunbridge Wells or Brighton.

Sexually, as liturgically, Tom's time at Lancing strengthened his awareness of his own orientation. During the holidays he even took to using make-up – 'a powder compact and a little rouge'.[35] At school, he had a crush on E. J. 'Jimmy' Watson, a slightly younger boy in another house, but the passion was unrequited and un-consummated. Soon after first catching sight of Watson, Tom celebrated the event in a poem called 'Minutes of My Life':

> I saw Jimmy first on the Quad,
> Ragging about; I thought 'My God!
> What a topping boy that chap there looks:
> Who is he?' Just then he dropped his books
> And rushed off with a shout; so I went over there,
> And looked at 'em – *Kennedy's Latin Grammar* –
> 'Is his name written in it?' 'Yes, there it is.' 'Where?'
> ('Here's the Head Master's wife, God damn her!')

In another poem written at the time, Tom referred more obliquely to his torments of the flesh:

> The body is a sepulchre, wherein
> The chafing soul is pent; she, restless, strives
> To win again that light which all our lives
> We spend in exile from: the bar is thin . . .

Until his last year at Lancing Tom's sexual restlessness was ex-pressed mostly in words rather than deeds. There may have been occasional furtive gropes, but he was uncharacteristically circumspect about them. Under the patronage of Roxburgh he rose steadily through the ranks, his reputation untouched by scandal. He was appointed head librarian and head sacristan; in September 1923, the start of his final year, he became head of his house and deputy head of the school.

A respectable achievement, one might think, especially as he lacked the sporting qualifications usually preferred. But Tom was bitterly upset at being a mere deputy. The head boy in whose favour he had been passed over, a youth named Gibbs, was everything Tom was not – 'straight, square, glowingly healthy and clean-minded'.[36] Tom, a natural rebel, had played the game according to the rules laid down by the authorities and had lost. There was no longer anything to gain from self-denial. He made sexual advances to a boy in his dormitory, who promptly reported him to the housemaster.

The punishment would normally have been immediate expulsion. But the school authorities were worried by the effect that the scandal might have on Tom's mother, coming so soon after the death of her husband. The headmaster, a charitable old cleric called the Reverend Henry Bowlby, determined on 'keeping the whole trouble from Mrs Driberg, who is a widow in poor circumstances and devoted to this – her youngest – child'.[37] Tom's brothers, Jack and Jim, were discreetly summoned to Lancing to discuss the problem.

A deal was struck. All news of Tom's disgrace would be kept from Mrs Driberg. He could stay on until the end of the Christmas term in a form of solitary confinement, working and sleeping in a small bedsitting room. He must not attend lessons or have any contact with other boys. He could take meals in the house dining room, but even here he was segregated: he sat on a dais with the housemaster, his wife and the matron. At the end of term he must leave, but his mother would be told that this was because he needed private tuition for his second attempt at the Oxford scholarship.

This arrangement did nothing to relieve Tom's distress. 'I felt so utterly miserable that I went up one night to a high place – the top of the "Masters' Tower" – and tried but failed to summon up enough courage to jump from it.' On the last day of term he had to endure an interview with Bowlby, who told him that 'if you have enough faith in Christ, he will see you through.'

Tom's early departure turned out to be no bad thing. The tutor who was engaged to 'cram' him for his second attempt at the Oxford scholarship, a young man from Orpington called Colin Pearson (later Lord Justice Pearson), taught Tom how to bluff his way through the papers in which he was weakest; and in March 1924 T. E. N. Driberg was awarded the third classical scholarship at Christ Church, Oxford. It was worth £80 a year.

No sooner had the award been announced in *The Times*, however, than rumour of his conduct at Lancing began to reach the ears of the Dean of Christ Church, who immediately dashed off an anxious letter to Bowlby at Lancing. In reply, once again, Bowlby was generous beyond the call of duty. After praising Tom as a 'distinctly able fellow – with tastes and interests outside his pure Scholarship', he tried to calm the Dean's fears:

In reply to your confidential questions, I should like to reassure you absolutely on the point at issue. There was no definite charge of immorality; otherwise we should have removed him from the School and could not have recommended him to any College authorities. More than this, the undue intimacy which he apparently wished to establish with a younger member of the House was discovered at once; and he himself protested that we had placed too severe an interpretation upon his action. However, with all our officials we maintain the standard of 'Caesar's wife', and therefore degraded Driberg from his position as a Captain of his House and of School Prefect.

You inquire further whether I consider 'there is no reasonable probability of a recurrence of this morbid state'. Again I can answer unhesitatingly that I feel sure the boy has learnt his lesson; quite apart from the fact that the circumstances of University life are wholly different, and that views on such matters change quickly when School has been left behind.

This was one of the great misjudgments of modern times, but it satisfied Christ Church.

Tom showed no gratitude for his old headmaster's kindnesses. He rejoiced when, shortly after retiring from Lancing, Bowlby was arrested and charged with molesting little girls on a train. The trial ended in acquittal, but Bowlby suffered grievously from all the publicity. 'Perhaps,' Tom gloated, 'I should not have felt a slight twinge of *Schadenfreude*.'

With six months to fill before taking up his place at Oxford, Tom spent the summer term teaching English at a prep school in Bournemouth. This seems to have been an unmemorable experience, redeemed only by the opportunities for corrupting the minds of his pupils with poems by Edith Sitwell and other modernists. The boys' smooth, hairless bodies were left well alone: he was still badly shaken by the fright of his expulsion from Lancing. Besides, he explained, they were 'too young for me'.

CHAPTER TWO

OXFORD RED

... National Service had not been suggested,
  O-Level and A- were called Certs,
Our waistcoats were cut double-breasted,
  Our flannel trousers like skirts:
One could meet any day in society
  Harold Acton, Tom Driberg or Rowse –
May there always, to lend a variety,
  Be some rather odd fish at the House ...

— W. H. Auden's toast to Christ Church,
  proposed at Gaudy dinner, Oxford,
                     22 June 1960

No generation of Oxford undergraduates has been so unflaggingly mythologised as that of the mid-1920s. The hyperbole is well caught in the title of Martin Green's book about them, *Children of the Sun*.[1]

Is it because these were uniquely brilliant youths who went on to make the world catch its breath? Hardly. W. H. Auden, a contemporary of Tom's at Christ Church ('The House'), became a poet of international reputation; yet he is of less interest to chroniclers of the sun-children than figures such as Brian Howard and Harold Acton, also both at Christ Church, or Peter Quennell and Cyril Connolly. Brian Howard, the most lionised of undergraduates, was paralysed for the rest of his miserable life by his inability to live up to the adulation he had enjoyed at Oxford. Some of the sun-children were Marxists, some were reactionaries; some – Alfred Duggan and John Strachey – were reactionaries who later became Marxists.

What they all had in common, according to Martin Green's theory, was a determination to challenge the hegemony of Victorian and Edwardian 'consensus humanism'. They defied 'the "mature" modes of seriousness that our culture sponsors'.

The weapons most favoured were dandyism and aestheticism. The use of the word 'weapon' is not inapt. Harold Acton, who recited *The Waste Land* through a megaphone from his balcony to bemused passers-by in Christ Church meadows, said he would crush the enemies of aestheticism with mockery 'and, if need be, with violence'. His brother William Acton, another Oxford dandy of the period, once knocked down a 'hearty' who had sneered at his bottle-green suit and raspberry *crêpe de chine* shirt.

More often the violence was in the other direction. When Tom arrived at Christ Church in the autumn of 1924, he wasted little time in equipping himself with a pair of Oxford bags, a fashion popularised by Harold Acton. Tom's were bright green and as baggy as he could get: at least two feet wide in each leg. They looked, as Auden said, more like a skirt than a pair of trousers. What happened next was inevitable, and will be familiar to anyone who has read the opening scene of Evelyn Waugh's *Decline and Fall*. A group of fifteen or so Bullingdon Club types came charging up Tom's staircase in Peckwater Quad one night, howling his name. As Waugh wrote, 'Any who have heard that sound will shrink from the recollection of it; it is the sound of the English county families baying for broken glass.' Within moments Tom's green trousers had been torn from him. They were paraded round the quad and then cut into strips, which were hung in the Junior Common Room like hunting trophies.

But it would be a mistake to think that the battle lines were as simply drawn as that incident implies. Tom soon became quite friendly with the leader of the party that debagged him, Tim Shaw. Brian Howard, the *arbiter elegantarum* of the dandies, used to join Bullingdon members on window-smashing forays. And Paul Pennyfeather, the unfortunate victim in *Decline and Fall*, who lived within his allowance and always ate in Hall and never drank to excess, would have seemed as contemptible to the aesthetes as to the hearties. For the rest of his life Tom remembered how 'irresistibly exhilarating' he found it when, during his first interview with his tutor, a rich undergraduate put his head round the door to announce that 'I shan't be coming to any tutorials or lectures this term, because I've managed to get four days' hunting a week.'

Not that Tom would miss lectures to chase a fox through the mud. But he loved the insolence of it, the idea that one was free to cut tutorials, drink wine, drive out to the country in a fast car for lunch, throw parties in one's rooms – and not be punished. It was quite a change from school; even from 'liberal' Lancing. Almost from his first day at Oxford Tom gorged himself on this delicious freedom. The obligations implied by a scholarship were quickly forgotten. 'I was preoccupied with interests outside – politics, art, sex, parties and so on,' he said later. 'There was just no time for any academic work.'[2]

The Oxford of the 1920s could not have been better suited to his expression of those interests. He found that his growing enthusiasm for the *avant-garde* – for Diaghilev and Stravinsky, Jean Cocteau and Picasso – was shared by most of his new friends. He obtained a copy of *Ulysses* from Paris and 'toiled my way through it with delight'; when he painted an abstract water-colour for a student art exhibition shortly afterwards, he named it 'Marion Tweedy Bloom' in honour of Joyce's heroine.

The epochal event for all the Oxford aesthetes of Tom's generation was the publication of *The Waste Land*. As Eliot's biographer Peter Ackroyd has written:

It was not with the reviewers . . . that the reputation of *The Waste Land* was first made but rather with undergraduates and young writers who saw it as the revelation of a modern sensibility. With its 'jazz' rhythms, its images of urban and suburban life, its fashionable use of anthropological myth, its introduction of quotation and parody – this was, as Edmund Wilson said, 'the great knockout up to date'.[3]

Cyril Connolly said that he and some others developed 'a total preoccupation'[4] with Eliot. Harold Acton promoted the poem with the urgency and zeal of a missionary trying to save the unconverted.

Tom and W. H. Auden discovered *The Waste Land* together. They 'read it, standing side by side in [Tom's] rooms, in a copy of the first issue of Eliot's review, *The Criterion*; read it, at first, with incredulous hilarity (the Mrs Porter bit, for instance); read it, again and again, with growing awe.'[5] Or so Tom claimed. This is slightly surprising. W. H. Auden did not go up to Christ Church until October 1925, a year after Tom; and he said later that the poetry he wrote in his first term at Oxford was influenced mainly by Hardy and Edward Thomas because he had not yet seen *The Waste Land*. So the historic moment of revelation in Tom's rooms, which was to have such an effect on Auden's verse, cannot have happened earlier than 1926. Yet the first issue of *The Criterion*, which did indeed carry *The Waste Land*, appeared in October 1922. It was widely noticed. Could Tom, normally so alert to anything new, really have taken more than three years to discover the poem? Apparently so: Auden once inscribed a book 'To Tom Driberg, who made me read *The Waste Land*', which seems pretty conclusive. But Tom's slowness in spotting it was an unusual lapse.

More characteristic was his early championing of Sacheverell Sitwell's *Southern Baroque Art*, published in 1924, which inspired the fashion for Italian baroque and rococo followed by such influential undergraduates as Harold Acton and Edward James. (James was a fabulously rich and exotic young man, rumoured to be an illegitimate son of Edward VII. He was a great patron of the aesthetes and paid for Tom's tickets to the Diaghilev ballet in London.) Tom enhanced his reputation by being able to claim acquaintance with the author: he had met both Sacheverell and Osbert Sitwell while he and his mother were at the Hotel Bristol in Rapallo in December 1924, during his first Christmas vacation from Oxford.

Staying in the Hotel Bristol that Christmas were several other English artists and *literati* who became friends of Tom's: the composer William Walton, who had written *Façade* with Edith Sitwell a couple of years earlier; Richard Wyndham, who was making drawings of *campanili* for his book on southern baroque towers and drove round in an open-topped grey Rolls-Royce; and the novelist Ada Leverson, Oscar Wilde's old friend, who took Tom to see Max Beerbohm in his little rooftop study in Rapallo. Also in town was Peggy Guggenheim: on New Year's Eve Tom had to rescue her from a fracas in the casino in which her drunken husband had got involved.

Just as memorable, from Tom's point of view, were the indigenous males. 'I can almost forgive my mother for the well-meaning errors of my upbringing,' he wrote, 'when I recall that she was responsible for my first experience of Italy and, unwittingly, for my first taste of Italian sex.' He and his mother went over to Portofino one day and walked along the headland to the *faro*. She slipped and hurt herself slightly, so Tom climbed the lighthouse on his own. He found at the top a 'sensuously attractive' twenty-five-year-old lighthouse keeper. Their eyes met. 'Contact was instant, consummation almost as quick; he had clearly not had any sex for some days. Within five minutes or so I had rejoined my mother. "What a long time you were up there, dear." "Well, it was a lovely view, mother." '[6]

Tom's sexuality fitted into mid-Twenties Oxford as happily as his artistic tastes. 'We were the last generation of womanless Oxford,' Cyril Connolly wrote. 'Men who liked women were apt to get sent down.'[7] Connolly himself was later a famous womaniser, but even he was affected by the prevailing homoerotic ethos of the time. So were others who went on to suppress their homosexual inclinations after leaving university: John Betjeman had sex with W. H. Auden for £5, and we have already seen Evelyn Waugh rolling on a sofa with his tongue down another man's throat. Homosexuality, or at least some semblance of it, was not merely acceptable but almost *de rigueur*. One of Tom's Oxford friends, the historian A. J. P. Taylor, noted that 'the strange one-sexed system of education at public schools and universities had always run to homosexuality.' In Victorian times it was 'sentimental and ostensibly innocent'. At the *fin de siècle* it was 'consciously wicked'. In the 1920s it was neither innocent nor wicked. 'It was merely, for a brief period, normal.'[8] Tom was something of an oddity nevertheless; for he had no desire to sleep with his social and intellectual equals. Throughout his life he believed that sex was enjoyable only with someone he had never met before and would never meet again.

He cut an attractive figure, even in his Oxford bags: tall, lean, darkly handsome. He had shed his schoolboy glasses. His withdrawn, rather diffident, apparently aloof manner – a consequence of having spent so much of his childhood on his own – now seemed to give him an air of mystery. The hint of wickedness behind that saturnine countenance merely heightened its allure. Christ Church had plenty of undergraduates who would undoubtedly have been delighted to sport their oak with Tom; yet he seems not to have gone to bed with any fellow-students during his three years at Oxford. While Evelyn Waugh mooned over young Richard Pares, and John Betjeman swooned over Hugh Gaitskell ('Hugh, may I stroke your bottom?' 'Oh, I suppose so, if you *must*'), Tom sought sex where he had always found it, in the shadows. He haunted public lavatories; he ambled along the canal towpath at twilight. A favourite memory was of 'romantic walks' with a milk roundsman 'who seemed to smell deliciously of milk'. There was a brief fling with a don, but this was – in the first instance, at least – a case of mistaken identity: when they met in a gents' lavatory in Bear Lane the man 'looked far from donnish'.

His pursuit of young working-class men was sometimes too energetic. At A. J. P. Taylor's twenty-first-birthday dinner, Tom kept leaving the table for what were, Taylor assumed, visits to the lavatory. In fact Tom was chasing the waiter. Finally, the harassed servitor strode up to Taylor and issued an ultimatum: 'I am a respectable married man and if that gentleman comes out to me again I shall go home.' When Tom was reminded of this incident by Taylor fifty years later, he remembered the waiter perfectly and was quite unrepentant. 'What,' he asked, 'had his being a married man to do with it?'[9] The last evening that A. J. P. Taylor and Tom spent together, only a few months before Tom's death, ended appropriately: as Taylor was leaving, Tom said that he wanted to 'stay behind and have a word with the waiter'.

Alan Taylor, a studious Lancastrian, was out of the usual run of Tom's Oxford friends. What brought the pair together was the fact that they were members of the Oxford University Communist Party. Indeed at one point they were the entire membership: Tom was the Secretary, Taylor the rank-and-file.

Oxford in the mid-1920s was not hospitable to left-wing politics. The weekly report of Oxford Union debates in the *Cherwell* was headed by one of Evelyn Waugh's woodcuts, which bore an apt slogan: 'Europe Listens Where Oxford Sleeps'. The international political ferment that had been started by the Russian revolution went all but unnoticed at the university. At Oriel A. J. P. Taylor discovered that even the Liberal Asquith was regarded as a dangerous revolutionary and that anyone with socialist opinions was well advised to keep quiet about them. Taylor made the mistake of talking freely. 'Oriel being a civilised college, I got off lightly. All I suffered was a stream of drunken men calling each evening in an attempt to convert me away from Communism. When this became intolerable, I had to keep away from my rooms until late at night.'[10] A Communist at Merton called Ieaun Thomas was treated more roughly: in just one term he had his books burnt twice and his wardrobe four times. 'People talk of a persecution complex,' Thomas grumbled. 'It is easy to have a persecution complex if you are a Communist at Merton.' Before long Thomas became so weary of the guerrilla raids on his room that he quit Oxford altogether.

Graham Greene and Claud Cockburn, who were a year senior to Tom, were Communists too, but were not active in the Party. The only other member at Oxford was a brash, boastful Australian Rhodes scholar called Tom Stephensen. He regarded Greene, Cockburn, Driberg and Taylor as incurably frivolous, and preferred to spend his time working with Oxford trade unions. This left T. E. N. Driberg and A. J. P. Taylor on their own.

The monthly meetings of the Oxford University Communist Party were therefore cosy affairs. They were held in Tom's rooms in Peckwater Quad. The curtains were drawn; the only light was from candles. Tom, wearing a dressing-gown, would shuffle round the room to the strains of a jazz or blues record that he had just bought – Bessie Smith, perhaps, or Ethel Waters. Taylor would report on his lack of success in recruiting converts from the Labour Club (to which he belonged as well, in contravention of the Labour Party's recently instituted ban on dual membership). Tom would then speak of his achievements in selling the CP's paper, *Workers' Weekly*, at the gates of factories in Cowley – which, as Taylor pointed out, 'enabled him to become acquainted with the better-looking factory workers'. Perhaps Tom Stephensen's accusations of frivolity were justified. Taylor later admitted: 'I did not take my political activities very seriously.'

While Oxford slept, the British labour movement was stirring. On 22 January 1924 James Ramsay MacDonald had become the first socialist ever to form a British government, but from the start he had taken pains to calm any fluttering hearts by proving himself a respectable, statesmanlike fellow. In particular he wanted to emphasise that, though his government had recognised the Soviet Union and signed treaties with it, at home he was as robust an anti-Communist as any Liberal or Tory. To this end, his attorney-general announced that the editor of *Workers' Weekly*, J. R. Campbell, was to be prosecuted for sedition. There was uproar from Labour supporters, and in October the prosecution was dropped. It was then the turn of Conservative MPs to be outraged: they managed to push a motion of censure through the House of Commons, which automatically brought about the dissolution of Parliament. In the ensuing election Labour lost 42 seats, the Liberals lost 118. In November 1924 Stanley Baldwin, who had been evicted from office only nine months earlier, returned to 10 Downing Street.

It was inevitable that sooner or later the new government would find itself dragged into a confrontation between unions and employers; it was almost as inevitable that the coal industry was to be the battlefield. The mine owners, a notoriously bone-headed breed, reacted to a sharp fall in coal exports by insisting that miners should have their wages reduced and their working day lengthened. The Miners' Federation refused. In July 1925 Baldwin averted what might have become a general strike by offering to subsidise the miners' wages while a Royal Commission considered the problem. Peace was bought for eight months. But the Commission's report, issued in March 1926, recommended among other things that the subsidy should be stopped from 30 April. Once again the mine-owners said that wage cuts were essential; once again the workers declined to agree. On 4 May 1926 Britain's first General Strike began.

The news took A. J. P. Taylor by surprise. 'Perhaps,' he thought, 'the revolution was coming after all.'[11] Since he and Tom would presumably have to lead the revolution in Oxford, they drove up to London at high speed in Taylor's fishtailed Rover sports car to get instructions from the Communist Party's HQ. To their surprise, the office at 16 King Street was shuttered and bolted. Hot for insurrection, the two undergraduates banged at the door until an elderly Communist called Bob Stewart appeared. 'There's no one here,' he said with a scowl. 'I'm only the caretaker. Get along hame with ye.' (According to Taylor, 'these were the only instructions I ever received from the Communist Party of Great Britain.') Taylor was so disillusioned that he drove off to Preston to help his striking father instead. But Tom decided to wait in London for a day or two. He arranged to stay at his brother Jim's flat in Park Crescent, by Portland Place.

Tom eventually prevailed on the curmudgeonly Stewart to give him a job. He was ordered to collect a bundle of strike bulletins, and then had to rendezvous with another comrade who would drive him north through various provincial cities, distributing the bulletins as they went. Tom had only just started to load the papers into the man's car when the police arrested him. He was interrogated for several hours, first at Bow Street police station, later at Scotland Yard. Then he returned to Park Crescent. Since Jim and his wife were both Tories, Tom had not explained to them why he was in town; but they already had their suspicions, 'and were furious when, immediately after my return from the Yard, a copper took up his position on the opposite pavement and proceeded, very obviously and crudely, to watch their flat'. After this, Tom seems to have played little part in the strike.

Back in Oxford, scores of undergraduates were enlisting as special constables and strike-breakers, imagining heroic roles for themselves. 'It was August 1914 all over again,' A. J. P. Taylor recalled. 'The volunteers saw themselves gallantly at war against the revolution. One of them said to me, "I wonder if I shall ever come back." The enrolment was Tom Brown's Last Stand.' The Labour Club held a meeting to protest at the university's encouragement of the blacklegs. A. D. Lindsay, the Master of Balliol, came along to explain that the university was not taking sides; it was merely allowing government recruiting officers to use its premises.

Support for the strikers in Oxford was led by the socialist don G. D. H. Cole, a patron of the Labour Club, whose group of undergraduate followers included John Dugdale (later a Labour MP) and Hugh Gaitskell. Tom had little time for Cole's reformists, though he speculated later that 'maybe I would have been more interested if I had known that Cole, besides being one of the most brilliant and attractive of the younger dons, had homosexual tendencies.'[12] Cecil Day Lewis drove a car for the Trades Union Congress in London for the duration. W. H. Auden volunteered his services, too, and was asked to collect a car belonging to a sympathetic history don from Oriel, George Clark; it was to be moved from Old Marston into the centre of Oxford. Auden was too embarrassed to admit that he had never driven a car before. The two-mile journey took him two days.

An even more improbable class warrior was John Betjeman. As his biographer, Bevis Hillier, has pointed out: 'John might easily have become a strike breaker. Nothing could have been more tempting to him than the prospect of driving a train or a bus.'[13] But he was persuaded by Dugdale and Gaitskell to side with the workers, and travelled to Didcot in Dugdale's Morris to collect messages for the National Union of Railwaymen. 'I do not recall their having any messages for us to take,' Betjeman wrote; but he thought it a 'lark' all the same.

On 12 May, after nine days, the General Strike ended with a suddenness that shocked most of those involved: the TUC had, in effect, capitulated. Some workers refused to go back; others found that they had no jobs anyway. There was a legacy of great bitterness and poverty, especially in mining villages, where most of the strikers stayed out until the winter. But at Oxford it was all soon forgiven. Had undergraduates on either side seen it as anything more than a lark? Perhaps not. As the strike-breaking students returned to Oxford, A. J. P. Taylor found that 'they had developed a respect for what they called "the other side". They were not offended at what I had done. On the contrary, it created a bond between us; and we were far more friendly than we had been before. Their disapproval, so far as they had any, was directed against the "shirkers" who had stayed in Oxford and not taken sides at all.' It was not the winning that counted but the taking part. One can almost hear a ghostly voice exhorting 'Play up, play up, and play the game!' The miners who never worked again after 1926 could be forgiven for taking a less sporting attitude to the struggle.

Tom himself did not treat the General Strike as frivolously as most of his Oxford contemporaries; indeed he described it as 'a most unfrivolous, brave and tragic event'. But he was ashamed of his own flimsy contribution. During vacations from Oxford over the next year he tried to atone for his 'humiliating flop' by volunteering for duty in the editorial office of the *Sunday Worker*, one of the Party's newspapers. While doing this penance he often slept rough, since he was no longer a welcome guest at the flat of his brother Jim; but sometimes he would walk the streets until he found a man who was prepared to pay for the privilege of taking him home for the night.

His reports for the *Sunday Worker* were published anonymously, lest a copy might by some bizarre circumstance fall into the hands of someone who knew him or – worse – his mother. But in the spring vacation of 1927 he emerged from the shadows for long enough to be recognised. On the weekend of the boat race between Oxford and Cambridge, the *Sunday Worker* could not resist boasting that its correspondent was himself a varsity man. And thus it was that Tom had his first by-line in a national newspaper, above a front-page report that is worth quoting in full, headlines and all:

BOAT RACE ORGY

Varsity 'Bloods' Run Amok in West End

TOW-PATH SNOBS

Fewer Workers Trouble To Turn Out For Boss Event

Cambridge beat Oxford by four lengths. Time 20 min. 16 sec. Record time 18 min. 29 sec. (Oxford, 1911). Last year's time, 19 min. 29 sec. Races rowed, 79; Oxford won 40; Cambridge won 38; dead heat, one. Course: Putney to Mortlake (4½ miles).

BY T.E. [*sic*] DRIBERG
(Christ Church, Oxford)

The banks of the Thames were yesterday lined as thickly as ever with enthusiastic crowds who had come for miles to see the Oxford and Cambridge boat race.

Working-class people were conspicuously fewer than in previous years. Perhaps the Workers are beginning to realise that there are better ways of spending a Saturday afternoon than in struggling for some hours on a crowded towpath for the doubtful privilege of watching a few young cubs from the 'varsities engaged in what is probably their nearest approach to hard work.

But the middle classes and the wealthy unemployed were of course there in full force, and were no doubt vastly relieved to find this important spectacle almost entirely free from the contaminating presence of their social 'inferiors'.

'What a lot of nice people one sees here,' I overheard one elegantly-dressed young thing say to her boyfriend, a youth in Oxford bags and a monocle which failed to hide the vacant arrogance of his stare.

PECKSNIFF BALDWIN

She may have been referring to Mr Pecksniff Baldwin, who with his wife and daughters, and his son Wyndham, was present in the Cambridge enclosure.

A few women in expensively simple tailor-made and some typical plus-foured products of the bosses' principal dope-factories gladly paid a mere guinea or two to get a better view of the race from a luxurious launch.

However, most were content to make the day a kind of social function like Ascot or Henley on a smaller scale – for from the tow-path the race itself is actually visible only for a couple of minutes or so.

'REVELRY'

The most important part of the day was, as usual, the evening's revelry in the West End. Never before has this been of a more extravagant character.

Money and champagne flowed like water and all night young bloods were to be seen rushing about the streets completely drunk, holding up the traffic and pushing mere common people, young or old, men or women, rudely out of their way.

Scenes of disorder were witnessed in restaurants and night-clubs; and in one of the most exclusive of these damage was done which is estimated to amount to more than £200 – a mere nothing, of course, to these future rulers of our nation.

HOOLIGANISM TOLERATED

But all this hooliganism was treated by the authorities with a smile of indulgent approval. After all, the great English tradition of law for one class and licence for the other must be maintained.

Workers will remember that there is probably not a single one either of those who took part in the actual boat race, or of the West End rowdies of last evening, who did not in the general strike do his utmost by blacklegging to keep for his class the privileges which were so well illustrated yesterday.[14]

Afterwards, Tom seemed faintly embarrassed by this spirited début. 'I doubt if the article converted anyone to Communism, and it may have antagonised some readers,' was all he had to say about it in *Ruling Passions*. 'It should probably have been dismissed as a "Left deviation".' One reader who was strongly antagonised was an old buffer called John Hodgkin, who spotted the article while perusing the *Sunday Worker* in – of all places – the Constitutional Club. He hastened to a writing table and penned an outraged letter to the Dean of Christ Church.

Dear Sir,

In case you should not have seen it, I venture to call your attention to an article in today's *Sunday Worker* written by 'T. E. Driberg (Christ Church, Oxford).' I, of course, do not know whether such an individual is or is not a member of 'The House', but should he be so, I can only condole with you on possessing such an undesirable person (as he seems to be) on your books. It would not surprise me to learn that he was not a member of the University, graduate or otherwise. Apparently from his patronymic he is a foreigner. Should you not have seen the article you will forgive my calling your attention to it.

I am, Sir, Yours faithfully, John Hodgkin. (an old Magd. Coll. School-boy, early '70s!)[15]

Rather than flinging this poisonous little note in the waste-paper basket, the Dean filed it approvingly. He had not forgiven Tom for standing for the presidency of the Oxford Union as a 'Communist candidate' a month earlier, at the end of the spring term. To make matters worse, Tom had done surprisingly well, winning 75 votes against the 132 for C. S. M. Brereton (Balliol) and 155 for J. Playfair-Price (New College). This, Tom explained, was because 'Christ Church people, whether they were hunting men or not, voted automatically for a Christ Church candidate and they just didn't notice that I was on the extreme Left'.[16]

The *Sunday Worker* article, and the complaint it had provoked from the old Magd. Coll. (School) busybody, gave the Dean an opportunity for retribution. When Tom returned to Oxford for the start of the summer term he was given a 'severe dressing-down' for bringing the College's name into disrepute.

Summer 1927 was Tom's final term at Oxford. That he had survived for a full three years without being sent down was quite an achievement, if we are to believe his boast that he did 'practically no work at all'. The only reason for disbelieving him is the recollection of the actor Emlyn Williams, another Christ Church man, that before the previous year's exams 'Greenleaves, Lennox-Boyd, Auden, Rowse and Driberg all seemed to be working at fever pitch'.[17] No other contemporary recorded this sudden and implausible diligence. But Tom had indeed been at 'fever pitch', literally: he had avoided the second-year exams by eating 'a certain substance' which sent his temperature up sharply, earning him an aegrotat.

The same trick could not be carried off twice. He would surely have to sit some exams eventually, which would equally surely reveal that his reading in the previous three years had included few of the recommended classical texts. Tom seemed unconcerned by the imminence of his nemesis. Instead, he threw himself into a project that would again push his name into the pages of the national press: he booked the Holywell Music Room for a concert to be called 'Homage to Beethoven', in honour of the centenary of the composer's death. The title gave no clue that the evening would be anything other than a respectful canter through some of the great man's works, so elderly dons and their wives – 'a nice collection of old ladies from North Oxford in silk shawls,' in John Betjeman's words – filled the hall on the evening of Sunday 27 May. ('The air,' according to Tom, 'was thick with the aroma of moth-balls.') They were disabused as soon as Tom took the stage: through a mega-phone, he curtly requested the audience to 'commit no nuisance'.

The reviewer for *Cherwell* described the scene thus: 'Into an atmosphere of good dinner digesting, and indifferent cigars reeking, Mr Driberg hurled his staccato and repressive challenge.'[18] There-upon the small orchestra behind him sprang noisily and discor-dantly into life. In front of the stage, a plaster bust of Beethoven frowned suspiciously. As John Betjeman recalled in his verse auto-biography, *Summoned by Bells*:

> The nice North Oxford audience, velvet-dress'd,
>   Waiting a treat whose title promised well:
> HOMAGE TO BEETHOVEN the posters show.
>   'Words: Thomas Driberg. Music: Archie Browne'.
> Good wives of Heads of Houses, do you know
>   For what it is you've given your half-crown?[19]

The orchestra was made up of four-handed piano, a string section, some woodwind and an imposing array of typewriters and 'other domestic conveniences', playing a score in three movements composed for the occasion by Archie G. Browne (under the pseudonym of Kerreth Guinn-Kinney). Over the tinkling and clat-tering, Tom began to recite, through his megaphone, 'Homage to Beethoven', a long poem in three parts. He started as he meant to go on:

> A pound a day makes country women's holiday
>   Gay day holiday and holidays mean member
> But once fell the laughter from Parthenon dead
>   For Dick goes tomorrow to visit December
>   remember remember
> The wrinkled pinhead sky must come
>   The shady tomb, the shady tomb
>   december

There was more, much more. As with Edith Sitwell's *Façade*, which had been premiered at the Aeolian Hall in London four years earlier, the sound and rhythm of the words – delivered in a rhythmic, curiously impersonal monotone – was far more import-ant than any meaning they may or may not have had. (The idea of delivering the verse through a megaphone was also taken from *Façade*.) Some of it was little more than a modernist version of 'hey-nonny-nonny':

> boom ya yelling ho ho hanks thanks not at all
> tonks tanks hangs hands across the sea and
> a few kind words words words verbal verbal
> vernal verbal ah vernal we try vernal we try to

Elsewhere Tom pelted the gawping audience with jumbled, quasi-Biblical images of antelopes and green slugs, fingernails and waterfalls, Satan and Sion. There was sex, too:

> If I forget thee, Sion, Sion,
>   may all my members lose their skill,
> For there a modest phallus beckons
>   in blushing starkness from the hill.

Tom's acquaintances in the hall were naturally on the look-out for *double entendres*, and were rebuked for it afterwards by the critic from *Isis*. 'The most appreciative part of the audience were those who were taken most by surprise,' he reported. 'On the other hand, those who in cumbrous conversation endeavoured to interpret the work's (sexual or other) significance must have taken much less real pleasure in it. It should be pointed out to them that the line "We'll whirl magenta hoops through that red town" does not, as I have heard it suggested, indicate Mr Driberg's left-wing political sympathies.'[20] The *Isis* reviewer praised Tom's contribution. 'Mr Driberg evokes excitement by words; not the sophisticated romantic excitement, but the simpler excitement arising from a perception of form.' Michael Dugdale[21] from the *Cherwell* was even more enthusiastic:

Mr Driberg has already thrown out small crumbs of his verse to the Oxford public, but this is the first time that we have heard a great deal of it, all at once. The effect is very pleasant. The phrases are too soothing to astonish us painfully, his associations too surprising to let our attention wander. We feel it inevitable, such is the magic of his sonorous phrases, that the theme, hitherto zoological, should in half a sentence be concerning itself with the late Lord Mayor of Gloucester.

There was indeed rather a lot in 'Homage to Beethoven' about the late Lord Mayor of Gloucester, who was described as a 'leprous puma'. But he had disappeared from view by the time the poem came to its bathetic end:

> To eat all this is no tangle, cried the deep one in Miranda.
> She was so young she didn't know how to pin down little spirals.
> But little spirals is alabaster and we were the first that ever burst
> And alabaster is alabaster five six pick up sticks.

Notwithstanding Michael Dugdale's favourable review, *Cherwell*, under the editorship of John Betjeman, did its best to sabotage Tom's success. On 14 May Betjeman had accepted for publication a poem by Tom, 'Spring Carol', which was later incorporated into the third part of 'Homage to Beethoven'. It included such lines as

> Destitute, destitute of caramel.
> White water comes to take its place.

and ended with a typically impenetrable couplet:

> 'Calm; and Free' (Wordsworth).
>   /Quite Abstract.

The next issue of *Cherwell*, which appeared the day before the premiere of 'Homage to Beethoven', printed an anonymous parody of Tom's work. According to Bevis Hillier it may even have been written by Betjeman himself, who was fond of Tom but could not resist teasing him for his *avant garde* affectations:

> MR DRIBERG'S NEXT POEM?
> An aard-vark, Aaron's-beard aback:
> Abacus, Abaddon, abaft abandon
> Abase, abask.
>
> A, ab, absque, coram, de:
> Y, yaffil, yapp:
> Zeppelin, zonave, zygote:
>
> Destitute, destitute of meaning –
> The Concise Oxford Dictionary comes to take its place:
> The beginning and the end –
> Between A and Z
>   quite obviously %.

Unperturbed by the ribbing, Tom remained convinced of the merits of 'Homage to Beethoven'. Three years later, in 1930, he persuaded the Parisian magazine *Échanges* to publish a revised version of the recitation under the title 'Metropolitan'. It was dedicated to Edith Sitwell.

What of the music? The orchestra provided what was, by all accounts, a fitting accompaniment to Tom's megaphonic nonsense verse. According to Eric Walter White, an admired undergraduate poet who played one of the piano parts, 'the typewriters had been silent during the first movement, and their entry in slow triplets over a slowly moving ostinato bass in common time, followed by a union glissando punctuated by warning bells, was undeniably moving.'[22] At the end of the second movement, following a drum-roll, the orchestra rose to its feet. The audience shifted nervously, wondering whether the National Anthem was about to be played. Suddenly the drum-roll stopped. Somewhere off stage a lavatory was flushed. A door slammed. This, it turned out, was the opening of the third movement.

Michael Dugdale thought the music admirably restrained: 'Sometimes the dry click of a typewriter would accentuate a well-turned phrase; once a member of the audience, by disregarding the preliminary exhortation, added to the richness of the orchestration; but when the reader drew to a close we were allowed to hear what some twenty musical instruments crowded into a small space could do. We were not disappointed. The music like the verse was admirable, and only failed to dispel the scowl from Beethoven's plaster features in front of the stage because that composer was unfortunately deaf.' As the third movement drew to a close in a tintinnabulation of typewriters, Tom raised his megaphone for a last time. 'Please,' he exhorted, 'adjust your dress before leaving.' He was cheered to the echo – or, as Michael Dugdale put it, the audience 'reacted so strongly to the emotional suggestion of the music and words that I felt that Mr Driberg's parting request was not misplaced.'

As well as drawing favourable notices from the university magazines, Tom's concert was noticed in the next issue of the *Sunday Times*, under the heading 'Musical Innovation'.[23] For the second time in as many months the names of Driberg and Christ Church appeared in the national press in a context that cannot have pleased the college authorities. The *Sunday Times* item was also drawn to the attention of Aleister Crowley, the legendary black magician who rejoiced in the title of 'the wickedest man in the world' or, more concisely, 'The Great Beast'. It is not certain why Crowley was so interested in the report of 'Homage to Beethoven'; perhaps word had reached him that Tom's weird lyrics included references to Beelzebub. Whatever the reason, Crowley invited Tom to lunch at the Tour Eiffel restaurant in Percy Street. Tom, with his love of anything dangerous, scandalous or bizarre, could not but accept. The Great Beast did not disappoint him. 'Pardon me while I invoke the moon,' Crowley intoned as they sat down to their meal, and then proceeded to recite some mumbo-jumbo by way of a grace. The two men met again from time to time after this lunch. One day Crowley announced that Tom was mentioned in the Egyptian Book of the Dead: the passage in question read 'From no expected house shall this child come' – and what, Crowley demanded, could be less expected than 'The House', as Christ Church was known? 'It was often hard to tell if he were serious or joking,' Tom wrote, 'as when, soon after this, he told me that he had decided to nominate me as his successor as World Teacher.' Tom speculated that, because he was at Christ Church, Crowley may have assumed he was rich. Crowley continued to labour under this misapprehension for some time. Even twenty years later, when a young convert called John Symonds put himself at the disposal of the Beast, the Beast replied by sending him 'the names and addresses of nineteen persons, among whom were Madame Wellington Koo (the Chinese Ambassadress), the late Viscount Tredegar, and Mr Tom Driberg, with instructions to call on them and raise funds'.[24] Yet it was Tom who made money out of Crowley, not *vice versa*. By rather dubious means he acquired Crowley's manuscript diary, bound in red morocco and encased in baroque silver, which recorded 'his daily magical and sexual doings'; many years later Tom sold this for a handsome sum to Jimmy Page, the guitarist with the rock group Led Zeppelin. In 1973 Tom raised more money by auctioning at Christie's several volumes presented to him by Crowley. They included a copy of *The*

Book of the Law, inscribed 'To True Thomas of the Eildon Hills with all best wishes from Boleskine and Alertarff'. In the same lot was a letter from Crowley urging Tom to study the Koran: 'I also hope that you will be pleased by the sincerity and simplicity of the Mohammedan faith, and learn up the words, so as not to make any more howlers like "Moslems".'[25]

Tom's meeting with Crowley confirmed his exotic reputation among his Oxford contemporaries. 'It was Thomas Driberg who now appeared to dominate the obvious and outer and smarter intellectualism of the university,' observed Geoffrey Grigson, then a young undergraduate at St Edmund Hall. Grigson wrote this extravagant account of visiting Tom at Christ Church:

I was taken round to see the great man in his rooms at the House by a friend of mine who had been with him at Lancing, but I was too small an atom for his notice. The black hair, the white face, the nervous insolence, the elegant tailoring – Stendhal might have seen him and modelled upon the sight a young priest, machiavellian and subfuscly burning with ambition; or Balzac might have transformed him from the brilliant undergraduate into a schemer sliding into power through the *salons* of Paris . . . I have felt since that this exceedingly able man was born and fashioned at the very least a hundred years too late, and perhaps in the wrong country . . . Here was the white embryo of a dark cardinal or a Pope or a prince of the Renaissance.[26]

Grigson did not like Tom's poetry, which he derided as 'versifying in the mode', the mode in question being a 'blend of Eliotese and Edith-Sitwellese'. Grigson's lifelong crusade against Edith Sitwell had already commenced, and he had a chance to spy on the foe at close quarters when she came to speak in Oxford, at Tom's behest, in June 1927.

Tom had been pressing his attentions upon Edith Sitwell for some time. Five months earlier, in his last Christmas vacation from university, he had invited her to tea at Rumpelmayer's in St James's Street; to his delight, she had accepted. For her Oxford performance he appointed himself impresario, stage manager and master of ceremonies. Holding up a copy of Eliot's *Criterion*, he spoke of 'the delights of intellectualism and modernism'. He introduced Edith

Sitwell with fulsome praise for the 'synaesthetic' qualities of her poetry. She returned the compliment handsomely. After comparing the poems of Noyes and Binyon to rolls of linoleum, she turned to Tom and laid her long, birdlike talons on his shoulder. 'This young man,' she informed her audience dramatically, 'is the hope of English poetry.'

Keen to capitalise on this testimonial, Tom sprang up from his chair at the end of Edith's speech to recite a poem of his own, 'Cottage Squalor':

> The beneficial forms of greenness
>   fall upon a green tablecloth,
> flickering to the plush and stealing
>   red ink from the undergrowth.
>
> Sunlight is green and grandmother beams,
>   the dirty girl prepares the greens,
> the network and the spider's blot
>   are grey and green flickering and dirt.
>
> She scrubbed sunlight, wet wood
>   wet wood smells green this morning.
> Dirty girl prepares greens.
>   Grandmother looks netted haughty.

The audience chewed pensively on these morsels. It was, as Grigson said, a rococo evening.

Having already been anointed as Aleister Crowley's heir, Tom now found himself publicly revealed by Edith Sitwell as the man on whom the future of poetry depended. His notoriety swelled until it seemed it might burst. As the summer term drew to a close, he could reflect that his university career had been an unimprovable success: he had begun to make a name for himself outside Oxford; he had cultivated the right friends; he had conquered his shyness; he had learned to eat and drink with discernment and pleasure. But by the more formal measurements of academe his three years in the nurturing womb of Peck Quad had been a failure. The moment of discovery could not be postponed. At the end of the summer term, at long last, he had to sit his Schools.

There was no feverish last-minute cramming, nor even any lead-swinging. The condemned man ate a hearty breakfast – or, to be strictly accurate, he attended a Commem' Ball the night before the first exam. White tie and tails happened to be the obligatory dress for both events. After drinking until dawn, he strode into the examination room still dressed from the night before, and still squiffy. Within minutes he was fast asleep.

And that was that. The college authorities told him to pack his bags forthwith. 'Completely disgraced', he left without a degree. 'Oxford,' he wrote, 'had finished with me.'

Not so. Tom avoided Christ Church for a few years after leaving, but in the 1950s and 1960s he was a regular and welcome guest. In 1965 he gave evidence at the public inquiry which killed the idea of building a main road through Christ Church meadow; perhaps in gratitude for this service, the then Dean, Cuthbert Simpson ('a dear old boy'), awarded Tom an honorary MA of the House. Simpson explained that the honour was given to people who were either too stupid or too lazy to pass exams but who later achieved some distinction. 'I think some Scottish nobleman was also an honorary MA,' Tom said, 'but whereas I was too lazy to pass exams, he was too stupid.'[27] One drawback was that the MA applied only while Tom was in the precincts of Christ Church. When visiting the House in his later years he loved strolling about in his MA gown, but he had to remove it as soon as he stepped out of Tom Gate into the street. Even at the age of seventy he was genuinely fearful that some sharp-eyed proctor might seize him.

CHAPTER THREE

TARTS AND DEBS

Tom left Oxford in the summer of 1927 with no degree and no money, but in high spirits. His undergraduate exhilaration was punctured as soon as he returned to Crowborough: 'My mother, her small house, and the whole place seemed to have shrunk, almost physically, into near insignificance.'[1] This was no sort of place from which to launch a literary career. A poet could live in a truly grand house or in a garret, but could not live in the stockbroker belt. Most of the aesthetes he had known at Oxford – Harold Acton, Bryan Guinness, Brian Howard – were rich young men with enviable addresses. For Tom, the only choice was to seek a garret.

He found it in Soho, a part of London to which he was drawn by memories of 'a certain deep and dark doorway in Rupert Street, in which [during Oxford vacations] I had stood for hours at a time enjoying the quick embraces and gropings of other young layabouts'[2] – a pleasure 'even more dangerous, and therefore more thrilling' than cottaging in public lavatories.

The explanation he offered his mother for his flight from Sussex was that he had decided to become a journalist (poetry being too uncertain a living) and would need to visit newspaper offices often. She was reluctant to let him go. Could he not write articles at home and post them to London? He pointed out that the subject matter available locally was rather limited. A series of features about Crowborough – its dull houses, its dull afternoon bridge parties, its dull golf courses – was unlikely to excite many Fleet Street editors.

His garret was a small room at 66 Frith Street, which he rented for 12s. 6d. a week. 'The stairs and the bed creaked so loudly, and the walls were so thin, that I hardly ever risked taking anyone there.' He still frequented the deep and dark doorway in Rupert Street. One of his pick-ups there – 'rather too ruling-class for my taste' – took him to the Guards Club, where he had sex on a sofa. He spent a happier evening lying on Hampstead Heath in the moonlight with a youth from the East End. 'I think we ad a verry, hapy time,' the boy wrote to him afterwards.

To pay the rent, Tom pawned his few valuables, including a silver cigarette box from Asprey's given to him by his mother as a twenty-first birthday present. He enrolled with a theatrical agency, which occasionally found him work as a film extra for a couple of pounds a day. Sometimes he even made money from casual prostitution: a businessman gave him thirty shillings for being wanked off in a telephone box.

It was not enough. Evicted from his room, Tom took a job as a waiter and washer-up in an all-night café nearby which paid him five shillings a week plus bed and board on the premises. The bed was a large double which Tom had to share with the cook, a burly Irishman called Paddy. Tommy, the café manager, slept in a single bed in the same room. Paddy rebuffed Tom's sexual advances with some ferocity, though 'he didn't mind a non-sexual embrace, and we often slept in each other's arms'.[3] Tommy was rather more game, and tried to clamber into the double bed; but as he turned out to have gonorrhoea Tom was obliged, regretfully, to decline the offer.

All the other rooms above the café were occupied by huge prostitutes, whose clients – usually small, weedy men – liked 'burying themselves for hours in those great earth-mothers' mounds of flesh'. Tom took the women trays of food which ensured that their figures stayed the requisite shape. Paddy, who prepared these meals, fell in love with one of the blubbery women. He wept and threatened her with a loaded revolver on learning that his passion was not reciprocated.

Tom had seen little of his Oxford contemporaries since coming down from university, and when he did meet them it was usually by chance. Evelyn Waugh had recorded one such encounter in his diary towards the end of October: 'Sunday. Feeling a little less ill I went to church in Margaret Street where I was discomposed to observe Tom Driberg's satanic face in the congregation. He told me he was starving but would not come to luncheon. It is so like *Sinister Street*, meeting school friends at Mass. I gave him a penny.'

But there was one literary friend who still opened her door to the Soho mendicant. On Saturday afternoons, in the couple of hours before the café opened at 6 pm, Tom would spruce himself up and slip off to Edith Sitwell's flat at 22 Pembridge Mansions, Moscow Road, Bayswater, to attend her famous tea parties. He had kept in touch with her since the rococo evening in Oxford; she in turn had drawn him in to her literary plots and controversies, treating the twenty-one-year-old as if he were a figure of some consequence. She urged Tom to write a letter of protest to the editor of the *Weekly Dispatch*, who had commissioned her to write a regular column but kept excising her enthusiastic references to Matisse, Picasso, Stravinsky and other luminaries of the modernist movement. 'He *won't* have anybody under eighty mentioned,' she grumbled.

When Tom moved to London, Edith began sending him invitations to her Saturday afternoon gatherings. Though the company was impressive, the setting was not. Her flat was five storeys up in a block described by Brian Howard as looking like 'an inexpensive and dirty hospital'. The fare was cheap and unchanging – sticky halfpenny buns and strong Indian tea. There were seldom flowers in the room. Nevertheless, every Saturday the flat was almost as crowded as a tube train in the rush hour, jammed with literary eminences and Edith's young protégés.

Having to deal with customers in the café – who tended to be on the rough side – had helped Tom conquer what remained of his aloof diffidence. But at Edith Sitwell's parties he often suffered relapses. He would sit in a corner, tongue-tied, gawping at writers such as H. G. Wells, Arnold Bennett, Aldous Huxley and T. S. Eliot. Of Wells, Tom could recall only that 'he was there and was voluble.'[4] All he remembered of Bennett was his stammer ('What Siegfried [Sassoon] needs is a m-m-m-*mistress*'). Huxley was 'very tall and graceful, myopic and a little stooping, gracious yet distant'. The difficulty of communication was greatest with Eliot, partly because of the special awe in which Tom held him and partly because he was quite as shy as Tom. Edith liked to mimic Eliot's conversational openings: 'I rather – hesitate – to – suggest . . .'

At Pembridge Mansions Tom met Gertrude Stein for the first time since she had come to speak at Oxford – 'massively common-sensical, like a reliable *hausfrau*, in brown boots and black woollen stockings'. Mrs Patrick Campbell appeared once, but only once. Tom suspected that she was cross at finding in Edith 'a majesty that even her imperious presence could not outshine: at any rate, she told her friends afterwards how sorry she was that Edith had to live in such horrifying squalor, and sent her a dozen silver tea-spoons.' Another guest was Tom's old acquaintance from Rapallo, Mrs Ada Leverson, 'smiling and nodding with the constant pretence of understanding' but deaf as a post. She dressed in black, her head topped by an orange wig and a tulle-swathed black hat. Osbert Sitwell claimed that the headgear was in one piece: she could not take off her hat without removing the wig too.

Edith sometimes asked Tom to come an hour before the other guests on Saturdays, so that they could discuss his poetry. For his first few weeks in London he managed to avoid telling her how he was living: he said merely that he was doing 'a rather humdrum job'. But eventually he blurted it out, fat prostitutes and all. She was horrified. She rebuked him for not telling her sooner about his plight. The following Monday, while waiting to meet her parents at the Curzon Hotel, she scribbed him a note:

You must have thought me an absolute brute on Saturday, but I am much more upset than you can imagine . . . I have been thinking a lot about what to do; I do *hope* you don't think I am unsympathetic. Osbert has consulted Beverley Baxter of the *Daily Express*. Not very hopeful, but you could send him up articles on the chance, mentioning O's name.

Miss Vaughan of the *Daily Sketch* (who is married to Sava, the sculptor) is going to speak about you to Maurice Elvey, the producer. Also she is going to ask you to tea. Mind you go. She will or may be useful.

The Sitwell lobbying machine, once switched on, was formidable. The place of Edith Sitwell's poetry in the literary canon may be arguable – *The Times*'s obituary gallantly pointed out that 'Poets as good and as different as W. B. Yeats, Mr Robert Graves and Mr Roy Campbell all at different times found something to praise in her'[5] – but her reputation as a cultural impresario is secure. She devoted as much energy to promoting young people whom she admired as to nursing her feuds with F. R. Leavis, Wyndham Lewis and other enemies of the tribe of Sitwell. She now set about helping Tom in earnest. She badgered the editor of *Vogue* to appoint Tom as film critic. Alas, the job was already promised to Frank Wells, H. G.'s son. She wrote to Richard Jennings of the *Daily Mirror*; he had no vacancies. She asked her publishers, Gerald Duckworth & Co, to hire Tom; again with no success. 'How maddening,' Edith fretted. But she urged him not to despair:

These things always happen at first – I have the greatest hope that next year will be a much happier one than this for you. We will all work for this. Poor Tom, what an awful time of it you have had. But something will and shall be done, so that it never happens again. You really deserve good fortune, and you shall have it.

His best hope now seemed to be the *Express*, where he was interviewed just before Christmas 1927 by the features editor, Reginald Pound,[6] and sent off to write a sample article on London's nightlife. 'I need not tell you with what anxiety I shall wait to hear the result of your article for the *Express*,' Edith wrote to Tom the day after Boxing Day. 'You can scarcely be more anxious to hear the result than I am.' In a postscript to this letter she apologised for sounding 'rather vague and disjointed. But I've just smashed a tooth, and am in considerable anguish.' As Tom remarked, a smashed tooth is an emergency which many people would make an excuse for not writing.

Edith's recommendation, and Osbert's quiet word with the *Daily Express*'s editor, Beverley Baxter, ought to have counted against Tom. Lord Beaverbrook, the newspaper's owner, held pronounced anti-Sitwellian views. To quote a memo he sent a year or so later:

Lord Beaverbrook wishes to know who engaged Edith Sitwell to write the leader page story. He says he has stood in the breach for ten years defending the paper against the publicity stunts of the Sitwells. His Lordship is betrayed from time to time and he would like to know who gave to the Sitwells the keys of the gate . . . This family group is less than a band of mediocrities.[7]

The editor seems to have been the culprit on that occasion, as on several others. In 1927 Baxter had employed Evelyn Waugh on the strength of an introduction from Sacheverell Sitwell. And in January 1928 the Sitwells' young friend Driberg was given the keys of the gate. The *Express* liked Tom's article on nocturnal London and hired him as a reporter on a six-week trial. He was to be paid £3 a week.

By the time Tom arrived, Waugh had already departed. 'Had he stuck, and hardened into a full-time *Express* newshawk, we might not have had those novels,' Tom mused many years later. 'Had I not stuck, and hardened into a full-time columnist, I might have become a good poet – which Edith Sitwell thought I was and wanted me to be but effectively prevented me from being by getting me this job.'[8] This seems rather ungracious – and uncharacteristic, for Tom usually missed no chance to admit his debt to her. (When his *Express* columns were collected in *Colonnade* (1949) he dedicated the book to Edith, 'in lasting admiration and gratitude'.) It is risible to suggest that she 'effectively prevented' him from achieving the poetic success that would otherwise have been his. Tom got nowhere as a poet because his poetry was not very good. But no one worked harder than Edith to disprove that, even after he had entered his new career as a journalist. Her very first letter to him after he was hired by the *Express*, written on 17 January 1928, makes this plain: 'You don't know what a happiness it is to me about you and the *Express*. I do *hope* with all my heart it will last. I don't think even you can be happier about it than I am.' She then goes on, immediately, to more serious matters:

The poem, as usual, shows this remarkable unfolding power of yours. 'And a corpse grows greyer' is so *fearfully* good. So is 'the booming pastes an aged statue.' I have such great hopes for your future as a poet.

Can you please send 'Homage to Beethoven', 'Metropolitan' *as soon as possible* (in a few days) straight to Monsieur Roger de Leval, 84 Avenue de la Toison d'Or, Brussels and say you are sending it at my request. Tell him it's the poem I wrote about to him.

She continued to plead his case for many years, in spite of her inability to persuade anyone else of his poetic talents. The poem referred to in her first paragraph was a long work titled 'Hell' which he had sent her. Like most of his poetry at the time, it was still all too recognisably written under the influence of Eliot, as these few stanzas should demonstrate:

> Is it too much to stagger for a mile,
> To pass this leering semblance of a janitor,
> To climb these stairs, ten weary flights of stairs?
>
> (The filthy Jew of Malta is spilling water from the hall-bucket.)
>
> Climb all these stairs, rocketing, buzzing, blind.
> Climb, there, inveterate dizziness.
> This is his lordship's room, and here he often sits,
>   Most bloody and most rich.
> Dead youth surrounds him, rouged corpses attend him.
> Will you await him, having climbed these stairs?
> That is the colonel's chair.
>
> My father's arm is there.
>   In that dusty case.
> Rust is gnawing the vital woodwork of that table.
>
> The vast and streaking brownwork
> inspires the contemplation
> of a brain-working brown one
> and a corpse grows greyer.
>
> The drum drum and orchestration
> drives up from down, a cloud
> of chatter, and the wrinkle
> sings with furrowed courage.
>
> The booming pastes an aged statue.
>
> Do you understand, now, now?

Most of the well-known Eliot devices appear sooner or later, such as lurches into foreign language ('What's done cannot be undone. Nec ut soles dabis iocos') and the sudden colloquialisms ('Pardon./ Granted as soon as asked. Cold beef and vinegar' – reminiscent of Eliot's 'Well, that Sunday Albert was home, they had a hot gammon'). In a companion piece, a poem called 'Purgatory', the echoes were even stronger:

> The shadow of a rainbow fell
> Across her face, and she was no more dead.
> Come along, time. Time. Time please gentlemen.
> Hurry along there please. Time. On on. Time 'tis time.

Which, of course, is remarkably similar to lines from *The Waste Land*:

> HURRY UP PLEASE ITS TIME
> HURRY UP PLEASE ITS TIME
> Goonight Bill. Goonight Lou. Goonight May. Goonight.
> Ta ta. Goonight. Goonight.

Plagiarism? Or a deliberate *hommage*? Either way, the derivative verse Tom was writing hardly seemed to justify Edith Sitwell's enthusiasm. Yet her faith was unwavering. A few years later she even commended Tom's poems to the author of *The Waste Land* himself. 'They seem to me to show really remarkable promise and, at moments, achievement,' she wrote to Eliot in June 1935. 'He is very greatly under your influence (though not in form; he needs more shaping). But then, who is not?' She asked Victor Gollancz to read the poems, offering to write a preface if he would publish a collection. Nothing came of it. After leaving Oxford, Tom only once had his poetry accepted for publication – and this was not the sub-Eliotian meandering for which he and Edith had such hopes, but a page of jolly nonsense verse which appeared in *Pall Mall* magazine in September 1928. It was as derivative as his other poems; this time, however, the inspiration was clearly Belloc's *Bad Child's Book of Beasts*:

> Come let us join our cheerful songs
>   to praise the caddish GLOOT
> And give the lie to those who try
>   to make it out a caddish brute.

Nay rather, let us humbly view
    each cupid lip, each modest leg,
And marvel most at its proud boast:
    'Each night I lay a peppermint egg.'

Another verse, illustrated with a whimsically surreal drawing by his brother Jack's wife, Pearl Binder, praised the Thrumming Willuar:

With ringing cheer and loud huzzah
    (appropriate approbation)
Exalt the THRUMMING WILLUAR,
    the flower of the Wild-goose nation.

Discovered by a former Shah
    of Persia at Newcastle-
On-Tyne, the Thrumming Willuar
    was smuggled in a parcel

Of anthracite to Boston (Mass.),
    and with it all its chattels
Consisting of a pint of Bass,
    Fifteen Decisive Battles,

And eighteenpence, and so became
    the flower of the Wild-Goose nation,
Which earned for it a lasting fame
    and world-wide admiration.

This literary slumming seems not to have muted Edith's enthusiasm for her protégé. Her song of praise for his 'serious' work may have been an unaccompanied solo, but it was none the less *allegro vivace* for that: poems such as 'Hell', she reassured Tom,

really *are*, as I've said a hundred times, *most remarkable*. The habit you have of suddenly developing a majestic and grave rhythm out of chaos is most moving. And they have great beauty . . .

    I admire the poems very greatly, and am deeply moved by them. They are most evocative, and have a strange beauty and insight. As you know, I've always felt this – and the poems last. One does not see them differently.

Tom's complaint was thus the wrong way round: his poetry sank in spite of Edith's endeavours, not because of them. As a poet, he would never have risen above the lowliest ranks. As a journalist, he found his voice and wrote himself into Fleet Street's history.

The quality every good reporter needs is curiosity, which Tom had in abundance. Barely a month after he joined the paper it brought him his first scoop. Having heard from friends at Oxford of an odd American evangelist, Dr Frank Buchman, who had surfaced in the city and was recruiting students to his cause, Tom attended one of the Buchman group's Sunday evening meetings in a private room at the Randolph Hotel. 'Fully a hundred and twenty-five men were present,' he reported, 'almost all undergraduates.' He continued:

The public confession of sins has been a frequent feature of the Sunday evening meetings. Such an ordeal naturally involves a violent emotional strain and, in the case of one or two young men of nervous temperament, the unfortunate results of their 'conversion' have provoked severe comment, and are said to be attracting the attention of the university authorities.

Academic and ecclesiastical opinion was mixed. Canon B. H. Streeter of Queen's College approved of the group's proselytizing. Dr A. E. J. Rawlinson of Christ Church, Tom's old college, thought the Buchmanites 'extremely peculiar – one might almost say grim'. Father Ronald Knox said that 'a revival of specifically "enthusiastic" religion was about due. These revivals usually come in cycles of about a century.' Buchman himself was unavailable for interview.

Tom's first report on the Buchmanites was printed on the front page of the *Daily Express* on 27 February 1928, under the headlines 'Revival Scenes at Oxford. Undergraduates' Strange New Sect. Prayer Meetings in a Lounge'. Its tone was unmistakably quizzical, not to say mocking. Perversely, the same day's *Express* carried an editorial arguing that the religious revival in Oxford would 'fortify the soul of the coming generation', and should not be mocked.

A further instalment of Tom's story, as irreverent as ever, appeared on 28 February. The Buchmanites could bear no more. That afternoon four of them presented themselves at the *Express* office and complained to Baxter about his reporter's hostile attitude. The next morning's paper had yet another report from Tom, but it was markedly more restrained than before.

The group's meeting the following Sunday had to be moved from the Randolph Hotel to St Mary's church to accommodate new recruits who had been attracted by all the publicity. An anonymous follower wrote to tell Buchman what had happened: 'The writer of the scurrilous articles in the *Express* last week turned up last night with some 20 odd fellows from Christ Church headed by one who used to be at Princeton with the hope he could disturb the meeting. They did not realise it had been moved to St Mary's.' Finding the ballroom empty, Tom and his friends had allegedly thrown a few chairs and then left. Another letter claimed that 'some of the men responsible for these articles have come into the group and told us of the half-cynical, prankish frame of mind which combined with fertile imaginations to produce them'.[9]

Tom's articles were the first reports in a popular national paper of a movement which was soon better known as the Oxford Group and eventually, in the 1940s, won international fame – or notoriety, according to taste – as Moral Re-Armament. Tom became MRA's most unrelenting scourge, accusing them of 'zeal amounting to fanaticism, persistent crude invasions of physical and spiritual privacy ... an obsessive and often impertinent harping on sin, especially sexual sin'.[10] The Buchmanites repaid the insult – and proved his point – by compiling a dossier on his sexual habits. One Buchmanite, J. P. Thornton-Duesbery (the Master of St Peter's College, Oxford), was so stung by Tom's tireless hostility that in 1964 he published a book whose sole purpose was to defend Moral Re-Armament against Tom. 'There is documentary evidence,' Thornton-Duesbery wrote, in outraged tones, 'of seventy-one public attacks made by him [Driberg] upon Dr Buchman, the Oxford Group and Moral Re-Armament since that day in 1928 when he obtained his first big scoop in Fleet Street by attacking them.'[11]

Later in 1928 Tom returned to Oxford to write an article for the *Express* about a Group house-party, held during the summer vacation. This time he did meet Frank Buchman, who strode across a sunlit lawn to greet a gaggle of devotees which included the gents'

outfitter Austin Reed. 'Hi there, Mr Austin Reed!' Buchman hal-
loed. 'How's that lift-boy of yours coming along?' Tom was impressed that Buchman cannily remembered to use the English word
'lift' instead of the American 'elevator'. Shortly afterwards Tom
was granted a private interview. He asked Buchman suspiciously
about the group's finances, especially its reluctance to publish
accounts. 'Why,' Buchman laughed, not at all offended, 'who'd be
interested in our little accounts?' Tom persisted. Where did Buchman's money come from? Simple, the evangelist replied cheerfully.
See the overcoat hanging on the door? An admirer had been 'guided'
by God to give Buchman that. See the big car outside? Divine
'guidance' again. It was, Tom wrote, 'the gentlest possible brush-
off'.[12]

Many of Tom's journalistic duties at this time were rather more
mundane. Fire, theft and accident were his everyday beats. Once –
'it would have been unprofessional to do it too often' – he interviewed a bereaved husband, telephoned his report to the office and
then returned to the man's house to go to bed with him, 'providing
consolation that he was unlikely to get from any other source that
night.'[13]

As tends to happen in newspaper offices, no one noticed when the
six-week trial was over. Tom decided to continue turning up until
someone asked him to leave. After a few more months, he had
another scoop: an exclusive report of the great 'bathing suit' party
of July 1928.

By the summer of 1928 Fleet Street had begun to notice the antics
of the Bright Young Things, a generic term for Harold Acton, Brian
Howard, Elizabeth Ponsonby and their comrades. It could hardly
not notice: a favourite Brian Howard performance, for instance,
was to lead a line of two dozen friends into Selfridges and then play
follow-my-leader – 'up and down in the lifts, in and out of the
departments, and even over the counters'.[14] And, of course, there
were the parties, always guaranteed to get a popular newspaper
licking its lips. The previous year Tom's friend Gavin Henderson
(later Lord Faringdon) had given a dinner party near Henley after
which guests poured sixteen gallons of petrol into the Thames and
'set the river on fire'. Then there had been an 'impersonation

party', at which everyone had to go as somebody else. Tom had impersonated Brian Howard.

I simply had to make up my face, giving one of my eyebrows much more of an exaggerated twist. One of Brian's was always raised in that mocking, satirical twist. I wore the same sort of suit he usually wore – plain, loose, dark blue – and carried a package of twenty Gold Flake cigarettes in my hand. Brian would never put one in his jacket pocket in case it spoiled the line. He was staggered when I confronted him – the near-mirror image.[15]

Tom was the only person in Fleet Street who could write about these frolics as an insider. Other reporters might lurk in the shrubbery, hoping to glimpse scandalous revels through a window or witness a body tumbling down the front steps. Tom was admitted through the front door in his white tie and tails – or, in the case of the party given on 13 July 1928, in his swimming trunks. The invitation was strict on this point:

Mrs Plunket Greene, Miss Ponsonby, Mr Edward Gathorne Hardy and Mr Brian Howard request the pleasure of your company at St George's Swimming Baths, Buckingham Palace Road, at 11 o'clock, p.m. on Friday, 13th July 1928.
    Please wear a Bathing Suit and bring a Bath Towel and a Bottle.
    Each guest is required to show his invitation on arrival.

The party lived up to – or, perhaps, down to – its promise. From time to time in the course of the night Tom rushed out to a nearby telephone box to dictate an extra paragraph for the *Express*. At breakfast-time the next morning, while the police were trying to persuade the last bedraggled guests at the swimming baths to go home, *Daily Express* readers were regaled with Tom's on-the-spot report. It began in suitably splashy style:

The Bath and Bottle Party organised at the St George's Swimming Baths last night was justified, if by nothing else, at least by the weather.
    Bathing costumes of the most dazzling kinds and colours were worn by the guests. Dancing took place to the strains of a negro orchestra, and the hardy leaped later into the bath, of which the water had been slightly warmed.
    Great rubber horses and flowers floated about in the water, which was

illuminated by coloured spotlights. Many of those present brought two or three bathing costumes, which they changed in the course of the night's festivities. Cocktails were served in the gallery, where the cocktail mixers evidently found the heat intolerable for they also donned bathing costumes at the earliest possible opportunity. A special cocktail, christened the Bathwater Cocktail, was invented for the occasion . . .

Two months later, on 13 September, Tom was transferred to a corner of the paper where his social contacts could be exploited more often – as assistant to Colonel Percy Sewell, author of a daily column of social chit-chat called 'The Talk of London'. He was at last given a proper contract of employment. His salary was raised to seven guineas a week.

Sewell was a lonely, mysterious, melancholy figure. He believed that every man is born with a fixed number of orgasms in his body 'and that when you've come this number of times you're finished sexually'. In spite of their differences of opinion on such matters, Tom and the colonel liked each other. (According to Tom, one rumour advanced to explain Sewell's hangdog demeanour was that he had fallen irrevocably but unrequitedly in love with a lesbian.) Sewell would spend most of his afternoons on the golf course or at the races, leaving Tom to fill whatever space was left.

Neither man's name appeared on the column. It was signed merely 'The Dragoman', a word which *Chambers' Twentieth-Century Dictionary* defines as 'an interpreter or guide in Eastern countries'. Precious little interpretation found its way into 'The Talk of London'. Sewell wrote harmless gossip about middle-aged or elderly aristocrats, in a style that even then seemed archaic: a typical Sewell sentence, Tom once suggested, would start: 'Lady X, who is of course Lord X's third wife, was charming in blue'. Tom's items for the column were often no less inconsequential; but they were at least more entertaining, and the stock characters in them rather younger. He was a vigilant recorder of fads and trends. 'The new drink is green beer,' he suddenly informed *Express* readers one morning, adding that it could be found only at the 'enterprising Bury-street restaurant where Londoners were first introduced to *champagne rosé, champagne nature* and camel soup'.[16] Another day he announced that a fashionable club in Bond Street 'is, I believe, the first to provide brown candy sugar with coffee, instead of the ordinary white lumps'.[17]

Sewell's reports of dances and first nights were always entirely straight. 'The most important of last night's dances was that given by Lady Newborough at her house on Bruton-street . . . The hostess wore a black dress . . . her daughter, the Hon. Stella Wynn, for whom the party was given, looked very pretty . . . Princess Andrew of Greece was an imposing figure in gold . . . That interesting newly-engaged couple, Lord Bective and Lady Clarke, were dancing together, and looking radiantly happy . . .'[18] Tom had a keener ear and eye for the absurd. Sent to report on an exhibition of furniture that was opened by Sir John Lavery, for instance, he came up with this:

Lady Lavery, who accompanied her husband, wore a mauve skull-cap, and was presented with a bunch of pink carnations.

She turned with one of her gracious smiles to greet Lord Berners when he arrived with Mr Evelyn Waugh.

'How nice to see you,' she said, 'and Mr Wuff, too.'

A few minutes later she turned to Lord Berners again.

'Where is Mr Wuff?' she asked.

'Mr Wuff,' said Lord Berners, 'has left for Abyssinia' – and was thereupon engaged in conversation by the chairman, who thought he was Lord Burnham.[19]

In later years Tom betrayed a certain guilt at the column's political stance, or lack of one. He invented the following justification:

. . . the tone of the column, as far as I could influence it, became more and more satirical. I described in detail the absurdities and extravagances of the ruling class, in a way calculated to enrage any working-class or unemployed people who might chance to read the column; at a time of mass unemployment I felt that I was doing something not without value to the Communist Party, to which I was still attached.

This does not quite convince. If unemployed readers were likely to be enraged by reading about aristocrats, their class hatred might just as well have been ignited by Sewell's reports on the Aga Khan's racehorses or Lady Windermere's fan as by Tom's notes on the progress of young debs. Besides, Tom's satirical intentions were hobbled by the fact that, as he admitted, he 'never ridiculed my Oxford friends'. Since these friends made up most of the *dramatis personae* who flitted through his paragraphs every day, that did not leave him with much to ridicule.

Still, his contributions were lively and energetic. And some of the friends about whom he wrote were, as he put it, 'intrinsically interesting' figures such as Nancy Mitford and Evelyn Waugh. *Decline and Fall*, Waugh's first novel, was published in September 1928, just as Tom began writing for 'The Talk of London'. Christopher Sykes recalled the moment:

I was in a nursing home when *Decline and Fall* came out, and Tom Driberg visited me and brought a copy. He began to read out some favourite passages and was literally unable to read them to the end because he and I were so overcome with laughter. This was one of hundreds of such scenes in London in September 1928.[20]

Waugh's great success with *Decline and Fall* made him a newsworthy figure – and no one was better placed than Tom to take advantage of this. Waugh understood the uses of publicity. In September 1930, when Waugh was received into the Roman Catholic Church, Tom was surprised to find himself the only person invited to attend. He hadn't seen much of Evelyn since Oxford; he was not a Roman Catholic. Why choose him? To quote Christopher Sykes again,

Since Evelyn had not asked Tom to avoid any mention of the matter in his column, it stood to reason that he would mention it, since Evelyn was now 'news', and his conversion to the Catholic faith was almost in the class of a scoop. So Tom, of course, did mention it. Tom, in fact, had been used by his friend as part of an ingenious stratagem. If Evelyn's conversion was reported in the widest-selling newspaper in the country, then he would be spared the labour of writing numerous letters.[21]

The service took place at the Church of the Immaculate Conception in Farm Street. Afterwards Tom and Evelyn dined at the Café de Paris, where there was a new black singer from Los Angeles whom Tom wanted to hear. And the next day Tom duly reported Waugh's conversion in the *Express* – though he did not exactly shout it from the rooftops. That morning's 'Talk of London' column began with several items about the death of Lord Birkenhead. Then there was a frivolous piece by Tom about the Imperial Conference:

Motor cars flying little pennants, and with official cards stuck inside the wind-screens, moved swiftly about a sunlit London yesterday.

In them rode innumerable busy officials, all dressed up in their little black coats.

And in them, too, went a few of the delegates to the Imperial Conference, which opens to-day.

From one stepped the Maharajah of Bikanir, unexpectedly dark of complexion, his magnificent black moustache sweeping grandly to the skies.

And in another was a somewhat nervous official who told me later of a startling experience he had had that morning.

'Would you believe it,' he said. 'I was driving along just now when a man in another motor-car leaned forward, looked straight at me, and suddenly blew out his cheeks, contorting his face in a horrible grimace.'

Outraged officialdom was calmed only by an explanation of this phenomenon by a third party.

'It's a game called Bulgy,' he explained, 'and I believe it was invented by Lord Berners as a substitute for the word "Snap" in the card game.

'Instead of saying "Snap" when your card is the same as your opponent's, you bulge out your face, and the one who laughs first loses his cards.'

And now, it seems, the game has been extended to the streets, and two people in a motor-car bet whether they can make people laugh before they do so themselves.[22]

After this foolery came the obligatory theatrical report ('An American duchess, an electric earl, and a wolf-taming baron added considerably to the smartness of the usual first-night audience which greeted *Leave It To Psmith* at the Shaftesbury Theatre'). Only then did the Dragoman turn his attention to the Café de Paris, whither, he noted, some of the Wodehouse first-nighters had gone on for dinner:

Here, too, were Lady Ravensdale, lately back from Russia, but wearing an exquisitely capitalist evening dress; and Miss Tallulah Bankhead, who was with the Hon. David Herbert; and the Marquis de Casa Maury; and, watching critically from the balcony, Mr Evelyn Waugh, who had earlier in the evening been received into the Roman Catholic Church.

Mr Waugh is leaving London shortly for Abyssinia, where he will attend the coronation of Ras Tafari as – to quote the official title – 'Emperor of Ethiopia, King of Kings, and Lion of Judah'.

Having done his duty by his old schoolfriend, Tom immediately turned his attention to more pressing matters, describing the 'immense excitement' that had been caused at the same restaurant, later that evening, by the performance of 'two roller-skating acrobats, who were formerly employed at a night-club in Chicago by Mr "Al" Capone'.

Waugh seems not to have minded Tom's *sotto voce* revelation of his scoop. The arrangement had worked to both men's satisfaction, and thereafter Waugh often used the *Express* as a tribal noticeboard. When, a couple of years later, *Black Mischief* was denounced in a signed editorial in a Catholic weekly, the *Tablet*, Waugh retaliated by writing Tom the following letter:

Two aspects of *Tablet* article: –
(a) an unfavourable criticism,
(b) a moral lecture.

The first is completely justifiable. A copy of my novel was sent to the *Tablet* for review, and the editor is therefore entitled to give his opinion of its literary quality in any terms he thinks suitable.

In the second aspect he is in the position of a valet masquerading in his master's clothes. Long employment by a Prince of the Church has tempted him to ape his superiors, and, naturally enough, he gives an uncouth and impudent performance.[23]

Tom, egged on by Evelyn, published the letter in his *Express* column and provoked a predictable controversy.

The neatest example of Waugh's skill in what is now known as 'news management' was his second marriage, four years later. His first wife had deserted him after only a few months. Once he had obtained an annulment from the Vatican, he became engaged to Laura Herbert. 'It is not to be announced until after Xmas,' Waugh wrote to Lady Mary Lygon in July 1936. 'So you must not tell people I am engaged or Driberg will put it in the papers.'[24] But when Waugh was ready to announce the betrothal, just after Christmas, he made sure that Driberg would put it in the papers by sending the following letter:

My Dear Tom,

I have got engaged to be married & shall be announcing the fact early next week. I don't imagine the story will be of great news value but if you care to publish it you can have it a day ahead of the *Times*. In return could you oblige me in one particular? I think that by now most people have forgotten or have never known that I was married before. The marriage has been annulled by the papal courts and it would be very painful both to me & my young lady to have it referred to. (1) because in ecclesiastical circles they get embarrassed if annulments are given publicity (2) because my future wife is a near relative of my former wife's and there are numerous mutual aunts who would be upset. So may I rely on you not to bring the topic up?

Apart from that you can have all the details you need . . . I can give you a photograph of her if you want one for Tuesday's paper – announcement Wednesday . . .[25]

It may have been Evelyn Waugh who bequeathed the *Vile Bodies* generation to posterity, but it was Tom Driberg who first brought them to public notice. In the late 1920s and early 1930s, he introduced readers of 'The Talk of London' to Brian Howard, 'Babe' Plunket Greene, Harold Acton, John Betjeman, Nancy Mitford and Peter Quennell. He noted the sartorial eccentricities of the Hon. Stephen Tennant – clad in 'pink vest and long blue trousers' at one party, in 'football jersey and earrings' at another. Of David Tennant, Stephen's cousin, *Express* readers learned that 'when in London he drives about in an electric brougham of the Edwardian period. He says it is like riding in a bow window.' Christopher Sykes was revealed to have two ambitions: '(1) to be elected Pope, and (2) to conduct a great orchestra in Wagner.' Elizabeth Ponsonby was summarised thus: 'Eternal sophistication looks out, a little wearily, from under her heavy eyelids, and her mouth, smiling as enigmatically as that of the Gioconda, can utter all knowledge and all wisdom.'

All this, Tom admitted, was 'pretty frivolous stuff'.[26] As Adam groaned in *Vile Bodies*: 'Oh, Nina, *what a lot of parties*.' In Waugh's novel there were

Masked parties, Savage parties, Victorian parties, Greek parties, Wild West parties, Russian parties, Circus parties, parties where one had to dress as somebody else, almost naked parties in St John's Wood, parties in flats and studios and houses and ships and hotels and night clubs, in windmills and swimming-baths, tea parties at school where one ate muffins and meringues and tinned crab, parties at Oxford where one drank brown sherry and smoked Turkish cigarettes, dull dances in London and comic dances in Scotland and disgusting dances in Paris – all that succession and repetition of massed humanity . . . Those vile bodies . . .[27]

Waugh was not improving on reality by much. The party where one had to dress as somebody else, like the swimming-bath party, has already been mentioned. Norman Hartnell threw a Circus Party in July 1928. The Wild West Party was hosted by Harold Acton and friends in March 1929 ('Some of the smartest and prettiest women in London have been searching wildly for a dress appropriate for a Wild West Party, and cowboy costumes are at a premium,' the *Evening Standard*'s 'Woman's World' column trilled). And the Greek Party, the *ne plus ultra* of Bright Young Thingery, was given by Babe Plunket Greene on 4 April 1929 in honour of Brian Howard's twenty-fourth birthday. It was officially titled 'The Great Urban Dionysia'. Each guest, the invitation ordered, 'must be dressed as a *definite* character in *Greek* mythology, and is bringing wine. Extraordinarily beautiful dresses, which are not expensive to make, may be copied with great ease from the Greek vases in the British Museum.' Brian Howard designed the invitation himself, under the influence of *Blast* and Marinetti's *Futurist Manifesto*. Beneath the heading 'J'Accuse' he listed his dislikes of the moment, among them Anglo-Catholics, Public Schools, Gertrude Stein, 'Tell-tale-tits, slit-tongues, lickspittles and all social snippet writers' – any of which might have been an implicit jab at Tom. But Brian Howard was in fact an admirer of Tom's, and on the right-hand side of the invitation a 'J'Adore' column displayed a defiantly modernist taste which matched Tom's own – Picasso, Epstein, Kokoschka, Jazz, Russian Films, Cocteau, Stravinsky.

Tom did, indeed, manage to smuggle into 'The Talk of London' some of the aesthetic causes that he and his Oxford contemporaries championed. Osbert Sitwell, Constant Lambert and W. H. Auden all made regular appearances. His belief that the description of Dionysian revels could ignite a working-class revolution may have been fanciful, but his other plea in mitigation – that the column promoted artistic radicalism – has some force. As he put it in *Ruling Passions*:

I did manage more and more – particularly when writing for Monday's paper on a Sunday, if Sewell was off and I was left in charge – to introduce references to more serious subjects, such as capital punishment, Soviet films (praised, and the monstrous Home Secretary, Joynson-Hicks, attacked for banning them), modern architecture and *avant-garde* movements in the arts; this greatly to Baxter's distaste, since he said that nobody was interested in ballet, that nobody had ever heard of Stravinsky or *Façade*, and that Epstein and D. H. Lawrence were 'ugly'.[28]

When Radclyffe Hall's novel *The Well of Loneliness* was attacked in an *Express* editorial as 'flagrant and infamous', Tom defended the book in his column.

With Tom and Colonel Sewell tugging in opposite directions, their column came more and more to resemble an uncoordinated pantomime horse. To take a random example, 'The Talk of London' for 7 October 1930 carried two photographs: that on the left showed a grinning Marchioness of Blandford out shooting at Hackwood Park, the Marchioness Curzon's home; this was balanced on the right-hand side of the page by a detail from a wood-engraving called 'Workers Resting', by a Ukrainian artist, which was on display at a Soviet Art Exhibition in Bloomsbury. The incongruity was reflected in the text. The first two-thirds of the column were filled with Sewell's blitherings ('Those who believe in "following the money" with their racing investments may be interested to hear that a very large bet was made yesterday on Friendship for the Cesarewitch'; 'News reached me yesterday of a most successful bag of 709 brace of partridges made in one day at Six Mile Bottom, near Cambridge, by Captain Cunningham-Reid and eight other guns, which included Colonel Wilfrid Ashley, Captain Cunningham-Reid's father-in-law, and Sir Bolton Eyres-

Monsell, Chief Conservative Whip . . .'). Tom was then allowed the final few paragraphs for the opening of the Soviet art show. Even here, he cunningly appeased Sewell and Baxter by contriving to introduce at least one titled lady:

Most of those present represented radical tendencies in art or politics; and it was from a variegated sea of dark beards, green shirts, and the mysterious oval faces of young Russian women that I observed emerging the brown tricorne and the immense gold earrings of Lady Ottoline Morrell.[29]

Colonel Sewell's retirement in 1932 gave Tom more freedom, but only within the restraints of the 'house style' he had inherited: Beverley Baxter did not much care for Tom's attempts to extend the range of 'The Talk of London'. It was a gloomy and frustrating period. Tom was depressed by the thought that he had abandoned an apparently promising career as a poet merely in order to produce oleaginous tittle-tattle. One evening in April 1932 Robert Bruce Lockhart, who was writing the *Evening Standard*'s diary as 'The Londoner', bumped into Tom at a West End nightclub called the 43 and found him 'very unhappy' in his job. 'He writes poetry,' Bruce Lockhart recorded in his diary. 'He said that if he died now and I had to write his obituary would I ring up Edith Sitwell and she would tell me all about him. He said he *must* get away, go round the world as a steward in a ship – anything. But has he – have any of us? – the courage? I doubt it.'[30]

The editor may not have offered Tom much encouragement, but an even more important figure at the *Daily Express* was quietly impressed with his work. Lord Beaverbrook, proprietor and 'Chief Reader', had long ago grown weary of the simpering drivel about milady's boudoir. 'Goddammit,' he had often complained to Sewell, 'write about people who *do* things – who do real work – not about these worthless social parasites and butterflies.' Beaverbrook did not like all the artists whom Tom promoted; even so, they were more interesting than witless baronets or neighing débutantes. But Tom was still strapped in the restricting corset of 'The Talk of London'. In Beaverbrook's opinion a completely different style of dress was required for the column.

First it was given a new heading, 'These Names Make News . . .' – a slogan stolen from *Time* magazine, whose diary page bore the message 'Names make news: last week these names made this news'. Beaverbrook then encouraged Tom to jettison the lingering parasites and butterflies. Instead of reporting Mayfair parties, the Dragoman would profile two or three people every day – people who *did* things, of course. Lest any readers had failed to notice the change, on 12 May 1933 Tom printed this brusque manifesto at the top of his column:

STATEMENT OF POLICY:
Discerning readers of this column will have noticed, during the last few weeks, a distinct change in its character.

It has ceased to be a diary of events, a causerie, or even (except implicitly) a commentary. All of those things it has tended to be in the past.

It is most emphatically not a social gossip-column (not that it ever has been in the ordinarily accepted sense of the phrase).

It has become an intimate biographical column – giving day by day anecdotal character studies about men and women who happen to be prominently in the news.

Men and women who work. Men and women who matter. Artists, statesmen, airmen, writers, financiers, explorers, stage people sometimes, dictators, revolutionaries, fighters . . .

Mayfair may find this new departure boring – but not half so boring as the rest of the world finds Mayfair.

Social chatter about the eccentricities of gilded half-wits is dead.

Occasionally I may ornament my page with the photograph of some lovely but idle débutante. This will be for decorative purposes only.

In general, any woman who is 'in Society', and has no other justification for her existence, will be out of this column.

I believe that this experiment is on the right lines.[31]

That day's column, by way of example, included: a photograph of Anna May Wong; short assessments of Sir Algernon Aspinall (secretary of the West India Committee) and Lord Cecil ('He is not a great platform speaker. Nor is he impressive in Parliament'); a story about the Prince of Wales inspecting a new office building; a bulletin on the health of Malcolm Sargent, the conductor; and a 'curious fact', namely that 'the four outstanding dictators in the world today are vegetarians'. (The four in question were Hitler and Mussolini, and – 'using the word dictatorship in a broad sense' – George Bernard Shaw and Mahatma Gandhi.)

The following Monday, 15 May, Tom reported readers' reactions to his statement of policy. Almost all, he claimed, were approving. 'Tell us about our politicians,' a woman from Birmingham had begged. 'About the women MPs as well as the men MPs. And tell us not only about those who have been lucky or astute enough to sink into a comfortable seat at Westminster, but about those who are still carrying on the fight in the constituencies.' Tom obliged by interviewing Susan Lawrence, formerly Labour MP for East Ham North, who was hoping to stand for Stockton-on-Tees at the next election. In the next few days he wrote about two other prominent socialist women, Leah Manning and Jennie Lee.

Tom was smart enough always to keep half an eye on the Chief Reader. In his item on Susan Lawrence, he inserted the gratuitous revelation that 'Miss Lawrence admires Lord Beaverbrook.' And on 25 May he filled the first half of his column with a fifty-fourth-birthday tribute to the proprietor. 'I told Lord Beaverbrook yesterday that I proposed, with his consent, to write about him in this column,' he reported. '"I don't mind," he said, "so long as you don't flatter me."' Flattery was just about avoided, but the tone was warily polite: 'He never stops working. And he has a better idea of what goes on at Parliament than if he spent half his days at Westminster . . . His resonant Canadian voice comes through on the telephone well and intimately . . . He enjoys the pleasures of life in moderation . . . His spectacles are of the unassuming, old-fashioned, steel-rimmed kind . . . He reads a good deal, especially the Bible.' He added that Beaverbrook 'will, when the time comes, be a fascinating subject for a full and analytical biography'. Twenty years later, just such a biography of Beaverbrook appeared; Tom wrote it.

Now that the column had a new title and a newish cast of characters, Beaverbrook decreed that a change of by-line was also necessary. At the end of May the Dragoman was buried. Tom adopted the pseudonym of William Hickey, after the eighteenth-century diarist and rake.

CHAPTER FOUR

DARLING BILL HICKEY

In November 1932 the 'Talk of London' column printed a dozen photographs of babies who had later achieved fame, under the heading 'When We Were Very Young'. The caption on 19 November read: 'No. 12 – Here, to wind up this domestic series, is The Dragoman at a tender age. Note the alert and critical poise of the head.' The photograph showed a very young Tom Driberg sitting upright, wearing a dress.

Fifteen months later, on 15 February 1934, the photograph was again printed in the *Daily Express*. This time the caption ran: 'William Hickey. He's changed – a little.'

Just so. In his transformation from Dragoman to Hickey, however, Tom had to endure a spell in purgatory. When the new column began, in May 1933, it was strictly controlled by the Chief Reader, whose desire for 'people who *do* things' turned out to mean a glutinous daily diet of flattering titbits about dull Canadian provincial businessmen. Nearly every day Tom would have to go to Stornoway House, Beaverbrook's London residence, and take down 'a lot of rubbish'[1] which he would then print exactly as dictated.

When Beaverbrook was satisfied that William Hickey was delivering what he wanted he left the column alone – insofar as he could ever bear to leave anything alone. Whole weeks passed without a summons to Stornoway House. But his influence lingered in the extraordinary style Tom was ordered to adopt for the column, a 'staccato telegraphese' inspired by *Time* magazine. Few conjunctions and verbs. Even fewer definite and indefinite articles.

Abbreviations like 'tho'' and '&'. Strange portmanteau words like 'cinemagnate' (a Hollywood tycoon) and 'radiorator' (a speaker on wireless). Short, jerky, adjective-stuffed sentences. Random example:

Shilling-anywhere post-7pm trunk calls seemed great boon when they started on 1 October 1934.

They are. But boon has snags.

Trunk calls anywhere are quick now, most of the day. After 7 there's congestion, long delay.[2]

Whatever this was, as Tom admitted, it was certainly not English. But over the years the 'angular barbarism' developed into a style that was as readable as it was distinctive. 'The first harsh experiment may even have been beneficial, leaving a certain residue of tautness and crispness,' he wrote, 'just as pure cubism, though a dead-end in modern painting, enhanced the structural quality – "the skull beneath the skin" – in the later work of its practitioners.'[3]

Those who know the *Daily Express*'s William Hickey only in its gossipy, post-war form would be surprised by Tom's columns from the 1930s. Unlike Lord Castlerosse in the *Sunday Express*, Lady Eleanor Smith in the *Weekly Dispatch* and Lord Donegall in the *Sunday News*, Hickey was not purely – or even mainly – a social columnist, filing his despatches from Berkeley Square. He was a political reporter, a foreign correspondent, a pundit and an entertainer. 'A columnist,' he wrote, 'must be interested in a large variety of special subjects. *The real secret is not to appeal to the majority but to appeal to as large a number of minorities as possible.* This will in effect get you a majority readership.'[4] One of his tricks was to skim dozens of periodicals catering for special interests – beekeeping, drink, architecture, boxing. They were often quotable. In an obscure missionary magazine, for example, he found advice from a priest in Zanzibar on how to behave when attacked by a python. ('First thing to remember is not to run away. Python can move faster than you. It may be 20 or 30 feet long.'[5])

The most ordinary throwaway remarks might be seized upon and transformed into a Hickey item:

I am glad to see Rumania's King Carol described as 'a young man with . . . an unmistakable moustache'.

This confirms my view that middle age begins later and later as the years roll on. Carol is 43. Tory politicians, novelists, barristers go on being rising young men till they are much older than that.

It is also a good thing that Carol has an unmistakable moustache. People are always annoyed if you mistake their moustaches for cigarette ash or egg stains.[6]

Mixed into the jokes and whimsy, however, was a strong dash of political tabasco. After attending a 'Lucullus-on-the-Dole' lunch, hosted by a right-wing MP who wanted to prove that one could eat well while living on the cheapest possible food, Tom reported:

'Cheapest possible food' consisted of: –
  Giblet soup.
  Baked huss (alias dog-fish) with crab stuffing.
  Mock chicken (alias rabbit) pie.
  Curly kale. Chive potatoes.
  Apple Charlotte.
'Except possibly for the crab stuffing,' said MP Michael Beaumont, presiding, 'it is a lunch that could be provided in the humblest homes.'

I wondered how much contact he had had with people who are really, not just playing at being, 'on the dole', people who can't afford even the British Medical Association minimum weekly diet.

It was a little embarrassing to meet chairman Beaumont, for I had intended to refer to him again as 'chubby pro-Fascist' – adjectives which he queried, I justified, last week. He said to me with grave, courteous dignity, 'We have exchanged acerbities.'[7]

Hunger and unemployment were subjects to which Hickey often returned in the 1930s. In 1937 Tom sent a Christmas card to a thousand readers chosen at random from his correspondence files, informing them that the much-quoted angelic utterance – 'Glory to God in the highest, and on earth peace, goodwill toward men' – was an inaccurate rendering. It should read 'peace toward men of goodwill', a category which (he wrote) would exclude 'those who make war for greed or material gain, those who obscure clear issues with sophistical evasions; bullies, bad landlords, slanderers, those who say, "Oh, the unemployed don't really *want* work, you know";

all who live only or first for their own profits and privileges. For them I wish a change of heart or quick extinction.' Goodness knows what the recipients made of this douche of cold water. One of Tom's friends complained that it was 'calculated to cast a damper on any festivities'. Three days after Christmas, however, the message from the card was quoted in full in the Hickey column. Christiansen printed it without a murmur.

As Tom learned what he could get away with, William Hickey's political views became more and more explicit. In May 1938, George VI visited Scotland; Tom went too and wrote a column on 'Where The King Did Not Go', describing Clydebank tenements where fifty people lived in fourteen rooms:

We knocked. Husband McIlveney let me in. This family have what is known as room-and-kitchen. Mostly they live in the kitchen. The 'room' is a small space in which husband and sons sleep.

In the kitchen sleep wife and three daughters. The bed is fairly big, but the wall by it is usually damp, which is bad for Mrs McIlveney's sciatica. They also eat there. On the floor, among discarded shirts, were some stale slices of bread. On the radio set stood a shaving-brush, a comb, a bowl containing one gold-fish, a crucifix with a dusty palm-cross stuck in it, a picture postcard of some priests.

This kitchen-bedroom-living-room's proportions are not bad. It is fairly lofty. It is about the size of, say, one of the older bathrooms at Claridge's; but has only one tap, above the sink by the window.

The lavatory is outside. In the Yard also is a dark, ill-ventilated wash-house which has to do for 12 families; so that each of them gets at it about once a fortnight.

McIlveney is not in work. A 20-year-old son works at John Brown's as a beater. They pay £1 10s. a month rent.

'You're an old soldier,' says doctor. 'You'd do better in a tent.' McIlveney wishes he could find one.[8]

Ten months later he spent a few days in South Wales, interviewing unemployed miners and their families. 'It is good for pampered Londoners,' he wrote, 'to be brought in direct contact with such modest standards, with extreme poverty, with men who have been in strikes, in jail, are still engaged in a violent struggle to live. I had known, in an academic way, but had never before fully realised that there are many people in Britain so poor that they cannot afford a newspaper.'[9]

Tom was not a very active Communist by now, mainly through sheer lack of time, but he did keep himself informed of party affairs by drinking occasionally with other Fleet Street comrades – printers, mostly – and CP veterans such as Robin Page Arnot and Dave Springhall. His party contacts put him in touch with men and women whose plight would make good copy. They also arranged for him to meet Arthur Horner, the South Wales Miners' President, whom Tom accompanied to a Communist fancy-dress dance at Cardiff's City Hall. Horner nearly walked out in disgust when he saw that one guest had come dressed as a Nazi storm-trooper. 'Horner's hatred of Fascism is intense,' Tom reported admiringly; he was 'still as staunch a Communist as before he had to mix with coal-owners'.[10]

Like George Orwell, Tom had a rather romanticised vision of the working class, and especially of working-class men. (In Tom's case it was both political and homo-erotic: those sinewy thighs and rough hands, that heroic nobility in adversity, the sweat of labour . . .) Unlike Orwell, however, he was too fond of the comforts available to 'pampered Londoners' to become anything more than a tourist. Tom's visits to the depressed areas – like his sexual encounters with working-class men – were passionately arousing but also impersonal and brief.

His discovery that some working-class households lived in near-starvation did not inhibit his own enjoyment of a good meal. He was an enthusiastic member of the Wine and Food Society, which was founded in October 1933 by A. J. A. Symons and André Simon with the professed intention of improving the standard of cooking throughout the country by educating the general public to make the best possible use of available materials. As Tom conceded privately some years later, the Society did not even begin to live up to this noble purpose: it was, rather, 'a clique of convivial dilettanti dabbling in exotic dishes and elaborating a *mystique* of wine which always slightly amused and puzzled the wine-growing French. They were, in fact, gastrosophists rather than gastronomes.'[11] The Society's first 'demonstration' was a lunch where all the food and wines came from Alsace, for which members were charged 10s. a head. As the *Manchester Guardian* commented at the time, 'Only the incurably insular will be inclined to reflect that many a housewife could do the whole family rather well on ten shillings and without going any nearer Alsace than the village shops which she ordinarily frequents.'[12]

But the Alsatian luncheon was modest by comparison with what followed. Each feast or banquet seemed more extravagant than the last; all were written up for the Society's magazine, *Wine and Food*, in prose that teetered on the edge of self-parody. There were solemn critiques of meals at which various vintages were 'shown' (never served) and 'discussed' (not drunk). Claret would be 'deployed' in 'batteries'. The Society celebrated the end of its first year with 'the most sumptuous and elaborate banquet held in Britain for more than a hundred years' – a forty-two-course dinner at the Royal Pavilion in Brighton. Dishes were modelled on those served to the Prince Regent a century earlier by the great chef Marie-Antoine Carême, and were washed down with sixteen carefully chosen wines and liqueurs.

Quite how this was supposed to raise the cooking standards of ordinary kitchens was never explained, though an editorial in *Wine and Food* three years later continued to insist that 'it is very important to teach the humbler housewives how to make the best use possible of the foodstuffs within their means. We are also aware that, when it is good, plain food is best, and that English food can be both plain and best'. What of the out-of-the-way wines and the exotic meals? These, the editorial explained, were merely 'to introduce just an element of novelty likely to rouse more interest in and attract more attention to our Society, its aims and its work'. In other words, forty-two-course banquets and the like were merely a tiresome duty, necessary to drum up support for the more lip-smacking business of teaching working-class housewives to cook cabbage properly.

This disingenuous logic deserved the sarcasm of William Hickey at least as much as, say, the Lucullus-on-the-Dole lunches at which he sneered so readily. (The inner circle of the Wine and Food Society, consisting of diners who were prepared to spend up to £5 a head on a meal, actually called itself the Lucullus Group.) But Tom could hardly mock the Society's excesses; he was himself an accomplice in them. Here, for instance, is the beginning of A. J. A. Symons's account in *Wine and Food* of a characteristically affected evening presided over by Dick Wyndham, whom Tom had first met eleven years previously in Rapallo:

The place: The Savoy Hotel.
The date: 2 September 1936
The host: Richard Wyndham.
The guests: Tom Driberg, Montague Shearman, Hon. David Tennant, R. J. Brock, Arden Hilliard, E. A. Boyce, St John Hutchinson, KC, Ralph Keene, Peter Quennell, John Heygate, Sacheverell Sitwell, Curtis Moffat, Freddy Mayor, Desmond Flower, Hon. Patrick Balfour, Major W. R. Barker, Capt. J. S. Poole, Capt. F. O. Cave, and A. J. A. Symons.
The fare: Paw-paws.
            Peanut soup.
            Turtle fins.
            Roast partridge; Egg plant and pimentos.
            Mango fool.
            Corn on Cob.
The wines: Tio Pepe.
            Piesporter Goldtropfchen 1925.
            G. H. Mumm, Cordon Rouge 1923.
            Martell 1906.
            Mead.

The invitations for this remarkable dinner had read:

To welcome home Aginejok.
Richard Wyndham invites you to a Dinka dinner to be held in the Bahr-el-Ghazal Room, Savoy Hotel, at 8.0 pm on September 2nd. *It is hoped that after-dinner speakers will stand on one leg.*

Readers of Wyndham's excellent book, *The Gentle Savage*, will remember that 'Aginejok' was the native name for the friendly district commissioner who had been his host in the Sudan. 'Aginejok' (Captain J. S. Poole) completed his term of service this year, and his former guest conceived the pleasant idea of welcoming him back by an African dinner in London.

Expectation was high when the guests arrived, and it was not disappointed. The dining-room door opened to disclose a tropical scene. Walls and ceilings had been shrouded in thin gauze, from behind which gentle lights diffused the blue glow of Eastern twilight. Fifteen-foot palms hid the corners. At one end of the room a camp bed, protected by mosquito nets, awaited use. The long dining table was lit by candles standing in empty wine bottles. Two impassive Africans, at least six feet six high, naked save for leopard-skin loin cloths, with painted faces and huge spears, stood at the head of the table; and invisible drums sounded the tom-tom invitation to the feast . . .[13]

Symons reported that the 'agreeably glutinous' turtle fins formed a perfect background for the cool champagne which accompanied them and the rich madeira sauce in which they were served. 'I began,' he wrote, 'to revise my ideas of the hardships of African life'.

These were the people whose company Tom most enjoyed. Dick Wyndham was the host of what Tom recalled as 'the best weekend parties I have ever attended', at Tickerage Mill in Sussex. Four or five old friends would usually make up the party – Peter Quennell, Constant Lambert, John Rayner (who was by now a colleague of Tom's on the *Express*), A. J. A. Symons, Cyril Connolly. Some might bring their latest wives or girlfriends, but these were essentially masculine gatherings and Tom, for one, would have preferred them to be exclusively so. The fare was sumptuous enough to be noticed in *Wine and Food* from time to time. Symons described with awe a Tickerage dinner where lobster was served, 'not boiled at all, but kept alive until needed, then killed by a knife through the head, cut in half, and grilled'. Tom's abiding memory was of the wine: 'from Dick's marvellous cellar, ranged on the sideboard and decanted well before dinner, would stand six or more magnums of chateau-bottled claret of the finest years.'[14] Between meals there would be croquet and long walks, all-night games of Lexicon and ninety-mile-an-hour drives to Lewes in Wyndham's Railton. (Wyndham was always an ostentatious motorist: he had been driving a grey, open-topped Rolls-Royce when Tom encountered him in Rapallo.)

Other weekends would find much the same group at Brick House, Finchingfield, Essex, the country residence of A. J. A. Symons since 1931. Symons is remembered today only as the author of a strange and wonderful biography of Baron Corvo. His house bore witness to his other interests: weekend guests would be woken, and summoned to dinner, by the twangling of Symons's large and valuable collection of musical boxes; they would admire his thousands of first editions (Symons had founded the First Edition Club); they would be taken on a candle-lit tour of his well-stocked cellar (he was the Wine and Food Society's Secretary). And they would be expected to share their host's intense enthusiasm for games of all kinds – table-tennis and croquet, Monopoly and Nyner (a cross between bagatelle and shove ha'penny). Symons had devised a house game in which each guest would be armed with a toy pistol that fired little balls of paper; Oscar Wilde's son, Vyvyan Holland, mounted an 'epic and successful defence of the back staircase when his side had been seriously depleted by casualties'.[15] In another version of the game, the hall was fortified by two barricades of furniture from behind which the two sides sniped at each other. It is probably no coincidence that one of Symons's most wily table-tennis opponents, Francis Meynell, was the dedicatee of Stephen Potter's *Gamesmanship*, in which he was ennobled as 'Gamesman No. 1': he came from a top-class stable. When *Gamesmanship* appeared, incidentally, Tom gave it a long and favourable review. In the sequel, *Lifemanship*, Potter praised Tom as a 'noted Essex Lifeman' who 'has done a good deal of work on Counter Cottaging' – the ribald pun being, presumably, intentional. What Counter Cottaging meant here was Tom's suggestion as to how one should reply if asked 'Are you going down to your cottage this weekend?' (The correct answer is 'Yes' followed by some such qualification as 'We've had to close the south wing altogether', or 'We're just having the octagon room done up'.) Though not quite as serious about games as A. J. A. Symons, he was a keen competitor at country-house croquet or canasta. Years later, at Easter 1950, he stayed up all night playing canasta with John Freeman, then the MP for Watford; at eight in the morning the two of them were served with breakfast at the card table. They played on until 11 o'clock.

Beaverbrook was amused by the apparent incongruity between Tom's political affiliation and his *bon vivant* habits. According to

Tom, it was the proprietor himself who dictated this teasing item for the *Evening Standard*'s 'Londoner's Diary' in May 1938:

THE CAFÉ COMMUNIST

The Café Communists are one of the more modern products of our modern social life.

They are the gentlemen, often middle-aged, who gather in fashionable restaurants, and, while they are eating the very fine food that is served in those restaurants and drinking the fine wines of France and Spain, they are declaring themselves to be of Left Wing faith.

One of them is Mr Victor Gollancz, not actually a member of the Communist Party, but a staunch Left Wing supporter, who lunches each day off the best fare that London can provide. Another is Mr John Strachey, a prominent member of the Communist Party, who may from time to time be seen supping in a certain grillroom.

REPLY

Another is Mr Tom Driberg, the columnist. When taxed with this incongruity between his views and his surroundings, Mr Driberg retorts that he does not see why he also should be a victim of the malnutrition which is an endemic disease of capitalism; that clear-thinking need not imply poor feeding; that since the most painful part of his job is to associate occasionally with the rich and powerful, he naturally, on such occasions, needs an anaesthetic; and that he has yet to discover a really 'fine' Spanish wine anyway.[16]

Oddly, the *Standard* neglected to inform its readers that 'Mr Tom Driberg, the columnist' (of whom few had heard) was the famous William Hickey of the *Daily Express*.

The idea that socialists ought never to enjoy themselves is a wearisomely persistent right-wing misconception. Still, it was true that the company Tom kept was not conspicuous for its revolutionary zeal. The worthless débutantes who had so riled Beaverbrook in 'The Talk of London' did not disappear altogether with the coming of Hickey: Tom was an energetic party-goer and night-clubber, and he continued to report the comings and goings of The Young Girl when he spotted her. The most famous of the breed, Margaret Whigham (later Margaret, Duchess of Argyll), has left a picture of the West End in which both she and Tom were to be found most evenings during the mid-1930s:

I was quite capable of having dinner with one young man, pleading tiredness and going home at 10.30, only to sally forth again to meet another beau at the Embassy or the Café de Paris, where we would dance until the doors closed at 2 a.m.

Then we would float on to the late nightclubs such as the Florida, the Silver Slipper, the Bat, or Uncle's, ending up by having eggs or bacon at dawn . . .

This was the era of the famous Big Bands — Tommy Dorsey or Paul Whiteman would come over specially from America to play at the Kit Kat Club; Roy Fox always played at the Monseigneur, and Carroll Gibbons at the Savoy.[17]

At the Kit Kat club in Haymarket a singer called Harry Ray used to bellow out — to great applause — a number called 'My Girl's Pussy'.

Tom was a popular figure with Margaret Whigham and her friends, and not only because he could put their names in the paper. 'He did attract people,' says John Rayner, an *Express* colleague who often accompanied him on nocturnal excursions. 'The rich, grand women at the Embassy and the Café de Paris adored him. With his dark hair and long nose he looked as though he had Indian blood — the son of a Maharajah.' At least one aristocratic woman made a determined effort to lure him into her bed. Needless to say, she failed.

Though Tom enjoyed the company at the Embassy, he preferred to end the night in more raffish surroundings — perhaps the Nest in Beak Street, near Liberty's, or the Blue Lantern, opposite the Windmill Theatre, which had a pianist named Hetty Wade. Many of the Soho clubs that he liked were owned by an Italian called Gino Callegani who styled himself 'Gino the Night-Club King'. Gino ran the Slipp Inn, the Bobbin, the 43 and — Tom's favourite — the Shim-Sham Club in Frith Street. Most of the staff and customers at the Shim-Sham were black, but Tom's column brought it to the attention of fashionable white people who fancied themselves as Bohemians. A few years later the Night-Club King wrote, in his broken English, to thank Tom for 'the way that a great journalist Mr Hickey helped me by bringing Society made the place a success. Remember your first party at the Shim-Sham. Nora Stuart Brown, Mr Dryburgh [sic], Lady Ashley, Douglas Fairbanks and several other nobilities who off hand I cannot remember. I still remember those wonderful nights . . .' Tom sometimes went to the Shim-Sham with the composer Constant Lambert, who struck up a friendship with the club's cigarette girl, Laureen Sylvestre. When Laureen gave birth to a baby girl, Cleo, both men agreed to act as godfathers. Tom always claimed that Constant Lambert was in fact Cleo's real father.

Yet another Soho club, Frisco's, was run by a large black man in a top hat – the eponymous Frisco – who often sang 'Lullaby on Broadway' at Tom's request. Tom thought the song fitted perfectly the mood of Soho at dawn: 'Sleep tight, baby, the milkman's on his way.' At the height of the Abdication crisis of 1936, when Wallis Simpson issued a late-night statement describing her situation as 'unhappy and untenable', a party from the *Express* office roared into Frisco's at 2.30 in the morning, after the last edition had gone to bed. To the tune of 'St Louis Blues' Tom composed a topical lyric:

> Say, boys, the crisis is over,
> Mrs Simpson's got it on the raw,
> Her situation is unhappy and untenable,
> Da-da-di-da-dida-da . . .[18]

'We formed a crocodile,' the *Express*'s editor, Arthur Christiansen, recalled, 'with Frisco in his top hat, white tie and tails, leading us round, and we sang and sang.'

All this revelry, all those dinners at the Café Royal and the Savoy Grill and Quaglino's, did not come cheap. As one friend put it, Tom was never happier than when 'spending his last fiver (or better still someone else's last fiver) on sharing a bottle of good wine or a finely cooked meal'.[19] He was a lavish host, and he lived beyond his means.

Not that he was badly paid. Tom's weekly wage at the *Express*, which had been seven guineas when he joined in 1928, was 13 guineas plus £6 guaranteed expenses at the start of 1932. By the end of the year this had been put up to 16 guineas; the expenses were now nine guineas. In March 1934 he had another pay rise, to 21 guineas. Beaverbrook was a generous employer. In the Hickey column one morning Tom described himself, jokingly, as a wage slave. Beaverbrook was on the phone to Christiansen at breakfast time the same day. 'If there are any wage slaves on the staff of the *Daily Express*,' he rasped, 'set them free.'

For his first four years at the *Express* Tom had lived in shared or borrowed flats, seldom staying for more than a few months. In the early weeks of 1932 he was at John Rayner's flat near Paddington, but that March he ended his nomadic existence by taking a lease on 5 Queen's Gate Place Mews, SW7 – a perverse choice, since he disliked Kensington intensely. He hired a live-in manservant and chauffeur, Albert Westlake, to look after him. At the same time he bought a rather dashing second-hand Studebaker for £60.

Tom never learned to drive, just as he never learned to cook or type: he always assumed that one could charm or pay people to take care of these tiresome chores. 'You expect everything to be done for you,' John Rayner once rebuked him. 'If ever I can't get everything done for me,' Tom replied, 'I hope I die.'[20] Albert Westlake's previous job, suitably enough, had been as a lavatory attendant. He arrived with an unhelpful reference from his last employer, the head porter at the Palace Hotel, who revealed that Westlake 'was discharged for absenting himself from duty without leave. Otherwise I found him a very smart industrious man. I have nothing against him, only what is stated above.' Tom took him on regardless, installing him in a small spare-room. Westlake's hours were unpredictable: sometimes he would have to wait up until the early hours to drive his master home.

Tom was not kind to menials, as a rule, unless he wanted to seduce them. His abominable treatment of waiters in restaurants was notorious: he would always find fault with something – the wine, the sauce, the cutlery, the cruet – and complain loudly about it. Westlake seems to have been a fortunate exception. Relations between the two men were chaste but affectionate. Westlake called his master by his Christian name; Tom coined the nickname 'Oi' for the servant, so that he could shout down the staircase 'Oi, can you do this please?' They were both inexplicably amused by the joke.

The rent for Queen's Gate Place Mews, Westlake's wages and the cost of running the car all ate further into a salary already depleted by too many good dinners. Tom had taken the little mews house unfurnished, and asked the department store Peter Jones to equip it with carpets and mattresses, kettles and mirrors, sofa and chairs, desk and divan. They even provided his address die and cocktail shaker. The bill was £157 16s. 2½d., almost three months' pay from the *Express*. He had already acquired his lifelong overdraft habit.

Beaverbrook knew of Tom's hopelessness with money, and baled him out on several occasions: a loan of £200 in November 1935, followed by gifts of £250 in February 1937, £50 towards the cost of his holidays in October 1937, £125 in April 1938, £200 in May 1939. On 7 March 1940, when Tom had debts of almost £2,000, he wrote to Beaverbrook begging for a loan. The next day Beaverbrook's manager at the *Express*, E. J. Robertson, sent for Tom. 'We have a strict office rule against such advances,' he said. Tom's heart sank as he contemplated his imminent bankruptcy. 'But,' Robertson added, 'Lord Beaverbrook has instructed me to make you a free gift of £1,000. Here is a cheque.' Lord Castlerosse, a gossip columnist on the *Sunday Express* whose debts were often settled by Beaverbrook, called the proprietor 'my never-ending lord of appeal'.[21]

It was entirely thanks to Lord Beaverbrook that in November 1935 no Fleet Street paper reported a sensational story: that Tom Driberg, better known as the columnist William Hickey, was in the dock at the Old Bailey charged with indecent assault. 'In theory and principle I deplore such suppression of news,' Tom wrote, 'if what is kept out is newsworthy (which my trial perhaps, just marginally, was); but I am bound to admit that when it is something which concerns one personally, the suppression is jolly welcome.'[22] As well as persuading his fellow newspaper-owners to turn a blind eye, Beaverbrook paid Tom's defence costs. Only two references to the trial crept into the press: it was listed in the official calendar of forthcoming cases in *The Times*, albeit in print so small as to be almost illegible; and when the ordeal was over the trade paper *World's Press News* remarked enigmatically, 'That was a curious case that Fleet Street was talking about last week. Not all names make news.'

It was a curious case indeed. On the night of Tuesday 29 October 1935 – or, to be precise, in the early hours of the following day – Tom was stopped by two men on a street corner while he was on his way home. They turned out to be unemployed Scottish coal-miners, forced south by the search for work, who introduced themselves as Alexander Livingstone and James Kitchener Reid. They had nowhere to sleep. Could Tom suggest anywhere? He mentioned a few doss-houses and Salvation Army hostels, but the men deemed all these unsuitable – some were already locked up for the night, others were too seedy and lice-infested. After talking to the men for another couple of minutes, Tom invited them to stay with him.

Both men were quite young – Livingstone about thirty, Reid perhaps twenty – and neither was unattractive. Tom was honest enough to admit afterwards that if they had been older and uglier he would probably not have taken them home. But he insisted that sex was not on his mind. He believed that the *Daily Express* should report on the miseries of unemployment in the Scottish coalfields; if he could bring Livingstone and Reid into the office the following morning and introduce them to the news editor or features editor, it might prod the paper into action. Besides, it was 'genuinely difficult, at this time of night, to advise them where to go; and it was not a warm night'.

Only when they reached Queen's Gate Place Mews did Tom confront a problem which, if we are to believe his account, had not hitherto occurred to him: where were the miners to sleep? The house had three bedrooms. One was his, furnished with a bed which was slightly wider than an ordinary single. The second room was occupied by the sleeping Westlake. The third, which was tiny, had no bed in it and was being used as a boxroom. He could have put them downstairs, on the sofa in the drawing-room, but he was afraid that they might scarper with his 'few things just worth stealing' in the middle of the night. They had been under stress 'and might yield to temptation'. One suggestion was that Reid could sleep downstairs while Livingstone shared Tom's bed, as a kind of surety. But Livingstone, already suspicious about Tom's intentions, refused to be left alone with him. There was only one thing for it: as if in a scene from an Aldwych farce, all three men ended up in Tom's bed, with Tom in the middle. The bed was three foot six inches wide.

In these cramped circumstances physical contact could hardly be avoided. At about seven in the morning Reid jumped out of the bed and accused Tom of trying to seduce him. Livingstone joined in, saying that he knew about perverts because a man in Canada had once tried to seduce him. He vowed to give Tom 'the biggest thrashing of his life'. Tom pleaded that if he had touched either of the men it was an accident. The argument continued for some time downstairs, until eventually Tom ordered them out of the house, showing them to the door in his pyjamas.

And that, he believed, was that. But in the afternoon Tom was rung at the *Express* by the faithful Westlake, who said that the police had been round and would be returning at 7 pm. Tom went home early to await them, expecting that they would ask a few questions and go away again. Instead, as soon as the officers arrived they arrested him. He was cautioned that anything he said would be taken down and might be used in evidence against him. What he did say was not too taxing on the police's shorthand: he uttered one word, 'Fantastic!' He was then taken to Kensington police station and locked in a cell for the night. In the morning he was transported in a Black Maria to the West London magistrates' court, where he was committed for trial at the Old Bailey on a charge of indecently assaulting Alexander Livingstone and James Kitchener Reid. He was given bail.

As soon as he was bailed he went to see Arthur Christiansen at the *Express* and told him the whole story. He then called on Lord Beaverbrook. Tom could not conceal the scandal from either of them, but with their assistance he might yet conceal it from most of the British public – and in particular from his mother, still living in Crowborough and still wearing the black crinoline of her widowhood. If he had been prepared to take advantage of his position slightly earlier he might not have been charged at all. 'Why didn't you tell us who you were?' the arresting sergeant asked in astonishment when, a few days later, he discovered that Tom wrote the William Hickey column. After the trial, Beaverbrook happened to mention the case to the Lord Chief Justice, Lord Hewart, who said he had been told that it was 'a mistake'. The implication of both remarks was that a man of Tom's rank should not have to undergo the humiliation of being taken to court by a couple of penniless nobodies.

The suspicion that the case was being decided by what one might call 'class justice' was strengthened during the trial itself. The defence counsel, J. D. Cassels KC, made an effective speech and cross-examined competently enough, but Tom was convinced that what really swung the verdict in his favour was the evidence of his two character witnesses. The first was Colonel the Hon. Wilfred Egerton, a moustachioed, straight-backed, Edwardian figure, a friend of one of Tom's maternal uncles. He testified that he and his wife had often met Tom, and had always found him 'perfectly honourable' and of excellent character. The second character witness was Lord Sysonby, who gave his address as St James's Palace (whereupon 'one could sense a delicious *frisson* running through the collective consciousness of the jury', according to Tom). He said that Driberg's reputation was 'exemplary'.

If the case had been judged on Tom's true character, he would have been guilty as charged. This, after all, was a man who had been expelled from Lancing because he couldn't keep his hands to himself. But the court knew nothing of that. Here was a fine young man of rank and education, a man who enjoyed the friendship of colonels and peers — peers who lived in St James's Palace, no less. The jury took little time to reach their verdict: not guilty.

Was justice done? It certainly seems an extraordinary coincidence that, of all the people against whom these Scots miners could have made false accusations, they should have happened upon someone who was indeed a groper. It would be just like Tom to give one of the men an exploratory fondle. Woodrow Wyatt claims that Tom admitted to him years later that he lied in court.

Suppose this is true; is it necessarily reprehensible? Should he have pleaded guilty to a charge that, were he a heterosexual, would never have been brought in the first place? He had not been accused of rape. All he had done — if he did anything — was to make a preliminary, tentative touch, to see if his lust was reciprocated. He would certainly not have tried to go any further without the man's cooperation; there were two of them and one of him, and he risked a severe beating if he tried to force himself on either of them. Tom's sexual taste was, anyway, not one that could be forced on an unwilling partner. All he ever wanted to do was to suck men's erect cocks; an unconsenting cock would not be erect.

But he may have been innocent. For the rest of his life Tom insisted to friends – except Woodrow Wyatt, apparently – that he really hadn't laid a finger on the man, however incredible it might seem. And in *Ruling Passions*, where he gleefully confessed to any number of homosexual adventures and close shaves with the law, he maintained that it had all been a 'misunderstanding' caused by squeezing three men into a bed made for one.

Although Tom's trial was kept from the newspaper-reading public, by word of mouth it became common knowledge in political and journalistic circles, in predictably garbled form. Almost eight years later, after dining with Lord Beaverbrook at Cherkley one Sunday evening, Robert Bruce Lockhart made the following entry in his diary:

Max [Beaverbrook] then told me how he had once helped Tom Driberg out of a very bad scrape. Tom was going home late one evening when he met two men who said they were Welsh miners and were homeless. Tom took them home, put one miner into his sitting room and the other (whom he made take a bath first) into his own bed. The next morning the miners accused him of indecent assault. Tom tried to buy them off, but they took proceedings. There was a case which Max helped Tom to defend by supplying him with money for counsel and by arranging for the minimum of publicity. Tom was acquitted.[23]

Hardly anyone, however, used the story against Tom. When he first stood for Parliament, seven years after the trial, a lawyer in the constituency tried to start a whispering campaign by telling three local families of their candidate's alleged habits. 'One family,' Tom noted with pleasure, 'did not understand what he meant; the second did not believe him; the third didn't mind.' The only other public reference to his appearance at the Old Bailey, and a pretty oblique one at that, was made in 1945 by Anthony Eden, Churchill's wartime Foreign Secretary. Bruce Lockhart again recorded the occasion in his diary:

[Eden] is also very anti-Tom Driberg whom he scored off harshly in Parliament. Driberg had been attacking Anthony for flirtations with kings. Almost without knowing what he was saying Anthony retorted: 'I do not know how far the Hon. Member is an expert in flirtations or in what kind of flirtations.' Tom Driberg went as white as a sheet. The House rocked. I asked Anthony if he knew the story of how Max had saved Tom Driberg in a very dirty homosexual case with two poor miners. He said of course he did. After the debate Driberg came up to him and said: 'That was a very neat retort you made,' and pretended to laugh the matter off as if there were no inner meaning.[24]

Bruce Lockhart may have been mistaken, however, in assuming that Tom's levity was a pretence. In-jokes of the Anthony Eden type held no great terrors for him, just as he didn't mind at all when the *World's Press News* published its knowing little paragraph the week after his trial. (He was much more bothered by 'having to go back to the office, on bail, each afternoon when the Court rose and write a light-hearted Hickey column'.) Of course Tom feared exposure, as any homosexual in public life did; but he courted it, too, regaling colleagues and acquaintances with stories of his escapades. Living dangerously gave him an almost sexual thrill. 'Drinking with him for an evening was like listening to a sort of underworld Arabian Nights,' the Labour politician John Freeman recalled. 'I didn't believe most of it at the time: now I suppose that most of it was probably true.'

The fright of the Old Bailey case, like his expulsion from Lancing, did cool his ardour for a while. But fear of the consequences could not deter him for long – 'any more than fear of the rope deterred the average murderer', to use his own rather ill-chosen analogy. His liking for rough trade became known far beyond Westminster and Fleet Street. Sometimes he received anonymous letters at the *Express* implicitly threatening him, of which this is a fairly mild example:

Dear Sir,

If a regular reader may make so bold, as I read your column the thought crosses the mind 'how mellowed & improved this fellow would be if he took unto himself a wife!' Yes, a wife & what is more a woman who by birth is a member of that class, the 'privileged class' you presume to despise!

A healthy, intelligent, practical individual with a sense of humour, both capable and artistic. Someone who could 'swallow' those less creditable incidents in your past, interest herself in your present & help you make that promising future which lies before you.

I think you would find something would be brought into your life that now seems to be lacking, an anchorage which the spirit subconsciously seeks, a certain sweetness and contentment.

Think it over!

But plenty of *Express* readers remained in happy ignorance, including a number of women who decided that he was the man of their dreams and wrote to suggest that he should indeed take unto himself a wife. One swooning admirer turned up at the *Express* office in person to propose to him, but her nerve failed her in the foyer and she left him a note instead. Another 'ardent reader' plucked up the courage to write and ask if he 'could find time to have a cocktail with me'. She helpfully appended her vital statistics: 'If you are sufficiently interested I am five foot eight inches in height, weigh 120 lbs, hair shaded from brown to blonde & grey eyes & work as a model.' Tom left her to waste her sweetness on the desert air.

The most ardent reader of all was a woman in Taunton, who had fallen for a photograph of Tom that was printed in the column one day, and who begged him to send her another picture. He ignored the letter, but she was not to be put off that easily. On 23 April 1937 she wrote to Hickey again, addressing him as 'darling Bill':

I was so hoping you would send me a photograph because the newspaper cutting I have is getting so worn, I look at it so often. I always take it to bed with men and kiss you goodnight. Then I lie in bed and imagine you are with me, fondling me and making passionate love to me. Oh Bill darling you can't imagine how much I love you. I have tried to fight against it but your handsome face always comes before me . . . I shall probably end up marrying some stodgy person like George, whom I mentioned in my last letter, so please be good to me and give me a little thrill now by sending your photo and perhaps just a wee letter.

She assured him that her appeal was not 'some kind of hoax or anything like that', a necessary precaution in view of what came next:

There is a woman come to live at the Grange near us and the other day I was talking to her, she was having tea at our house, and she picked up the *Daily Express*. I asked her if she ever read your column and she said she did. I shall not tell you her name as I am going to tell you a secret about her. From the first time we met she seemed to be rather fond of me. I visit her a good deal and she always kissed me before I left. Other women sometimes do this but her kisses are different. They are the kisses you only give to a person with whom you are in love. A few weeks ago she vowed she was in love with me. I found this rather thrilling, because I had never heard of a woman being in love with another before.

She invited me to dinner one night and after the meal we went to her boudoir. She made passionate love to me and I was quite thrilled. When she found I was responding she became more intimate. She slipped off her evening gown and gently took off mine. We were soon lying together on the divan, both nude, in a passionate embrace. Since that time she has lost no opportunity of repeating the love-making. Now she wants me to go away for a week-end with her but I don't know if I ought to do that.

Now please Bill darling do drop me a line and *please*, *please* send me a photograph.

The lesbian scene was no doubt meant to set darling Bill Hickey's loins a-quiver with lust. It left Tom cold. The poor woman never got her photograph.

Tom's celebrity was of a curiously anonymous sort. William Hickey was a name that opened doors, impressed women and elicited grateful handshakes from club-owners; but who had ever heard of Tom Driberg? He could walk down the street unrecognised. In the circumstances it was perhaps not surprising that someone else should try to pass himself off as Hickey. Tom learned of the impostor when a reader rang to ask if he had been at a music-hall called the South London Palace the previous weekend, behaving in a 'rather lively' way. He hadn't. Then two other readers telephoned with the news that someone calling himself William Hickey was to be found at the South London Palace every night, standing drinks in the bar, boasting in a loud voice of his newspaper column and chatting up a young female dancer from the show.

Accompanied by a couple of friends and a private detective, Tom set off for the Palace, near the Elephant and Castle. The detective was told to lurk in the background while Tom and his companions hunted their prey. They found him, as expected, in the bar. He had a weak chin and nicotine-stained fingers, but a 'rather pleasant' face; he was wearing a shabby coat and a floppy felt hat. Tom contrived an introduction and then strung the man along for the best part of an hour, spouting all the inanities that were usually put to him: 'What an interesting life you must have . . . What a lot of interesting people you must meet . . .' The bogus Hickey said with a world-weary sigh that it was a bore to have to lunch with tycoons when he would rather be playing shove ha'penny in his local pub.

'How do you get such a job?' Tom asked keenly. 'What are the qualifications?'

'Oh you just have to have flair, old boy,' the impostor replied, not inaccurately. He added: 'The screw's jolly good, but it's a hell of a life. Most of the money goes to the brewers in the end anyway.'

After a while, the small gaggle was joined by the eighteen-year-old show-girl whom the man was courting. The moment of dénouement was near. As Tom watched the youth he felt only pity and curiosity – and a twinge of lust. 'Hickey' seemed to have plenty of money, and always stood his round. There was no question of him obtaining money by false pretences. What was his motive?

'I think this has gone on long enough,' Tom announced suddenly. 'Will you tell me why you are passing yourself off as Hickey?' The man looked straight ahead and murmured: 'I don't know what you mean.' He then took Tom aside and asked if they could talk elsewhere: he didn't want his girlfriend to hear.

It was to impress her, he explained when they were outside, that he had invented his alter ego. 'I wanted to *be* somebody. I thought she wouldn't look at me.' Tom offered some sententious advice to the effect that, if she was worth having, she would love him for himself; but the fake Hickey was unconvinced. 'I can never face her again,' he groaned. 'I just worship her. I've let her down.' He refused to go back and explain to her. Instead, he accompanied Tom to the

West End for a drink, and then to Queen's Gate Place Mews; there the real William Hickey fell to his knees and paid sexual homage to his impersonator.

It was only in the early hours that Tom remembered the private detective, still loitering obediently at the Elephant and Castle and awaiting further instructions.[25]

CHAPTER FIVE

NO WAR THIS CRISIS

Claud Cockburn called the 1930s the devil's decade. To W. H. Auden it was a 'low, dishonest decade'. Tom's preferred epitaph for the period came from another Auden poem:

> 'O where are you going?' said reader to rider,
> 'That valley is fatal when furnaces burn,
> Yonder's the midden whose odours will madden,
> That gap is the grave where the tall return.'[1]

As William Hickey grew in confidence and reputation, he rode into that fatal valley more and more often. At home, he toured towns that were scarred and wounded by unemployment, sending back reports that sat oddly in the pages of the *Daily Express*. Abroad, he visited the Soviet Union, the United States, the Middle East, France, Germany and Spain. Some of these journeys were undertaken in his own time – during leave or holidays – to save himself the trouble of having to persuade the editor to send him. If Tom had asked to cover the Spanish Civil War, for instance, he might well have been refused because of his Communist sympathies. So he went in his annual holiday, wrote it up as a series of articles on his return and dared Christiansen not to print them. It worked. Christiansen was wary of Tom's politics but he admired his writing.

Tom's first trip to Spain, in September 1937, was an eccentric little odyssey. For one thing, he insisted on taking his car (driven by the uncomplaining Westlake) and entering Spain as a tourist. For another, he followed a most indirect route, travelling via Brussels,

Cologne, Nuremberg, Milan and Perpignan to reach the Spanish border. 'Oh, we couldn't issue documents for Spain,' said a shocked young man at the Automobile Association before he left. 'I mean, there isn't a government, is there?' On hearing of the expedition, Tom's insurance company refused to cover the car at all, because of 'war risks'. He took his revenge in a Hickey column after his return. 'War risks?' he wrote. 'Insurance company have simply lost a nice premium. Spending a whole week in Madrid, driving out several times to various front lines – things were unusually quiet, it's true – I never saw a shot fired in anger; only damage to car seems to be that the cigar lighter has fused.'[2]

It took a fortnight to reach Madrid, not least because Tom insisted that Westlake must drive slowly; for he was terrified of speed. The previous year, after being driven across Paris by Prince Bernhard, he had written with horror of the Prince's reckless motoring: 'The toughest fiend I have ever had the misfortune to be driven by . . . Even Paris taxi-drivers turned pale as he roared past.' He had in fact been the victim of a leg-pull by the *Express*'s Paris correspondent, Sefton Delmer, who was a friend of Bernhard. 'As an unkind joke on Driberg,' Delmer recalled, 'I had asked Bernhard to drive him as fast as he could, knowing that Tom hated going at anything faster than twenty miles an hour.'[3] This particular joke back-fired. Queen Wilhelmina of the Netherlands, whose daughter Bernhard was to marry, had the Hickey piece drawn to her attention; she gave her prospective son-in-law a stern talking-to about the dangers of speeding, and told him that in future he must not exceed forty mph, even on the autobahn. 'Forty! I ask you. Forty on the autobahn!' Bernhard complained to Delmer.

It was the magnificence of the autobahns that Tom found most disconcerting as he made his stately progress through Nazi Germany on the way to Spain; more sinister, even, than the sight of Hitler Youth on the march. He met an Englishman who fulminated that 'only a madman would spend so much on roads when the farms and villages look as dilapidated and poor as they do in Germany'; but Tom, recalling that the roads' primary purpose was military, 'foreheard in my mind's ear the rumbling of army lorries in the Central European night . . .'

In Milan Tom tracked down Aldo, an Italian whom he had last seen during the Christmas holiday that he and his mother had spent in Rapallo twelve years earlier. Then, Aldo had been a ragged, penniless youth of seventeen, who was happy to let Tom give him a blow-job plus a few lire. They had exchanged letters since, and Tom had sent him some more money. ('Why not? When there is heavy unemployment and no social security what else can such boys as Aldo do?') Now, under the Fascists, Aldo was flourishing: he had a good flat, a well-paid job in the municipal bureaucracy and a wife. His brother, however, had been out of work for seven years, during which time he'd read the whole of Dante. For old times' sake Aldo came back to Tom's hotel for sex, and Tom again gave him a *pourboire*. Aldo seemed nervous as to whether Tom would disapprove of his working for the Fascists. What, he wanted to know, did the English think of Italy these days? Tom replied that the English thought of little but football.

Reaching Spain at last, after driving through the South of France, Tom was greeted at the frontier by an unshaven militiaman who raised a clenched fist and shouted a cheerful '*Salud!*' Once in the country, Tom managed to avoid the 'war risks' about which the insurance company had been so fretful. On the night he arrived in Valencia, the war-time capital, an American woman greeted him with the news that 'You've just missed a dandy air-raid. Pretty as a picture it was.' (Not so pretty for the twenty-two dead, as Tom remarked later.) Valencia, Barcelona and Madrid were all being bombed by the Fascists, but Tom did not see a single aeroplane. Once or twice, over dinner in Madrid, his cutlery rattled slightly at the distant thud of shelling. And one night, eating at the Madrid flat of Sefton Delmer, who was now the *Express*'s resident correspondent, Tom thought he might be about to witness an air-raid: surely that was the unmistakable drone of a high-powered bombing plane? 'Oh no,' Delmer replied. 'That's the refrigerator cooling the champagne.' In his apartment in the Hotel Florida, Delmer had huge stocks of wine that had been looted from the cellars of the royal palace and then sold by an Anarchist pub off the Puerta del Sol. He was particularly proud of a Château Yquem 1904, of which he had bought several dozen at sixpence a bottle.

Tom travelled with Delmer to Valencia, where they were kept under the watchful eye of the foreign press censor, a dark, handsome woman called Constancia de la Mora Cisneros, whose husband was chief of the air force. She had been educated at Cambridge, and Tom was charmed by her combination of an aristocratic background with Communist politics. The attraction was mutual: when the *Express* reporters and their driver could find no hotel-room in Valencia, she put them up at her cottage in a secluded mountain village. (She emphasised that this was done only as a favour to Tom; Delmer, in her view, was objectionably right-wing. In her memoirs she complained that 'Sefton Delmer, who in London is notorious as something of a dandy, dressed deliberately badly in order to demonstrate his contempt for the Republic.') She warned the men that on their way to the cottage they would come to a road-block, where they would be expected to switch the car-lights on and off twice, hoot the horn once and shout a password or phrase. The hooting and flashing were left to Westlake, who managed well enough; but Tom had some difficulty making the guards understand his pronunciation of the Spanish for 'We shall avenge the innocent blood!'

At Constancia's house Tom breakfasted on Spanish omelette, pimentos and melon. Only the absence of fresh milk for their coffee hinted that there might be a war on. In Valencia itself, the clues were more conspicuous: 'food queues, dense crowds in not very uniform khaki, many with slung arms, bandaged heads or newly vacant eye-sockets'.[4] The dining room at the Hotel Victoria was crammed with medical officers and army officers, diplomats and spies. Ernest Hemingway and Martha Gellhorn were there too, learning to cope with the scarcity of supplies: one night Tom joined them for a meal of stewed cat.[5] When Tom found himself stuck without petrol he turned to Hemingway for help; in next to no time the Spanish Foreign Minister's private secretary, glad to be of assistance to any friend of the famous American novelist, gave him an authorisation for 200 litres (about 44 gallons). Thus replenished, Tom left for Madrid before dawn the next day.

The drive from Valencia was, scenically, as perfect as a dream. Tom wrote a brief, lyrical account for the *Express*:

Moon and starlight to start by. Before sun-up an eggshell-green glow in the sky on our left. Then — we were climbing steeply — craggy hills that looked cut out of silver-grey cardboard, like a Drury Lane set for *Don Quixote*.

Then, in the sun, fertile uplands: gashes of red earth, a far more vivid red than Devon cliffs.

Then wildly, romantically barren country; long-ruined towers growing out of the very rocks.

A high wind. All the way we were more or less 2,000 feet above sea-level. Magpies. Mongrel dogs racing the car. Mules shying away from it.[6]

The Madrid into which Tom came was still holding out against the Fascist siege. The trams and the underground were running, the telephones worked, there were elegant shirts in the windows of gents' outfitters. But every wall carried huge posters urging the populace: 'EVACUATE MADRID. TRUST YOUR FAMILY TO THE REPUBLIC.'

On the outskirts of the city Tom visited front-line trenches, some of which were in a park beside a large country house:

To reach the trenches we walked along stately avenues, the first leaves falling. The peace was only broken by an occasional shot a few hundred yards away: easy to imagine it was just another guest potting rabbits.

There was an ornamental lake, too. It was not full. They had just had to drain it. Presence in it of dead Moors had become unpleasantly noticeable.[7]

Naturally there wouldn't be much shooting at the moment, the troops in one trench explained: it was lunchtime.

Tom saw no serious fighting on this first trip to Spain. He had gone as a tourist, and he had had a holiday of sorts. He arrived back in London with the Studebaker's dashboard registering 4,001 miles more than on his departure. The car was thick with Spanish dust, in which could still just be read the message that had been traced by an unknown finger: 'VIVA LA REPUBLICA.'

'Who will win?' he asked, in a 'back-from-holiday column' for the *Express*. 'How should I know, having seen only one side for only a fortnight? I only know that I can't believe that the inflexible courage, humour, spirit I saw can ever really be beaten.'

Tom's enthusiasm for the Spanish Republicans was not shared by the *Daily Express*, but his reports were printed nevertheless. 'Within limits,' he wrote a few years later, 'I was given freedom to express, or at least to imply, political views different from those of the newspaper I was working for.' He did not dissemble or deceive: 'We had our fierce arguments daily, often triangularly – proprietor, editor, columnist. In retrospect, I pity the editor most.'[8] Tom promised to show Arthur Christiansen anything controversial or political before it was sent to be typeset. Christiansen found him 'scrupulous in observing the agreement', adding that 'I helped him to rewrite in suitable "implied" form more Left Wing stuff than I ever put on my spike.'[9]

Still, there were tensions. Christiansen was more eager to perform his 'tricks with type' and design eye-catching news stories than to get lured into the awkward business of politics. On the great issues of the day, he was happy to do as the proprietor told him. He did feel sick when he heard Neville Chamberlain on the wireless describe Czechoslovakia as 'a far-away country', and he telephoned Lord Beaverbrook to express his revulsion. 'Well,' Beaverbrook replied severely, 'isn't Czechoslovakia a far-away country?' Christiansen agreed that it was, and went back to producing his newspaper without another whimper.

In the couple of years before the outbreak of the Second World War, when Neville Chamberlain returned from Munich promising 'peace in our time' and the *Express* was telling its readers that 'there will be no war', Tom found the restrictions on his work so frustrating that he wondered if he should leave the paper. 'But many friends (including John Strachey) urged me to stay, partly because I was part of the open underground resistance within the *Express* office, partly because the space which I filled daily might otherwise have been filled by more positively objectionable material.'

The Hickey column was vigilant to the activities of British Fascists and their sympathisers. In March 1938 it reported on a pro-Franco meeting at Queen's Hall ('platform bore rich load of furs, jewels, spats, paunches'). While the Spanish anthem was played, Tom and his colleagues at the press table remained seated, taking notes. 'Stand up!' cried angry women in the audience. A year later Tom was given more frightening proof that the press table was no longer the inviolable sanctuary he had once assumed it to be, when he attended a Fascist meeting at St Pancras Town Hall. After a speech by Sir Oswald Mosley urging Britain to live in 'manly friendship' with Nazi Germany, there was a question-and-answer session chaired by the Fascists' political director, A. Raven Thomson. The tone of questions and answers became increasingly anti-semitic; at every mention of the Jews there were howls of hatred. Suddenly, from near the front of the hall, a man shouted: 'What is Mr Hickey of the *Daily Express* doing at the press table there?' Other voices were raised; people stood up and pointed at Tom. He heard shouts of 'Jew!' and 'He's a Jew!' and 'Hickeystein'. From the platform Raven Thomson said that he had been 'keeping an eye' on Tom during 'our Leader's' speech, and that while Mosley had been delivering his precious message Tom had taken no notes but had sat there twiddling his pencil. 'I wish I could get a job like that,' Raven Thomson jeered. In fact, Tom had filled almost eight pages in small handwriting during Mosley's speech. He held up his open notebook as evidence. 'Yes, I know, you made some notes,' Raven Thomson allowed. 'But it struck me that you were just writing down those points which might be twisted against Mosley.' At this point a steward sidled up to Tom and quietly advised him to leave by a side door. What, Tom asked, was wrong with the main door? 'Well, we don't want any trouble,' the steward whispered. 'Some of the boys might get rough.' Meanwhile Raven Thomson was still declaiming from the platform. The press had a right to cover these meetings, he said, 'but we do wish they'd do a little more for us sometimes in exchange for the unfailing courtesy they receive at our meetings'. Hickeystein left shortly afterwards, the hatred of the mob still scalding his ears.[10]

Tom had a sharp eye for anything that might give aid and comfort to the Nazis. He rebuked *Peace News* for devoting 'a remarkably large amount of space to material friendly to Nazi Germany'.[11] (The magazine had pleaded for 'understanding' of Goebbels, and argued that Hitler did not want conquest or world domination but merely 'economic independence' for Germany.) He monitored the *Anglo-German Review*, which 'appears to be mainly filled with pro-Nazi propaganda', and criticised Sir Wyndham Childs, a former assistant police commissioner at Scotland Yard, for contributing to it. He suggested that Childs was an 'elderly' man who 'should know better'.[12] Childs sued for libel, complaining that Tom had portrayed him as 'an almost senile old dodderer with pro-Nazi views'. The *Daily Express* pleaded fair comment. Its counsel, Sir Patrick Hastings, read passages from the issue of the *Review* in which Childs's article had appeared, including an editorial assurance that the *Führer* 'has no territorial ambitions so frequently attributed to him by all anti-German propagandists. He will be known to future generations as Hitler the peacemaker.' The old dodderer stood revealed as, at the very least, a useful idiot. Judgment with costs was given for William Hickey and the *Daily Express*.

As well as harrying Nazi apologists at home, Tom managed to slip away to the Continent several times, to observe the enemy at first hand. He drove to Germany (or, rather, was driven by Bert Westlake) on the eve of Chamberlain's Munich agreement, in August 1938. Coblenz, his first stop, seemed peaceful enough. But the next day he moved on to Bayreuth, Wagner's home town, about thirty miles from the frontier with Czechoslovakia, and found a menace that was only half-submerged:

By day South Germany is a smiling land: the rowan trees red with berries, girls with flaxen pigtails, steep-timbered houses, geese in the streets.

By night other powers wake. You can't see the trees; girls and geese are sleeping. Instead you are startled, hurrying to your bed at Bayreuth well after midnight, to pass great buildings – in the remote countryside – with every window lit, their inmates busy.

You can't see if they are factories or barracks. They are big, square, new-looking blocks, just far enough back from the road to make it difficult to identify them without leaving the road, which might not be wise. One that I passed at about 11.30 pm certainly was a works of some kind. Furnaces were blazing, there was a roar one could hear from far in the still night. All Sunday too, I noticed, smoke poured from factory

chimneys. I don't know what sort of factories. They weren't
labelled.[13]

Just south of Bayreuth, the German army was on manoeuvres. Tom
asked about them. 'You cannot go there,' he was told frostily. 'The
roads are too bad for your car.' He drove on to Czechoslovakia.

In Prague he booked into the Alcron Hotel. 'No "grand hotel"
novel,' he wrote, 'could deal adequately with one of these Central
European capitals when there's a crisis on.' It appealed hugely to his
love of intrigue. He sat in the hotel lounge scrutinising his fellow
guests, imagining spies and arms salesmen everywhere. That red-
haired woman in a black veil *might* be a housewife from Bratislava
up for a day's shopping, but then again . . .

The Alcron was also the temporary home of Lord Runciman,
who had been sent out a month earlier by Neville Chamberlain to
'mediate' between the Czechs and the Sudeten Germans. Runciman
was a former President of the Board of Trade, 'ostensibly chosen for
his supposed skill in settling industrial disputes', as A. J. P. Taylor
wrote, 'but perhaps more for his ignorance of the issues at stake'.[14]
On Tom's first night in Prague he saw Lord Runciman dining in the
hotel restaurant with the Czech prime minister, Hodza. Hitherto
Runciman had spent most of his time with the pro-Nazi Sudeten
Germans, but that morning he had seen President Beneš, and now
here he was in intense discussion with Hodza. What deal was he
trying to foist on the Czech government? For more than three hours
Tom tried desperately to eavesdrop. However, the tables next to
Runciman had been taken by functionaries sitting on their own,
reading papers, and throughout the evening the orchestra loudly
worked its way through an interminable selection of Mozart pieces.
Tom couldn't hear a word. All he could report about the meeting
was that Runciman and Hodza had dined on tomato soup, sole
meunière with carrot, chicken mayonnaise and mixed ice, and that
when Runciman eventually went up to his room the orchestra broke
into a light-hearted Lehar Serenade. 'This,' he informed his *Express*
readers, 'was what is called being present when history is made.'[15]

On his last day in Czechoslovakia Tom travelled to 'the geo-
graphical heart of the problem' – German minority territory two

hours north of Prague. Elsewhere in the country the sense of impending conflict had been merely implicit. But here there was no mistaking the threat of German invasion: fortifications were being hurriedly erected everywhere, new barbed-wire fences lined the road, tree-trunks were lashed together into barricades, soldiers crowded the villages. In Warnsdorf, a town near the frontier, he listened to the Germans' complaints of Czech 'oppression'. There were genuine grievances, he concluded, but 'that Nazis should be righteously indignant about such "persecution" suggests a lack of mote and beam proportion.'[16]

Tom's own vision was not entirely unclouded. Through 1938 and 1939 he vacillated between suspecting that war was inevitable and believing that it could be avoided. When an eighteen-year-old reader in Morden wrote to ask if William Hickey could find another young person 'who wishes to get away from this mad world ... I mean, shoulder his pack along with me and work a passage over to Canada ... to wrench himself away from the approaching disaster,' Tom replied severely: 'No I cannot. All I can do is give the sour advice: There is no escape. If "disaster" came, don't you think you would be involved in Canada, USA, anywhere else? Or if you weren't, would you feel quite easy about having left your people and friends at home?'[17] Yet Tom often persuaded himself that 'disaster' need not happen.

His attitude was not, of course, as complaisant towards Germany as that of his newspaper and its owner. 'It is impossible,' the Express had stated with characteristic certainty in April 1938, 'that the British government should pledge us to fight to hold together the ramshackle state of Czechoslovakia.' A month later it was even more emphatic: 'Britain will not be involved in war. There will be no major war in Europe this year or next year. The Germans will not seize Czechoslovakia. So go about your business with confidence in the future and fear not.'[18]

Tom was rather less sanguine about the Nazis' intentions. Nevertheless, he was infected all too often by the bright optimism that had spread through the rest of the paper. On 15 September, a fortnight after returning from Czechoslovakia, Tom flew with Neville Chamberlain to Munich, where Chamberlain told Hitler that he did not object to the detachment of the Sudeten Germans from the rest of Czechoslovakia 'providing the practical difficulties could be overcome'. In his column the next morning Tom ventured no opinion on this act of appeasement. Instead he filled his space with an account of the journey and of Chamberlain's arrival in Germany. On the day after that he reported Chamberlain's return from Berchtesgaden, and announced his own intention of taking a few weeks' holiday.

William Hickey was therefore absent from the office when the *Express*'s wishful thinking reached its apogee. A fortnight after the talks at Berchtesgaden, Chamberlain was back in Munich to sign an agreement which effectively abandoned Czechoslovakia to Hitler. The front page of the *Daily Express* reported this deal under a huge, triumphant headline: 'PEACE'. Scarcely less prominent was the message above the headline, emblazoned just below the masthead: 'The *Daily Express* declares that Britain will not be involved in a European war this year, or next year either.'[19] The following day's splash headline quoted Chamberlain: 'IT IS PEACE IN OUR TIME, YOU MAY SLEEP QUIETLY.' Elsewhere on the front page the exhortations to stop worrying even spread into the brief announcement of the end of summer time: 'Forget the crisis but remember to put your clock back tonight.'[20]

It was a ghastly misjudgment. But when Tom resumed his column, on 18 October, he did not try to distance himself from it. 'I left you just after Berchtesgaden, but before Munich,' he reminded his readers. 'There really didn't seem to be anything I could do. Also I had arranged to take my holiday then, and it seemed more English to finish one's game of bowls. Also, we here knew – hadn't we been telling you? – that there wasn't going to be a war this year.'[21] He did at least forbear to add 'or next year either', but it was not his finest hour. Ten years later, when he produced a book of his Hickey columns, he suppressed every one of his 'no war' predictions. Instead he inserted a rather disingenuous footnote: 'I was certainly conscious that war was almost inevitable.'[22]

In one corner of Europe, the war was almost over. Soon after celebrating the New Year of 1939,[23] Tom set off on his second visit to Spain, where the Republicans were desperately beleaguered.

Barcelona had fallen. Hundreds of refugees were heading for France. The imminence of defeat was apparent as soon as Tom crossed the border, 'for, trudging up the road towards us and towards the French frontier, alone and carrying a pack, was a stout middle-aged figure whom I suddenly recognised: he was Alvarez del Vayo, Foreign Minister of Spain.'[24] (It turned out that he was not fleeing the country but taking some official documents for safe keeping in France.)

Tom had hitched a lift into the country with two fellow-Communists from Fleet Street, Lou Kenton and Harry Harrison, who were driving a food lorry to Spain for the Printers' Anti-Fascist Movement. At La Junquera, the first town on the Spanish side of the border, crowds swarmed round them crying 'Bread, bread!' Anguished women clawed at the lorry. Tom and his comrades found it almost unbearable to have to explain that they were taking the food to the central depot and could not hand it out there and then. In a column for the *Express* he described the throng of refugees as 'the most horrifying and miserable sight I have ever seen'.[25]

The lorry was held up for several days near the frontier by the 'refugee traffic jam'. Tom began to worry: he had with him some insulin which he had been asked to bring in for Spain's chief censor, José-Maria Quiroga, who was diabetic. Would Quiroga expire before they could reach him? Eventually they cleared a route through the human road-blocks and drove with haste to Figueras, the temporary capital following the fall of Barcelona, where they were relieved to find that the chief censor was still hard at work. In his ante-room there was a lone poster, bearing the message: 'Exaggerated optimism assists the enemy'. Quiroga was a quiet, bespectacled man who had been Professor of Spanish Literature at the University of Salamanca. He was grateful for his insulin; in return he invited Tom to attend one of the last meetings of the democratic Spanish parliament, the Cortes.

Some said the Cortes meeting was to be out at an obscure village. Such stories were perhaps spread deliberately so that Franco's spies should pass them on. In fact, it was at the castle, late at night; not till we were starting off for it in our cars were the drivers told where to go.

The old castle was in darkness – but for MPs' cars' lights, which must have given the show away if enemy planes had been watching – when we drove, through many archways, into its enormous quadrangle. We stood about, talking for some reason in undertones. Quiroga marshalled us, led us through yet more archways . . .

We came into a vast, echoing, round-vaulted crypt, with roughly whitewashed walls and pillars. Part of it was set apart for Parliament's meeting. There was some semblance of pomp – carpets, gilt chairs, a table hung with red brocade, the Republican colours above it. Naked electric bulbs, hastily rigged up, shone overhead; Parliament was only an oasis in this long, cathedral-like cavern, in whose dim aisles soldiers sat about smoking.[26]

The Speaker installed himself at the red brocade table. At his right, on one long bench, sat a dozen ministers – including Del Vayo, whom Tom had last seen strolling towards France a few days earlier. 'Few Parliaments,' Tom wrote, 'have ever met in more dramatic circumstances.' The speeches, mostly long, were sombre: there was much talk of the shortage of weapons and the weariness of the soldiers. But when the session ended, well after midnight, each MP and minister stood up in turn and said, simply, '*Si*'. The vote was unanimous: the war would continue. There was a shout of '*Viva España!*' Was this, Tom wondered as the House rose, the 'exaggerated optimism' against which the censor's poster had warned? Or simply an inextinguishable hope?

He returned home via Paris, by air. When fog forced his plane down at Kenley he fell into conversation with a young RAF officer, who was interested to learn that Tom had been with the Republicans in Spain. 'D'you know,' the airman said, 'in a way I'd like them to win. They're putting up a dam' good show.'

It hardly mattered. A month later, Franco had won. His aristocratic supporters in London held a victory celebration at the Queen's Hall, which provided 'the charming spectacle of English ladies and gentlemen gloating over a fallen foe', Tom wrote bitterly in the *Daily Express*. Franco was described at the meeting as 'Our generalissimo', 'A military officer as honest and patriotic as any anywhere', 'Our ruler and guide' and 'The heaven-sent chieftain'.[27] The only moment Tom enjoyed was when a meek little man stood up and asked quietly: 'Might a member of the public denounce you as traitors?' The answer was no: the revellers shouted 'Throw him out!', and out he went.

Though Tom continued to assure his readers that there would be no war, he seems to have had some premonition that easy travel might soon be only a memory. In the spring and summer of 1939 he was continually dashing abroad, gathering sights and experiences like a squirrel preparing for hibernation. He was in Rome for the funeral of Pope Pius XI in mid-February, and then again for the Coronation of Pius XII a month later. These ceremonial occasions gave Tom an opportunity to exercise his 'tiresome knowingness' (as he himself termed it): he was always a great pedant on matters of ritual, especially religious ritual. In his despatches from the Vatican he loftily reproved other English newspapers for falling into 'some strange errors' in their coverage of the funeral. *The Times*, for instance, had said that the lying-in-state was in a chapel on the south side of St Peter's. Actually, Tom reported, it was on the north, 'though in a less learned journal the mistake might have been overlooked, for St Peter's "faces" west instead of east'.[28] While in Rome he spent much of his time with the novelist Hugh Walpole, who was covering the events for the Hearst press syndicate in America and who, on Tom's suggestion, wrote a book about the papal transition, *Roman Fountain*. Most of it was written in the weeks between funeral and coronation, when Walpole found himself at a loose end because 'Tom Driberg, whom I had immensely liked, had gone back to London.' Tom had a cameo role in Walpole's characteristically theatrical rendition of the crowd-scene on the steps of St Peter's during the coronation:

There, also, I saw Hilaire Belloc eating sandwiches and drinking out of a bottle. At once there was a little group of us – Belloc, Tom Driberg, Michael, Hillman – all of us on the edge of the crowd looking up to the balcony where the new Pope would be . . .

And then I felt myself lifted and knew that I was carried off my feet. I was helpless and the sense of that was so ominous to me that it was as though I were about to be crushed to death.

'So this is the end of my Roman adventure!' I thought.

I fancied that I had a last vision of Hilaire Belloc, lifted up, transcended, in air, waving a sandwich. I heard people call out, 'The steps! The steps!' I saw Tom Driberg in his elegant evening dress and white gloves, still smiling and courteous although he seemed to be bent sideways. 'The steps! The steps!'

. . . I saw a woman disappear. A great wave hit us in the back. I saw Driberg's white gloves. I slid. I slipped. I slid. I was almost down. I was up again. I rushed, as though I were eagerly greeting a friend, to the outer wall. I stayed, breathless; my waistcoat was torn, my shoes trampled to pieces.

I looked to the balcony, but the ceremony was over.

I never saw Pope Pius XII crowned.[29]

Tom, on the other hand, saw everything; and he recorded it in obsessive detail for the *Express*. 'He went on to the throne. The plumed fans were set up on either side. While the choir sang the *Kyrie Eleison*, chasubled dignitaries went up to the throne to do homage. Cardinals kissed the Pope's foot and hand; archbishops and bishops kissed his foot and knee; mitred abbots his foot only. The homage ended. They rearranged his flowing alb over his feet. Then they lifted the alb back again; held a big missal before him . . .'[30] And so on, for well over a thousand words.

At Easter, Tom took a few days off and caught the ferry to Boulogne. He was kept awake until after three in the morning by English holidaymakers bawling 'The Lambeth Walk' outside his hotel window, but in spite of this inconvenience he much preferred Boulogne to his other port of call, Le Touquet. Boulogne was full of 'workers on long-saved-up-for day-trips', who were much jollier company than the 'golfing stockbrokers and expensive cuties' who made up the English contingent in Le Touquet. Nevertheless, curiosity drove Tom over to Le Touquet for a few hours. In the Casino he was accosted by an English gent with a red carnation buttonhole and an even redder face. 'Wrote about me once,' the man snorted. 'Didn't like what you said. Nothing against me, what? Didn't like what you wrote in your – hah – rag.' Tom couldn't remember ever having mentioned the man in his column. What, he asked, had he written? 'Can't remember,' the aggrieved gambler snapped. 'Know I didn't like it. Don't ask me what it was.'

Three weeks later Tom was off to New York. Again he pursued pleasure with the intensity of one who guessed that there was little time left for blithe carelessness. He spent an exhilarating day at Coney Island racing along switchbacks with names such as Thunderbolt and Cyclone and soaking up the 'invigoratingly raucous company of about a million working-class New Yorkers'. He gorged himself between rides on frankfurters, corn-on-the-cob, chocolate-flavoured popcorn and a species of ice-cream called frozen custard. (The fastidious gourmet and patron of *avant-garde* art liked to wallow in vulgar food and entertainment occasionally; this, after all, was a man who found his salvation in public lavatories as well as cathedrals. But the vulgarity had to be *in its place*. The sight of, say, an HP Sauce bottle on his dinner table in a smart hotel would provoke him to petulant rage.)

At the World's Fair he wandered curiously through pavilions full of scientific gimmicks. There was an electric eel which, every half-hour, would set a radio playing and a model railway working. ('Poor thing, it looked dead beat last night.') In the Medical Building's Hall of Man, where the processes of human birth were displayed, Tom overheard a bewildered woman asking an attendant: 'At what point does the soul come in?' 'I don't have that information, lady,' the attendant replied. 'You'll have to ask the supervisor.' Then there was the exhibit in the American Telegraph and Telephone Company's building:

From long queues always waiting in there, a few are chosen by lot for the privilege of making free long-distance calls – the only condition being that the several hundred others can listen in by earphone.

This is really a beautiful stunt. It gratifies on the one hand the eavesdropper, on the other the exhibitionist, as well as giving careful out-of-towners, who feel they've been spending too much, something for nothing. Also, many of the chosen free-callers are excellent comic turns.

When I was there a stout priest from the Middle West had won a call. I think he regretted it as he stepped up into the glass-sided booth and the crowd, all earphoned, waited to hear him talking to his distant family.

His brother answered. 'Is that Martin?' said the priest. 'This is brother John. I'm speaking from the World's Fair, they give us a free telephone call, you know.'

'Why, that's swell,' said Martin. 'How're you making out up there? We're all fine, but –'

'Listen, Martin,' said the priest, with an anxious glance at us, 'be careful what you say. [Laughter.] There's a whole lot of people listening.'

'What's that?'

'I said don't say anything special, there's about four hundred people listening in.'

'What makes you think so?' said Martin – and went ahead to talk about family worries.

Mother, it seemed ('You know how bad her legs are'), had 'fallen all the way downstairs and bruised herself up.' Roars of laughter from the unfeeling crowd. Then that business about auntie –

'Hey, Martin,' cried the priest, in agony. 'I told you there's a lot of people can hear us. Can't you hear them laughing?'

'No,' said Martin, obviously not believing a word of it.

Brother John was gladder than the crowd were when his five minutes were up.[31]

But it was not all bread and circuses. In Yorkville, New York's German district, most bars and shops were adorned with portraits of Hitler and swastikas. Tom observed that the German–American organisation *Bund*, which had 100,000 members, was indistinguishable from the Nazi party in opinions, methods, salute and swastika emblem. Its leader, Fritz Kuhn, had a portrait of Hitler above his desk; yet he denied being influenced by the Nazis. 'We have no liaison with Germany,' he said when Tom went to interview him. 'No money from there, no orders, no ideas.' Tom was puzzled. Didn't Kuhn accept the racial theories of National Socialism? For instance, would he expel any of his members who married a Jew?

'Most certainly. I should hope so!' he said, explosively – then quickly added, 'I didn't like the way you put that question. We are not against the Jews. We do not want to deprive them of their rights. We simply ask that we shall keep our own company. For, after all,' he went on – and the lightning tangents of his argument left me following far behind, dazed – 'after all, you, coming from England, should know even better than I do that the Jews are the root of all evil.'

'Why specially England?' I asked.

'The British Israel Secret Service,' he said, 'is the most powerful in the world.'

'The what?' I asked.

'The British Israel Secret Service,' he repeated, with melodramatically guttural emphasis.

'We never hear about that,' I said. 'I suppose we are not allowed to?'

'Hah! That is so,' he said, glad that I was getting the hang of it.

He also seemed surprised that I had not heard of a petition signed, he said, by two million Englishmen who were against war with Germany.[32]

As Tom had advised the teenage reader in Morden, there was indeed no escape. It was impossible to talk to anyone for more than a few minutes without the conversation turning to war, and rumours of war. After returning to England he found sinister or melancholy reminders everywhere. On a grey and windy morning in Brighton he heard a workman on the pier whistling 'Deutschland über Alles.'

The Nazi–Soviet Pact was signed on 23 August. Leftists at the *Express* were appalled: Dick Plummer (who was later a Labour MP) burst into Tom's office and shouted 'You can include me out as a friend of the Soviet Union'; Willie Forrest, another of the reporters who had covered the Spanish civil war, resigned from the Communist Party. Tom was plunged into gloom. In his column on 25 August he reproached a milk bar-maid who had been heard to say 'It's not as bad as you read in the papers. They make it up. It gets them more money.' 'I wish,' Tom wrote testily, 'one could take as light a view.' The next day, however, he seemed to have cheered up. 'My tip: no war this crisis,' was his rash message. This must have puzzled those readers who recalled that only a fortnight earlier he himself had denounced a spiritualist pamphlet for peddling optimism ('They won't fight,' it had predicted, 'but most people will believe that they are going to fight in September . . . Remember, no war!').

On 28 August he found another seer to mock. He reviewed an 'astrological' book called *Hitler's Last Year of Power*, which predicted that 'Poland will not emerge unscathed', that the days of late August 1939 would be 'critical', but that 'through negotiations a catastrophe can be avoided'. Tom commented:

I do not blame the publishers for quoting this passage ecstatically in their advertisements. Nor do I blame them for not quoting the passage, four pages earlier, which states in emphatic italics that 'It will be impossible for the gulf between Germany and Russia to be bridged' so long as Hitler and Stalin remain in power.

On Wednesday 30 August, after a visit to his barber at Trumper's, Tom reported: 'Lord Stanhope had been in on Monday: he said that things looked better than on Sunday. (Not that I would trust his judgment; but his information should be good.)' In the early hours of the morning of 1 September the Germans attacked Poland.

The British declaration of war was not immediate. By the evening of Saturday 2 September, Neville Chamberlain was still babbling that 'if the German government should agree to withdraw their forces then His Majesty's government would be willing to regard the position as being the same as it was before the German forces crossed the Polish frontier. That is to say, the way would be open to discussion between the German and Polish governments on the matters at issue.' But at 9 o'clock the following morning Chamberlain was eventually forced to issue an ultimatum. When it expired at 11 am, Britain was at war.

Tom was in a taxi on his way to work at 11 o'clock that Sunday morning, clutching his gas-mask. Searching for somewhere to listen to Chamberlain's broadcast, he and the cabbie found a vicar and a few other people huddled round a wireless set at the door of a church. They all listened. 'That's that,' said the vicar briskly when Chamberlain finished. 'Well, I'd better tell them to start the service.'

Tom stayed for matins, and for the air-raid warning that sounded minutes after the Prime Minister's announcement. Then he walked to Fleet Street to compose his first wartime despatch.

'Well,' he began,

you can't complain that there's 'nothing in the papers nowadays'; nor can we complain of having nothing to write about. If only I had room to print all that we have thought, heard, felt in the last day or two . . . I must apologise for prophesying wrongly nine days ago that there would be 'no war this crisis'. I overestimated the Nazis' shrewdness. I was wrong in exalted company. All the spirit messages and stargazers' reports that I have seen foresaw 'no war'; especially emphatic was a book of alleged spirit writings on the crisis which a Spiritualist newspaper attacked me for criticising recently. I at least claimed no supernatural authority for my opinion.

It was not a handsome apology, but it was all he was prepared to offer. Being wrong about the imminence of war was, in his view, a minor crime compared with being soft on Nazism. And he had never been guilty of that, unlike many in the British Establishment. Hence the surprisingly boastful conclusion to his column on the first day of World War II:

Now I suppose we just have to set to and win.

Some of us have, in a sense, been in the war since January 1933, when paganism and persecution became officially okay in Germany; but we can't sit back and say 'I told you so.'

We're all in it.

CHAPTER SIX

FAMOUS LAST WEEKENDS

It was at this inauspicious moment that Tom became a man of property. In the autumn of 1939 he moved into Bradwell Lodge, a mansion on a remote Essex peninsula.

Had anyone suggested a few years earlier that he might ever do such a thing, Tom would have scoffed at the idea. Throughout his childhood he had longed to live in London; he was irresistibly fascinated by its garish pleasures and squalor. 'Having always been told that living at Crowborough was "living in the country",' he explained, 'I wrongly identified English country life with interminable calls on elderly ladies whose favourite topic was the servant problem.'[1] After ten years in London, however, he had discovered that even metropolitan sensations could pall. Meanwhile, his weekends at the country houses of friends had given him a taste for rural escape.

The original ambition was modest enough: he wanted a small cottage or *pied à terre* no more than an hour from London by car. He was soon persuaded by A. J. A. Symons that he should confine his search to Essex. Weekends with Symons at Finchingfield had taught him that it was a much maligned county, 'consistently underestimated by Victorian romantics, who wallowed in the melodrama of mountain and torrent. They called it "flat and uninteresting".' In fact, as Tom pointed out, the area round Finchingfield and Saffron Walden, in the north of Essex, had 'small-scale but exquisitely undulating' hills. And although the southern and eastern half of the county was moderately flat, it was anything but uninteresting, with its muddy estuaries and enormous Dutch skies; this was the landscape Tom preferred, a place where 'you may walk for miles along a sea-wall track, raised between rich marsh pastures and mysterious saltings, and see no sign of human activity but the white fleck of a sail far out in the turbulent estuary'. Essex was the least spoiled of the home counties. Unlike Surrey, Sussex and Kent, it had escaped the inter-war ravages of speculative builders: Tom always maintained that this was because it had the worst train services and 'the most tedious and squalid road exit from London'. For the same reason houses there were cheaper than at comparable distances to the north, west or south of London.

And so, on occasional free Saturdays in the summer and early autumn of 1938, Tom had set out in the Studebaker with Bert Westlake, armed with sheaves of orders-to-view from estate agents. He gave the agents reasonably precise specifications of his needs – quiet surroundings, tiny garden, small house or cottage, preferably Georgian, not Tudor, and, if modern, certainly not Tudoresque. They in turn sent him off to view huge disused Victorian schools, baronial piles in rolling deer-parks, and ramshackle bungalows a few feet away from roads where lorries thundered by.

Late in the afternoon of one October Saturday, having seen four properties of varying degrees of unsuitability, Tom sat in the car feeling weary and discouraged. He wanted a drink, but the pubs were not open yet. He glanced at the one order-to-view that remained. Yet again the estate agents had ignored his wishes: this was clearly too big – a rectory with sixteen rooms and twenty-seven acres – and too far from London, out at the eastern tip of a promontory jutting into the Blackwater estuary. He was still twenty miles away, and darkness would be falling by the time he arrived.

But the name of the village, Bradwell-juxta-Mare, caught his fancy. And then he noticed, in the typewritten details, a mention of decorative work by Robert Adam. It was always worth seeing an Adam house. He asked Westlake to drive on to Bradwell.

They found the house with difficulty. The door was answered by an elderly clergyman, Canon Ithel Owen, who led them along a dark corridor into a room which was even darker, where the Canon's wife greeted them. Tom thought it all rather gloomy. He was alarmed, too, to see heavy Tudor beams on the ceiling. Where were the Adam decorations that had been promised? But then Canon Owen led Tom through a door and switched on a light. 'We were suddenly in a spacious hall, arched and domed and with delicate plaster-work and Wedgwood-blue plaques; and within a few minutes I felt absolutely sure that, whatever the difficulties or the expense – for even in the half-light of evening one could see that there was much that needed doing – this was the house for me.'[2] It was one of the critical moments of his life.

Canon Owen explained that though the house was largely owned by the church, some of it belonged to him personally. It had been the Rectory of St Thomas's, Bradwell, for generations; but since he had been preceded as Rector by his brother and father, for the past seventy years it had been occupied by his family. (During his brother's incumbency one frequent guest was Erskine Childers, who wrote *Riddle of the Sands* at the Rectory.) Now that the last of the three Canons Owen was about to retire after seventeen years in the job, the church had decided to sell the house and use the proceeds to build a more modestly sized Rectory. It had been on the market for some time. Duff and Diana Cooper, and 'Chips' Channon, were among those who had looked at it but had rejected it as too small.

Tom inspected the other rooms in a euphoric daze, while the parson told him more of the house's history. It was a peculiar hybrid, with a Tudor end dating from about 1520 and a Georgian half which had been added by the Reverend Sir Henry Bate Dudley towards the end of the eighteenth century. Dudley, a former editor of the *Morning Post*, was a combative character. He arrived at Bradwell in 1782 straight from Newgate Jail, where he had served a year's sentence for libelling the Duke of Richmond. In London he was known as a duellist; he fought a famous duel in Vauxhall Gardens to defend the honour of an actress called Mrs Hartley, whose sister he married. In Bradwell he was an energetic harrier of smugglers, who used to bring casks of brandy ashore: he had a room with a 360-degree view – a belvedere – on top of the house so that he could watch out for them. ('Lawless he found them,' wrote one historian of the Bradwell villagers; 'he succeeded in bringing law and order.') The belvedere was used as a studio by Gainsborough when he came to Bradwell to paint his portraits of Bate Dudley and his wife.

Bate Dudley's architect, John Johnson, built the new part of the Rectory separate from the original section, with a carriageway between them. But after a couple of years Dudley was fed up with having to trudge through the rain and cold to get from one room to another. He hired Robert Adam to build a hall that would connect the two halves. At the same time Adam installed decorative fireplaces in other rooms, including one marble chimneypiece inlaid with panels painted by Angelica Kauffmann.

Tom felt a throb of excitement at the idea that these Georgian treasures were almost within his grasp. He must have them.

The parson was anxious to sell soon, for he was already seventy-five. He could see that such an odd house was not to everyone's taste. And any buyer would have to spend heavily on repairs and improvements: both the church authorities and Canon Owen had for many years left undone those things that ought to have been done. For all these reasons, he agreed on a price of £3,800, which, even by the standards of 1938, was cheap. For another £200 he would include two properties on the edge of the Rectory grounds. One was a small Regency gatehouse, the other a Victorian red-brick cottage which was occupied by tenants.

Could Tom afford it? As a well-salaried bachelor he should have had no difficulty raising a mortgage for most of the cost, but he was also a free-spending bachelor with a large overdraft who proposed to buy a house that needed underpinning and other expensive surgery. Besides, even if he could get a mortgage, where would he find a deposit? He had no capital at all.

The latter problem solved itself first, albeit rather painfully. He was invited to the opening-night party of a new restaurant in Jermyn Street, A l'Écu de France. Afterwards a French journalist offered him a lift. 'It was late at night, and the streets seemed deserted,' Tom recalled. 'Through inattention or reckless folly, he began to cross the red lights: safely once, safely twice – then, at the third crossing, a big lorry came fast from the side turning and we hit it smack on.'[3] Tom's nose and right knee-cap were broken, and he was off work for several weeks.

The Frenchman's insurance company paid Tom about £500 compensation — enough to cover the deposit on the Rectory (or, as it would henceforth be known, Bradwell Lodge) as well as a convalescent week in Brighton. At the same time Tom decided to postpone the question of a mortgage by simply buying the house on an increased bank overdraft, which he persuaded his mother to guarantee. It was not until 1940 that he took out a mortgage with a building society.

This left one other bill to be met. During the spring and summer of 1939, Bradwell Lodge was uninhabitable while the builders and decorators went to work on it. Steel girders were put in the cellar to stop further subsidence, the old bathrooms were replaced, fitted carpets were laid, the whole house was repainted. A rudimentary form of central heating was installed, with radiators in the hall and on the landings fired by a coke boiler. The cost of all these improvements was £1,500, almost twice as much as Tom had anticipated.

Here again he was saved by a profitable stroke of bad luck. Just before dawn on 13 July 1939 his mother died of leukaemia. Tom's share of her estate — when it eventually reached him, a year later — was enough to pay off the builders and all his other creditors.

Tom felt no grief at the death, but remorse gnawed at him. Remorse that he hadn't known her better, remorse that he had visited her so seldom, remorse that only a week earlier he had chosen to spend a day in Brighton spooning with a young Persian student instead of going to the nursing home in Crowborough where his mother lay dying. Remorse, above all, that relations between them were always so awkward. Conversation with her, never easy, was almost impossible in her last years as her behaviour became more and more eccentric. She started talking to the bees that she kept in her back-garden at Crowborough. She sent Tom enigmatic little messages. One day in the mid-1930s he returned to his flat to find an envelope from her, delivered by hand. Inside was a leaf from a tear-off calendar of the thought-for-every-day type. It read:

Avoid society which is likely to mislead you; flee from the shadow of sin.

NEWMAN

Had she discovered something about his sexual adventures? Tom never knew. He yearned to talk to her about sex – and politics, and everything else that mattered in his life – but it was too late for honesty. A few weeks before her death she asked him whether she would recover from her illness. 'Of course I should have told her the truth,' he wrote ruefully many years later. 'If only we could have had a real "heart-to-heart" talk then . . . but I had always responded with an embarrassed lack of warmth to her displays of affection and to any attempt by her to achieve intimacy or to pry into my life.'[4] So, as usual, he preferred to lie than to upset her. He forced his face into a grin. 'Of course you're going to get better!' he told her, suffering another jolt of remorse as he did so.

Amy Driberg's last words before she died were 'All men are liars.'

Tom organised the funeral. St John's, Crowborough, had for many years been moderate in its habits, a place of candles but no incense – what Tom derided as a 'middle stump' church. But in the 1920s, much to Tom's delight and the horror of most of its congregation, a vicar called the Revd Basil Gurdon had transformed it. He introduced the Mass, he encouraged genuflexion, he kissed the cross; the church was alive with bells and smells, and as high as a well-hung grouse. Or, as Tom would say, it was 'what every Anglican church should be – uncompromisingly Catholic'. The local hostility amused Tom. It reminded him of nineteenth-century anti-Tractarian propaganda that he had come across as a boy, such as:

> God give our wavering clergy back those honest hearts and true
>   Which once were theirs ere Popish snares their toils around them
>   threw;
> Nor let them barter wife and child, pure hearth and happy home,
>   For the drunken bliss of the strumpet kiss of the Jezebel of Rome.

At last the strumpet had reached the stockbroker belt. During the new priest's first Christmas Communion Tom had spotted the change straight away, and whispered excitedly, 'Mother, *it is the Mass!*' Mrs Driberg took to the new order rather well; but through the 1920s and 1930s low-church evangelicals in the town continued to grumble that St John's had been stolen from them by a Popish snare. These were the very people – the golfing stockbrokers, the genteel ladies – whose infestation of Crowborough had made Tom hate the place so much. His mother's exequies gave him one last opportunity for *épatant les bourgeois* by flaunting his ultramontane tastes.

There was a full Requiem Mass, celebrated by the latest vicar of St John's, Father Olive. Father Charlton, a previous incumbent, performed the Absolutions, 'circumambulating the catafalque to cense it and sprinkle it with holy water, to the shocked horror of some old friends of my parents, firm Protestants, who had turned up. I took pleasure in handing them unbleached candles to hold, and lighting these at the correct places in the service.' The clouds of incense wafting around the corpse 'mingled with, but could not quite disguise, a slight whiff, already just noticeable, of carnal decay'.[5]

The *bourgeois* were duly *épatés*, and not only those who actually attended. After reading a report of the service a Mr E. T. Stoneham wrote a furious letter of complaint to the local paper. Tom's reply was no less outraged:

It is certainly unusual to make a funeral – with its tender memories, its intimate solemnity, its mingling of mourning and hope – the occasion of partisan controversy. Mr E. T. Stoneham has done so, in reference to a funeral reported in your issue of 22 July. He hopes he will not be thought 'unkind'; but thinks it better to risk wounding the feelings of relatives and friends than to miss the chance of airing his apparently inadequate and perverted view of the Church.

After a few more smacks at the wretched Stoneham, Tom aggressively defended the legitimacy of Catholic liturgy and ritual:

The funeral itself was, despite Mr Stoneham's disapproval, in strict accordance with the principles of the Church of England, the ancient Catholic church of this country.

The church at which the funeral was held has borne witness since 1839 to truths which were half-forgotten in the Church of England's 'dead' centuries, before the Methodist and the Catholic Revivals. There, for instance, the Communion of Saints is a reality, not an empty phrase for recitation once a week. There the souls of the Faithful Departed are prayed for, in accordance with Bible teaching. There the sacrament of the altar has been given the central place in Sunday morning worship which the Book of Common Prayer clearly intends for it, and is celebrated with those Catholic accessories which are not merely permitted but actually ordered by that book – however distasteful Mr Stoneham may find the fact.

It was a defiant farewell to Crowborough. There was no longer any reason for him to visit the place, except to arrange the sale of Uckfield Lodge and the auction of its contents – and, a few years later, to install in St John's a memorial to his mother, a Madonna commissioned from Sir Ninian Comper.

In spite of being the youngest son, Tom now assumed the position of head of the family, such as it was. His brothers were in no condition to assume responsibility for anything. After brilliant early careers, both had become sad, bruised figures by the time of Amy Driberg's death. 'Both,' Tom wrote in *Ruling Passions*, 'were distinguished in their professions, but at a crucial point in their lives something went wrong – through their own faults or not I cannot tell – and they suffered humiliation and even disgrace.'[5]

The eldest, Jack, is still remembered with respect by anthropologists. He was a curious, tolerant man – too tolerant for his own good, in the end – who between 1912 and 1926 served as a District Commissioner in the Colonial Service, first in Uganda and then in Sudan. His administrative style was unconventional. He strode about his territory naked save for a khaki kilt, and settled disputes by fighting duels with spears against local champions. He spoke at least eight African languages – Kiswahili and Luganda (Bantu), Galla (Hamitic), Didinga and Topotha (Half-Hamitic), Lango and allied dialects (Nilotic), Lugbara and Kakwa (Sudanian). He also had a large menagerie of wild animals. At one time he was followed by no fewer than five lions; he wrote occasional articles for the *New Statesman* about one of them, Engato. His *Times* obituary recorded that 'he won the confidence of the natives to a remarkable extent by his unorthodox methods, participating fully in their life, hunting – very successfully – with native weapons and becoming a "blood brother" of at least one tribe.'[6] The initiation rite for his 'blooding' included training in sexual endurance, which, according to Tom, 'later enhanced his standing (in every sense) with some of the women of Bloomsbury'. Jack told Tom that he had twice had to eat human flesh. The first was an old female witch who had been killed for failing to produce a good harvest (and who also failed to make a good meal: 'the meat was stringy'). The second was a baby that had been killed in his honour; he found it 'rather like *poussin* in the average London restaurant – a bit tasteless'.[7]

Jack Driberg became the first District Commissioner of Nagichot, in the south-eastern Sudan, after it was taken over by the British in 1920. He built his own log cabin and planted English flowers from the garden at Crowborough. Because of his bald head he was known as *Bwona Tong* – 'Mr Egg'. When Tom went on a sentimental journey to Nagichot in 1952, he was pleased to find that 'an old man called Loki – who walked ten miles up the hill today to greet me – is one of many Africans who remember my brother kindly.'[8] But Jack Driberg's colleagues in the Service were not so fond of him. 'He had,' Kingsley Martin wrote in the *New Statesman*, 'long outraged British Colonial opinion in East Africa.'[9] In 1926 the Colonial Office finally seized its chance to throw him out. The pretext was that he had invented – and prevented – an atrocity.

He had been ordered to lead a punitive expedition against a hill tribe which had raided British-protected areas. He refused, saying that he knew the people concerned and could pacify them without force. His masters in Khartoum, the capital, were coldly insistent: it was an order, not a request. A couple of weeks later, Jack told HQ that he had carried out the expedition, killed the offenders, burned down their villages, and so on. Unfortunately for him, some British officers had been looking forward to taking part in the raid and were furious at having missed the fun. Their inquiries quickly revealed that Jack's report was pure fiction. Not a single hut had been burned, nor any natives killed. No raid at all, in fact. Jack Driberg was immediately dismissed from the Service.

Back in England, he studied anthropology at the London School of Economics, and began to teach and write. He wrote several well-received books, including *The People of the Small Arrow* (1930) and *At Home With the Savage* (1932). As Kingsley Martin remarked, he had an unusual approach to his subject, because he knew the tribes about which he wrote 'not from the outside investigator's point of view, but as a friend and tribal member'. His academic colleagues respected his methods more than his Colonial overseers had. In 1934 he was appointed University Lecturer in Anthropology at Cambridge, where his students included the young Jomo Kenyatta. He was an eminent figure in his field.

But he was miserable. Eviction from Nagichot had been like banishment from Eden. Pining for Africa, he tried desperately to rehabilitate himself with Whitehall and begged for a posting of some sort. He wondered if Tom had any contacts in the government who might be able to intercede on his behalf. The answer was always no. His marriage broke under the strain. By 1939 he was a weary and disappointed man.

His brother Jim was in an even more wretched condition. Whereas Jack's downfall was caused by his courageous defiance of unjust orders, Jim was ruined by nothing more heroic than whisky.

Yet even Jim Driberg had had his noble moments. Having qualified in medicine just before the outbreak of the First World War, he had gone to the Front with an ambulance unit. He was captured by the Germans but then repatriated thanks to an appeal by the American Ambassador to Belgium. Later, as a surgeon in the RAMC, Jim was present at some of the ghastliest battlefields of the war, including Loos. He was awarded the Military Cross. 'On one leave, I remember,' Tom wrote,

he spent much of his time sleeping in an easy chair in front of the smoking-room fire – and his sleep was restless, punctuated, as a dog's sometimes is, by twitching of the limbs and faint moaning sounds. My mother put these phenomena down, no doubt correctly, to the nervous strain of his experiences at the Front, and when, later on, his career ended in disaster, she still blamed all his misfortunes on the war.[10]

Apart from the drowsy twitchings, however, Jim's shell-shock did not reveal itself during the war. When home on leave he was cheerfully generous to Tom and his mother: he brought them presents, took them on jaunts to London and otherwise compensated for the lifelessness of John James Street Driberg, whose health was by then in its long final descent. Sending Tom a present of a bagatelle board, Jim referred to his father's enfeebled state in an accompanying note: 'it will be a good game for you and daddy to play together, as daddy is not able to read or write.'

In the years immediately after the war, there was still no indication of the collapse that was to come. Jim built a successful Harley Street practice as a consultant specialising in orthopaedic surgery. He married, and moved into a splendid flat in Park Crescent. He was handsome and prosperous. He was a member of White's Club.

Then he went to pieces. Perhaps, as his mother said, the war had belatedly caught up with him. Whatever the reason, in the late 1920s he began to drink and gamble heavily. His wife left him. So did many of his patients: he was seldom sober enough to practise as a surgeon. His gambling debts forced him into bankruptcy.

In 1931, awash with drink and despair, he sought help from Frank Buchman, the founder of the Oxford Group and Moral Re-Armament. It was an extraordinary decision – and, for Tom, highly embarrassing. Only four years earlier Tom had written the first exposés of the Group, soon after joining the *Express*. Now his own brother had gone over to the enemy. Jim could have pointed out that this was merely tit-for-tat, since he in turn had been embarrassed when, during the General Strike, his flat had been placed under surveillance because of Tom's subversive activities. But he did not fall into the arms of the Oxford Group in order to make things awkward for Tom. His motives were more straightforward. Lonely, desperate people are the most susceptible to cults and religions, and Jim was lonely and desperate. Here is his own account of how he was led to Buchman:

Men drink for various reasons – for company, for consolation, to celebrate or to forget. I drank simply because I was thirsty. I loved to drink. I drank mostly alone. I would go to my room with a bottle of whisky and a novel and not appear again until both were finished.

It was after an all-night session in my flat spent in the usual way that I found myself facing an early London morning, with a hangover, a foul temper, and no more drink. I was extremely thirsty, and there being no supply available anywhere at such an hour, I strolled round to a friend of mine to knock him up and ask him for a drink. This friend was an equerry to the Prince of Wales and lived in St James's Palace.[11] He did not much like being disturbed at this unearthly hour and, in fact, was pretty fed up with me and my habits – as indeed were all my friends.

'I'll give you a drink, Jim,' he said, 'on one condition.'

'What's that?' I said cheerfully. I would willingly have promised him the moon. I wanted a drink!

'That you go round and see a friend of mine – I think he could do something for you.'

'Certainly, old man. I'll go round and see the King of England or the Pope of Rome. I want a drink.'

'Well, he's a fellow called Frank Buchman and he stays at Brown's Hotel. I met him on board ship and I'm sure you ought to see him.'

I had my drink and I kept my promise. We got on well from the start. We had many friends in common and Frank was full of stories. Pretty soon I found myself telling him my own story. Frank was a good listener. The only trouble was that talking made me thirsty, so I asked Frank for a drink. Frank said nothing but pressed the bell and the waiter came in. At that very moment an extraordinary thought struck me. It came with the force of a clap of thunder. 'This is the last drink you will take.' I quickly added a PS of my own, 'Well, you'd better make it a double.' I did. And it was! Before I left Frank that day we prayed together.[12]

This account was obviously written soon after the event: it has all the breathless zeal of the convert. And for some months Jim Driberg was indeed a model Buchmanite. He corresponded almost daily with his new mentor. According to Buchman's biographer, Jim became 'a source of help and inspiration to many who met him. The Bishop of London, Mahatma Gandhi and C. F. Andrews were among many who were struck by the obvious change in his behaviour.' He visited his old Oxford college, Brasenose, as the guest of the Dean, a former drinking companion. Hoping to keep the conversation away from alcohol, the Dean asked: 'How is your golf, Jim? What's your handicap?' 'Mine's drink,' Jim replied. 'What's yours?'

Tom was predictably shocked by his brother's new allegiance, and remonstrated with him over the telephone. 'I knew you could sink very low, but I never thought you would sink so totally as to associate with those people.'

Jim left the Oxford Group as suddenly as he had joined it. In

February 1932 he happened to see a letter from Buchman to another person, in which Buchman claimed that Jim had been sent to him by the Prince of Wales and the Duke of Kent, 'through their ADCs'. The exaggeration shook Jim's confidence. He wrote to Buchman that, in spite of his 'deep, deep gratitude for all you have done for me', their correspondence must cease. Buchman abased himself – 'forgive and forget my mistakes,' he wailed, apologising for his 'legally incorrect statement' – but added that he was 'puzzled that you should take such drastic action'. Jim was nevertheless adamant.

Refusing to accept the explanation that had been offered, Buchman cast about for another reason why Jim might have shunned him. Humphrey Butler, the equerry who had sent Jim to Buchman in the first place, suggested that it was one of Jim's 'brain storms', which were 'the fault of the war'. Buchman consulted Jack Driberg, who (according to Buchman) attributed his brother's behaviour to the 'mental factor which has now and then sent Jim off on absurd tangents'.[13] Buchman concluded that Jim was an 'ambulance case'.

However baleful the Oxford Group's influence might have been, it had at least kept Jim sober. Even Tom acknowledged that this was 'greatly to Buchman's credit'. Once Jim had cut loose he was soon drinking again. For years afterwards Moral Re-Armament spread the rumour that it was Tom who, out of 'sheer wickedness', had lured his brother back to the bottle, but in fact Jim was quite capable of returning to his old habits without any assistance.

A year or two later Jim made one final attempt to flee from his demons. He emigrated to Brazil, where he scratched a living in remote parts of the Andes by treating peasants' illnesses and injuries in exchange for food and shelter. Amy Driberg worried about him continually. Was he drinking again, had he fallen into bad company, was he in debt? In 1937, when she was already seventy years old and in poor health, she startled Tom by announcing that she would take the boat to Rio and investigate for herself.

Jim, who was living in Belo Horizonte, received this news sullenly. When his mother arrived in Brazil she telephoned and asked him to see her in Rio de Janeiro; he replied that he couldn't afford the train fare. She sent him two pounds; he returned the money, saying it was inadequate. She advanced him twenty-five pounds; he pocketed it but still told her to come to Belo Horizonte – even though it was the hottest season of the year, and the train journey would take eighteen hours or so. She rang him with an ultimatum: 'You can come to Rio and see me or I shall take the next boat to England and you can rot in Brazil.' Jim, desperate for her money, grudgingly heaved himself into the train and chugged his surly way to Rio.

A journalist in Brazil, H. E. Walker, had been asked by Tom to keep an eye on Mrs Driberg during her visit. His despatches back to London were not encouraging:

I know your mother gave him [Jim] seventy-five pounds later to settle with people who kept coming to the hotel to see him; whether she gave him other money for past accounts I do not know, but I did advise her (at her request) about putting up several hundred pounds to set him up in practice in BH [Belo Horizonte] when, and if, he is licensed; I advised that she should consult you two brothers in England before she took such a step, as she said she would have to use her capital.

I found your brother very charming but he seems to be very weak in character from a financial standpoint. He owes considerable money to various persons and firms in Rio; your mother paid his entire expenses while she was here. I only had a drink with him the first night I met him because I knew he was spending the mother's money. He used to spend hours at a neighbouring hotel with English people whom he knew before, sitting around a bar table; this happened almost daily *but your mother never knew it*. I'm not criticising except from the point that it wasn't his own money he was drinking up. Your mother told me that she thought he was not as black as he is painted, but she thought he could not stand liquor because just a little affected him; all she understood was what he took with her.[14]

Amy Driberg stayed in Brazil for several weeks longer than she had intended, so that she could 'study' Jim thoroughly. She then sailed for home, professing herself satisfied. 'I am afraid,' Walker wrote, 'her position as a mother blinds her somewhat.' But she may not have been all that blind; more likely, she had concluded reluctantly that – as Walker himself put it – 'if a man of his age [forty-six] cannot stand on his own feet financially then he is never going to be able to do so'. She continued to pay Jim's debts, just as she had baled out Jack from time to time. In 1938, a year after returning from Brazil, she changed her will so that Tom would inherit £2,000 more than each of his brothers, to compensate for all her previous donations to them. Tom was ungrateful. 'Why, in any case, should we have been "entitled" to anything at all?' he wondered. 'Money, and quarrels about money, are the most sordid aspect of the whole family complex.'

His high-minded objections did not prevent him from accepting the extra £2,000. It was this inheritance – or at least the promise of it – which enabled him to have Bradwell Lodge fit for habitation by the end of 1939.

Tom's first house-guests came to stay at Christmas that year. In the week before their arrival he panicked hourly. There was still furniture to be shifted, linen to be bought, boxes to be unpacked. And what were they to eat? He had plenty of food in the house (rationing had not yet begun), but the skills of the newly-hired domestic help were limited to cleaning and bed-making, and Tom himself couldn't even boil an egg. Panicking again, he hired an expert cook through a London agency. 'She was a highly superior Scottish matron who had, in the past, it seemed, held posts in ducal households. She did not conceal her pained surprise at our inadequate, indeed chaotic, kitchen arrangements. Never before, for one thing, had she worked without the assistance of a kitchen-maid.'[15] She cooked splendidly, but her forbidding presence chilled the festive spirit. Tom was relieved when she left.

The guests that Christmas were Jack Driberg, Constant Lambert, Joan Rayner, the writer Patrick Balfour (who had recently succeeded to the title of Lord Kinross) and his wife. John Rayner, Joan's husband, was unable to come but sent a house-warming present of a magnificent visitors' book, an inch and a half thick, bound in leather, which was printed with the name of the house and Tom's initials.

Over the next few months, many appreciative friends signed their names in the book. At one weekend party in January 1940, the guests were Dom Bernard Clements, a Benedictine monk who was Vicar of All Saints, Margaret Street; Isabel Delmer, an artist who was then the wife of Tom's *Express* colleague Sefton Delmer but later married Constant Lambert; and Lord Berners, the eccentric musician and painter, described by Tom as 'one of the wittiest men I have ever known'. According to Berners's entry in the visitors' book, during the weekend he 'made a tangerine soufflé and a madrigal'. Berners sent a fulsome letter of thanks a few days later: 'I must congratulate you again on your house and the way you have arranged it. It is, as far as I can see, without a flaw – save possibly Liverpool Street – but that is made up for by the delightful rurality of the railway – and even Liverpool Street has a certain Monet-esque charm on a foggy morning.' Berners was so taken with Bradwell that he lent Tom several paintings to hang in the house, including a Max Jacob and a Dufy.

Tom delighted in bringing together disparate characters. His talent, he sometimes said, was that of a Madam in a high-class brothel: one weekend the guests would be an MP and a clergyman; the next he might invite a novelist and an actor. Isabel Delmer recalled with excitement a Bradwell house-party after the war that consisted of herself, Constant Lambert and Aneurin Bevan: when they assembled for breakfast on Sunday morning, the newspapers bore headlines such as 'Blood-bath Bevan Won The Day'. 'Many people spent pleasant days and nights at Bradwell,' she said. 'Always good food and wine, and conversation on all subjects, word games and Lena Horne singing in the evening.'[16] Even John Freeman, who thought of Tom as a Jekyll-and-Hyde figure and was deeply suspicious of the Hyde aspect, admits that at Bradwell Lodge he was always Jekyll – 'engaging, cynical, funny, erudite and graceful'. Freeman's memory of Bradwell was of weekends spent 'in total tranquillity and with a delightful host'.

In the eerily peaceful months after the start of the Second World War the rococo signature of A. J. A. Symons appeared often in the visitors' book, garlanded with curlicues and flourishes. He was enraptured by his first visit to Bradwell Lodge. 'This,' he told Tom, 'is the most beautiful house in Essex, and *therefore* the most beautiful house in England, and *therefore* the most beautiful house in the world.' In another letter, he wrote: 'How is the House? I think often and with envy of its octagonal room, its park and its privileges, and look forward with Essexian zeal to a Pilgrimage.' Their friendship had survived a slight fracture in the autumn of 1939 when, in a moment of irritation, Tom had said: 'When we come to power, my dear A. J., *you* are one of the first people we shall have to bump off. Regretfully, of course, but it will have to be done.' Symons was startled. He complained to his brother, the writer Julian Symons. 'I have always been a Socialist,' he insisted, much to Julian's surprise, 'even if I have not always avowed my faith publicly – I have always been a Socialist because I have always believed that Socialists were trying to ensure a freer, fuller life for mankind. But if they are going to imprison men of good will, harmless collectors of musical boxes and first editions, then I shall have to think again.'[17] Julian Symons suggested that Tom had been joking, but the harmless collector would have none of it: he believed the threat was perfectly serious.

Britain hardly felt like a country at war during that spring and early summer of 1940. Guests came to Bradwell most weekends, snoozing in the shade of the huge ilex tree in the garden after Saturday lunch, playing canasta until far into the night, walking out the next morning to see the ancient Saxon church of St Peter-ad-Murum in a field just outside the village. In June they ate potatoes and gooseberries from the garden; one evening Tom served a bottle of Château Margaux 1900. A croquet lawn was laid out, on which Tom triumphantly beat the inveterate gamesman A. J. A. Symons at the 'particularly wild and hazardous' brand of the sport that was favoured in Essex.

As the days again grew shorter, one frequent guest took to writing in the visitors' book 'Famous Last Weekends, 1', 'Famous Last Weekends, 2', and so on. The phoney war, like the gooseberries and croquet, could not outlast the summer. On a sunny evening in September, Tom and a couple of neighbours were picking fruit from an old mulberry tree on the lawn, their fingers stained red with its ripeness, when suddenly 'there was a curious pattering among the leaves, as of hailstones. High above we could see fighter aircraft engaging the German bombers: the Battle of Britain had begun.'[18]

Bradwell Lodge was requisitioned soon afterwards for use as the Officers' Mess of 'RAF Bradwell Bay'. (There is no bay at Bradwell;

the reverse, in fact. Tom wondered if the RAF station was given this inappropriate name to confuse the enemy.) Most of his furniture was sent into store, the wine cellar was bricked up and the Adam fireplaces were boarded over. He rented River View, a small house near Bradwell Quay, as a weekend cottage for the duration. 'There, much later in the war, in a bar of the Green Man crowded with airmen, one could sit on a wide window-sill and watch the VI doodle-bugs chug-chugging clumsily in overhead.' Bradwell, being on the east coast, was a 'restricted area', where residents had to show permits as they approached their homes.

The RAF officers at Bradwell Lodge were hospitable to their dislocated freeholder, giving him a standing invitation to join them for a drink in the Mess before Sunday lunch. He was often asked to parties in the evening, too, but these were a mixed pleasure since the airmen lived each day as if it might be their last:

It was difficult not to wince as robust young men slid down the Adam staircase on trays or threw chamberpots full of beer from end to end of the hall. But any remonstrance would have been unthinkable: these young men were going out night after night (as they put it, with self-mocking irony) 'dicing with death'; and almost every night too many of them did not come back. One, a Canadian, asked me to get him a new cigarette lighter (difficult then to find). I gave it to him. Next night he was killed.

After the war a memorial was erected to the 121 airmen who flew from Bradwell and never returned. Many of them were from the Royal Canadian Air Force and the Royal New Zealand Air Force.

As the number of squadrons at RAF Bradwell Bay grew, the Officers' Mess overflowed the confines of Bradwell Lodge. Nissen huts appeared on the lawn, serving as extra dining-rooms and kitchens. WAAF quarters and air-raid shelters were built elsewhere in the grounds. Having only just begun to restore order to the house and garden, Tom had to watch the place become an eyesore.

But there were consolations, not least in his enjoyment of the company of servicemen. Like many of the institutions that he inhabited in his life – Lancing, Oxford, the Communist Party, Fleet Street, Parliament – the armed services celebrated masculine comradeship, which he found most congenial. Besides, he had always been turned on by the sight of young men in uniform. During the war he seduced black American sailors, Canadian pilots, English marines and countless others, though more often in London than Bradwell. He commemorated one of them – an American GI – in a poem called 'Soldier's Love', written in April 1942:

> The Yale and a creaking shove; at once, the stink of cheap sex.
>> He stayed in the dark by the door for a moment of doubt.
> Over the sharp rosy glow an indigo dragglement draped.
>> The gas-fire popped and roared; so put the light out.
>
> He stripped like a boy for a bathe; unfurled, sloughed off his white
>> smooth shoulders the layer of khaki and grey.
> With – was it a sigh to greet the rare ease, or a groan?
>> by the gas on the greasy Axminster, rigidly passive, he lay.
>
> The stroking of muscles – the contours of silk – the terminal jets of
>> passion:
> He saw in the gas a log-fire, crackling free, horses about a white
>> house, blueberry pie, a shot of rye with dad,
> – and wept for the woe of a secular doom that must be.[19]

In this respect, the requisitioning of Bradwell was a gift from heaven, and he missed few opportunities to flirt – at the very least – with the dashing young men who had occupied his house. He even helped serve their meals. One serviceman who was stationed at Bradwell in the war, Wilfred Beard, reminisced in a letter to Tom years later:

You used to serve in the canteen there and you conversed in a very friendly manner with us when ever we visited the canteen. I remember you once invited me to stay the night at your home, but I could not as I was on guard duty that evening. I met you in the 'Green Man' one evening. I ordered a Martini and you inquired where I had learned to drink them. I was a member of the Communist Party at the time and you informed me that you were also a member of the party. You showed me your party membership card, also some correspondence you had entered into with Mr John Strachey with regard to the war then in progress . . .[20]

There was plenty to correspond with John Strachey about. It was Strachey who had persuaded him not to leave the *Express* in the late

1930s, when Tom had been sickened and frustrated by the paper's pro-appeasement exhortations. Now that war had been joined in earnest, and Christiansen and Beaverbrook had been proved wrong, Tom assumed that the old restrictions on his column would be eased. As he had written the day after war was declared: 'We're all in it.'

He soon discovered that not everyone was in the same 'it'. The defeat of Hitler was a common purpose. But how? And what then? Chamberlain's replacement by Winston Churchill in May 1940 had helped to placate some critics and malcontents, but there were still arguments that would not go away, however many appeals for national unity issued from the Prime Minister's lips. As George Orwell wrote in his famous wartime essay 'The Lion and the Unicorn':

What this war has demonstrated is that private capitalism – that is, an economic system in which land, factories, mines and transport are owned privately and operated solely for profit – *does not work*. It cannot deliver the goods . . .

As soon as one considers any problem of this war – and it does not matter whether it is the widest aspect of strategy or the tiniest detail of home organisation – one sees that the necessary moves cannot be made while the social structure of England remains what it is. Inevitably, because of their position and upbringing, the ruling class are fighting for their own privileges, which cannot possibly be reconciled with the public interest.[21]

This was certainly borne out by Tom's experience. His left-wing opinions, which in the pre-war years had sometimes been allowed into the paper as evidence of amusing eccentricity, could no longer be tolerated so easily. There would be no more teasing paragraphs from the Chief Reader in the *Evening Standard* about 'Café Communists'. Lord Beaverbrook, who had himself been something of a licensed eccentric for years, was in May 1940 appointed Minister for Aircraft Production. The *Daily Express* was now owned by a leading member of the government. Arthur Christiansen, nervously trying to anticipate his master's wishes, spiked more and more of Tom's Hickey items. Tom was not allowed to call for the requisitioning of West End houses, nor even to publish a little gentle mockery of the Wine and Food Society; Christiansen suspected it was all 'Communist propaganda'. Tom chafed and grumbled and sighed and sulked and, eventually, poured out his resentment in a long memo to the editor:

As I express myself more clearly on paper than in conversation, I hope you will accept this note.

1. If it is 'Communist propaganda' to pillory the follies of the rich, much that has been printed in the *Express* – in Opinion, in news stories – must come under that head. Certainly, Priestley's article in the *Sunday Express* must be 'Communist propaganda' – still more Michael Foot often in the *Standard*. The Hickey column was always intended to be provocative, satirical, debunking, disrespectful to those of high degree, as well as informative; not a 'sunshine' column.

2. If a paragraph is only 'Communist propaganda' when I write it, because I am known to hold left-wing views and my writings are therefore suspect, that seems an extremely difficult handicap to work under. I believe that only a Leftist could have conducted the Hickey column in the way in which it has been conducted all these years – satisfactorily in the main, I believe; only a Leftist has the sense of social analysis, the sceptical reaction to official dope, the indignant impulse to expose injustice and resist repression, which must underlie such work. If my work is to be censored more drastically than other people's *because* I am a Leftist, I am, therefore, being penalised for the very qualities essential to a columnist of my type.

3. I don't think the comparison with Swaffer and Cassandra[22] altogether irrelevant. They are my 'opposite numbers'. To some extent I compete with them. It is, to say the least, galling to see them constantly printing the kind of stuff which is constantly killed when I write it.

I remember you said that C got away with it because he is funny. But if I were to try his kind of slapstick humour, his violent ridicule of personalities, the lawyer would certainly object. As it is, I often attempt to give a witty turn to my paragraphs. In any case, that doesn't apply to Swaffer, who often writes in a burning rage. (So, sometimes, does Cassandra.)

Yesterday, the *Sunday Express* advocated in a leader the requisitioning of west-end houses. I realise that you killed this the other day because of EJR's[23] objection to the idea – but doesn't he also control the Sunday? Why should they have more freedom than I?

4. Friday's column was deplorably scrappy. But almost an entire column was killed – including, I still think, three good items. (The Wine & Food

par. I had shown to Rayner before sending it down; it amused him, and he saw no 'Communist propaganda' in it.)

I am sorry that I left the office so early. I was anxious to get a good night's sleep in the country. My daytime engagements had been such that I had had altogether, from Sunday to Thursday, 12½ hours' sleep. This week I hope to organise that necessity better.

5. Altho' I find it discouraging, as a writer of independent spirit, to be reduced to such a position of hack impotence that 'all that is wanted' from me is 'Cockney humour' and stuff of that calibre, this is not a mere personal bleat.

The more serious the situation, the more urgent it surely is to preserve freedom of individual comment and criticism. I recall with apprehension the years of officially-inspired gagging before the war – lay off. Ribbentrop, mustn't offend Italy, etc – and note the mess that the policy of appeasement, of which that gagging was an integral part, has landed us in. If the war is allowed to reduce us to a nation of yes-men, Hitlerism will have won the war even if Germany is defeated.

Even from the point of view of conservatives who wish to prevent any drastic change in the social order, I should have thought it wiser to allow in the Press a few safety-valves for the expression of complaint and criticism which masses of ordinary people are muttering. They cannot destroy grievances by not recognising their existence.

From the point of view of the Press it surely pays to have a reputation for championing the downtrodden. Then, even if the worst (as conservatives would see it) came about, we should at least have made to ourselves friends of the mammon of unrighteousness.

6. I have raised wider issues than Friday's column alone, but they do to some extent arise out of it. I must add that I feel no resentment at all against you personally, and I am so sorry to trouble you with so long a note at a time when you, naturally, have greater worries than any of us. My resentment is entirely against the forces of dictatorship and repression, which seem to me to menace us even on our own side in the war and – to take a small instance – to use newspapers as their unwitting or unwilling tools when journalistic openness is restricted.

A little more openness was discernible in the Hickey column after Tom's complaints. He had been forbidden to argue that Mayfair hostesses should have their houses taken from them, but in January 1941 he was permitted to write a long exposé of illegal West End gambling parties attended by the same gilded citizens. Through a friend he obtained an invitation to one of these occasions, held in a suite at a Mayfair hotel. The party was due to start at 4 pm prompt; Tom arrived at midnight and found it in full swing. From the open doors ahead came a warm, luxurious buzz that reminded him of Le Touquet or Monte Carlo.

Then a middle-aged man approached me quickly, sizing me up intently through his spectacles. 'Have I the pleasure of your acquaintance?' he said (with no indication that my acquaintance would give him great pleasure).

I explained that a friend whom I was expecting to meet here had given me a card. He did not recognise her name. 'I must ask you to leave at once,' he snapped. Then he saw that I was looking in at the open doors of the party. 'Shut those doors at once,' he shouted, rather melodramatically. There was a great bustle of minions.

He seized my invitation-card, put it in his pocket. 'I shall have to check up on this card,' he said. 'All our cards are coded . . .'

'What? Just for a private party?' I said, innocently.

'Oh yes,' he assured me.

By this time I was in my hat and coat again, being firmly shown towards the stairs. Then someone who had recognised me whispered to my inhospitable host who I was.

He at once became extremely agitated. 'You understand that we don't want anything about this in the papers,' he said.

'I quite understand that,' I said.[24]

Downstairs in the hotel lounge, Tom met a woman he knew. 'I heard you were here, darling,' she said. 'I can get you in if you like.' This seemed unlikely after his tussle upstairs. He contented himself with asking her what she thought of the party. 'I'm adoring it,' she gurgled. 'It's terrifically hot – real Casino atmosphere.' They had been served a 'lovely, wonderful' dinner – buffets laden with rationed and unrationed food, caviar, sandwiches made with butter, and 'masses of champagne'. Who else was there? She named various Mayfair socialites known to Tom. 'It's so absurd,' she said, 'what they say about officers being "lured" to these parties and "fleeced". I've only seen one officer here tonight. I think it's so nice that people can still have all this fun nowadays . . .' She and her friends usually stayed until seven or eight in the morning, she revealed.

'Well,' Tom concluded when he wrote up his story for the *Express* the next day,

that's the story of my only experience as an unsuccessful gatecrasher. Personally, I *don't* think it's 'nice' that, to adapt a famous saying, a few of the people should have all of the fun all of the time. I am not against gambling as such. I have often gambled myself. It might be a good thing if the state licensed casinos, taxed them heavily. But I think that fun carried to these lengths of lavishness, for private profit, is, at the moment, unseemly.

This attack on private enterprise was evidently deemed by Christiansen not to be Communist propaganda.

Thus emboldened, a few weeks later Tom dived into another controversy of the moment, over whether the indiscriminate bombing of German civilians was acceptable:

A Briton in prison hospital in Germany writes home that a 'sweet little' 6-year-old German girl named Hilda has been visiting him. She reminds him of his own child. 'She is never tired of perching by my bed and looking at the photographs of you and the baby.'

This will upset Sir Robert Vansittart's fans – the simple-minded folk who regard all Germans as 'Huns', fit only to be bombed indiscriminately.

'Give the brutes a taste of their own medicine.' Bomb them all. Bomb Hilda.[25]

Again the editor let it through; but he was nervous. He asked Tom to inform him if anyone complained about the item. Seeing a way of involving readers in the controversy, Tom replied to Christiansen in the Hickey column itself, six days after the original item:

Memo Hickey to Editor:–
You asked me to let you know if there were any reactions to a short recent paragraph ending 'Bomb Hilda.'
So far twenty-three people have written in about this. Of these, twenty-one say, in effect, 'Yes, bomb Hilda.' Only one supports my view. (One, the usual egregious literalist, takes my irony straight and reads 'with disgust' that I 'approve of the destruction of children'.)
One must allow for the fact that people are always more likely to write to a newspaper to express disagreement than agreement . . . But I doubt if

'We have no quarrel with the German people' (still official policy) now corresponds with the emotions of the majority.[26]

Of the twenty-one bomb-Hilda letters six were reasonably written, with some semblance of rational argument that bombing of German civilians would shorten the war and therefore save more lives in the end. The other fifteen, Tom reported, consisted largely of hysterical abuse and wishful fantasy.

Several suggest, seriously, the total extermination of all Germans. None explains how the mass execution of 65 million people is to be organised, or how their land is then to be populated.

Several others say, Yes, bomb Hilda, *because she will grow up to be a Nazi*. What do such people think the war is about? How long do they expect it to last? They are gloomy prophets.

A Croydon reader advises me to study Churchill's views. I have. I am glad to say that he has shown himself consistently aware that our bombers' real business is to destroy military and industrial objectives. A Rochford reader is convinced that Hilda (at 6) is trained in Nazi propaganda; that our men in German prison hospitals are besieged by troupes of sinister Shirley Temples.

A week later Tom returned to the question. The score had evened slightly: his postbag now had thirty-seven letters in favour of bombing Hilda and twenty against. 'Rather fewer letters than I would have got if I had attacked dogs or the Royal family,' Tom noted. Nevertheless, the letters showed the strength of the saloon-bar passions that he had aroused. '*We want revenge*,' wrote a reader in Romford. 'Believe me, none of us are interested in the invasion ports being bombed, we want all German cities bombed and burned, we want their women and children treated the same way as we all are suffering.' Tom's last words on the subject in his column were a typically defiant taunt:

One thing puzzles me. All my bomb-Hilda readers scream for a 'total war' on German civilians; but none advocates immediate big-scale gas and bacterial attacks on Germany. Why not? The more horrifying the better, is their idea of war; surely they cannot be restrained by any moral scruples or considerations of expediency?[27]

Christiansen, like many of his readers, did not care for Tom's sermons on this divisive topic. It would be much better for morale if Hickey would instead extol the plucky, we-can-take-it spirit of the blitzed British cities. Thus in the spring of 1941 Tom was sent to Glasgow, Newcastle, Coventry, Manchester, Liverpool, Bristol and Exeter in search of tales of simple heroism among the workers.

What he found in Newcastle was rather more pleasurable: the Vic-Wells ballet were in town, accompanied on piano by his friend Constant Lambert. For some years Tom had had a private joke with Lambert whereby each set the other impossible limericks to complete ('There was an old man of Stoke Poges . . .'). So, without warning Lambert of his presence, Tom went into the theatre early and left a card on the piano's music-stand, on top of the ballet score. He then seated himself at the front of the stalls. In due course Lambert entered, made a stately bow, sat down and looked at his music – only to see a card reading 'The Bishop of Glasgow and Galloway / Preferred Artie Shaw to Cab Calloway . . .' He stiffened for a moment but then began to play, as fluently as ever. By the first interval he had completed the limerick.

This was a rare diversion in Tom's otherwise grim itinerary. 'Coventry seemed the most cataclysmic, then Manchester shook me; each bombed town in turn seems to impart a sharper pang than the last.'[28] He reached Wallasey – which he could identify in the *Express* only as 'a Merseyside residential area' – just after its worst blitz, and found a town of 'smudged, dazed faces'; he lent a hand putting straw into mattress cases at the emergency rest-centre, where the newly homeless slept. In Liverpool he stayed in a big air-raid shelter that was exuberantly noisy all night long. Hardly anyone slept: 'Some play mouth organs, some cards. A woman changed hats with a sailor, raucously singing that she was Popeye the Sailor Man. A Norwegian cracked another over the head with a *full* beer bottle, the waste of beer being what distressed us most.'[29] From Liverpool he travelled to Bristol, where he endured 'a night of constant fire and noise – the bombers returning with maddening repetitiveness to the flames that they themselves had kindled'. In the lounge of his Bristol hotel there was the usual bomb-proof couple sitting calmly through it all. When the whole building shook violently from one particularly powerful blast, the woman looked up from her knitting: 'Was that a *bomb*? . . . it *sounded* rather like one . . .' 'M-m-m-m-m,' her husband grunted from behind his copy of the *Tatler*.

Like many Britons, Tom came to expect sleepless nights in 1941 – though unlike most of them he was already hardened to insomnolence by his years of pre-war training at Frisco's and the Café de Paris. Late one evening in April, back in London from his tour of the provincial rubble, he was asked by the news editor to go to Broadcasting House to investigate 'a pretty big incident' (ARP jargon for bomb damage). He arrived at Portland Place to discover that the BBC building itself had narrowly escaped but dozens of shops and offices nearby were destroyed. Trudging through 'an ankle-deep porridge of glass and water', Tom gazed at the wreckage of a pub. 'There was usually 20 or 30 of 'em in there at that time,' a policeman told him. Tom was glad of the ARP wardens' company as he explored the rest of the 'incident'.

All this time, intermittently, more bombs were swishing down. As each fell, or as a plane sounded like diving, we stepped back a pace or two into the gaping shop, crouching instinctively in unison, hardly needing to say, 'Here's another.' Again instinctively, with a protectiveness that might have been pathetically futile, the men would shield each others' bent shoulders with their arms. Twice, as we crouched, the blast – a foul, hot, giant's breath – swept sighing through the shop, tore its way through glass at the far end.

A rose judgment-day glow shone down on us. Some of the men moved over the road to a darker place . . .

Turning a corner, they came upon a tall building in flames. An ARP man called Henry whom Tom had befriended was aghast: he told Tom that many retired nurses and other old women lived in the house. A girl they met said that there were still a few inside.

Henry dived straight into the house. The sparks danced about him; he vanished behind fallen, flickering timbers. 'Henry, come back, it's no use,' cried the girl who had spoken before.

It was five anxious minutes before we saw him again, on the stairs, helping two firemen undo a knot in the hose they were playing up the liftshaft. Their figures stood up darkly against the evil red light – three men walking unharmed in the midst of the burning fiery furnace.

Before we had time to think that this night could be nearly done – so timeless seemed its incidents, so endless the treadmill of its grim routine – we looked up . . . and the light in the sky was not all from the fires.

The chill dawn wind fluttered burned paper into our faces. Already men were sweeping up the crunching glass. A big lorry switched off its lights as it stole past us.[30]

The blitz came even closer to home in November 1941. Bradwell Lodge itself was bombed, though no serious damage was done to the house. The gardener, Isaac Thurgood, who lived just over the road and had worked at Bradwell Lodge for the previous twenty-three years, had his cottage bombed too. But Tom missed it all: by then he was on an extended trip to the United States. His secretary at the *Express*, Elsie King, wrote to reassure him that his solicitor and surveyor were taking care of everything.

The journey to America had taken almost a month, travelling on a Norwegian cargo boat which had to keep changing course to avoid the German submarine blockade. There were two other passengers, signed on (like Tom) as nominal deckhands: Sven Oftedal, a Norwegian journalist who was on his way to take up a new posting as his country's press attaché in Canada; and an *Express* reporter named Charles Foley, with whom Tom shared a cabin. 'It was,' Tom wrote, 'a salutary exercise in patience, self-control and mutual tolerance: no radio (except for occasional news in Morse), no sex, no drink (it ran out quite soon).' Oftedal, a teetotaller, watched with amusement as the *Express* men painfully readjusted their drinking habits. The food was surprisingly good in the circumstances, enlivened with tinned anchovies, herrings, mussels and asparagus. But it was a relief to reach the New World. Coming from a London of ration-books and black-outs, Tom emerged blinking into the 'blinding canyon of light' that was Broadway. 'For the first night or two,' he cabled back to England, 'one gets a kick out of realising that one's own bedroom lights are among those negligently shining out a mile up in some skyscraper. One longs to put one of the ample pats of butter in an envelope and air-mail it home.'[31]

America in the autumn of 1941 reminded Tom of Britain in the late 1930s: it was inching towards war in a tortoise-like fashion, urged onwards by the 'up and at 'em' brigade, shooed back by appeasers and outright fascists. Lindbergh speaking at an 'America First' rally in Madison Square Garden was just like Mosley at Olympia – a muddle of 'fanatics, honest peace-lovers, plump, smug middle-class dupes, and virulent pro-Nazis all jammed together in a jamboree of flag-waving and blue spotlights'.[32] More sinister still was Yorkville, where newspapers from Stuttgart and Berlin were freely available at news-stands, alongside pamphlets about Roosevelt's alleged Jewish ancestry. In a Yorktown bar German youths started throwing beer-mats at Tom, clearly preparing themselves for a full-scale brawl. He scribbled his signature on several of the beer-mats, calmly told the waiter 'I think those gentlemen were asking for my autograph' and then scarpered as fast as he could.

Hostility to Britain was not unique to Nazis, however. On a train from New York to Philadelphia, a sailor told Tom that he resented the British: 'We're doing your job for you, aren't we?' This seemed such an amazing inversion of the truth that Tom asked what on earth he meant. 'Well,' the man explained coolly, 'we're producing the stuff you need, aren't we, and now we're seeing it safely over to you, see?' The danger of transporting 'the stuff' through hostile waters was the only risk he acknowledged. 'It hadn't occurred to him,' Tom wrote, 'that anything – fighting, for instance – was done with the stuff after delivery.'

Everything changed after the Japanese attack on Pearl Harbor on Sunday 7 December. Tom was in Chicago at the time but caught an overnight plane to Washington, taking off in a snowstorm. Senators, naval officers and journalists were all converging on the Capitol at once: the city was 'a fantastic hubbub of traffic jams, armed guards, cordons, diplomatic comings and goings'. Tom's cab took twenty minutes to drive two blocks. A hotel charged him the equivalent of twenty-five shillings to use the bathroom for half-an-hour. There were no bedrooms to be had: Tom had to sleep in a cubicle of a Turkish bath for the next few nights.

Shortly after noon on Monday the President was to address a

joint session of House and Senate, and hundreds of reporters were begging and scrambling for tickets to the press gallery of Congress, which had space for only 100. Tom strolled through the doors with insouciant ease: 'Wearing an innocent look and my English accent, I said to the Marine who barred my way: "There's a ticket waiting for me inside – I have to collect it." The good fellow let me through.'[33] Tom grabbed a place at the front, right above where the President was to stand. He made the most of his ringside seat: readers of the *Express* the next day were expected to wade through a long article which not only reported what Roosevelt said but also described the paper on which the speech was written and the desk from which he delivered it. ('The rostrum bristled with a dozen mikes; they encroached even on the desk from which the President was to read his speech. Beside it stood a jug of water and a glass covered with two dusters. Below it stood a cuspidor . . . A secretary placed the President's message on the sloping desk before him. The typescript was in a black, looseleaf binding. From where I sat, just above, I could see clearly how widely spaced was the typing.'[34]) As at the Pope's funeral or the King's coronation, he had a pedantic, obsessive need to record every minute detail of the ritual.

Later that week Tom flew to California. Or, rather, he flew as far as Wichita, Kansas, where the plane was grounded by yet another snowstorm; he finished the journey by train in the company of two Hollywood actresses, Carole Landis and Linda Darnell, plus a carriage-load of naval recruits hurrying to join their ships. It was his first visit to the West Coast, and he stayed for more than two months – mostly as a guest in the Bel-Air house of Alfred Hitchcock, whom he had met through Sidney Bernstein.

Though Hitchcock was hospitable enough, he was slightly preoccupied with making *Saboteur*, a film about a munitions worker who is wrongly accused of sabotage. At the end of each day's shooting Tom would watch curiously as the producers and screenwriters – Peter Viertel, Joan Harrison and Dorothy Parker – gathered at Hitchcock's house to discuss progress. Joan Harrison's brother had been a schoolfriend of Tom's at Lancing; he liked her at once. He was less impressed by the mega-wit Dorothy Parker, who was 'too drunk to sparkle' and 'would tell us the witticisms that she had written into her three-weeks late script that day, repeating them at intervals to make sure we had all grasped them'.[35]

Tom went on the film set from time to time, and lunched with James Cagney, but he soon grew weary of hanging around in Hollywood. The town was enervatingly trivial, parasitic and ephemeral. Having laughed at them the first time, he soon grew to hate the shops with names like 'Dog Togs – smart things for dogs to wear', and the 'doll hospitals' where rich girls' toys could have their broken limbs fixed. To the amazement of his Hollywood hosts, he took to spending his evenings in the rougher corners of downtown Los Angeles, in black dance-clubs and Chinese restaurants, bowling alleys and underground dives. Their 'highly-flavoured, indeed gar-licky, atmosphere' was refreshing after the synthetic fragrance of Hollywood. He spent one evening in a Mexican bar, sitting at the edge of the dance-floor with a uniformed policeman who was paid a dollar an hour by the management to control customers and chuck out drunks every few minutes. Tom was impressed by the man's keen sense of duty:

Suddenly he flashed his torch in the face of a young man dancing with a girl. The youth looked round. 'Take your hat off,' bawled the cop.

I remarked I didn't think that that would have mattered much at a dump like this. He replied, grimly, 'If a guy's any kindova gentleman, he'll take off his hat when he's dancing with a woman.'

It was some time before I disclosed to this cop that I was English. 'I couldn't figure what it was,' he said, 'but I could tell you had a kindova odd brogue.'

Other customers included two rather bogus Texas cowboys on the bum, who insisted on playing guitars and yodelling, and argued that beer was improved by the addition of salt; and a New Zealand sailor, straying far from his ship, who attracted a curious circle of Mexicans. 'He talks English as good as us,' they said in surprise.[36]

Even more to Tom's taste was San Diego, where he spent his last few days in California – 'a great naval port with a bar on every street-corner and several dozen sailors in every bar'. The sailors were, he found, 'ready and willing for anything, and in need of a few bucks'. He gorged himself gratefully and paid them well. 'My expense account became exorbitantly swollen, but Lord

Beaverbrook, I reflected, would strongly approve of my spreading good-will towards Britain in the United States Navy.'[37] Tom then set off for Newfoundland to catch a plane home. Five months earlier, his westward Atlantic crossing had taken almost a month; the eastward journey, aboard an RAF bomber, lasted just nine hours.

CHAPTER SEVEN

HONOURABLE MEMBERS

After almost six months abroad, Tom arrived back in Britain with more than the usual displacement fatigue of a returning traveller. He felt deracinated. He had lost Bradwell Lodge for the duration; he had lost Bert Westlake, the good and faithful servant, who had joined up and was now Cadet Westlake of 202 OCTU in Southend; and he had lost 5 Queen's Gate Place Mews. Before boarding ship for America the previous autumn he had given up the lease rather than waste five months' rent on an empty flat. He still had the tenancy of River View in Bradwell, but he could hardly commute from there to the *Express* office every day. He was all but homeless.

Fortunately, with so many people having left London to escape the bombing, accommodation was easily available and cheap. He found a second-floor flat at 28 Great Ormond Street, near the children's hospital, for £90 a year. His friends thought it rather poky – two rooms and a bathroom, none in splendid condition – but Tom loved it. He would draw visitors' attention to the 'noble staircase'; he would mention that in the eighteenth century the house had been part of the French embassy (or so he had been told). He was glad to escape from 'aloof, smug Kensington' to the more civilised and Fabian pastures of Bloomsbury.[1] Best of all, he was within walking distance of public lavatories – at Jockey's Fields, Russell Square and elsewhere – that offered excellent cottaging. Over the next twenty years he became almost as sentimental about Flat 4, 28 Great Ormond Street, as about Bradwell Lodge.

There was another loss, however, that could not be so easily replaced. It hurt him much more deeply than his temporary homelessness or Westlake's departure: not long before leaving for America in 1941, Tom had been expelled from the Communist Party.

His own account of it, in *Ruling Passions*, was brief and mystified:

This shattering news was conveyed to me in a curiously hole-and-corner manner. I was on my way to a branch meeting with the comrade whom I liked best in Fleet Street, a print-worker named Harry Kennedy. He had called for me at the *Express* office. We stopped at a pub for a drink; he was rather silent and seemed ill-at-ease. Then he said, in an unnaturally formal way: 'I have been instructed to inform you that you are no longer a member of the party . . . You have been expelled.' I protested furiously and asked why. Harry didn't know: he was merely a messenger. I went to see the most influential party members I knew, Robin and Olive Page Arnot and Dave Springhall (who was later jailed for espionage). *Why*, I asked: was it because of sex? Or religion? Or something I had written in my column? They were acutely embarrassed but seemed genuinely as much at a loss as I. And there was no appeal.[2]

There was, of course, one very obvious reason why he might have been thrown out: after the Nazi–Soviet pact in 1939 he had been publicly at odds with party policy. 'I have often wondered,' he mused in *Ruling Passions*, 'whether this deviation was one of the reasons why, a year or two later, I was expelled from the Party.' Harry Pollitt, the Party's general secretary, had been forced to resign his post in October 1939 for the same heresy – though he was reinstated in 1941, when Hitler's invasion of the Soviet Union forced the CPGB to perform a quick *volte-face* and support the war after all.

Four years after the posthumous publication of *Ruling Passions*, a sensationally different explanation for Tom's expulsion was proposed. In his book *MI5*, published in 1981, the author Nigel West claimed that Tom had for many years been an agent of the Security Service, secretly reporting on the activities of the Communist Party of Great Britain to Captain Maxwell Knight, head of MI5's counter-subversion section, B(5)b. Soon after regaining the Party's general secretaryship, Harry Pollitt had learned of Tom's duplicity and expelled him.

West's account had the hilarious improbability and cracked logic so characteristic of spy-writing. Tom, he alleged, had 'joined the CPGB on Knight's instructions'. (Since Tom was a paid-up member of the CPGB while still a schoolboy, this was no mean feat of talent-spotting on Knight's part.) The story continued as follows. Tom would feed Knight gossip that he picked up from his party comrades, which Knight would then write up and circulate in MI5, referring to his source only as 'M8'. One day Anthony Blunt happened to notice a report by Knight which mentioned M8. Blunt was employed by MI5 at the time, while secretly working for the Communists; he was horrified to learn that someone had pulled the same trick in reverse, belonging to the Communist Party while secretly working for MI5. He must tell his KGB controller at once. Fortunately, Blunt was able to put a name to M8. 'The secret report mentioned a book by M8,' Nigel West explained, 'and Blunt immediately realised that M8 was none other than Tom Driberg.' Tom was summoned to King Street and told by Harry Pollitt that his membership was being withdrawn:

When Driberg demanded to know why, Pollitt accused him of being M8. Driberg naturally denied the charge, never before having heard his own code name. But when the incident was reported to Knight the MI5 officer realised that there could only be one explanation – a hostile agent inside the Security Service. Knight was appalled and launched an investigation to track down the source, but he never succeeded. Blunt was furious at the way in which his information had been handled and complained that the network had been unnecessarily put at risk.[3]

Blunt nevertheless survived for another twenty years before being forced to confess that he was a Soviet agent.

West's source for all this (though he didn't identify him in the book) was Anthony Blunt, who was hardly a disinterested or reliable witness. Blunt's story also reached the ears of Peter Wright, a former MI5 man. At about the same time as Blunt was briefing West, Wright was busily unburdening himself of a lifetime's secrets – and paranoid anti-Communist obsessions – to Chapman Pincher. The Pincher version, which surfaced in *Their Trade is Treachery* in 1981, differed in some details, as stories tend to once they have been passed from second to third hand:

Blunt was asked by 'Henry' [Anatoli Gorski, his Soviet controller in London] to discover the identity of 'M8', but after trying for six months, he failed. 'Henry' then informed him that Soviet intelligence had discovered that 'M8' was Driberg. With unusual clumsiness, the Russians immediately alerted Harry Pollitt, who summarily expelled 'M8' from the Party.[4]

Since then the rough edges of the tale have been smoothed out by continual retelling. Here, for instance, is a passage from Anthony Masters's biography of Max Knight, *The Man Who Was M*, published in 1984:

[Driberg] submitted written reports to Knight and these were identified as reports from M8, though Driberg himself was not aware of his label. Blunt . . . saw a copy of such a report in someone else's office . . . He showed the content of the report to his Soviet case officer who instructed him to discover the identity of M8. Because of B(5)b's independence from the main body of MI5 this was extremely difficult to achieve, and six months elapsed before Blunt could make any progress. Then he saw another report from M8 which mentioned a book that Driberg had recently published, and Blunt was able to identify him at last.[5]

In 1988, John Costello included the story in *Mask of Treachery*, his biography of Anthony Blunt:

Ever since [Blunt] had joined B(1)b in late 1940, one of his standing instructions from 'Henry' was to help identify the MI5 moles in Britain's Communist party. He spotted one, code-named 'M8', in a routine report on the CPGB . . . From a reference to a book that had been written by 'M8', Blunt deduced and passed on to his controller that this particular informant was Tom Driberg, then a *Daily Express* journalist.[6]

Another member of the queer fraternity of spy-writers, Andrew Boyle, praised Costello's book for being 'brilliantly researched'. True, unlike most of his rivals, Costello was honest enough to admit (in a footnote) that he had no source for the story other than Nigel West, who in turn had heard it from Anthony Blunt. But the account of Blunt's discovery of 'M8' has appeared in print so often that it is now treated as an Authorised Version, neither susceptible to nor needing further investigation. The crucial detail that lends verisimilitude is the bit about Tom's book.

It is not true, however. The suggestion that Tom was recruited by MI5 while still a schoolboy may strain credulity but is at least within the bounds of theoretical possibility. That he was betrayed by 'a reference to a book that had been written by "M8"' is not. As Costello and West and others of their persuasion could have discovered in a moment's research, brilliant or otherwise, by the time of his expulsion from the CPGB in 1941 Tom had not written a book. His first book, *Colonnade*, a collection of his Hickey columns, did not appear until 1949 – 'abominably produced by a mushroom publisher who went bankrupt on the day of publication',[7] as he complained.

So what did happen?

Charles Henry Maxwell Knight was one of the more bizarre figures of modern times. After serving in the navy for the last year or two of the First World War, he worked as a clerk in the Ministry of Shipping and then as a prep-school master. But he longed for romantic adventure, inspired by *Greenmantle* and *The Thirty-Nine Steps*, and in 1925 he eagerly accepted an offer to go and work for MI5. For the next twenty years he threw himself enthusiastically into the great game, running agents and hatching plots, sniffing out Communists and 'subversives' (sometimes inaccurately, as in the case of Ben Greene, a harmless pacifist who was interned for twenty months during the war on the false evidence of one of Knight's *agents provocateurs*). He was known by his colleagues simply as 'M'. In spare moments he played the drums in a jazz band at the Hammersmith Palais. After the Second World War, finding that his unconventional talents were not appreciated by the new Director of MI5, Knight began another career. He had always been a naturalist: his house teemed with snakes, monkeys, tarantulas, ferrets and any other creatures that caught his fancy; he had once incubated a nest of adder eggs in his pyjama pocket. From the late 1940s, while still employed by MI5, he was a regular guest on BBC programmes such as *Country Questions* and *Naturalist*. On *Nature Parliament*, a show that went out at Sunday lunchtime, he developed the persona of Uncle Max, 'a familiar, rich voice that exhorted children to become nature detectives, looking under logs, in hedgerows and in fields to discover the natural history world.'[8] After retiring from the Security Service, he wrote *Pets and Their Problems*.

Tom certainly knew Max Knight. But he did not know him when he was at Lancing. Still less was he 'instructed' by Knight to join the Communist Party at the age of fifteen: he became a Communist out of genuine political conviction. From the evidence of those of Tom's engagement diaries that survive, he seems to have met Knight in 1931. He was probably introduced to him by Dennis Wheatley, whom Tom had come across in his capacity as 'The Dragoman' and who was a near-neighbour in Queen's Gate. Wheatley and Knight were close friends. Both wrote atrocious thrillers, though Wheatley's sold rather better than Knight's. (Knight's second novel, *Gunman's Holiday*, was dedicated to Dennis and Joan Wheatley. Wheatley returned the compliment: his novel *The Scarlet Impostor* bears the dedication 'For Max'.) They also shared a voracious interest in the occult, and were awed to learn that Tom knew Aleister Crowley. They begged for an introduction. Tom obliged, as Dennis Wheatley recorded in his memoirs:

We had Crowley to dinner several times. His conversation was fascinating. He gave me much useful information and several of his books, but never attempted to draw me into his occult activities. Later, when Driberg asked me what I thought of him, I replied: 'I think intellectually he is quite wonderful, but I don't believe he could harm a rabbit.'
    'Ah!' said Tom. 'You are right about that now, but it has only been the case since that awful business in Paris.'[9]

Tom then told Wheatley and Knight of how Crowley had tried to raise Pan in a hotel on the Left Bank.

The furniture from a room under the roof was removed and it was swept clean. In the evening Crowley, in his magician's robes, went into it accompanied by MacAleister (son of Aleister), one of his disciples. He then told the other eleven members of his coven that whatever noises they might hear in no circumstances were they to enter the room before morning.
    The eleven went downstairs to a cold buffet, very nervous. A little after midnight they heard an appalling racket in the upper room, but obeyed the Master's orders and did not go up. When in the morning they did go

up, they knocked on the door but there was no reply, so they broke it in. Both MacAleister and Crowley had had their robes ripped from them and were naked. MacAleister was dead and Crowley a gibbering idiot crouching in a corner.

It was as a consequence of these encounters with Crowley that Wheatley began writing the novels about black magic for which he is best remembered. According to Knight's nephew, Harry Smith, Wheatley and Knight jointly applied to Crowley as novices, and were accepted. 'But my uncle stressed that his interest – and also Wheatley's – was purely academic.'[10]

In 1934 Wheatley was a founder-member of a club called The Paternosters, which held monthly lunches for authors, critics and publishers at the Cheshire Cheese in Fleet Street. After being elected chairman the following year, he announced that he 'wished to broaden the basis of the club'. He proposed a number of gossip writers for membership, including Lord Donegall of the *Sunday Dispatch* and Tom Driberg of the *Daily Express*. Wheatley's argument for admitting gossip columnists on the same terms as literary critics was simple: 'it will be readily understood that for every person who reads literary criticisms in their papers, ten read the gossip column; so mentions of new books in such columns are of great value to an author.'[11] Among the novelists who would doubtless appreciate this line of reasoning was another new member who had been proposed by Wheatley at the same time – Max Knight, author of the unforgettable *Gunman's Holiday*.

Joan Miller, who during the Second World War was both personal assistant and mistress to Knight, has pointed out that 'the Communist threat was something about which M felt very deeply indeed; his views on this subject, you might say, amounted almost to an obsession. He was equally adamant in his aversion to Jews and homosexuals.' Tom and Max might therefore seem an incongruous pair. But Knight was not all he seemed. As Joan Miller added:

M never allowed his prejudices to interfere with his appreciation of the work done for us by a couple of highly valued [German] agents, one homosexual and the other Jewish; as I've said, his intolerant attitude wasn't altogether consistent. Partly because of this, and also because he would sometimes pretend to be parodying himself, I never saw anything particularly outrageous in the way he kept referring to these *bêtes noires*. Everyone, I reasoned, had a topic on which they were liable to become unreasonable.[12]

Knight missed no opportunity to parade his loathing for homosexuals. He once drew Joan Miller's attention to some male prostitutes in the street, 'and explained how they used a special way of walking – like girls', only more pronounced – as an intermittent form of self-advertisement. When they weren't on the lookout for potential customers, he said, their gait was likely to be as normal as anyone else's. He spoke with extreme annoyance and contempt.'[13] Knight, who was married three times, cultivated a reputation as a ladies' man, like a hero from one of the John Buchan novels he so admired.

However, it seems that none of his marriages was actually consummated. Nor was his affair with Joan Miller, although they lived together for a couple of years. At first she put this down to her own inexperience, combined with the after-effects of his unsatisfactory second marriage. 'It was very difficult to associate M with incapacity in any area. I was assured that the problem was temporary, and largely created by me and my incompetence, and I was grateful to M for not making more of a fuss about it. He kept telling me not to worry, that it would be all right in the end.' But it never was. The unsatisfactory love-life began to 'worry and plague' her. One afternoon in 1942 she discovered Knight's secret:

He put an advertisement in the local paper that went something like this: 'Gentleman requires help from motorcycle expert afternoons at weekends.' It was true that he was obsessed with the things and kept three in the barn at Camberley, including the one he'd bought for me; still, I must say something about his sudden need to consult a mechanic, not to mention the way he went about acquiring one, struck me as odd. I was sure a more orthodox channel for obtaining this service existed . . .

An applicant duly appeared one Saturday and accompanied M to the barn where the two of them were closeted all afternoon. I caught a glimpse of them as they crossed the lawn. M's mechanic – a bus driver, I think – was a slim young man with a nervous way of gesticulating. Whatever he was hired to do, he did it well. M professed himself entirely satisfied with the young man's competence . . . the bus driver was back the next weekend, and the one after.

This new enthusiasm of M's left me feeling rather out of things. On the third Saturday I took a book up to my bedroom and installed myself in the window-seat . . . I watched [M] make his way back towards the barn, where the bus driver was standing in the open doorway. M had no idea he was being observed. For the first time he was off guard, and so fell into a posture he must have found pretty natural. I recognised it for what it was, for he had pointed it out to me himself, when we passed a couple of male prostitutes in the street.

As I sat there watching this avowed opponent of homosexuality mince across the lawn, a number of things became clear to me.[14]

As well they might. And though Joan Miller believed that Knight's tastes were generally in the direction of 'rough trade', she noticed that he made an exception for his friend Driberg. Max was 'sexually besotted by Tom'.[15]

Tom saw a good deal of Max Knight in the early 1930s. They would meet for lunch every couple of months, usually at Hatchett's restaurant, the Overseas Club or the Grosvenor Hotel. Sometimes Knight would drop in at 5 Queen's Gate Place Mews on a Saturday afternoon. They liked each other's company. It is unlikely, however, that Tom would have encouraged any advances made by the besotted spymaster.

If Knight's anti-homosexuality was a cover for his own appetites, what of his anti-Communism? It would be pleasing to think that he was working for the Comintern all along, but in fact his obsessive fear of 'subversives' was real enough. It remained with him until his death in 1968. 'He was worried about student unrest in the Sixties,' his nephew recalled, 'believing it to be the perfect breeding ground for Russian infiltration.'[16] But as Joan Miller noticed, he was capable of self-mockery, and sometimes deliberately exaggerated his opinions for effect. The same was true of Tom. As they exchanged gossip and prejudices there must have been many a sly wink.

And gossip was almost all that Tom could, or would, offer. He was unable to pass on the innermost secrets of the CPGB for the simple reason that he didn't have them. Besides, Knight was already well-informed about the activities of leading Communists, having managed to infiltrate two agents – Olga Gray and the crime novelist John Dickson Carr – into the party HQ at King Street.

But Tom had other information to give Knight. Spy-writers who have speculated on the relations between these two men have all overlooked the fact that Knight's section of MI5 was responsible for 'counter-subversion', not merely counter-Communism. As Knight explained to Joan Miller when she was recruited, B(5)b's task was 'blocking the threat to British security from the Right as well as the Left'. Indeed, Joan Miller's first assignment for Knight was to join the Right Club, posing as an ardent fascist from the War Office who wanted to leak military secrets to Germany, in order to trap Hitler's fifth columnists. Knight may have been a roaring anti-semite and anti-Communist but he was not such a blithering idiot as to ignore the very real menace of Nazi sympathisers in Britain. Tom was alert to the same danger, keeping a close eye on the Mosleyites, the Cliveden set, the Anglo-German Fellowship and anyone else who thought that Hitler wasn't such a bad sort. Their conversations over lunch at Hatchett's were as likely to dwell on the British fascists – or the peccadilloes of staff at the *Daily Express*, or what Lord Beaverbrook had told Tom at dinner the previous night, or which jazz band of the moment was hottest – as on the Communist Party of Great Britain.

Nevertheless, it would be foolish to deny that Tom gossiped about his fellow Communists. He was a man who gossiped compulsively about everyone and everything. Does this prove that his attachment to the Party was essentially bogus? His great enemy Chapman Pincher, whose delusions about Communism and homosexuality are even more paranoid than Max Knight's, has no doubt: 'It would have been no more than just if Driberg had been betrayed, for the overall verdict on him – in journalism, in politics, and intelligence – is that, eventually, he betrayed everybody.'[17] When Pincher first made his allegations, a rather more elaborate analysis of Tom's conduct was offered by the Labour MP Leo Abse:

Driberg walked all his life on a tightrope and gained his thrills in public and private by a never ending series of adventures, courageously and foolhardily oscillating from one role to another almost every day of his life. Distinguished journalist, grammarian and Churchman, he could be as punctilious about ecclesiastical ritual or a semi-colon as he was obsessional in his trawl of the 'cottages' of Britain: his fastidiousness was never extended to the unkempt delinquent youngsters who, in his prowling, he compulsively pursued. The spy is a man of identities and each day he must act many parts. Driberg could have played the part of the spy with superb skill, and if the officers of MI5 were indeed inept enough to have attempted to recruit him, then, in turn, Tom Driberg would have gained especial pleasure in fooling and betraying them.[18]

So far, so plausible. But Abse then lurched off on a wild Freudian detour, arguing that 'treachery is uncomfortably linked with disturbed homosexuals unable to come to terms with their sexual destiny . . . It was always so: did not Judas embrace and kiss Christ as he betrayed him?' The link between disturbed homosexuality and treachery, he added, 'is the child's lack of reconciliation between his hatred and love of his father'. Ah well.

The Revd Gerard Irvine, who knew and understood Tom better than Pincher or Abse, had a more persuasive explanation. 'He was greedy for experience, the more bizarre the better. Partly this was a journalist's instinct; but not wholly. It had to be not just experience or knowledge as such, but *his* experience and *his* knowledge.' His tolerant interest in human perversity made him a first-class journalist, and 'had he been more discreet in the use he made of such knowledge, he would have been also a first-class confidant. This, regrettably, he was not.' But indiscretion is not synonymous with betrayal. His fondness for an institution (or person) did not inhibit him from gossiping and joking about it. As Irvine said, 'Everything Tom loved, he mocked.'[19] He did not consciously harm the Communist Party by fraternising with Knight; there was no Judas kiss here.

Quite how the CPGB discovered Tom's association with Knight remains a mystery. It was certainly not through Anthony Blunt reading a report by Knight which mentioned a book Tom had written. Blunt may, however, have played a part. He and Tom certainly disliked each other. Michael Harbinson, a former lover of Guy Burgess, claimed that there was some sexual rivalry:

I knew all about cottaging . . . It was dangerous but Blunt did it because he loved danger. Everyone knows the toilet he used at Hyde Park, the big one near Speakers' Corner. He used to go to the one at Russell Square as well but he didn't like that as much because Tom Driberg was there for two or three hours every day, holding his mac over his arm.[20]

But King Street could equally well have learned about Tom and Max Knight from other sources, since their liaisons were not exactly clandestine: they were seen about town together, in restaurants and clubs and bars, without so much as a cloak or dagger to protect them. If Tom had been seriously engaged in betraying the Party to MI5, rather than merely exchanging gossip and enjoying the attentions of a man who was infatuated with him, he might have been more careful.

After their initial over-reaction, the Communist leaders came to realise this. There was no lasting grudge on either side: Tom continued to campaign for the lifting of the government's ban on the *Daily Worker*, 'a ban which seemed particularly absurd now that Russia was in the war'; Harry Pollitt bantered amicably with Tom when they appeared on a BBC discussion programme a few years later. And the expulsion turned out to have its advantages. When Tom stood for Parliament as an Independent in 1942, 'I was able truthfully to tell the electors that I belonged to no Party.' No one asked if he had ever belonged to one.

If Tom had been born fifty years later, he would probably never have got into Parliament. Candidates today are expected to learn the trade by fighting in two or three unwinnable constituencies first, or by serving a few terms on the local council; then they can begin the long search for a safe seat, slogging round dismal meeting-rooms in towns they have scarcely heard of, taking rejection with a smile before dashing off to catch the last train. Tom could not have endured such a marathon. True, he was capable of hard work; but he was also easily bored. To quote Gerard Irvine, 'He crammed more, and more varied, activities into a day than most men into a month.' There is nothing 'varied' about political selection committees. The idea of presenting himself for interview month after month, in the uncertain hope of one day being rewarded, would have been hideous to him. He was too impatient to accept deferred gratification.

The peculiar circumstances of 1942 were thus ideal. Churchill's coalition partners had agreed a wartime truce whereby, when a Member died or retired, the other parties would not contest the subsequent by-election. In the absence of any opposition candidates, it was possible for an Independent to stand for Parliament on impulse and have a reasonable chance of being elected. The only requirements were a deposit of £150 and ten electors' signatures.

When Tom landed at Prestwick in March 1942, at the end of his chilly and uncomfortable flight from America, he 'had not the faintest idea' that within three months he would be a Member of Parliament. But perhaps a seed had already been sown. Before leaving the United States, he had been discussing the progress of the war with some morose British visitors. Two battleships that had been sent to Singapore on Churchill's insistence, the *Prince of Wales* and the *Repulse*, had been sunk by the Japanese; on 15 February Singapore itself fell, and the 80,000-strong British defence forces surrendered. 'They seem to be making a pretty good mess of the war,' said one of Tom's companions. 'We'd better go into Parliament and show them how to run things.' It was not a serious suggestion, but it lodged in Tom's memory. Back in London, he spoke one evening at a meeting to protest at the continuing ban on the *Daily Worker*. Afterwards the editor of *Picture Post*, Tom Hopkinson, complimented Tom on his speech and said he ought to think of standing for Parliament.

Public dissatisfaction with the government was increasingly apparent at parliamentary by-elections. On 25 March an Independent candidate, W. D. Kendall, won a sensational victory in the hitherto Conservative seat of Grantham; on 29 April the Conservative candidates in Wallasey and Rugby were both routed by Independents. These results were welcomed in the William Hickey column:

'Hosanna! This is good news for England,' cried W. J. Brown after his Rugby victory yesterday.

The news of these Independent victories is good for England because they represent a challenge to the electoral truce; the merit of some of the candidates likely to get in if the reaction against the Party machines continues is more questionable . . .[21]

For once, Tom was in step with his newspaper. Lord Beaverbrook had resigned from the War Cabinet in a huff at the end of February, so criticism of the government was now permissible. An *Express* editorial on 1 May argued that the victories of Brown at Rugby and G. L. Reakes at Wallasey would give Hitler no comfort, for, although they had stood against Tories, they were still 'Churchill men'. If anything, the *Express* was more enthusiastic than Tom: 'Here,' it rejoiced, 'is a plain indication that the nation wants a halt called to the game of party politics. It is a most refreshing sign of healthy democracy in vigorous action.'

A fortnight later, listening to the evening news on the radio at his flat, Tom learned of the death of Colonel Sir Edward Ruggles-Brise, Conservative MP for Maldon – the constituency that included Bradwell-juxta-Mare. It seemed a propitious coincidence. He wondered aloud if he should put up for the seat himself. This brought a derisive hoot from his pick-up for the night, a Canadian soldier who was lying naked on the carpet in front of the gas-fire: 'You'd never do it – and if you did, you'd never make it.' The challenge strengthened Tom's resolve. The next day he went to Lord Beaverbrook and asked for three weeks' leave to fight a by-election. Beaverbrook was not greatly accommodating. Tom was free to stand for Parliament, but until the week of the poll he would have to keep writing Hickey most days. The proprietor had one piece of advice for his columnist – to buy a hat. 'The British electors,' he warned, 'will not vote for a man who doesn't wear a hat.'

Since Tom's chief claim to fame was as William Hickey of the *Express*, and much would probably be made of this during the campaign, Beaverbrook decided that the paper must state its position without delay. On 25 May, under the simple heading 'Our Staff', it published a leader that must have left readers puzzling over whether the *Express* was endorsing its employee's candidacy or disowning him:

Mr Tom Driberg, who writes the William Hickey column in the *Daily Express*, is to stand as Independent candidate in the by-election in Maldon, Essex.

The *Daily Express* does not support his candidature. But, of course, members of the *Express* staff are permitted and encouraged to exercise all their rights as private citizens, no matter what political viewpoints they may hold.

It does not make any difference to the *Daily Express* what views they hold. They may be in complete disagreement with the policy of the paper.

There is often some diversity of political viewpoint between the *Express* and Mr Driberg. That makes no difference. He can stand for Parliament, and personally we hold him in the highest esteem.

Tom began his campaign with a visit to Braintree, the largest town in the constituency and the source of most Labour votes. (At the 1935 election the Labour candidate had won 9,264 votes, against the 17,072 for Ruggles-Brise.) He trawled the local pubs incognito, asking drinkers – as if he were no more than an interested observer – what they thought of the contest. The reactions were promising. He repeated the exercise in Maldon, and was again encouraged. The landlady of the King's Head used the pulpit of her saloon bar to extol Tom's virtues. *Ad hoc* groups of well-wishers started canvassing.

His platform was that the Prime Minister was admirable and indispensable, but too many of the people around him were not up to the job. One of his slogans, suggested by a *Daily Telegraph* journalist, was 'A Candid Friend For Churchill'. Whether Churchill wanted a candid friend was another matter. In spite of the *Express*'s disclaimer, he suspected that Tom's candidacy was an anti-government ploy organised by Beaverbrook, especially as it was rumoured (wrongly) that Frank Owen of the *Evening Standard* might be standing in a by-election as well. 'The fact that Mr Driberg and Mr Frank Owen are standing as Independent candidates in two by-elections,' Churchill wrote to Beaverbrook, 'will of course be taken by everyone as indicating that you are running election candidates against the Government. This would be a great pity from many points of view.' In the first week of June, the Prime Minister also sent a letter of support to Tom's Conservative rival, Reuben J.

Hunt, an ironmaster and alderman who was standing as the National Government candidate. 'It is still my convinced opinion,' Churchill wrote, 'that in these days when the future of our country and indeed of all civilisation is in the melting pot, by-election fights are completely out of keeping with the gravity of the times. I hope, therefore, no one will show such levity of mind as to provoke an unnecessary and meaningless contest.' Tom's riposte was that precisely because times were grave Parliament should be reinforced 'with men who subordinate all prejudices and all profits to total victory and are in touch with the developing ideas of the younger people who will have to build the peace.' But how did Tom, as a pro-Churchill candidate, explain the fact that Churchill was apparently not pro-Driberg? Simple: the PM's letter to Hunt was not his own work. 'This,' Tom told reporters, 'is the routine document which the Conservative Party machine-minders require their titular leader to sign. He signs it – it is convenient for a busy Prime Minister to have behind him several hundred dummies who will say "Yes" to everything.'[22]

Bill Brown MP, the Independent who had won Rugby a few weeks earlier, pointed out that Churchill was arguing in effect that there should be no by-elections. 'It is an appeal to make permanent a situation in which the Conservative Party should possess something like three-quarters of the seats in the House of Commons when a General Election would probably give it no more than a quarter.' This was strikingly prescient. The famous Labour victory of 1945 is often presented as a totally unforeseen eruption – and, for the Conservative leaders, so it was. But politicians who were less insulated and remote had expected it for some time. At Maldon in June 1942 Tom soon discovered that the electors' support for Churchill would not automatically persuade them to vote for any old nincompoop or reactionary proposed by the Conservative Association. Reuben 'Bin' Hunt was a plain-speaking right-winger, described in one local paper as a man who 'by his stalwart appearance and robust outlook upon national and political life practically selected himself.' Voters of milder temperament were dismayed by the choice. Tories, Liberals and Socialists all presented themselves at Tom's house and campaign office to offer their assistance. A bank manager and a Ford car dealer from Maldon, neither of them socialists, backed Tom's candidature. So did the local scout commissioner, Jack Gold, a popular figure who had himself been asked to stand as an Independent. In a statement on 7 June, he announced: 'I have decided to stand down and support Driberg, as the Conservatives have chosen a reactionary county councillor. I offered myself to the Conservative Association as a non-party candidate.'[23]

There was one other candidate. A farmer named Borlase Matthews stood as an Independent, with a manifesto that differed little from Tom's. He, too, supported Churchill but thought the Conservative Party had too much influence over the government. He wanted to see the country run 'on progressive lines'. His only objection to Tom was that 'there were already too many lawyers and newspaper men in Parliament. It was about time practical men were returned.'[24] To prove his own qualifications in this respect, he regaled open-air meetings with stories of how he had learned to milk cows as a boy.

Tom could not match this, but he had other ways of wooing the masses. A campaign slogan described him as 'The Local Man With the National Reputation', and he drew attention to his celebrity by buying space in the local papers for weekly election bulletins that were laid out to resemble Hickey columns. At the top of each advertisement a paragraph in bold type reminded voters that Tom Driberg, Independent candidate in the forthcoming Maldon by-election, was William Hickey of the *Daily Express*. At the foot was a boxed announcement: 'DRIBERG – the only Candidate who lives in the Division'. In between, he hustled and badgered shamelessly. He noted, for example, that people who had reached their twenty-first birthday since June 1939 were not allowed to vote – 'but if every one of them who would *like* to vote for me will persuade at least three friends who *can* vote to do so, they will be making up handsomely for their disenfranchisement.'[25] He decorated each column with highlights from press coverage of his candidacy: 'Who is Mr Driberg? As William Hickey, of the *Daily Express*, he is the most brilliant columnist of the national Press; his writings are read by millions' (*Evening Standard*); 'A Parliament which contained Mr Driberg among its members should certainly feel itself buttressed by a unique safeguard against cant and humbug' (*Church Times*); 'A very useful resident' (*Burnham-on-Crouch Advertiser*).

Famous friends from Fleet Street such as Vernon Bartlett, Philip Jordan and Hannen Swaffer trooped down to the constituency night after night to address meetings in support of the useful resident. (Bartlett had himself won a by-election as an Independent four years earlier, at Bridgwater.) Those who could not come in person sent testimonials. J. B. Priestley wrote that Tom had the right ideas about the war and the peace which would follow; if elected, he would take part in 'sweeping away many sectional interests and clearing out some of the old gang who are still trying to preserve them'. A week before polling day a message arrived from George Bernard Shaw:

I have no rightful interest here in the Maldon election, but I find it necessary to remind the electors in Maldon and elsewhere that the Party truce does not mean a corrupt bargain between the two parties to vote just as they did last time and leave Parliament where it was before the war.

It means dropping the party lines and voting for the ablest candidate.

It not only means that Independent candidates are quite in order, but that the official party candidates are breaking the truce and are entirely out of order.[26]

Even Tom could not quite follow the Shavian logic, but he was grateful nevertheless.

More practical help came from Sir Richard Acland, the Christian socialist who was then sitting as an Independent MP but soon afterwards founded the Common Wealth movement. In spite of his reputation as an ascetic, rather holy figure, Acland was a brilliant organiser of by-election campaigns. 'As soon as I heard Tom was standing I asked to meet him,' Acland said. 'I recall asking him about organisation and he said he had none. I said: "It's now 13 days to polling day; we must spend nine days organising and four days winning."'[27] Acland immediately contacted Friends House, the Independent Labour Party, local left-wing vicars and anyone else who might be useful. He advised Tom how to control public meetings, how to use a loudspeaker-car (never speak while moving: the voice fading away is irritating) and how to create a network of committees. Tom used to say that 'Dick Acland can walk into any unknown town and four days later there will be a committee.'

The Labour Party and Communist Party were officially supporting the government candidate, but many of their members were unhappy at the selection of Reuben Hunt. Just before polling day the local Communists switched sides, after Hunt said that Britain was losing in North Africa 'because we've given too much help to the Russians'. The branch secretary of the CP, Harold Quinton, immediately advised his members to exert themselves for Tom. (He was subsequently disciplined by the national CP.)

As the campaign progressed, Tom began boasting to the press that more and more members of the local Labour Party, too, were working for him. The secretary of Braintree Labour Party, the Revd Jack Boggis, resigned his post to become secretary of the pro-Driberg committee. Boggis was also secretary of the Anglo-Soviet Friendship Society, and he had been won round by the fact that Tom was the only candidate to turn up at the opening of a new Anglo-Soviet bookshop in Braintree Market Square. Alarmed by this defection, the General Committee of Maldon Divisional Labour Party met on 14 June but concluded that there was 'no need to change the line of action previously decided': Labour members must 'give no support whatever to any independent candidate'. Sir Valentine Crittall, a former Labour MP for Maldon, was recruited to explain the attitude of his party at a number of public meetings. He pointed out that 'the present government is a coalition, formed for the one purpose of winning the war, and contains members of the Labour Party'. There was even a rumour – which turned out to be untrue – that Clem Attlee had been persuaded to send a letter of support to Reuben Hunt.

In the next thirty years Tom was to contest many elections; but he never enjoyed any so much as this Maldon campaign of '42:

It was fought in golden summer weather; most of our meetings were in the open air, in this loveliest and most unspoiled part of Essex. The big constituency embraced ancient villages like Finchingfield and quiet waterfronts like that of Burnham-on-Crouch; and Maldon itself, a favourite subject of such artists as Wilson Steer. At the King's Head in Maldon the splendid elderly landlady, Mrs Massingberd-Mundy, rallied all sorts of unexpected help. Dorothy L. Sayers, who lived at Witham, lent furniture for our committee-room there. (She thought better of it later; when I asked her in 1945 to help again, reminding her that we had been to Mass in London together, she replied that I appeared to be inviting her to commit inverted simony.) Another famous detective-story writer, Margery Allingham, lived at Tolleshunt D'Arcy: though personally friendly, she thought it wiser to leave everything to Churchill and not 'disturb people'.

But people *were* disturbed.[28]

One way and another, as he wrote later, 'we got things humming'. As victory seemed not just possible but likely, Tom decided to create an Independent version of a party machine. If he were elected, he said, his campaign committees would become a Maldon Constituency Association, which would pass on constituents' views and arrange 'the frequent and regular meetings at which I shall report personally on the kind of job I shall be doing in Parliament on your behalf'. This answered the suggestion sometimes made, especially by Labour Party officials in London, that Independent MPs were not responsible to anybody. 'I shall be responsible directly,' Tom promised, 'to the most important people of all – the people who elected me to Parliament.'

In the last of his Hickey-style advertisements in the local papers, on 19 June, he addressed himself to two other criticisms of Independent candidates:

1. Independents 'can't do anything in the House of Commons because they are on their own'. Right. Ask anybody to write down the names of the first 20 MPs he can think of. I'll warrant there'll be a disproportionately large number of Independents among them. Men like Vernon Bartlett, A. P. Herbert, Cripps, Hore-Belisha, *have* made their mark on public affairs. I don't say I agree with all the views of all these. But Parliament listens when they speak.

2. The official Tories are, of course, making great play with the Prime Minister's 'repudiation' of Independent support. They omit to mention that he has given several pretty big jobs lately to Cripps – an Independent. The present Secretary of State for War, Sir James Grigg, is also, like me, a non-party man, supporting Churchill, as I do.

The truth is that there are two Churchills: one is the great national figure whom no party can claim as its exclusive property; the other is the chief who was forced on the Conservative Party by the British people and who naturally now finds it 'convenient to have behind him several hundred dummies who will say "Yes" to everything.'

I have found Mr Hunt, the official Tory candidate, personally courteous and amiable; but I suggest that he conforms exactly to the old type of narrow, reactionary, commercially-minded Conservative. These men kept Churchill out of office for years. These men obsequiously upheld Baldwin in doing nothing and Chamberlain in doing wrong. These men did all they could to obstruct the alliance with Russia which might have checked Hitler years ago and made this war unnecessary.

How can a Socialist or a Liberal or a progressive Tory vote for such a man?[29]

If everyone who sympathised with his case would chivvy or wheedle their friends, families and neighbours into turning out for Tom, 'then we can beat the Old Gang next Thursday.'

Tom felt almost certain that he had won even before polling day dawned. On Wednesday 24 June he spoke at five eve-of-poll meetings — in Burnham-on-Crouch, Maldon, Witham, Silver End and Braintree — and was received by large crowds at each. Six thousand people pressed round his soap-box as he made his last speech of the campaign, in Braintree market square, even though he hadn't arrived until 10 pm. Sir Richard Acland and Hannen Swaffer had already warmed up the crowd, which was 'excited, but less hilariously so than at an ordinary peace-time election'. The war was still going badly, and only that week had come the shocking and inexplicable news that Tobruk had fallen to Rommel. The mood was serious, angry, fearful.

The next day the electors of Maldon went to the polls. Borlase Matthews received 1,476 votes; Reuben Hunt had 6,226; and Tom, surpassing even his own immodest predictions, won 12,219 — almost twice as much as the government's candidate. It was an astonishing triumph. His victory statement repeated the leitmotif of his campaign: 'I support Mr Churchill's leadership, as I am certain all who voted for me do, but there must be drastic changes lower down.'

Winston Churchill heard the news in Scotland while he was

boarding a train to London, having just flown back from the United States. He noted it curtly: 'It appeared that we had lost a by-election at Maldon. This was one of the by-products of Tobruk. This seemed to me to be a bad time. I went to bed, browsed about in the files for a while, and then slept for four or five hours till we reached London. What a blessing is the gift of sleep!'[30] Tom's old schoolfriend Evelyn Waugh was on a course at the Intelligence Training Centre in Matlock when he read of the result. 'Tom Driberg has been elected Independent Member for Maldon by a large majority,' he wrote in his diary. 'The newspapers have behaved very curiously over this by-election, giving no news of what any of the candidates are saying. In recording the result they simply describe him as a journalist and a churchwarden, which gives a very imperfect picture of that sinister character.'[31]

Tom's employer was no more generous. At lunch on the day after the election, when the outcome was still unknown, Beaverbrook told Brendan Bracken — the Minister of Information — that Tom would undoubtedly forfeit his deposit. When the scale of his misjudgment was revealed shortly afterwards, he ordered Christiansen to print another sniffy editorial about the errant columnist. It read:

Mr Driberg, who writes the William Hickey column in this newspaper, has won the Maldon by-election as an Independent. It should, of course, be made clear that the *Daily Express* has no share, no part in his triumph.

On 25 May this column stated:

The *Daily Express* does not support his candidature but, of course, members of the *Express* staff are permitted, and encouraged, to exercise their rights as private citizens. We do not agree with Mr Driberg's politics.[32]

Tom had his revenge in a tailpiece to his column the following Wednesday. After describing his first day at Westminster, he added: 'PS: The writer of this column is not responsible for the views expressed in any other part of this newspaper. He disagrees with many of them, anyway.'[33]

Parliament, like the Church, satisfied Tom's craving for exquisitely preposterous ritual. Instead of gilt censers and surpliced priests there were gilt maces and gartered Serjeants-at-Arms. 'It is,' he wrote, rather pompously, 'a grave and a great day in a man's life when he first goes to take his seat in Parliament.' It was like the Pope's funeral all over again:

The new boy and his two friends walk towards the Chamber. His heart is unruly, his throat dry . . .

Someone at the far end of what seems a purgatorial mile murmurs an invitation. 'Bow': they bow their heads. 'Left foot': they take seven paces in step. 'Bow': they bow the head again. Another seven paces; another bow; a few of the old stagers talking among themselves on either side are kind enough to emit the deep 'Hear, hear' which is described in Hansard as 'Cheers': this means that the rite has been performed correctly, so far.

Now the new MP's friends leave him. He is alone with the Clerk for the most solemn moment, the taking of the Oath . . .

He has handed over his blue Writ of Return. He signs a great book; the paper feels like vellum beneath his fountain-pen . . .

He is presented to Mr Speaker. He hears it proclaimed aloud that he is verily a Member of this venerable House.

It was certainly venerable in the more colloquial sense of 'aged-looking'. There had been no general election since 1935, and the rows of whiskery Edwardian Tories looked like an embalmed tableau of the Baldwin age – which, indeed, they were. The unreality was heightened by the setting. In 1941 the chamber of the House of Commons had been destroyed by incendiary bombs, 'as neatly extracted from the Victorian-Gothic environment of the Palace of Westminster (which was, otherwise, not seriously damaged) as an aching tooth from a healthy jaw',[34] Tom wrote later. The Commons had therefore taken over the Lords' Chamber, and the Lords had been banished to the Queen's Robing Room. Later in the war, when London was under attack from V2 missiles, the Commons moved to Church House in Great Smith Street, which was thought to be more bomb-proof.

Tom was impatient to make his mark at Westminster. Only two days after his introduction there was an ideal opportunity, when the House debated a motion proposed by a senior Tory, Sir John Wardlaw-Milne MP: 'That this House, while paying tribute to the heroism and endurance of the Armed Forces of the Crown in circumstances of exceptional difficulty, has no confidence in the central direction of the war.' The motion, tabled on the day of the Maldon by-election, had created great excitement in the British and American press, not least because it was seconded by Admiral of the Fleet Sir Roger Keyes and supported by a former Secretary of State for War, Leslie Hore-Belisha. Had Tom asked to be called in the debate, the Speaker could hardly have refused, since the Maldon vote was obviously germane to the subject. Sir Stafford Cripps, the Privy Seal, recognised as much in a memo to Churchill just before the debate:

There is no doubt that there is a very grave disturbance of opinion both in the House of Commons and in the country. But it is also clear that the Vote of Censure does not in any way represent the general reaction of the country to the news. At the same time the very significant result of the Maldon by-election, in which the Government candidate only polled 6,226 votes out of a total of nearly 20,000, was undoubtedly largely due to results in Libya, and shows the profound disquiet and lack of confidence of the electors. I do not think that the feeling is in any sense a personal one against the Prime Minister, but a general feeling of dissatisfaction that something is wrong and should be put right without delay.[35]

Convention demands, however, that maiden speeches be uncontroversial; and Tom was in awe of parliamentary convention. Besides, he wasn't entirely sure that he wanted to be seen as an ally of Wardlaw-Milne, an unreconstructed Chamberlainite of buffoonish mien. In the end, letting 'I dare not' wait upon 'I would', Tom decided not to put his name down for the debate.

This was just as well. What should have been a serious challenge to the government dissolved into farce when Wardlaw-Milne opened the debate by advocating that the Duke of Gloucester — a famously unimpressive member of the royal family — should be appointed Commander-in-Chief of the British Army. The debate never recovered. After conferring with two fellow-Independents, Richard Acland and Vernon Bartlett, Tom cast his first parliamentary vote against the motion of no-confidence. It was defeated by 476 votes to 25.

Another convention relating to maiden speeches is that nobody interrupts them, but this was not observed when Tom finally broke his silence in a debate on 7 July about the government's use of propaganda. After criticising the Ministry of Information for not being strong enough to overrule the Service Departments, 'which have frequently been responsible for some of the worst delays and muddles of the censorship and also for the publication of exaggeratedly optimistic reports', he clambered on to his hobby horse of the moment, the ban on the Communist Party's newspaper:

Another matter which I may mention in passing, since it also concerns the Ministry of Home Security, is that one valuable weapon of home propaganda still remains unused, although it would cost the Ministry of Information nothing to use it. I refer to the *Daily Worker*. I should like, if it is within the scope of this Debate, to say that –
The Temporary Chairman (Mr Charles Williams): I do not think that that matter is within the scope of the Debate.
Mr Driberg: I bow to your Ruling.

Slightly hurt by this rebuff, Tom spent the next couple of minutes denouncing the Foreign Office instead, before ending with a grand appeal for a better world. Propaganda, he said, could only be effective if it was based on facts.

It is no good preaching about equality of sacrifice if every housewife and every soldier knows that there is not yet really anything approaching equality of sacrifice. It remains true that the best propaganda is a victory, but as we cannot have military victories every day, let us have another kind of victory to proclaim to the world, a victory over the old impulses of private greed and profit, a victory over old prejudices and fears – fear of Bolshevism and of what it may do to Europe after the war, fear of yielding up our privileges in case we never get them back. I believe it is only in that way that we can convince all our own people and all our friends in other countries both that we are invincible and that we deserve victory.[36]

Yet another convention of the House is that a maiden speech must be complimented by the next speaker. As Tom sat down after his stirring finale, Lt.-Col. Sir Thomas Moore did the honours. 'Many of us have read for years past the wise, shrewd and witty comments made in one of our most popular morning papers by the Hon. Member who has just spoken,' he said. 'I can only regret that he has found himself, as I understand it, in some divergence with the political views of the paper whose ranks he adorns.'

Tom's speeches, questions and interjections during his first few months in the Commons established the tone of voice – or, rather, the tones – which he was to maintain over the next thirty years: flippancy and earnestness, pedantry and passion. It was an unsettling mixture. Just as Beaverbrook never understood how a Communist could enjoy 'the fine wines of France and Spain' with a clear conscience, and just as in later years there were those who insisted that a man who owned a substantial country house in Essex could not be a sincere left-winger, so some MPs assumed that he was merely a striker of poses. They watched for contradictions of style and posture which they could brandish as proof that his politics were nothing more than an affectation. He only does it to annoy, so the argument went, because he knows it teases.

He did indeed take pleasure in teasing and annoying, and he often exaggerated in order to provoke. But his opponents mistook means for ends. He was not teasing purely for the sake of it. He was, to use a phrase which the critic John Bayley once applied to Shakespeare, 'kidding on the level'. There was nothing affected about his hatred of racial prejudice, say, or his anti-colonialism, or his sympathy for victims of injustice. His first oral question in the House concerned a Communist called Jock Cunningham, a former combatant in the Spanish civil war who had recently been discharged from the Royal Artillery; Tom believed that Cunningham's treatment by the army was straightforward political victimisation, especially as there were about a dozen similar cases of prejudice against men who had fought in Spain.[37] In another early question, he asked whether Churchill was aware

that an unfortunate result of the presence here of American Forces has been the introduction in some parts of Britain of discrimination against negro troops; and whether he will make friendly representations to the American authorities asking them to instruct their men that the colour bar is not a custom of this country and that its non-observance by British troops or civilians should be regarded with equanimity.[38]

In a debate in September, he argued that India should be granted its freedom now and not after the cessation of hostilities. 'It is an inevitable preliminary to victory in the Far East that we should enlist the masses of the Indian people on our side. But you cannot impose enthusiasm for our cause by whippings or even canings, by terrorism or by the imprisonment of men who, however wrong-headed they may be, are regarded by millions of Indian people as their leaders.'[39]

Not all his contributions were quite so intense. He asked the Chancellor of the Exchequer whether he would consider issuing a $1\frac{1}{2}d$. coin; one Tory MP insinuated that this was a stunt to allow the *Daily Express* to raise its price to $1\frac{1}{2}d$. He also kept up his gleeful baiting of the rich, demanding a purge on anti-social lunchers at the Savoy Hotel:

Mr Driberg asked the Minister of Fuel and Power whether he will state the names and addresses of the owners of the private motor-cars whose registration numbers are HPD 849, FYL 480, GKE 465, GGO 280, COW 648, EYR 248, FOJ 373, GPL 892, EOV 524, HVW 440 and JPD 713, all of which vehicles were between 1.30 pm and 3 pm on Friday, 16 October, outside the Savoy Hotel, a place readily accessible by public transport?

Major Lloyd George: No sir. Such inquiries as I have been able to make in the time available show that there may well be a legitimate explanation of the presence of the cars.

Mr Driberg: Will not the right hon. and gallant Gentleman take steps to check this lavish and lazy use of petrol, which is causing the greatest dissatisfaction to thousands of people who have not got any at all?[40]

More surprisingly, he took the feminist side in an argument over whether it was seemly for female doctors to conduct medical inspections of male soldiers. MPs worked themselves into a state of spluttering outrage about this absurd non-issue: one complained of the blow to a man's 'innate sense of modesty' if a woman MO were to see him naked; another urged the minister to take 'a more robust and masculine line'; yet another said that anyone 'with a streak of masculinity in their nature' would recoil from 'the indignity of being examined by a woman in cold blood'. Tom, who could hardly shake hands with a woman without shuddering, might have been ex-pected to add his voice to the chorus. Instead he told his colleagues to calm down and keep a sense of proportion. There was, he pointed out, an acute shortage of doctors, and 'medical man-power, whether male or female, must be used in the most economical way possible.' He added:

To my mind, when we accept women in a profession, we must treat them in an absolutely cold-blooded way as equal professional partners: we cannot introduce, or allow to remain, this emotional sort of complex about them – which is really going part of the way to the Nazi idea of sending women back to the kitchen and not allowing them a public career at all. We must try to see this thing rationally and coolly: even if there is a sensitive minority of people who object, I think they have far worse hardships than this to put up with in the Army.[41]

Tom had promised the electors of Maldon that he would vote only on subjects he knew about or cared strongly about. Hitherto, it had not seemed likely that female emancipation fell into either category. But he was learning fast. He even took to speaking on behalf of 'the farming community',[42] a breed that had previously been as alien to him as women, and holding forth on the problems of Essex poultry auctions.

He was in Bradwell most weekends, but it took him a while to conquer his aversion to the fête-opening and baby-kissing now expected of him. The first public ceremony he attended in Maldon was a parade of ATC cadets, at which – to his alarm – he had to take the salute. He was unsure how a hatless civilian was supposed to carry it off, but solved the problem by standing stiffly to attention and 'glaring piercingly at each saluter'.[43] He also found himself invited to an intimidating number of vegetable and allotment shows, the wartime equivalent of flower shows.

A year or two before the war Tom had overheard a conversation between two Tory MPs, in which one grumbled at having to go to his constituency. 'Oh Lord,' the other sympathised, 'what an awful bore.' 'Yes,' the first continued, 'and the worst of it is, I shall have to go there next year too.' Tom was always ready to criticise the remoteness of Conservative Members from the people who had sent them to Westminster. He thought of himself as a diligent constituency man, and so he was at first, but this was mainly because he happened to enjoy spending his weekends in the Bradwell peninsula anyway: he had chosen to live there long before he ever thought of standing for Parliament. Years later, as the Member for Barking, an unprepossessing corner of Greater London, he was notorious for the infrequency of his visits. 'When he was offered the Barking seat in 1959,' one friend recalled, 'Tom told me that the people there only expected him to come to one meeting a year.'[44] In Maldon, by contrast, he would visit several villages every Saturday – especially in summer, when he spoke from a soap-box on the village green – and then tour local pubs, meeting the people. Once a month he held a meeting at the Jubilee Hall in Maldon, which usually pulled an audience of 350 or more.

On the tenth anniversary of his election to Parliament, Tom wrote an article about an imaginary 'MP for South Barsetshire' who was clearly a vehicle for Tom's own feelings:

Whatever his motives for putting in a pretty non-stop performance as South Barsetshire's MP, the habit grows on him and his constituents; it is one of those habits that, once acquired, cannot easily be shaken off.

True, in his periods of extreme fatigue, he does sometimes glance wistfully at the politically 'safe' and geographically compact urban constituencies that many of his colleagues represent . . . The rural MP, if he is giving continuous service, has to work far harder, at the constituency end of the job, than the urban MP. The urban MP has his special problems – bad housing more intensely concentrated, industrial difficulties more acute; but his 50,000 electors can all be canvassed on foot, a cheap tram ride will take him from one end of his constituency to the other in ten minutes . . . whereas South Barsetshire's 50,000 people are scattered over 800 square miles of countryside, in fifty or sixty separate communities, none of more than 12,000 people, most of 300–500: communities vary widely in character and each is entitled, and now accustomed, to expect a visit and a speech every now and then from its MP.

So the rural MP sometimes wonders if he shouldn't, like a footballer, get a transfer . . . But then he goes to speak for a friend in Birmingham or Bradford, and his spirit is weighed down by the sheer ugliness of wet Sunday slate roofs and Victorian Gothic town halls and pretentious super-cinemas and the rest of the paraphernalia of private greed rampant; and he returns with relief to his serene market towns, his villages huddled about their great churches, his Dickensian rustic inns, his rolling farms, and his old fishermen sunning themselves on jetties.[45]

It was hard work nursing Maldon; expensive, too. He had some help from Jeannie Hunt, who had been his mother's housekeeper in Crowborough for many years, and was now installed in the same capacity in his little waterside cottage at Bradwell. His entire parliamentary salary – £600 – was used to finance a constituency office that his supporters had opened in Maldon High Street, but it seemed a fair price to pay for the exhilaration of having the letters 'MP' after his name. He lived off his wages from the *Express*, which were by now £44 18s. a week, plus 12 guineas guaranteed expenses.

Just seven months after his election to Parliament, however, Tom's political career nearly ended as suddenly as it had begun.

One of the first people to volunteer assistance at the Maldon by-election had been Tom Wintringham, who had commanded the British battalion of the International Brigade in Spain.[46] From a soap-box in Braintree market place he praised Tom as 'the fellow who could put across the Independent mind and his own natural point of view.' Tom was always punctilious in repaying debts of honour – debts of money were a different matter – so when Wintringham stood as an Independent in the North Midlothian by-election of 1943 it was natural that William Hickey, now also famous as the 'Member for Tobruk', should travel north to help. His presence guaranteed a full house at Wintringham's meeting in the Usher Hall, Edinburgh, on Friday 22 January, but was not quite enough to carry the candidate to a sensational victory: the Tory crept in by 11,620 votes to 10,751.

That visit to Edinburgh branded itself on Tom's memory nevertheless. After speaking at the Usher Hall he had what was, apart from his Old Bailey trial, 'the narrowest shave of my life':

I was walking along Princess Street towards my hotel. The war was still on and the whole city was blacked out. In such dim lighting as there was, one could just make out the forms of passers-by – and I bumped into a tall figure in a foreign naval uniform. One of us struck a match to light cigarettes. He was a Norwegian sailor, typically Scandinavian in appearance, flaxen-haired and smilingly attractive. He may have had a few drinks, too: he was eager for anything, and perhaps lonely. (Loneliness is as strong an incentive, often, as lust.) I recalled that there was an air-raid shelter under the gardens a few yards from where we were standing. Neither of us could speak the other's language, but he readily came down to the shelter with me. Down there it was completely dark, but another match showed a bench running along one side of the shelter. There was no air-raid, nor alarm, on at the time, so we were alone. In a matter of seconds he had slipped his trousers half-way down, and was sitting on the bench, leaning well back. We embraced and kissed, warmly enough, but my interest was concentrated lower down, on a long, uncircumcised, and tapering, but rock-hard erection; and I was soon on my knees.[47]

Not for long. Seconds later Tom was dazzled by the beam of a torch. 'Och, ye bastards,' a gruff Scottish voice called out, 'ye dirty pair o' whoors . . .' It was a young policeman. They were caught, as he said later, 'almost wet-handed'.

The constable wanted to march Tom – and his friend with the tapering organ – to the police station at once, but Tom insisted on first producing a card which revealed that the bearer was Tom Driberg, Member of Parliament, also known as William Hickey of the *Daily Express*. The officer was flabbergasted. '*William Hickey!* Good God, man, *I've read ye all of my life!* Every morning!' He told the Norwegian to vamoose ('Get awa' oot of it, ye bugger') and then, having introduced himself as PC George Crowford, allowed Tom to argue the case for not being charged. 'I lied to him as convincingly as I could,' Tom recalled, 'swearing that if he would let me off I would never do such a thing again.' More truthfully, Tom pointed out that his arrest would be tremendous propaganda for the Germans. A British politician arrested *in flagrante*: just imagine what Dr Goebbels and Lord Haw-Haw might make of that. Of course PC Crowford had to do his duty, but perhaps one should consider the national interest, too . . . Crowford was persuaded. After chatting for a few more minutes, mostly about the Hickey column, they parted as friends. Tom liked him, 'but judged that it would be going too far, in the circumstances, to make a pass'. A week or so later he sent Crowford an edition of William Blake and six guineas' worth of book tokens. 'I thought it thoroughly decent – and Scottish – of him not to pretend that this was a surreptitious gift, or bribe, in any way connected with the shelter incident.' Crowford replied on 10 March with a letter of thanks whose phrasing was as primly archaic as the copperplate hand in which it was written:

Dear Sir,

I feel it would be presumptuous of me to approach you in your friendly style of dedication, but I never the less remain sensible to your great compliment.

I confess, your recollection of me came as a very pleasant surprise; please accept my most sincere and grateful thanks for your kind letter and handsome gift. The book is invaluable in itself but I doubly esteem as a gift from you.

My knowledge of Blake is decidedly limited, but I anticipate the pleasure of perusing his work, and comparing it with that of Burns.

With the tokens, I obtained a History of the Borders, my native shire, also a work on the law of Scotland.

I am still ploughing the lonely furrow of a Constable, patiently awaiting the day I get my feet on the promotion ladder, which in the past has proved most elusive. I am prompted to solicit your assistance in this respect, by your generous offer, and which I trust you will not view in the light of impertinence.

Were I free to consult my own wishes I would be delighted and honoured avail myself [sic] of your invitation and visit the House of Commons and renew our conversation. I have many times regretted the brevity of our meeting, but I assure you that it will remain a cherished memory and I will always feel indebted to your generous pen and kindness.

One would hardly guess from this absurdly polite message that the meeting whose brevity Crowford regretted had begun while Tom still had his mouth wrapped round another man's penis.

Although shaken, Tom soon recovered his poise. He told the story of his Scottish escapade to friends at the Commons as if it were nothing more than an amusing diversion. One of them – he thought it was either Bob Boothby or Harold Nicolson – mentioned the incident some years later to Compton Mackenzie, who was inspired by it to write *Thin Ice*, a novel about a homosexual politician. Mackenzie's version differed from the original in a few details: the setting was Glasgow rather than Edinburgh, and the politician, Henry Fortescue, was a sixty-two-year-old Tory. But the most significant revision – which offended Tom deeply – was in the conclusion, as related by Fortescue to his heterosexual confidant George 'GeeGee' Gaymer:

I thanked him [the policeman] and put out my hand. He would not take it. 'You'll excuse me, Mr Fortescue,' he said, 'but I'd rather not shake hands with you. I'm not letting you go because of yourself but because I won't give that bugger of a Haw-Haw the chance to open his dirty mouth over the wireless. And you'll be taking my meaning if I say a gentleman like you ought to know better than give such trash the opportunity.' With that he turned back in the direction from which he had come, leaving me, I'll be frank, Geegee, considerably abashed.[48]

In fact, Tom and George Crowford had shaken hands warmly at the end of their strange encounter in Edinburgh. The constable had even given a brief salute.

Henry Fortescue in *Thin Ice* was clearly not a facsimile of the MP for Maldon, but Tom must have felt occasional twinges of recognition as he read the book. 'Thank God, I am completely masculine, and shall be able to pass for one of those Victorian women-haters,' Fortescue says, ruminating on his wifeless state. 'The poor devils who are half women have a much harder task than mine. And I am such a woman-hater that they are displeasing to me as woman herself.' Tom's misogyny, likewise, spilled over into a contempt for homosexuals who were 'camp' or 'queeny'. He liked his men masculine. A young soldier from the Black Watch, reclining on the pillow after sex with Tom one evening in February 1938, had delighted him by announcing, in a broad Scottish accent: 'Only sissies like women. Real men prefairr male flesh.'

Like every homosexual MP, Fortescue in *Thin Ice* has to live with the daily fear of exposure and disgrace. His solution, he tells Geegee, is celibacy. 'I sound very sure of myself,' he says, 'but don't think it's as easy as all that. There are many moments when I ask why I should deny myself what for me is the normal expression of human passion as if I were testing a vocation for the priesthood. Why shouldn't I enjoy myself? Is it worth while to forgo pleasure for the sake of an ambition which may never be achieved? Chastity for the sake of discretion seems to stink sometimes. Pleasure wasn't the word to use; it is the perpetual thwarting of curiosity which is so hard to withstand.' Couldn't he continue to satisfy his curiosity but be discreet about it? 'That's what I was intending to be, until I realised that for me discretion was impossible. It had to be complete self-denial, or complete surrender. And walking about for ever on thin ice does not appeal to me.'

Tom, by contrast, enjoyed the thrill of stepping nimbly across the frozen pond, always one pace ahead of the cracking ice; nor could he contemplate self-denial. But he shared Fortescue's anguish and rage at the system which forced a politician to make such choices. As he pointed out, Ministers could be involved in divorce actions, often as 'guilty' parties, without jeopardising their progress up the greasy pole; one remarried divorcee, Anthony Eden, even became Prime Minister 'and thus, ironically, became responsible for the appointment of the bishops of a church which does not recognise the right of the divorced to remarry in a former partner's lifetime'. But no homosexual MP – 'and there have been a few, again including Ministers' – could survive the shadow of public scandal.

Not that this deterred him. 'If anything, I became more promiscuous after my election to Parliament, relying on my new status to get me out of tight corners.' He was once caught cottaging in a gents' lavatory in Jockey's Fields, near High Holborn, by a policeman acting as an *agent provocateur* (a common technique: the young officers who act as bait are sometimes known as 'pretty police'). He warned the policeman and his colleague that any charge would be vigorously defended by the grandest counsel in the land, up to the House of Lords if necessary; questions would be asked in the Commons, too, about the use of entrapment. After a few minutes of these indignant fulminations the police decided that a conviction would be more trouble than it was worth.

Tom sometimes boasted to friends that he was immune from prosecution: no government would ever allow him to be exposed, he said dramatically, because he 'knew too much'. The implication was that if he were disgraced he would drag down other public figures; one name he mentioned in this connection was Deryk Heathcoat Amory, a mild-mannered bachelor on the Conservative benches who rose to be Chancellor of the Exchequer in the late 1950s. He never revealed quite what Heathcoat Amory was supposed to have done, and he may have been bluffing, but it was certainly true that Tom was as well informed about other MPs' sex-lives as they were about his. There was a strong and confiding *camaraderie* among some bisexual and homosexual Members. On his first day at Westminster Tom was shown round the Members' lavatories – 'the most important rooms' – by the rich and homosexual 'Chips' Channon, Conservative MP for Southend. It was 'an act of pure, disinterested, sisterly friendship, for we had no physical attraction for each other'.[49] Their tastes were indeed discrete: Tom was amazed when Channon confessed to a craving for Sir Hartley Shawcross, Attorney-General in the Attlee government. Tom admired Shawcross's forensic intellect but 'could not bring myself to see him, even remotely, as bedworthy'. He was more attracted to Channon's son Paul, who, many years later, wound up as a famously accident-prone Transport Secretary in Mrs Thatcher's Cabinet.

Chips Channon's wealth, Tom noted enviously in *Ruling Passions*, enabled him to rent any man he wanted, including a German prince and an English playwright. 'His seduction of the playwright was almost like the wooing of Danaë by Zeus: every day the playwright found, delivered to his door, a splendid present – a case of champagne, a huge pot of caviar, a Cartier cigarette-box in two kinds of gold . . . In the end, of course, he gave in, saying apologetically to his friends, "How can one *not*?"' Loyalty to Channon inhibited Tom from naming the playwright: in fact it was Terence Rattigan, who showed his gratitude for all the caviar and Cartier by dedicating his play *The Winslow Boy* to young Paul Channon.

Some of Tom's parliamentary confidants – Harold Nicolson and Bob Boothby and, much later, Jeremy Thorpe – had at least a streak of homosexuality themselves. But energetic heterosexuals would do almost as well. Woodrow Wyatt, who met Tom during the war, wrote that 'he treated me as an elder brother might.' Not all elder brothers would agree, having read the following Wyatt story:

Once, on a Friday afternoon, when the Commons was almost deserted, I had promised Tom and another MP to drive them to some conference we all had to address. Kept waiting by Tom so long that we might be late, the third MP, who had last seen Tom going into one of the Members' lavatories, went to shout for him. A quarter of an hour passed before Tom arrived, furious. 'You bloody fool,' he cried, 'I was having one of the chefs. Don't you realise a policeman patrols outside those lavatories? Once you started shouting my name he might have tried to find out why I was there so long. How were we to get out together?'[50]

John Freeman recalled that 'much of the scandalous material now known about [Tom] he told me – and others – shamelessly and, for all I know, candidly . . . In the purgatorial boredom of the House of Commons he could be a life-saver, and I for one enjoyed the entertainment that he was prepared to offer.'[51] Another heterosexual socialist with a strong sex-drive, Tony Crosland, was less willing to listen. Susan Crosland has described a weekend when Tony Crosland and Tom were both staying with Jack and Frances Donaldson in Gloucestershire:

On Sunday, while Driberg went round for a pre-lunch drink with Evelyn Waugh who'd been at school with him [and who was a neighbour of the Donaldsons], Tony said to Jack: 'How on earth am I to endure driving Tom all the way back to London? All he really wants to talk about is his squalid sex life.'

'Well, you can't leave him here,' said Jack.

Halfway through lunch, Tony leant down the table to Driberg. 'Tom, I must be setting off for London, but there's a train that goes at 4.15. I'm sure you'd rather not rush through your lunch, and Jack can take you to catch the train.' Driberg said that would be very nice. Tony waved and was off.[52]

Tom was only too happy to talk carelessly about his adventures in the rough trade, and yet he evaded Nemesis: to some conspiracy theorists this is conclusive proof of a sinister influence at work. According to Chapman Pincher, for instance, the security services must have shielded him: 'Driberg's long relationship with MI5 solves the mystery of why such a notorious homosexual, who was repeatedly caught in the act publicly by the police, was never successfully prosecuted, though the practices to which he admitted in his biography were then serious crimes.' But there is no such 'mystery'. At the Old Bailey trial, he armed himself with grand character witnesses and expensive barristers against a couple of penniless Scottish coal-miners. In the other two brushes with the law – Edinburgh and Jockey's Fields – he pulled rank. Contrary to Pincher's implication, only a few homosexual Members of Parliament were ever 'successfully prosecuted'. In 1941 a young Tory MP and Royal Artillery officer, Sir Paul Latham, was cashiered from the army and sentenced to two years' imprisonment for 'improper conduct' with fellow-gunners. (When he learned that one of the men had betrayed him he tried to kill himself by throwing himself off his motor-bike. The authorities showed their generosity by charging him with attempted suicide as well.) In January 1953 the Labour MP William Field was fined £15 and forced to resign from the Commons for 'soliciting or importuning for immoral purposes', after police acting as *agents provocateurs* arrested him in a West End lavatory. Six years later a Foreign Office Minister, Ian Harvey, was caught late one night in St James's Park with a guardsman of the Household Cavalry. He was charged only with a breach of park regulations and fined £5, but he still had to give up his parliamentary seat.

To point out that MPs were infrequently convicted is not to diminish the grim menace of a law that forbade *all* homosexual acts between consenting males, whether in private or in public and regardless of age. Under the neanderthal Home Secretaryship of Sir David Maxwell Fyfe in the early 1950s there was a spate of prosecutions and jailings of well-connected men – Lord Montagu of Beaulieu, his cousin Michael Pitt-Rivers, the journalist Peter Wildeblood, the novelist Rupert Croft-Cooke. No homosexual, however exalted his status, could ever feel safe from zealous law-enforcers. At his back Tom could always hear the crunch of the Edinburgh policeman's boots on the gravelled floor of the air-raid shelter, and the raucous echo of 'Och, ye bastards – ye dirty pair o' whoors.' It had been a nasty scare: if charges had been brought, not even Beaverbrook would have been able to keep the story out of the papers this time.

Not that Beaverbrook would have wanted to. His fondness for Tom had waned since the Maldon by-election: he grumbled that the Hickey column was becoming dull (which it was, since Tom inevitably filled it out with too many Westminster jottings) and that Tom was contaminating it with 'all this left-wing propaganda'. But it was what Tom said as a politician rather than what he wrote as a journalist that finally brought about his dismissal. At the *Express* office one Friday in June 1943 the paper's industrial correspondent, Trevor Evans, told Tom of a rumour that Sir Andrew Duncan, the Minister of Supply, was thinking of leaving the government to take up a £25,000-a-year job in private industry. Tom made his own inquiries and confirmed that it was true. The next day, at an open-air meeting in Braintree market square, he denounced Duncan for deserting the government at this stage of the war and for – in effect – selling his knowledge of war production secrets to the highest bidder. He made copies of the speech available to the Sunday papers, which duly splashed it across their front pages.

Christiansen knew the source of Tom's information at once. He had held Evans's story out of the *Daily Express* the previous week, ostensibly on the grounds that it required 'further checking'[53] but in fact to save the proprietor's embarrassment: for Sir Andrew Duncan's predecessor as Minister of Supply had been none other than Lord Beaverbrook, who had had no compunction about quitting the government and returning to his business interests at an awkward moment in the war. On the Monday morning Tom was summoned to Christiansen's office and fired there and then for 'using outside the office, for partisan political purposes, information which I had obtained, presumably in a confidential conversation, in the office'. As A. J. P. Taylor pointed out, however, 'the real reason of course was that Beaverbrook did not wish to offend Duncan, who regretfully had to remain in office.'[54] The ever-excitable Hannen Swaffer was indignant on Tom's behalf. 'Beaverbrook's action,' he wrote, 'has stopped yet another of his staff from printing, or uttering publicly, views not in accordance with the

policy of his newspapers.' But Beaverbrook told Tom that he had
had nothing to do with the sacking, and had opposed it. Christiansen, he implied, had been over-zealous in trying to anticipate his
master's wishes. 'Whatever the reason for the severance,' the
Spectator commented, 'the *Express* looks like being considerably
the poorer for it. Mr Driberg has been responsible for the past ten
years for the column signed William Hickey, and it has been much
better worth reading, in my judgment, than any similar column in
the daily Press . . . if the new Hickey succeeds in maintaining Mr
Driberg's level he will have achieved something considerable.'[55]

The *Express* gave Tom a £1,500 pay-off, equivalent to six
months' salary. He left without regret: he had been thinking of
resigning anyway. Within weeks he was signed up by *Reynolds
News*, the Sunday newspaper owned by the Co-operative movement, which seemed an altogether more congenial prospect. A
weekly rather than daily deadline would not interfere with his work
at Westminster. He assumed, too, that in a left-wing paper there
would be none of the political restrictions that had bedevilled him at
the *Express*. Bill Richardson, *Reynolds*'s editor, offered him a fee of
15 guineas per column and a written assurance that 'Contributors
to *Reynolds News* have freedom of expression within the broad
limits of the paper's Left Wing policy.'[56] Tom might have paused to
wonder why Richardson could not end the sentence after 'freedom
of expression'; how broad, exactly, were these limits? But he was so
glad to be demobbed from the Beaverbrook army that he didn't
press the point.

Meanwhile, back at the *Express*, Christiansen was in trouble.
George Malcolm Thomson had tried his hand at the William
Hickey column for a few weeks but had admitted defeat, returning
to his previous job in Beaverbrook's secretariat. Another Beaverbrook favourite, Paul Holt, was called back from his post as
Moscow correspondent to write Hickey; he gave up within a couple
of weeks and was sent back to Russia. By the time Christiansen
retired from editing the *Express*, fourteen years later, there had been
no fewer than twenty-three William Hickeys — only two of whom,
he said, were any good at all. Christiansen complained that Tom 'set
such a standard that it was a heart-breaking job trying to find a

successor for him'. After the abdication of first Thomson and then Holt, the editor swallowed his pride and asked Tom, rather shamefacedly, if he would like to return to the *Express*. Tom declined. An ecstatic Hannen Swaffer filled his weekly column in the *Leader* with the news, smugly declaring that it was 'Fleet Street at its best'. The affair showed 'not only the invariable friendliness in which Beaverbrook's staff work – what other firm would forget and forgive so quickly? – but high-mindedness on the part of Driberg, who has turned down a lucrative salary for the sake of a principle. Christiansen wanted him back whatever his opinions were. Tom, for fear that his freedom of opinion might be jeopardised, said "No", but in all friendship.'[57] Tom was not so high-minded, however, that he neglected to tell *Reynolds* about Christiansen's offer before refusing it. 'We can never compete with the *Express* in cash attraction,' Bill Richardson replied in some haste, 'but if it will affect your decision I am confident I can get authority to go beyond this £15.15.0.'

At the same time Tom was seeking other ways to make up the shortfall in his income. Kingsley Martin commissioned him to write a parliamentary column for the *New Statesman and Nation* under the pseudonym 'Pontifex'. He was hired by the BBC's European Service to deliver a commentary every Friday in the programme 'London Calling Europe'. Once again, however, his politics tripped him up. After fifteen consecutive weeks of his broadcasts, on the evening of Thursday 14 October he was suddenly telephoned by the BBC and told that he needn't turn up the next day, or ever again for that matter. No explanation was given, but he discovered that some right-wing politicians had taken exception to his recent transmissions, particularly one in which he argued that 'people in this country are determined not to tolerate anything savouring of a return to the pre-war years of mass unemployment.' He had also criticised the Italian leaders who were now lined up with Britain as co-belligerents. When the BBC refused to drop him, the complainants lobbied the Minister of Information, Brendan Bracken, who insisted that Tom be taken off the air. 'Right Wing Gets Radio Ban on MP' was the outraged headline in the *Daily Mirror*. The paper protested:

If the Right Wing have their way Driberg will stay off the air. It isn't only Driberg they object to – they don't like what they call the 'Left' tone of the European service in general.

There are millions of people in this country who agree with Driberg's views. But the Right Wing has said Driberg must go off the air.

A LOT OF PEOPLE ARE GOING TO ASK WHY THE RIGHT WING SHOULD DECIDE THE MATTER.[58]

This was not Tom's first run-in with the BBC. Earlier in the summer he and two other MPs had been invited on to the first programme of a series called *Everybody's Mike*, which they had been led to believe was some sort of brains trust. When they reached the studio and saw a script they discovered that it was, instead, a comedy show, performed in front of a giggling audience. Tom and his colleagues were to be asked a number of silly questions and would be 'gonged' every time they couldn't answer. Following a walk-out by the outraged parliamentarians, the programme was abandoned.

The ban on his European broadcasts meant that *Reynolds News* was able to introduce its new columnist with a flourish when he wrote his first weekly article on 24 October. The front page carried an eye-catching boxed item:

BANNED!

Tom Driberg is an Independent MP and the most brilliant columnist in British journalism.

His weekly commentary helped to make 'London Calling Europe' one of the most forceful features of the European News Service – till the other day Right-wing pressure in high quarters caused the BBC to put a ban on Driberg.

He was accused of telling listeners in Europe that the British people were not prepared to tolerate a return to the bad old days of mass unemployment.

But if, for the moment, Driberg is 'off the air', he speaks his mind freely in *Reynolds News*.

When Tom had first discussed it with Richardson they had planned to call his column 'Inside Left', to describe both its political alignment and its position in the paper (on page two, below the leader). But at the last moment they changed their minds and settled for a boldly unimaginative title which stuck for the next twenty years: 'Tom Driberg's Column'.

CHAPTER EIGHT

DISTANT TROUSERS

At dawn on 6 June 1944, under the command of General Eisenhower, the Allies invaded France. By midnight the same day, 75,000 British and 57,000 Americans had landed. By the end of July more than one and a half million troops had gone ashore on the Normandy beaches. And on 22 August, chugging across the Channel in an old ferry called the *Princess Josephine Charlotte*, came yet more reinforcements: 500 Guardsmen – Grenadier, Coldstream, Welsh – accompanied by the beaming, khaki-clad figure of Tom Driberg, war correspondent.

He had good reason to be cheerful. He loved the company of soldiers, and had spent an enjoyable night running his connoisseur's eye over the men who were asleep on deck – 'the brutish, the coltish, the vacant, the knowing, the spotted cherub, the dark horse, the hard-bitten, the joker'.[1] It was a pleasure, too, to set foot on foreign soil after such a long captivity in blacked-out Britain. 'There is still an intense and poignant thrill in seeing France again,' he wrote in *Reynolds News* that weekend, 'in sharing the glorious aftermath of a four-year-long resistance to tyranny, in driving on the right of the road past houses with narrow slatted white shutters and absurdly steep roofs, in drinking red wine outside one's tent in a Normandy orchard, in rediscovering the small daily delights of this ravaged but still hospitable country.' At the hotel where he stayed for the first week, the Lion d'Or in Bayeux, he basked in the luxury of not having to observe the black-out strictly, leaving his bedroom windows open and curtains only half-drawn as he crept to bed by the light of a solitary rationed candle.

From Bayeux he wangled a lift to Paris, which had been liberated a week earlier and was *en fête*. 'The Parisians still offer you, on slight provocation, a highly emotional welcome,' he cabled back. 'Nor does this seem either artificial or superficial: it is genuine and moving – the almost unbearably joyful reaction from four black years. Most of the few British uniforms in the streets are worn by war correspondents. Elderly gentlemen are apt to stop one and shake hands, with cries of "Tommy!" – which I find a trifle embarrassing.'[2] There was one manifestation of pro-British feelings which he omitted to mention in despatches: during his few days in the capital he successfully propositioned several young Parisians. Thus nourished, he set off to join the front-line Allied troops in Belgium.

'It means quite a chase,' he wrote in *Reynolds News*, 'to catch up with front lines that move forward so fast as those of the Allies in these last stupendous weeks.' Within a week of leaving Paris, however, he had not only caught the troops but overtaken them. At 5.30 in the afternoon of 8 September Tom and G. K. Hodenfield of the *Stars and Stripes* newspaper were engulfed by ecstatic, flower-throwing crowds as they drove their jeep into Liège, the third largest Belgian city, several hours before the first Allied soldiers arrived. The retreating Germans had only just fled, and in the hotel that had been used as the Gestapo HQ the beds were still warm. For years afterwards Tom boasted that 'I personally liberated Liège.' He and Hodenfield were taken to dinner in the house of a grateful citizen; while they ate, children singing 'It's a Long Way to Tipperary' hammered at the window and begged for autographs. At 9 o'clock Tom heard a BBC news bulletin which reported that Allied troops were 'pressing on a broad front towards Liège'.

His progress through Belgium was not all flowers and bunting. At Fort Eban-Emael, where a few Germans were holding out after the surrender of most of their comrades, a young Allied soldier stumbled into Tom and whispered, 'I think I'm hit'; five minutes later he was dead. Another day, Tom's jeep was near the head of a long column of tanks rolling through the green countryside near Liège in bright sunshine, when suddenly they were shot at by Germans in a wood 100 yards to the left. Tom leapt out and took cover beside the jeep while a couple of tanks 'dealt with the enemy in a satisfactorily punitive way'. A few minutes later a small white flag was waved above the hedge at the side of the wood.

We walked across a field to meet the Germans. Two were left dead in the wood. Three others were wounded. These set up a tremendous moaning and boo-hooing as soon as they saw us; one, a boy of about 17, was indeed badly hurt, but I had the impression that they were piling on the agony deliberately to excite sympathy . . . Their yells, their exaggerations of their plight, merely irritated some of the Yanks. 'Don't cry so b— much,' snapped a sergeant from Texas. 'You started the b— war anyway.'[3]

Tom originally thought that the Belgians were treating collaborators less severely than the French. He was soon disabused. In Brussels he saw a Rexist, newly tarred and feathered, his face covered in bruises, being dragged along the road. Even more gruesome was the Hogarthian scene at Antwerp Zoo, where collaborators and suspects were being detained in the lion-house. There were two cages full of women, one of whom carried a Pekinese dog; each of the other cages held half a dozen men or boys. 'They pace up and down as tho' they were the original tenants; or lounge against the thick bars which form the front of their cages, hats pulled over their eyes; or lie huddled apathetically on the loose straw which is their only furniture.' A pale, blond youth of twenty-three stretched his hands through the bars at Tom in supplication. He had only been a member of a Nazi organisation for two months, he said, and had joined because he was so poor – the pay was good and he got extra rations.

Tom was unsympathetic: his attitude to collaborators and Nazis was merciless. In one of his reports from France he mocked the 'genteel squeamishness' of a *Times* correspondent who, in describing the execution of six young militiamen at Grenoble, had written that the criminals 'did not seem to be particularly debased specimens, to judge from their names and parentage . . . They were of good birth and education.' This provoked a snort of Dribergian derision:

But of course they were. Why be surprised? The quislings, the friends of

Nazism and Fascism everywhere are always drawn mainly from among those 'of good birth and education'. To the lowly, the workers, the 'debased', falls merely the glory of having resisted and conquered.

I should not have enjoyed watching these executions any more than the *Times* man did; but I understand and approve them.[4]

In Britain, which had never been occupied by the enemy, few could empathise with such implacable hatred of those who collaborated with the invaders. In the summer of 1943 several friends of his had been 'slightly shocked' by his speech in a debate at Plymouth, organised by the US Army, on the question of bringing the Axis leaders to trial after the war. One side, led by Major Vyvyan Adams MP, argued that spectacular public trials would provide a historic, unforgettable lesson. For the opposition, Tom said that such trials would not take place; and even if they did, they would not have the desired effect. Justice ought to be summary: once the Axis leaders were captured they should be 'securely confined, perhaps in island fortresses, or, better, shot (preferably by people of their own nationalities)'.[5] He added that he would 'feel a good deal surer of a just fate for the Axis leaders if the Russians got the whole gang'. Even if Britain and the United States did organise show trials, he said, they would be unsatisfactory: the big industrialists who had financed the Nazis, and who were just as guilty, would not be put in the dock; rules of procedure and laws of evidence could not accommodate a multinational inquisition; there would be a risk of giving guilty men a martyr's platform. Finally, the defendants would not be allowed to call witnesses. Otherwise, the Nazi and Fascist leaders might summon in their defence those well-born appeasers in Britain who, by sins of omission or commission, had assisted and encouraged them right up to September 1939.

At this point in the debate there was a disturbance in the audience. Lady Astor, teetotal queen of the Cliveden set, rose from her seat to shout abuse and shake her fist at Tom. Vyvyan Adams, Tom's opponent, came to his aid at once by denouncing Chamberlain and Cliveden, much to Lady Astor's annoyance. The chairman of the Plymouth Tories, Sir William Munday, later accused Tom and Adams of trying to make 'party capital' out of a non-party occasion. Since Adams was Conservative and Tom was

Independent, it was not clear which party Munday thought they were making capital for.

In Belgium a year later, Tom watched approvingly as the resistance applied its own summary justice. One night in September 1944, sitting in a café in Brussels, he was engaged in conversation by a dull young man with a Résistance brassard on his arm and a Soviet emblem in his buttonhole. 'Suddenly and quietly, two men – a tall young one and a short older one – came in and stood by him. They exchanged a few words – and the younger hit him smartly on the chin, while the elder held a pistol to his chest. He cowered with his face to the wall, his hands up, while they went through his pockets. They found that he had no right to be wearing the brassard. He had been recognised as a Rexist, they said. They took him away.'[6]

The Allied advance was gathering pace. On 17 September Tom rode with the British troops as they broke out of their bridgehead on the Escaut canal and swept through into Holland to try to join the paratroops who were landing – disastrously – at Arnhem. The road was ambushed on either side by Germans in the woods, who in turn were bombarded by British Typhoons. Tom noticed that the local cows, peacefully chewing the cud, seemed oblivious to the shelling – but every so often one would suddenly tip over and fall grotesquely dead. Pigs were wiser: whenever the noise started they would jump clumsily down into the slit-trenches. 'It is disconcerting,' he wrote, 'to find one in a trench beside you.' Leaving the convoy of tanks for a while, Tom walked through a plantation of young fir trees that had been splintered by a Typhoon attack. 'By the path lay a young English officer, his left arm torn out, his head battered,' he reported. 'A German sniper a few yards away seemed to have been killed by blast; his uniform was in shreds, his body curled up in horrible contortion, his greenish fingers clutching the air stiffly.'

There were many such scenes as the British and American forces pressed on towards Germany during the following winter. Tom flew back to London soon after Arnhem, but seven months later he returned to the Continent to witness a far ghastlier horror. 'It is easy to use words like "unforgettable" and "incredible",' he wrote more than thirty years afterwards. 'I simply know that of all the experiences of my life – and there have been some unpleasant and beastly ones – this was by far the worst.'[7] Its name was Buchenwald.

On Wednesday 18 April 1945 Eisenhower telephoned Churchill to reveal that his troops had just entered the concentration camp of Ohrdruf, near Gotha, and had discovered thousands of emaciated corpses of Jews, Polish slave labourers and Russian PoWs. The next morning a British officer, General Bedell-Smith, sent another message to Churchill: 'The Germany concentration camps which have recently been over-run by the Allied armies are even indescribably more horrible than those about which General Eisenhower spoke to you yesterday and of which photographs have appeared in the press today.'[8] One of the newly liberated camps, Buchenwald, was 'the acme of atrocity'.

At Eisenhower's suggestion, Churchill agreed to send a parliamentary team from Britain to inspect it at once. (An American delegation, Eisenhower had explained, 'might be too late to see the full horrors, whereas an English delegation, being so much closer, could get there in time'.) That afternoon, Churchill delivered a statement to the House of Commons. The camps, he said, 'far surpass anything previously exposed'. He proposed to send eight MPs and two peers to visit 'these gruesome scenes' and find out the truth. Members who wished to volunteer for 'this extremely unpleasant but none the less necessary duty' were asked to give their names to the party whips by the end of the afternoon. The delegation, representative of all parties and selected 'by the usual methods', would depart the very next day.

There were many volunteers; but Eisenhower had specifically asked Churchill to include a journalist or two in the party, so Tom was one of the ten parliamentarians who took off from London in an RAF Dakota on the afternoon of Friday 20 April. After spending the night in France they flew with Eisenhower to Weimar in the morning. From there it was fifteen minutes' drive to Buchenwald, along a neat road lined with fruit-trees in blossom and up into pine-clad hill country.

The peaceful, sylvan setting was hideously at odds with the carnage inside the gates. Although the Americans had been cleaning the camp for more than a week, the squalor was still overwhelming. Many of the survivors were unable to speak, lying in a semi-coma or following the MPs with unblinking eyes; others talked freely, displaying their scars and sores and bruises. 'All of them,' Tom wrote in the delegation's official report, 'were in a state of extreme emaciation. We were told by the US authorities that, since their arrival, the number of deaths had been reduced from about a hundred per day to thirty-five on the day before our visit. The usual clothing was a ragged shirt, vest or cotton jacket, beneath which protruded thighs no thicker than normal wrists. One half-naked skeleton, tottering painfully along the passage as though on stilts, drew himself up when he saw our party, smiled, and saluted.'[9] Tom was impressed by the calm of the one woman in the group, the Tory MP Mavis Tate, as she studied dead prisoners who were stacked on a cart. But beneath her *sangfroid* she was convulsed by grief; she died only two years later, and it was commonly said that she had never recovered from the shock of Buchenwald.

Before going to Germany, Tom had been frankly sceptical of some of the 'atrocity stories' that he had heard. 'I was doubtful, in particular, about those lamp shades said to have been made of human skin for the Nazi Commandant's wife, Frau Koch.' But, he added, 'having examined all the available evidence, visual and spoken, as carefully as possible, I feel obliged to accept even this fantastic horror.' He brought back with him a leather knife-pouch and part of a framed picture which looked like tattooed skin from a man's chest, on which nipples were clearly visible. These samples were sent to the government pathologist, Sir Bernard Spilsbury, who confirmed in a letter to Tom that both were indeed human skin. 'Frau Koch, I was told, was always quite nice and ladylike about this business,' Tom wrote. 'She would never let them stage actual parades of tattooed men. However, if one of the doctors or guards happened to notice a prisoner with a good specimen of tattooing, they would mark him down and later kill him (painlessly, with an injection).'

The official report was presented to Parliament and published within a week of the delegation's return. Tom also described the visit for *Reynolds News*, which trailed the article on its front page with a photograph of him talking to bed-ridden survivors, and a headline promising 'The Most Horrifying Story of the War':

Worse than any sight or sound was the smell that overhung the whole place, even after a week's intensive cleaning-up: a stuffy, sweetish-sour smell, not unlike the ordinary prison smell plus death and decay; a stench, compounded of excrement, dirty blankets, disinfectant and decomposing flesh, which seemed to seep pervadingly into every channel of our heads and cranny of our clothing and to linger in everything that one took away from the camp.

It may be partly my imagination, but this odour still permeates, for instance, a small document folded inside my notebook: opening it just now, I caught the smell; it rose up physically from the notebook to hit me, and at once I was back in the fearful gloom and squalor of Buchenwald. I think that carrion stink will always haunt me.[10]

It was, he said, not easy to eat the rather high Hamburger steaks that were served for dinner in the delegation's hotel that night.

The war in Europe was all but over. A week after the mission to Buchenwald, Hitler committed suicide in his Berlin bunker; and a fortnight after that London was celebrating VE Day. Tom roamed central London throughout 'The Day', watching people try to persuade themselves that they were now at peace. On the pavement in the Strand a buxom woman wearing an apron of Union Flags and a respectable-looking middle-class man whirled round in an exaggeratedly Latin-American dance while a passing accordionist played 'South of the Border'. As Tom picked his way down Coventry Street, he started guiltily when he heard a woman's cheerful yell: 'MPs – ye're off-duty tonight!' He then noticed that she was addressing two Military Police. But beneath the revellers' uproarious whoops Tom detected a desperate melancholy; there were ghosts on every corner. As dawn broke over streets strewn with torn paper flags and crushed ice-cream cornets, he saw a drunken and bleeding Canadian roll clumsily into the gutter. A cold voice was saying: 'There's a peace on.'

One of the first consequences of the peace was that he acquired a new secretary. Rosemary Say was, in her words, 'a nice middle-class gel', aged twenty-six, who had had an adventurous war working for the Special Operations Executive, the secret department that had been created in 1940 to organise subversion and sabotage in Occupied Europe. Arrested in Paris in December 1940, she had been interned for a year in Besançon and Vittel before escaping to Marseilles and making her way back to England through Spain and Portugal. When the war in Europe ended, Say and her colleagues were told to look for jobs elsewhere.

She was introduced to Tom by a mutual friend, the newspaper columnist Ian Mackay (whom she later married). Since Tom was without a secretary at the time he might have been expected to snap up a gel with such an impressive *curriculum vitae*. But he appeared strangely cautious. 'He went to John Rayner and got him to clear me through MI5,' Say recalled. (Rayner says he has no recollection of doing any such thing.) She concluded that Tom was playing a rather tiresome game with her. He hired her anyway.

Say installed herself in Tom's office in June 1945, and stayed for three years. She had a high regard for him as an 'incorruptible and painstaking' MP – in spite of his tendency to disappear to Prunier's restaurant for hours on end – but their relations were sometimes tempestuous. Tom could seldom endure any woman's company for long without becoming irritable. He was furious when he discovered that she and Jo Richardson, Ian Mikardo's secretary, were trying to unionise their colleagues in order to press for higher wages. He stormed into the office. 'Now look what you've done!' he yelled. 'You've really made a balls-up, Rosie. Some Labour MPs can't afford these pay rises, you idiot!'

One of her duties was to accompany him every Saturday morning to the *Reynolds News* office, near the ear-nose-and-throat hospital in Grays Inn Road, where she had to type his column. 'Sometimes he'd already written it, but sometimes he wouldn't start writing it until 10 on the Saturday morning – he was really impossible,' she said. He fussed endlessly over the tiniest details of his column. 'The printers would be screaming as he looked at his proof and said "Perhaps if I put this semi-colon here . . ."' He was, as all his secretaries discovered, a stickler for semi-colons.

In 1948, Say applied for – and got – a job as an editorial assistant at the *New Statesman*. Tom, who was in Jamaica when he heard the news, took umbrage. The letter he sent her from Kingston is a glorious specimen of the tetchy, cold self-pity that seized him whenever he was inconvenienced by people who were supposed to be serving him, whether cab-drivers or wine-waiters or secretaries:

Naturally I would not wish to prevent you from bettering yourself.

As you will have learned by now, I am *not* coming back the weekend before Parliament resumes; nor could I possibly now arrange to do so, even if I felt that I should. I take it that you start your new work full-time on November 8th. It seems to me quite essential that you should be available to me, at any rate part-time, during the week of my return (i.e. from the 1st to the 6th). There will be many details to discuss. I cannot believe that it should be very difficult to master the editorial routine of a periodical of the character of the *New Statesman and Nation*. A great deal must clearly be left to *ad hoc* last-minute indecision.

You will find it interesting and agreeable to work for Mr Martin; and you should have the opportunity of seeing a good deal more of Miss Woodman. [Kingsley Martin was editor of the *NS&N*; he lived with Dorothy Woodman.]

Several ladies are to be available for interview during the week of my return. I will choose your successor from among them. Please arrange this. By all means let Miss Gollancz be one of the candidates, if her shorthand and typing are of the first order; but I should not care for it if she were too earnest and hairy.

You had better advertise at once. Possibly the *New Statesman & Nation* would allow some discount on such an advertisement, in view of their somewhat sharp conduct in buying your services away during my absence abroad. The advertisement should be on some such lines as these (with any other necessary details): 'Labour MP needs secretary at once. Odd hours but long holidays. Must be imperturbable and able to use semicolons correctly . . . Write Box –'

I do not fully understand the final paragraph of your note. It bears traces of having been written in a flurry.

I wonder if W. Wyatt has had anything to do with this transfer.

Tom told Say that her departure was 'unforgivable bad manners'. But he did forgive her, and she him; twenty years later they wrote a book together.

Within days of Rosemary Say's hiring in June 1945 a General Election was called, and her new employer was forced to think seriously for the first time about his future. Since Oxford he had been borne along – on to the *Express*, into Parliament – by opportunity and chance. 'I never like using the word "career" of myself,' he wrote. 'I don't think I have had one, if the word implies an evolving pattern directed, perhaps by ambition, to a planned and foreseeable climax.' But now he had to look ahead. Friends on the Labour benches such as Ellen Wilkinson and John Parker urged him to join them, pointing out that few Independent MPs could expect to survive the end of the party truce. He dipped a toe in the water by becoming a member of the Fabian Society.

The Maldon Constituency Labour Party was in a quandary. It already had a prospective candidate, Morris Janis, but since his adoption he had been taken prisoner by the Japanese. As soon as the election was called, the General Management Committee met to discuss the problem. Some members wanted to persevere with Janis in the hope that he would be released from his PoW camp in the next week or so; some even believed that he should stand *in absentia* (though he would have been disqualified for not signing his nomination papers). But most preferred the obvious solution. Tom had worked hard during his three years in the House; his reputation in the constituency was good; he had all the advantages of incumbency; and, best of all, he was not languishing in a prison camp on the other side of the world. They argued for his immediate adoption. There was just one snag, as Tom revealed to the meeting: 'even at that late date, I did not particularly *want* to join the Labour Party.' He had not conquered his youthful impatience with Labour's clotted, *bourgeois*, 'middle-stump' moderation, and he told the committee that he would prefer to stand as an Independent with their support. The apparatchiks gawped at his innocence. Did he really think that a local Labour party would contemplate such an arrangement? He was soon put right. They liked him, but if he did not stand under Labour's flag he could expect no help at all. Tom hastily revised his position: with many an expression of gratitude and humility he said that *of course* he would be only too happy to accept the Labour nomination. He was given an application form for membership and thereby 'became, probably, the only Labour MP who had actually joined the party at his adoption meeting'.

It was a hectic campaign. The bitterness of the national elec-
tioneering – hysterical rants in the Conservative press, warnings
from Churchill of a socialist Gestapo – infected Maldon, and on
more than one occasion Tom denounced his Tory opponent, Major
Melford Stevenson, as a liar. 'It is always slightly shocking,' he
piously informed his readers in *Reynolds News*, 'to find that people
whom one knows personally – and would have said, offhand, were
fairly decent, upright, responsible citizens – will stoop to any lie to
catch a few votes.' Stevenson was a young, reactionary barrister,
notorious many years later as an old, reactionary judge. 'We gave
him hell!' Rosemary Say recalled. 'We put salt and sand in his car,
and did all those junior common room things.'[11] George Bernard
Shaw again sent Tom a message of support; other friends and
admirers made the pilgrimage to Essex – including John Arlott,
who delighted Tom by being both a policeman and a poet. The one
agony of the campaign was that it coincided with the height of
the hay fever season, so Tom's flights of oratory at village-green
meetings often crashed to earth in paroxysms of sneezing. (He
suffered loudly from hay fever, once claiming that the best summers
of his youth 'were ruined for me by this infuriating allergy, which
attracts little sympathy from those not affected by it'. In the
mid-1950s an ear-nose-and-throat man cured him permanently
with cautery – a whiff of anaesthetic cocaine up the nostrils
followed by a red-hot wire to seal off the nasal nerve ends. No pain,
and no more sneezes.)

The result was not declared until 26 July, three weeks after
polling day, to allow time for the forces' vote to be freighted back
from distant theatres of war. Tom's victory over the egregious
Melford Stevenson was no surprise, though the majority of 7,727
was gratifyingly robust. But the national verdict was better than
even the most confident Socialist could have expected. In the
new House of Commons Labour had an overall majority of
146 seats.

'The next Parliament,' Tom had written at the time of the
dissolution, in June, 'could be, literally, epoch-making: it could
inaugurate the Socialist epoch in Britain. It is for the electors to
decide. It is to be hoped that they will decide overwhelmingly for

Labour: a blurred, fifty-fifty result, leading to an unstable government, would in some ways be worst of all.'[12] He had his wish. Was this, then, the Socialist epoch? He thought again of the cheerful soldiers he had met on the evening of VE Day in Charing Cross Road. One had had a red flag; another – an RAF sergeant and navigator – wrote on it in ink: '"We will now proceed to the establishment of socialism" – Lenin, 1917.'

In fact, as he wrote nearly thirty years later, we did no such thing: 'it was too much to expect of the mild "Toynbee Hall Socialism" of Attlee and the other moderate and war-exhausted Labour leaders.' His verdict on the Attlee government, with hindsight, was disdainful:

There were some benign reforms, the establishment of a fairer system of social security, the (unavoidable) dismantlement of the Empire, and the transfer of some – mostly run-down and unprofitable – industries to the care of bureaucratically run public corporations, with excessive compensation to the former private owners. But there was no fundamental or lasting change in the economic or social structure of Britain.[13]

In spite of his lofty attitude, Tom managed to work up some excitement occasionally: at the end of the Second Reading debate on the bill to take the coal mines into public ownership, for instance, he was moved to see old miners trooping through the lobby in tears, and to hear them burst into spontaneous renditions of 'The Red Flag' and 'Cwm Rhondda'. But most of the time he was curiously detached: he approved of the nationalisation of coal and railways, or the creation of the National Health Service, as a mildly interested observer rather than a committed participant. 'The whole bloody business bored him,'[14] was Ian Mikardo's conclusion. Britain in the age of austerity was too dull; Labour's reforms were all too mechanical, too corporatist, to engage Tom's passion. During the late 1940s and early 1950s he looked abroad for excitement, to lands where wars were still being fought, empires were collapsing, blood was being spilt. Fleeing the country to escape the Attlee government was what wealthy landowners or characters in Evelyn Waugh novels were supposed to do, but Tom was poised for flight even as the election results were announced. He had heard from

Frank Owen, who was out in the Far East editing *SEAC* (the South-East Asia Command newspaper), that the troops in Burma felt themselves to be 'a forgotten army' now that Europe was at peace. Someone, Owen said, ought to go and report their struggle. On 30 July, only four days after being returned at Maldon, Tom wrote to the Supreme Allied Commander in South-East Asia, Lord Mountbatten:

I am presuming on a very slight acquaintance; you were good enough one night, a year or two ago, to drive me from Claridge's to the corner of Tottenham Court Road.

When Frank Owen was home a few months ago he urged strongly that I ought, as a Member of Parliament and a journalist, to visit SEAC. The long summer recess of Parliament seems to provide a suitable opportunity, and I am already making arrangements for such a visit. I shall go as a war correspondent on behalf of the newspaper for which I now work, *Reynolds News* – the only Sunday Labour paper. In the rather limited time available, I am anxious to visit as forward an area as possible.

Mountbatten was unreceptive to the suggestion. But Mike Wardell, his Assistant Deputy Chief of Staff responsible for information, urged him to make Tom welcome, not least because of the strong recommendation from Frank Owen.

Mountbatten was later thankful that he heeded this advice: he and Tom hit it off at once and discovered that they had much in common, including a sexual preference for men. ('Have you seen Dr Kinsey's fascinating book on the sex-life of the American male?' Tom asked him excitedly in 1948.) Mountbatten was a royalist and snob who nevertheless held left-wing views; Tom was a left-winger who nevertheless loved the monarchy. Both were treated with suspicion by their *confrères* because of these heresies, but with each other they could talk freely. In the years to come Mountbatten found Tom a useful conduit for passing on 'guidance' to newspapers and politicians. He also convinced himself, eccentrically, that Tom was a reliable barometer of public opinion. In 1946, when his nephew Philip was about to be engaged to Princess Elizabeth, Mountbatten suggested that Tom could pre-empt any xenophobic or republican rhetoric from Labour MPs by inviting some of them – John Freeman, Donald Bruce, Maurice Edelman – to lunch with the

Prince at the Commons. 'Thank you for being so kind to my nephew Philip,' Mountbatten wrote afterwards. 'He was tremendously thrilled with his day in the House, and very favourably impressed by you. It is most kind of you to say that you will help to give the right line in the Press when the news of his naturalisation is announced.'[15] After his appointment as the last Viceroy of India in January 1947, Mountbatten was preoccupied with negotiations in New Delhi and depended even more strongly on Tom to ensure that the press followed 'the right line' on the subject of his nephew. Tom whispered to left-wingers that they should not make a fuss about the betrothal, since Prince Philip was (hush hush, keep it under your hat) something of a socialist himself. 'I was agreeably surprised,' Mountbatten wrote from New Delhi on 28 July 1947,

to find that only the *Daily Worker* appeared to condemn my nephew's engagement on political grounds. Even if they knew the truth about him, I feel it would be too good a propaganda point for them to pass up altogether. I am so grateful to you for telling people the truth about him. As you know, I am an ardent believer in constitutional monarchy as a means of producing rapid evolution without actual revolution, but only if monarchy is wisely handled. I am sure that Philip will not let the side down in this respect.[16]

But Tom warned Mountbatten that there were growls of discontent in the Labour Party at the amount of money being spent on the royal wedding, and at the suggestion that Philip might be paid an allowance. On 3 August, less than a fortnight before Indian independence, Mountbatten found the time to write a long letter from the Viceroy's House providing arguments to deploy against the grumblers:

Thank you for sticking up for my nephew Philip among the infantile-Leftist readers of *Reynolds News* who do not understand the position. I am passing on to him your remarks about the substantial minority feeling against lavish allowances to him on marriage and the expensive use of scarce materials for the wedding. You can rest assured that he thoroughly understands this problem and indeed he spoke to me about it when I was home in May. I am sure he is entirely on the side of cutting down the display of the wedding, and his own personal feelings are against receiving any civil list for the very reasons which you give. I, however, have persuaded him that it is essential he should take something, for reasons which I will now explain.

As you know, the present dynasty in Greece was founded by King George I, brother of Queen Alexandra and younger son of the King of Denmark. The Danish Royal Family was by no means rich enough to endow a younger son with personal riches and wealth on taking up the Crown of Greece. Any small property the family were able to acquire in Greece from personal means was largely destroyed and swallowed up in the many revolutions and periods of exile. The Civil List salary of a Prince in Greece was never very big; and any rights that Philip may have had to a Greek Civil List, he renounced together with his rights of succession in 1944. To my certain knowledge his private means are very small and he is almost entirely dependent on his Naval pay which is slightly under £1 a day and after tax is paid I do not suppose amounts to as much as £300 a year.

His tiny little two-seater made a big hole in his private fortune, and except when travelling on an officer's warrant he usually goes Third-class by train. He has no complaints; he is very happy on his present Naval pay and could quite well manage as a bachelor with no official standing. As a future Prince Consort, however, I think you will agree that Third-class travel would be regarded as a stunt and a sixpenny tip to a porter as stingy. If he is to devote much of his time to public duties, then I submit the public must at least find the means to enable him to carry these duties out. He can not and should not spend his entire time merely accompanying his wife. I know he intends to go on serving in the Navy, and he is bound on many occasions to be separated from her and still carrying out public duties. What is he to do? Borrow money from his wife to pay for the hire of a car to go and open a War Memorial at Plymouth?

Be reasonable Tom, he cannot possibly uphold the dignity of this nation on £300 a year any more than the Prime Minister was able to uphold the dignity of his office on £10,000 a year! Mr Attlee had to have a very large tax-free allowance for expenses; and what I know is in Philip's mind is to ask for his expenses and either no Civil List salary or a comparatively small one.

It really amounts to this: you have either got to give up the Monarchy or give the wretched people who have to carry out the functions of the Crown enough money to be able to do it with the same dignity at least as the Prime Minister or Lord Mayor of London is afforded.

On second thoughts I am going to send a copy of your remarks, as well as a copy of my reply, to Philip, so that he may know what has passed between us. He realises that you are a well-wisher and represent a very important point of view in the country. But I simply cannot advise him to try and do the job on the pay of a Naval officer. He would be letting down his future wife and the whole institution of monarchy.

It is better to be criticised severely at the time of the announcement of an allowance than to spend the rest of your time being criticised for being mean and stingy and incapable of carrying out your duties except by sponging directly on your wife.[16]

Tom's apologias for the royal family sometimes landed him in trouble: a gushing article he wrote for *Reynolds News* to celebrate Elizabeth II's coronation in 1953, for instance, provoked many indignant letters. When he did make a mild republican gesture, by not supporting higher allowances for Princess Elizabeth and her new husband after their wedding, he hastened to reassure Mountbatten that he hadn't meant it:

I hope that you were not shocked (if you noticed it, which you probably didn't) by the fact that I was one of the majority of back-bench Labour MPs who voted for the 'token' lower figure for the Royal allowances. This was certainly not (except in a small minority of individuals) a veiled dig at the Monarchy. It was largely – and this you may not have heard, since it could never be published – the result of an extraordinary incident inside the Select Committee that considered the allowances: a disagreement caused by an emotional caprice of Churchill's which led to the abandonment of a position that had hitherto been agreed on unanimously.[17]

But it would be wrong to think that Tom's posture in his dealings with Mountbatten was one of nervous genuflection. He was not afraid to offer forthright advice (as when he complained that 'Princess Elizabeth and your nephew are still fairly solidly beset by old-guard Right-wing advisers') and uninhibited gossip. Once he even dared to publish a critical character analysis, in which he argued that Mountbatten lacked a 'fully developed humanity', seeing people as machines. 'I do not know if he is capable of compassion,' Tom wrote, 'or if he would recognise the innately equal value and rights of an unsuccessful or "useless" or warped human being.' Mountbatten seems not to have taken offence. As he exclaimed after Tom's visit to South-East Asia Command in 1945, 'I shall never cease to bless the day when Mike Wardell persuaded me to break my rule about MPs-cum-war-correspondents!'[18]

When Tom originally wrote to Mountbatten, in July 1945, he assumed that the war in the Far East would drag on for many months. But on 6 August and 9 August the atom bombs were dropped on Hiroshima and Nagasaki, and by the time Tom arrived in Asia a month later 'a kind of peace was breaking out'. His flight from England to Ceylon was a bumpy ordeal, in a York freighter plane with no seats: for two and a half days he and his six fellow-passengers sprawled as best they could on and around the cargo, which was mostly Red Cross packages for India. But as soon as they reached Ceylon, tempers mended magically: Mountbatten had sent his private aircraft — a superbly furnished, white-leather-padded Dakota — to carry them from Colombo to the Supreme Commander's HQ at Kandy.

Tom was almost immediately recruited as an unofficial adviser. On 6 September Mountbatten asked him to sit in on a meeting with seven members of the Patriotic Burmese Forces, which had been formed by the Japanese and had come over to the Allied side only in March 1945.[19] The British authorities were having difficulty persuading the PBF to disband and enrol in the regular Burma Army, and Mountbatten hoped that Tom might be a conciliatory influence. This proved rather optimistic. The meeting had some lasting value, however, since it introduced Tom to the founder of the PBF, General Aung San ('the Tito of Burma'), who impressed him deeply: 'unlike some of the older Burmese politicians, honest and incorruptible; a slight, boyish figure with a surprisingly strong, deep voice; physically and mentally agile, with an irrepressible sense of humour and a gift for cynical wisecracking which he exercised impartially at the expense of his Burmese friends and of the British.'[20] This first encounter with Aung San inspired Tom's lonely but tenacious campaign for Burmese independence, which he waged in Parliament over the next two years against the indifference of Attlee and the hostility of Churchill. Only Mountbatten's intervention eventually forced Attlee to set a date for the transfer of power, in 1948. Aung San did not live to see it: in 1947 he was assassinated, mown down by a machine-gun at a political meeting.

A few years later the government in Rangoon decided to confer honours on Mountbatten and the few Labour backbenchers who had championed the cause of independence for Burma, including Tom. The awards were to be presented by the Burmese ambassador at a reception in London, but at the last moment (so Tom claimed) 'their embassy was advised through diplomatic channels that, as a routine courtesy, their list of honorands should first be shown to the Foreign Office: they were surprised, but I was not, when the list was returned with the backbenchers' names struck out.'

Having met the resistance leaders in Kandy, Tom saw them a month later on home territory in Rangoon, when Mountbatten stopped there on his way to the Japanese surrender ceremony in Singapore. Aung San invited Tom to join him on the platform at a Labour rally attended by 10,000 working-class Burmans. 'His presence and his speech stirred the crowd to fervent enthusiasm,' Tom reported. 'He is unmistakably (as I know from other evidence as well) the popular hero of Burma.' But he was no hero to the old ruling class. At a victory dinner given in Rangoon's Orient Club, Tom and Mountbatten were outraged to discover that the elder statesmen of Burma had placed themselves at the top table while relegating Aung San to a seat in a far corner of the room and omitting him from the list of after-dinner speakers. Mountbatten told his hosts that he would not deliver his speech unless Aung San was called to speak too. 'This,' Tom wrote, 'was where I first appreciated Mountbatten's political acumen and his understanding of the new nationalist forces rising in Asia.'

Tom also noticed Mountbatten's ability to win the respect of newly liberated prisoners in Japanese PoW camps, many of whom were in bloody-minded mood and might have resented yet another visit by a brass-hat. At the Changi jail-camp in Singapore Tom was waylaid by four prisoners who had produced the handwritten 'camp magazine', *Exile*. One of them was a man named Paul Miller, whom he had known in London before the war; another was the artist Ronald Searle. Only one copy of each issue had been produced, because of the lack of paper, but it had been passed from hand to hand and was obviously a documentary record of potential importance:

I asked Mountbatten to come over and look at it, and introduced Miller, Searle and the others to him. I then said, a bit diffidently: 'D'you think we could take them back for a talk to Government House [where we were staying]? It looks as if there'd be some interesting material for me in this.' He said instantly: 'Tell them to get into the second jeep and follow along – yes, all four of them.'

A little later we drove back to Government House. In one of the vehicles in the Supremo's cortège rode four ragged, jail-worn prisoners (none of them an officer). It is typical of Mountbatten that, when we got to Government House, there was no question at all of segregating them. On the contrary, after drinks – the best and strongest rum cocktails – he invited them to stay to dinner. Even so soon after the war, dinner at Government House was once more a glittering formal ceremony. Mountbatten and the other men wore white mess-kit, with acres of medal-ribbons; Lady Louis wore a superb evening dress. There must have been fifty at the long table, mostly major-generals and brigadiers. Mountbatten sat half-way along the table, his wife opposite him; and he put the four men from Changi, unkempt as they were, in the places of honour on either side of her and of himself. Nor did they feel at all embarrassed, as anybody might have: both host and hostess put themselves out to put them at their ease, and no one knows better than they how to do that.[21]

When he mentioned this incident in *Reynolds News* he had a letter from Kaye Webb, acting editor of *Lilliput* magazine (to which Ronald Searle had contributed before the war), asking for more news of the artist. He put them in touch, and not long afterwards they married.

Tom himself missed the dinner for Searle and the *Exile* team; after cocktails he had to excuse himself to keep an engagement with another prisoner, the remarkable Dr Leonard Wilson, Anglican Bishop of Singapore. Wilson had been interned in March 1943, a year after the fall of Singapore, when the Japanese quite suddenly decided that he was the kingpin of an espionage and sabotage organisation. He had then been tortured for eight months. Wilson asked Tom not to write about him as a hero or martyr 'or anything like that', but it was impossible to comply. Wilson's story, Tom explained in *Reynolds News*, did not lend itself to any other treatment:

He described to me in detail his first three days of interrogation.

On the first night he had to kneel and was beaten about the shoulders for the space of two hours, 'but not severely'.

On the second day he had to kneel for a longer time, under a table, his hands strapped behind him and a triangular, sharp-edged rod fixed in behind his knees; the Japanese stamped and jumped repeatedly on his thighs, on which scars still show lividly.

On the third day he lay strapped on a table, face upwards, head hanging down over the end of the table. For many hours on end, guards in relays – seven men in all – flogged him from the waist downwards with threefold ropes. When he fainted they revived him and continued flogging. 'Naturally,' he says, almost casually, 'I was a complete wreck for days afterwards.'[22]

Wilson had often cried out in pain, but even at his worst moments had never cursed his torturers. This puzzled them. 'All the others swear at us,' they said. 'Why don't you?' He explained that, in spite of appearances, he believed them to be God's children. When telling the story to Tom, Wilson deflated the excessive piety of this remark by adding that 'I was a little sarcastic about it.'

Before leaving Asia, Tom visited Saigon. For years afterwards he boasted that on this brief stop-over he 'nearly prevented the Vietnam War' – which, like his claim to have liberated Liège, was a rather imaginative interpretation of his own part in events. What happened was this. Much to the alarm of the French, at the beginning of September Ho Chi Minh had created his independent North Vietnamese state; meanwhile the southern half of the country had been taken over by British troops under the Potsdam agreement. The French suspected that Britain and America might eventually hand the whole country over to Ho – certainly the Great Powers showed no inclination to recognise France's right to sovereignty in Indo-China. In the early hours of 22 September, French troops staged a violent raid on the Viet Minh HQ in Saigon, directly breaking a promise given by the French commander to Mountbatten and, in effect, firing the first shots of a bloody and pointless war that was to continue for thirty years. (Ho, forewarned of the French attack that night, managed to flee before they arrived.)

Tom was in Saigon at the time. He sent a message to Mountbatten revealing that through friends in London he had contacts with the Viet Minh, and suggesting that – in his capacity as a Member of Parliament – he could intercede. 'There was a slender chance of averting a bigger clash,' he wrote thirty years later, after the Nationalists' eventual victory:

I offered to try to see Ho Chi Minh and get talks going between the Viet Minh and British political spokesmen. The offer had to be referred for approval to the newly formed Labour government in London. At last authority for my *démarche* came through – just too late: one day earlier I had left for home, to attend the opening of the first post-war Parliament: as a new Labour MP, I felt that I ought to be there.[23]

This was slightly inaccurate. Mountbatten did not need to wait for approval from London: he gave it himself as soon as he received Tom's message, with the blessing of a minister who happened to be visiting South-East Asia Command Headquarters. The only delay was in the delivery of Tom's offer of mediation, which was sent on Monday 24 September but did not reach Mountbatten's desk until 28 September – the day on which Tom had to fly back to London, if he were to catch the opening of Parliament. Why did it take so long? The finger of suspicion points at General Gracey, the senior British officer in Saigon. He had supported the French invasion of Ho Chi Minh's premises in spite of Mountbatten's orders to the contrary, and it was he who carried Tom's note to Kandy. He knew that Mountbatten would probably accept the proposal; but he knew, too, that Tom could not remain in Vietnam after the weekend. If he could sit on the letter for three or four days, he could ensure that the meddling Driberg would not be able to strengthen Ho Chi Minh's position and embarrass the French.

A week after returning to London, Tom at last heard from Mountbatten:

Your offer to mediate with the Viet Nahm Republic only reached us on the Friday evening, which was the day that you said you would have to leave. However, I instructed Gracey, who was flying back, to accept your offer with thanks if you were still available . . . If only the French will be reasonable and come forward with an imaginative offer, the war in French Indo-China can be over. If it is continued through French intransigence, I hope it will be made abundantly clear that it is nothing to do with South East Asia.

The Dutch are even worse. They have been reviling Christison and Van der Plas for meeting the Indonesian leaders, Soekarno in particular, and yet were getting on splendidly with them until there was the interference from the Hague. Here again, the line surely to take is that it is the intransigence of the home governments that is making it difficult for people out here.

I can assure you that if I was left as free a hand in FIC [French Indo-China] and NEI [Netherlands East Indies] as I was left in Burma, I could solve both these problems by the same method; though it is heart-breaking to have to leave the political control to other nations when we are really in military control.

I need hardly ask you to keep the source of your information very strictly to yourself, and would be grateful if you could destroy this letter after you have read it, as I presume it is improper to write either to a journalist or an MP in the above strain.

I can't tell you how much I enjoyed having you on the trip, and am most grateful to you for all your help.[24]

This was characteristically indiscreet. Just as, in the 1930s, Winston Churchill used private briefings from the Chiefs of Staff when framing his parliamentary questions about Britain's unreadiness for war, so in the post-war years Tom had the benefit of Mountbatten's secret advice when criticising colonial policy. Compare the above letter, for example, with Tom's speech on Indonesia during an adjournment debate two months later, on 11 December 1945. Lambasting the French and Dutch empires for trying to restore the *status quo* in the Far East, he emphasised that no blame attached to 'the British commanders on the spot' – Mountbatten and his staff, in other words. 'I know that the troubles that have arisen there are no fault of theirs,' he told the House:

They have done their utmost in the way of conciliation, but they have been handicapped throughout by intransigent and unwise political directives emanating originally from Paris and from the Hague. If it had been left to the judgment and the discretion of the commanders on the spot to settle this matter, I believe that an amicable solution could have been reached without bloodshed, and both Indonesia and Indo-China might now have been well on their way towards obtaining self-government by peaceful means.

The evidence of that is manifold. General Aung San, the Burmese Nationalist Resistance leader, has paid tribute to the wisdom and liberality of the policy pursued by Admiral Mountbatten. Again, in Indonesia some weeks ago, when the Dutch were at their most difficult, General Christison was meeting and having dinner with Dr Soekarno the Indonesian Nationalist leader.

Tom admitted in *Ruling Passions* that Mountbatten's letters 'often provided useful material for speeches and questions in the House'. But the traffic in information went both ways. As Supreme Allied Commander in South-East Asia and later as Viceroy of India, Mountbatten often received bulging envelopes of political gossip and analysis from his man at Westminster. 'The Parliamentary Labour Party is in a highly agitated condition . . . Shinwell is President and is at present in a boiling rage . . . Attlee (who increasingly reminds me of Lady M's rebuke to Macbeth, 'Infirm of purpose!') has hardened on a *simpliste*, anti-Russian line, indistinguishable from Hearst, Churchill or the Vatican . . . Bevin, though patiently, grimly resisting all-out war-talk, has lost much ground, even with the Tories now . . .'[25] In his isolation, Mountbatten found these unofficial despatches more useful than they might seem, for his decolonising schemes in South-East Asia were being resisted or misunderstood not only by blimpish subordinates on the spot but also by the socialist government in London which was supposed to be backing him. 'Bevin is behaving like the *worst conservative diehard*,' an exasperated Edwina Mountbatten wrote to her husband from London – but at least Tom Driberg was coming to see her that evening 'so I'll get the Leftist views on Java etc.'

While he was in Asia in 1945 Tom paid a surprise visit to his brother Jim, who was running a military hospital in Chittagong. He arrived just in time: Jim was leaving for England the next day. 'So,' Tom recorded, 'there were convivial visits to officers' and sergeants' messes, and toasts to be drunk with matron, sisters and nurses. I could see that my brother – now fifty-five years old – still had a way with women: the staff seemed genuinely fond of him. On this special night I could not, of course, judge fairly if he was habitually drinking too much; but it was late when we turned in, pretty well canned.'[26]

Jim had had a surprisingly good war – the surprise being that he had had a war at all. In 1939 he had been sinking in his Brazilian morass, but by a remarkable effort of will he had hauled himself out of the mire and made the journey to Britain to volunteer for duty. On the strength of his record in the First World War he was again given a commission in the Royal Armoured Medical Corps. By the time Tom saw him in Chittagong he had been promoted to the rank of colonel.

Had the physician really healed himself, or was the war merely a pause in his self-destruction? Tom was soon to find out. After being demobilised, Jim had no job, no home in England and almost no money. Though Tom had no particular fondness for his brother, 'this maddening obligation of "blood ties" came into operation: he had, after all, been kind to me when I was a small boy and had made a creditable effort to recover from the degradation of Brazil'. So, as soon as Tom managed to get Bradwell Lodge back from the RAF, 'it was natural that he should come to stay semi-permanently'.

The derequisitioning of the house was no simple matter. First there were prolonged and complicated negotiations with the Air Ministry. Then, once Tom had regained possession, he had to restore the place to its former state. 'It was like starting from scratch all over again,'[27] he wrote gloomily. In the grounds, the RAF removed their Nissen huts from the lawn but left behind the concrete bases on which they had stood, each eighteen inches thick; the grass never quite recovered from these invaders. Inside the house, there was dry rot everywhere; Tom attributed it to the black-out and to the RAF linoleum laid on wooden floors, which had prevented the free circulation of air. Four experts from Winchester came to stay for several weeks, surveying every inch of the house from top to bottom, cutting out suspect timber and disinfecting every other scrap of wood they could see. 'You won't have any more of that trouble,' one of them said when they eventually departed. 'It's good for another fifty years.' There was another outbreak of rot within a decade.

While waiting for Jim to install himself in Bradwell, Tom was suddenly required to attend to the other surviving member of his family. For Jack Driberg, as for Jim, the war had been a glorious Indian summer. The British government had exploited his aptitude for languages – and his tendency to go native – by sending him on spying missions to the Near and Middle East, where he had, apparently, performed all that was expected of him; he had gone native so thoroughly that he converted to Islam and took to wearing Arab dress. After the war he was returned from Cairo to a job at the Ministry of Information in London – and, like Jim, he soon found himself slipping back into his old despair. On 3 February 1946 he had a slight fall, fracturing a rib ('a stupid accident', Tom said). He was taken into the hospital of Saints John and Elizabeth in north-west London. Two days later he had a coughing fit and died immediately.

'The aftermath of sudden death especially is grim,' Tom wrote that weekend. 'The yellow-brick mortuary, the inquest, the endless sorting of a chaos of papers, clothes, books, the bland voice asking if one would prefer a grave at £5 or £7 or £12.'[28] The aftermath of the death of a Muslim convert created extra problems: Tom had to arrange a funeral at the Islamic cemetery in Woking, with an *imam* from Regent's Park to conduct it. 'Islamic funeral tomorrow (Saturday), Brookwood Cemetery, Woking, 11.30 a.m.' was the deadpan announcement in *The Times*, as if this were quite usual for a son of the English middle class. Inevitably, something went wrong. 'There was a *contretemps*,' Tom revealed. 'The undertakers, despite my careful instructions, had laid on a standard, i.e. Christian, coffin, and as it was removed from the hearse at the graveside, we were shocked to see on the top of it a large brass cross. The *imam* seemed distressed: we hastily hid the cross with flowers. This would have amused my brother a great deal.'[29]

Tom's conviction that there was some sort of curse on the Dribergs was strengthened by his remaining brother's behaviour. Jim's genial, clubbable disposition made him popular in Bradwell village at first – especially in the local pubs, which he soon came to know well. But soon he was back in his old ways. Being in London during the week, and attending constituency meetings most weekends, Tom did not notice the decline until he began to receive absurdly large bills on his off-licence account from the King's Head in Bradwell, which worked out at a bottle of whisky a day. He investigated. Jim, he discovered, would wander over to the pub at opening time every morning, drink himself stupid for two or three hours and then stumble back home clutching the bottle of whisky he had just bought to see him through the afternoon.

At one point Jim was taken into hospital, where, because he seemed likely to die, he and Tom had their first and last intimate talk: 'We discussed our parents, his failed marriage, my homo-sexuality.' But Jim recovered, and started drinking even more heavily. One weekend Tom was staying with Lord Beaverbrook at Cherkley when the housekeeper from Bradwell rang to tell him that his brother had had a bad attack of the DTs and was defecating all over the bedroom floor. 'This,' Tom decided, 'was unbearable, and dangerous (he was in the sixteenth-century timber-framed part of the house); to put it cynically, it was difficult to get and to keep good servants.' Tom contacted his GP in Maldon, Dr David Cargill, who was a Labour stalwart and a good friend, to seek his help in getting rid of 'my crapulous old fool of a brother'.[30] The doctor persuaded Jim that the east coast was too bleak for a man in his poor health: he needed the warmer climate of the West Country. A room was found for him at a boarding house in Devon, where he eventually died in November 1956. Tom had to go to Exeter to identify the body:

I had performed the same melancholy office for my brother Jack, but had not been in a municipal mortuary before. I arrived after dark, but the big refrigerated room was brightly lit. The dead were in dozens of drawers, end-on, like the drawers of a filing-cabinet. The friendly, business-like attendant slid open a drawer. It contained a baby. 'No, no, let's see . . .' he said. 'Ah yes' – and he slid open another. This was the right one. It was brother Jim all right. I tried to feel pity and regret, but felt no emotion whatever. I put a finger on the cold forehead. It – not 'he' – felt like a Tussaud figure. Perhaps twenty seconds had passed; I must not waste the attendant's time; he was waiting to push the drawer back, stooping over it. He looked up at me and said, briskly and cheerily, 'All right, sir?' I nodded, and the drawer slid back and clicked shut. I spent a comfortable night at the hotel in the Close, and in the morning looked at the cathedral, ran into the Bishop of Crediton (who promised to remember my brother at Mass), and bought a pair of old lacemakers' lamps at an antique shop. It was a tidy finish to a largely unsatisfactory life and a cool fraternal relationship.[31]

Tom did not agree with Dr Frank Buchman on many subjects, but he might have seconded the old man's assessment of Jim. 'I am doubtful about ambulance cases like that,' Buchman had written to a friend in 1938, 'as they need very special handling.'[32] In the end, neither Tom nor the Oxford Group could save Jim Driberg from himself. The cause of death was morphine poisoning; not even Tom had known that he was taking morphia as well as alcohol. He died as he had lived, pretty well canned.

Tom's experience of coping with Jim might have given him some sympathy – respect, even – for Frank Buchman, who had laboured patiently in the same doomed cause in the 1930s. But he was above such considerations: the vendetta against the Oxford Group was pursued as fiercely as ever, even when Jim was living with him. In July 1946 fifty Labour MPs went so far as to issue a statement 'to dissociate themselves from the views expressed by Mr T. Driberg, Labour Member for Maldon',[33] after Tom had queried the Home Secretary's decision to grant 'high priority' permits allowing Buchman and dozens of his followers to come over from America. Raising the question in an adjournment debate, Tom argued that when transatlantic berths were in short supply Buchmanites should not be 'taking up space in ships or aircraft which could be used to bring men home on leave or on release'.[34] Although he insisted that it was not a question of religious intolerance – when conditions were better, 'individuals of whatever creed should, of course, be admitted to this land' – he could not resist the temptation to take a few swipes at his old foe. All the familiar charges were gleefully repeated: Buchman had falsified his *Who's Who* entry; he had once said, 'I thank heaven for a man like Adolf Hitler'; he had called Himmler 'a great lad'. This drew a shrill retort from Quintin Hogg, the Conservative MP for Oxford: 'Where are we getting to if people are to be refused admission to this country simply on the grounds of tittle-tattle of this sort which would not do credit to the senior common room of a girls' school?' The pro-Buchman forces on the Labour side were itching to join in, but Tom had spent so long on his denunciation that there was no time for anyone other than Hogg to speak before the Home Secretary replied to the debate. Unable to voice their anger in the chamber, they issued their 'public statement'.

He did have some defenders. On 3 August, fifty other Labour Members 'noted with regret' the statement signed by their colleagues the previous week. They published a press release 'deploring any attempt to limit or restrict the ancient privilege of an MP to raise in debate any subject that is not ruled out of order by Mr Speaker, and they consider that Mr Driberg was fully within his rights in raising the matter'.[35]

But the repudiation of Tom was what caught the attention, as a rare public acknowledgement of the mistrust many Members felt for him. Outside his immediate circle of drinking and gossiping companions – men such as John Freeman and Woodrow Wyatt – he was rather lonely at Westminster. According to Freeman,

He remained a mysterious, ambiguous and largely isolated figure among his parliamentary colleagues: a redoubtable ally if he happened to espouse one of your causes; a dangerous and malicious enemy if he turned against you. I don't think he was generally *disliked*: indeed quite a number of colleagues on both sides of the House were personally fond of him despite his less pleasing characteristics. But he wasn't generally popular either and was seen, I judge, by his Labour colleagues as a lonely, unpredictable figure who was not one of us, but whose heart was probably in the right place, who was a bit of a character – even though a character to be disapproved of.[36]

The reasons for disapproval were many and various. There was a belief in some quarters that he was not entirely serious, a dilettante who scorned the drudgery of Select Committees or the discipline of the party whip. As Ian Mikardo put it, 'He never did any of the bloody chores.' Some Labour MPs were suspicious of his friendships with Tory MPs, his social snobbery and the disproportionate importance he attached to good living. At an all-day conference of the National Executive one Saturday in the early 1950s, held at the Charing Cross Hotel, Tom solemnly moved an emergency resolution protesting at the poor quality of the lunch they had been served. When challenged by incredulous colleagues, who thought they had eaten and drunk quite adequately, he listed in detail what was wrong with each course of the meal – while the rest of the Executive waited with growing impatience to discuss land nationalisation.

His lofty, didactic pronouncements on trivial matters almost invited ridicule. 'Paper napkins! Ugh!' he wrote in his *Reynolds* column in February 1955. 'Even if not called serviettes, they are The End . . . I feel that a civilisation whose symbols of comfort and elegance include paper napkins deserves to be wiped out by the H-bomb.' This elicited a well-aimed counter-blast from Percy Cudlipp in the *News Chronicle*:

> The Bevanites heaved many a sigh,
>   Each bludgeoning his brain.
> 'We need,' said Nye, 'a rallying-cry
>   To launch our new campaign.
> Mikardo! Foot! Can't you compose
>   A slogan to inspire?'
> Then suddenly Tom Driberg rose
>   And to his Chief said, 'Sire!
>
> *The Paper Napkin Must Be Banned –*
>   *Let that our slogan be!*
> *Let every toiler in the land*
>   *Use decent napery!*
> *I'd rather perish out-of-hand*
>   *In radio-active vapour*
> *Than flout good taste and etiquette,*
> *And coarse inelegance abet,*
> *By using (Ugh!) a "serviette",*
>   *Or napkin, made of paper.'*
>
> 'That goes for me,' cried Jennie Lee.
>   'The symbol of our fight,
> Instead of a Red Flag shall be
>   A napkin starched and white!

Hugh Gaitskell (Ugh!) I'll lay a bet' –
   She spoke with withering scorn –
'Uses a paper "serviette"
   As to the manner born!'

A mighty shout of 'Good old Tom!'
   Arose from one and all,
And Nye forgot the atom bomb
   To voice this stirring call:
'With linen napkins, purchased from
   A reputable draper,
The working class shall gracefully
Remove the traces of high tea.
Fit only for the bourgeoisie
   Are napkins made of paper!'

However often he was mocked in the press or denounced by Labour MPs, his popularity among local activists did not suffer. At the party conference in Blackpool in June 1949 he was elected for the first time to the National Executive Committee, in the vacancy left in the constituency section by Harold Laski's retirement; he then remained on the Executive continuously until 1972, usually coming near the top of the poll. This puzzled and enraged his enemies. 'Activists in the party would say to me, "I don't know how Tom gets elected to the NEC,"' Ian Mikardo recalled. 'The answer was his column in *Reynolds News* – the celebrity factor. You see it now with the large votes for Ken Livingstone and Bryan Gould in NEC elections: people who appear often in the press, or on the TV and radio, get extra votes.'[37]

It was hardly surprising, then, that Tom often seemed to give his journalism priority over the business of the House: as a newspaper columnist he commanded the attention of thousands, many of whom had votes at Labour conferences. He was in any case disinclined to shed his old Hickey habits – such as foreign travel – merely to oblige the whips. During the years of the Attlee government, his absences from Britain became more and more prolonged. In the summer of 1946 he spent two months in the United States, visiting old friends and sending reports every week to *Reynolds News*. The following year he did not even confine his travels to the parliamentary recess: on 3 September he set off on a 10,000-mile journey by car through France, Western Germany and Berlin, Czechoslovakia, Yugoslavia and Italy, not returning until the end of November. (He had intended to be home earlier, but he ran out of money and had to stay in Villefranche-sur-Mer and then Paris for several weeks while awaiting the travellers' cheques that *Reynolds News* mailed him.) On 24 November Woodrow Wyatt sent a letter to Tom at the Hotel Vendôme in Paris, 'to tell you what has been happening in the political world since we all saw you last':

1). *Burma Independence Bill.* Second reading and Committee Stage. Absence of T. E. N. Driberg, MP for Maldon, noted and regretted.

2). *Various questions on Fascist Activities.* Absence of T. E. N. Driberg, MP for Maldon, noted and regretted.

3). *Royal Wedding.* (The biggest political function of all.) Absence of T. E. N. Driberg, MP for Maldon, noted and regretted.

When he came back the following week, Tom included in his column an airy apology – 'to anyone who may have noticed, or minded' – for missing some of the parliamentary session. Few Labour MPs were amused. It was bad enough that he was abroad when he should have been loyally trooping through the division lobby, but what made it worse was that he was so *conspicuously* absent: there he was on the leader page of *Reynolds News* every Sunday, interviewing Tito in Belgrade, sunning himself in Rome, visiting Matisse and Picasso in France.

Nevertheless, Tom's tendency to go AWOL – however infuriating – was a luxury that could just about be afforded during the years of the first post-war government, with its huge majority in the House of Commons. The election of February 1950 changed everything: Labour emerged with an overall majority of precisely five, and suddenly all the galley-slaves were required to row at once. But the Member for Maldon was soon wandering again, drawn by the sound of gunfire in Korea. On 16 August 1950 Tom set off on a 'survey tour of the Far East' for *Reynolds News*, saying that he expected to be away for 'about six weeks'. In fact it was three months before his colleagues were to see him again; by then, many of them were clamouring for his expulsion from the Parliamentary Labour Party.

The Korean war is, today, a largely forgotten conflict. Few people can recall – or believe – how vast and menacing was its shadow. The *casus belli* was provided by the North Koreans, whose forces crossed the 38th parallel into the South in June 1950, but the scale of the fight that ensued was the responsibility of America, which, deranged by McCarthyist paranoia and Cold War belligerence, saw an opportunity to 'roll back' the frontiers of Communism. By 1951 there seemed every likelihood that World War Three was at hand. General MacArthur – who was simultaneously in charge of the UN forces in Korea (including British troops) and of American forces in the Pacific – advocated the invasion of China; President Truman said that the decision on whether to use nuclear bombs was up to the commanders in the field. In the event President Truman retreated from that particular brink and sacked MacArthur, but the consequences of his futile adventure were still quite ghastly enough: by the time an armistice was signed in July 1953, leaving the frontier roughly where it had been in the first place, three million Koreans had been killed and the country was devastated.

One or two statesmen anticipated how dangerously the struggle might spread, and strove to prevent it. As early as July 1950 Pandit Nehru pleaded with both Stalin and Dean Acheson to stop the fighting but was ignored. When Tom arrived in New Delhi the following month at the start of his Asian tour, his first appointment was an exclusive interview with Nehru on the subject, which was splashed across the front page of *Reynolds News* on 20 August. The Indian Prime Minister, he reported, was still hopeful. The fighting had been going in North Korea's favour; MacArthur's troops, backed by the UN, were now almost falling off the edge of the country, pinned on the tip of the peninsula. If the Americans were forced to withdraw altogether, Nehru argued, there would be a 'breathing space' in which peace could be discussed.

This was based on the assumption that, once the Americans had been driven out of Korea, 'it would take them at least six months to

The infant Tom with his Kiplingesque father

'He looked like the son of a Maharajah' – a studio portrait of Tom in the early 1930s

Famous last weekends: Dick Wyndham, Tom, Cyril Connolly and
Stephen Spender at a party in the 1930s
'William Hickey fights a by-election': canvassing in Maldon, June 1942

Tom (second from right) in the Far East with Mountbatten (second from left) at the end of the war

'The most interesting wedding of the season': Tom with Ena in her Schiaparelli outfit

Bradwell Lodge: the chimneypiece in the drawing-room (below) was attributed to Robert Adam, with medallions painted by Angelica Kauffmann

With a R'Bab, a Russian musical instrument brought back as a souvenir after visiting Guy Burgess in Moscow, 1956

A night out with the Kray twins in the 1960s: Tom is in the middle with his hands on his knees, with Ronnie to his right and Reggie in front of him

A slightly classier night out, with Lady Diana Cooper in the 1970s

prepare a successful reinvasion'. But even as Nehru spoke, the Americans were already returning to the offensive. On 19 August their Superforts dropped 800 tons of bombs on three North Korean targets – including Chongjin, a port only forty-five miles from the Soviet border. Within a month MacArthur had launched a daring amphibious assault on Inchon, 150 miles to the north, and the North Koreans were retreating fast. By then Tom was in Korea himself. 'It is not only the Americans who believe General Mac-Arthur's amphibious offensive to be the turning point of the war,' he wrote from the front on 17 September. 'It is difficult for those who have seen the immense build-up of tanks, artillery and aircraft, ready for today's big push from Taegu, to see how the North Koreans can long maintain resistance in an orthodox military sense.' This proved true enough: the North Koreans were soon pushed back across the 38th parallel.

Here was a moment when the Western powers could have forced a negotiated peace. But MacArthur, intoxicated by power and success, pressed on past the frontier and up towards the Manchurian border. His intentions were clear. In a message to American War Veterans (which Truman ordered him to withdraw) he had already laid out his Far Eastern strategy, which was to turn the China Sea into an American lake: 'The chain of islands now running down the Pacific from the Aleutians to the Marianas forms a protective shield to all the Americas. From this island chain we can dominate, with air power, every Asiatic port from Vladivostok to Singapore.' A war that began with the legitimate aim of stopping aggression thus turned into a crusade to strengthen American domination of Asia by grabbing new bases. China, not unnaturally, felt threatened by MacArthur's provocative advance towards its border and his loud calls for the bombing of Chinese installations on the Yalu river. Eventually it retaliated: Chinese troops invaded Korea on 26 November, and were at the 38th parallel by Christmas. MacArthur's greed for conquest had wrecked the chance of peace.

Readers of *Reynolds News* learned almost none of this from Tom's despatches. He was in Korea for more than two months, from the end of August until the first days of November, but in all that time he never questioned MacArthur's intentions. His usual hostility to British and American imperialism, especially in the Far East, was muffled by his belief that the North Koreans had started the war and – above all – by his regard for 'our lads', the British marines who were fighting as part of the UN force. He was later to revise his opinion of the North Koreans' culpability, but at the time he had no doubts. 'Whereas the Communists say that the actual act of aggression last summer came from the South,' he wrote to an anxious constituent in December, 'I take the same view as that of the government, that the actual act of aggression came from the North.'[38] He did add, 'This does not mean that I approve or condone the things that are being done in South Korea', but his expressions of disapproval were saved for his return: in his reports from the front he avoided awkward political questions and concentrated solely on military tactics. As in France in 1944, his admiration for the British Tommy was boyishly unrestrained. He told a radio interviewer that the Royal Marines' landing behind North Korean lines 'seems to me, quite irrespective of the political background of Korea or anything like that, a superbly executed and planned operation – technically and almost artistically'.[39]

It was this artistic foreground that held his attention. His first cable from Korea to *Reynolds News* was typical, a long account of how he and twenty soldiers reached a platoon of the Argyll and Sutherland Highlanders that had been 'cut off' on top of a ridge of hills:

We started in jeeps along a rough track, circling the back of the mountain, the front of which was exposed to tank fire . . .

But the last three miles of the journey had to be done on foot – up a steep path and scrambling through dwarf conifers and young pines with which these hills are thickly clad.

What with these trees, and the swearing soldiers, one might almost have been in Perthshire.

By the time we reached the top, there was little breath left – even for swearing.

The supply party still had another 40 minutes to go down the other side of the mountain to deliver their load to company headquarters a thousand feet below.

I decided to stay where I was. And this was perhaps lucky for me.

Half an hour later there were sharp cracks and puffs of smoke below. The supply party had no doubt been seen; the slope they were descending was being subjected to mortar fire.

Three men were wounded.

Meanwhile an evening strafe from American heavy artillery behind us was beginning.

Shells whistled overhead like distant electric trains.

The first shell fell uncomfortably short of its target.

'Och, they're juist getting the range,' said a Jock affably.[40]

Tom liked danger as a spectacle. 'I don't say that I've got any particular physical courage,' he explained later, 'I haven't, and I intensely dislike physical danger, in war or anything. But none the less there is a curious sort of thrill about it, particularly enjoyed in retrospect.' But he was always ready to confess his own cowardice. 'When I've been a war correspondent and heard shots fired in anger,' he told one interviewer, 'I have ducked as rapidly as possible – more rapidly than anyone else, I think.'[41] In another interview he spoke of the 'absolutely paralysing, terrifying' fear of death that seized him when he was shot at by snipers while running across a paddy field near Seoul.[42]

According to The Times's correspondent in Korea, Louis Heren, Tom had more courage than he cared to admit. The two journalists were flying to Tokyo for a few days' rest at the end of September, when suddenly their plane – a Curtis Commando transport – flew into a typhoon. 'It was terrifying,' Heren recalled. 'I was terrified, the pilot was terrified. But Tom stayed calm. "You're a Catholic, Louis, aren't you?" he asked. I said yes. "D'you know anything about the 39 Articles?" I said no. He then began reciting them. I think we'd got to the 38th by the time we landed in Japan. It was one of the bravest things I've ever seen.'[43]

This was Tom's first visit to Tokyo, and before returning to the battlefront he sent a short feature to Reynolds News. 'It would be presumptuous, on such slight acquaintance,' he wrote, 'to generalise about the Japanese character and outlook' – but then proceeded to do so, apparently without irony: the Japanese 'walk busily about, with set, melancholy faces', they have 'a parrot-like imitativeness', they venerate their ancestors, they are scrupulously courteous and polite; and so on. Nor did he neglect the other great cliché beloved of Western journalists in Japan, the Madam Butterfly angle. To the American GI, 'coming from a country in which women are the dominant sex' (*sic*), Tokyo was 'a revelation of femininity obsequious and subservient':

The women flutter and fuss round him, skilled in every personal attention, flattering him till he really does feel himself the lord of creation and can forget the anxieties endemic in the unstable American society.

This is a general social, not only sexual, phenomenon; but its sexual aspect is conspicuous. A sample check of 480 GIs, taken recently by an American magazine, showed that more than 400 of them had formed 'steady' liaisons with Japanese women.

Many American soldiers can afford to buy their own houses in Tokyo or Yokohama and set up their mistresses in them.

This helps, incidentally, to keep the VD rate low.[44]

Tom's brief holiday had a 'sexual aspect', too, though he forbore to tell *Reynolds News* readers about it: while in Tokyo he did some energetic trouser-chasing, particularly of a youth called Kingo Suzuki. For once he was unsuccessful. But Suzuki's gracious and touching letter of rejection, delivered to his hotel, confirmed Tom's belief in the unshakeable politeness of the Japanese:

Mr, Tom. D.

I think → it is good not to see you againe. because, I can not became your friend. I hope, you find good friends, early.   END.
I want to say reason to you. but, I can not. because, I don't know how to write this reason by English.

Please (Pardon) help me this discourtesy and I hope you keep friends with Suzuki family that is excepted me.

Unabashed, Tom returned to war – and to his pursuit of British soldiery. His homosexuality became something of a regimental joke among the Marines of 41 Commando with whom he lived for the next month. Many of them were very young National Servicemen, eighteen or nineteen years old, who did not conform to the popular stereotype of tough Commandos. 'They are not muscle-bound supermen,' he noted approvingly. 'Many of them are quite slight and trim – physically compact.'[45] The sight of a Gorbals lad called

Johnny Mooney even moved him to scribble a verse, titled 'Lord of Creation: A Korean Snapshot':

> Acroflavine shadows glow
> On the stillness of the snow:
> Half a foxhole for a bed
> Tousles a fair and itching head.

Perhaps surprisingly, none of the Marines took offence at his unconcealed appreciation of young men. 'As a serviceman you get a broader outlook on life,' explained one of them, Michael O'Brien, who was just eighteen years old in 1950. 'You try a man out not on what his sexual activities are but on whether he's a *man*. Tom Driberg conducted himself as a man – landing in enemy country, coming on night raids – and that outweighed everything else. He was accepted as a chap. He was a bit bent but he was very well liked by the Royal Marines. We regarded him as a man of courage.'[46]

There was to be another reason for their admiration. British troops in Korea were paid less than GIs, a grievance that Tom promised to take up. Back in London he pestered the War Ministry until the men had an additional dollar a day. In the words of one Marine, Martin 'Tiny' Nesbit: 'We thought even more of him when he got us this extra money.'[47] Tom kept in touch with the men of 41 Commando for the rest of his life. In June 1952 he went to the Royal Tournament in London to watch some of them perform a cliff-climbing display; afterwards, Michael O'Brien recalled, 'he took about 20 of the lads to the pub and bought them a few beers, and then gave them a night out. There was no ulterior motive. That's the sort of chap he was.' Tom always attended 41 Commando's reunion dinners, where, according to O'Brien, 'he was genuinely welcomed'.

It was Tom's request to accompany the Marines on a night-landing behind enemy lines that made the greatest impression. 'As an eighteen-year-old lad,' Martin Nesbit recalled, 'I thought it was quite a brave thing to do, when he didn't have to – to come along and get into a small rubber boat in the middle of the night and land on an enemy shore where you didn't know who might be waiting. Very foolish and quite brave.' He was the only reporter present, and unlike the troops he was completely unarmed. 'He put his life in our hands,' O'Brien said, in some awe.

Tom joined 41 Commando first at the American Camp McGill near Yokosuka, in Japan, where he watched the youthful British recruits warily learning to handle American weapons and American food: one very young marine, having been warned to be careful what he drank in foreign countries, refused to touch Coca-Cola. After a couple of days at McGill, Tom and his Marines boarded an armed troop carrier called the *Horace A. Bass*, on which – much to his delight – he shared a cabin with no fewer than nine British lads. This ship was to be their home for the next month.

It was also to be the springboard for their landing on the coast of North Korea; but there were frustrating delays before Tom could satisfy his longing for action. When they put in at another naval base, Sasebo, for a night, they ended up staying for four days. Tom guessed that this was explained by the course of the war on the ground: the UN forces were approaching the 38th parallel, and the American and British commanders were waiting to see how the world might react to an invasion of the North. On 7 October the United Nations General Assembly passed a satisfyingly vague resolution which MacArthur took as a *carte blanche*. That very night the men from the *Horace A. Bass* – or, as the ship was fondly nicknamed, 'the galloping ghost of the Korean coast' – went ashore at last, near Chongjin in North Korea, only two hours after receiving a signal authorising the expedition.

Another message had arrived at the same time: a cable from the Government Whips in London ordering him to come home at once. MPs were being carried into the House of Commons on stretchers in order to maintain Labour's tiny majority, but Tom disregarded the summons without hesitation. He was impatient for adventure. 'You'll get me fired,' he muttered to the Commanding Officer, Major Dennis Aldridge. It was meant as a joke but it nearly came true.

The raid on Chongjin was once described by Tom as 'the outstanding experience of my whole life as a journalist'.[48] He wrote and spoke about it often, but the most immediate account appeared in *Reynolds News* a fortnight after the adventure. 'BEHIND THE

NORTH KOREAN LINES!' yelled a headline. 'A two weeks' silence from Tom Driberg, MP, our correspondent in Korea, ended last night when this vivid cable reached this office,' the newspaper revealed. 'Previously he had cabled that he was going on a secret mission. His report, held up for security reasons, has now been released.'

Tom was not best pleased to discover, when he finally obtained a copy of *Reynolds News*, that a sub-editor had cut his article 'pretty drastically' for reasons of space. Even so, he was proud of the work – 'a mere cameo portrait, but a cameo of matchless skill and daring'. It was, he believed, a story in a heroic tradition that went back at least as far as Thermopylae:

This is the moment of sharpest tension, the moment to which months of Commando training, weeks of planning, long nights and days of argument and calculation in wardroom and cabin have tended.

It is a moment of silence. The fussy chugging of the engine of the P-boat that towed us out from the ship has died fitfully away. We and the others no longer bob and jostle about the boat . . . The umbilical tow-rope has been unhitched. We are 12 men in a black rubber dinghy, gliding quickly by paddle towards a sombre range of hills.

We are less than a hundred miles from the Soviet frontier.

Our faces and hands are darkened: grease first, then boot blacking or cocoa (the joke was 'Troops will wear cocoa, officers Ovaltine') or burned paper; the administrative corporal, Ron Southworth, being an intellectual, uses carbon paper.

The hills loom nearer. (I never before felt the full menace of the verb 'loom'.) They stand up, steep and black, against the starry sky. We know them on paper, from maps and air reconnaissance photographs; we don't know how alertly they bristle. They do not, somehow, look as if they were asleep. If their watchmen are shrewd, they, too, will be silent – until just after we have beached.[49]

In fact the landing was unopposed, and Tom was soon helping the dozen Marines from his dinghy unload their essential cargo, on which they had been sitting: twenty 20 lb packs of plastic explosive and TNT. A few hundred yards up the hill was the target: a railway tunnel, on an essential supply line.

First, however, between us and the tunnel was a building on whose nature there had been much speculation. We called it 'the factory'. It was a large, long, blank building: it looked, just now, peculiarly inscrutable. It had to be cleared.

At his last briefing, the troop commander, Lieutenant Derek Pounds, had told the troops: 'Civilians are to be left alone if they stay indoors: if they interfere they get rubbed out.'

One section went on to do this job. Others – the 'powder train' – moved off circuitously to carry the explosives up to the tunnel.

The building was surrounded silently. (The men of the Commando wear very light rubber-and-canvas boots.) Our Korean interpreter, Lieutenant Commander Choi Byung Hae, thought it might be an Army barracks.

It turned out to be deserted: it seemed to have been used by fishermen. Beside it were a few poor dwellings: the Marines could hear women talking and coughing within.

A man came out, and wandered about uncertainly and perhaps inquisitively. He may have heard something. Some were for shooting him; but it was less noisy to knock him on the head.

In the text of his cable, Tom then added: '"I was sorry for him in a way," the marine who did it said afterwards, showing me the teeth marks on his rifle-butt, "but he oughtn't to have been there."' This was too much for *Reynolds News* to stomach, and was omitted from the printed version. Even without it some readers complained at Tom's callousness. His defence was that he had been attempting 'to imply an ironic comment on a tragic and anomalous situation', but few were persuaded. Certainly there was no indication anywhere else in the long article of ironic intention: his admiration for the Marines' derring-do seemed entirely unqualified. 'Even the most confirmed pacifist,' he wrote, 'could hardly fail to admire these men's absolute dedication to their mission – a ruthless mission, but no more so than war itself.' His only murmur of doubt came as he walked down from the tunnel to the beach with Dennis Aldridge after the explosives had been laid:

Just across the railway line were some more small houses. The people in them were going to get quite a shock when the tunnel went up.

'Can't you warn them,' I asked, 'tell them to get out?'

'It would only scare them out of their wits,' he said. 'They'd probably be too frightened to go. I don't think it'll do more than concuss them.'

He added: 'We could have destroyed those houses, but . . . well, one hasn't the heart.'

This conversation was interrupted by a loud scream from up the hill: Lieutenant Pounds had nearly electrocuted himself on a wire cut down from the factory. The scare precipitated their exit. An order to withdraw was given immediately, and Tom had to dive headlong into the dinghy as it moved through the surf. They paddled out to sea and waited for the explosion.

It came at last – at last, but dead on the scheduled time: a vast orange-red burst of flame, followed by a banging roar; soon a baleful black cloud drifted across the stars.

It was, they say, the biggest bang let off in any such raid this war. To those who made it, this final big noise was worth all the hours of nerve-racking silence that had gone before. Some two tons of explosive went up in it . . .

It is profoundly impressive to live with a Royal Marine Commando and be with it on the job.

His conclusion had no irony, however implicit; nor, as he admitted later, did it raise its eyes to the 'larger issues'. He was content to applaud a job well done. And he was hungry for more: elated by his little outing, he begged to accompany the Commando again the next night. 'He was told there was no room for him,' Martin Nesbit recalled. 'He was so desperate that he even tried to persuade someone to go with him in a little two-man boat, a five-foot dinghy. But no one would do it so he had to stay behind.'

In London, Labour MPs were fuming at Tom's continued absence – especially as rumours had begun to circulate that it was sexual pleasure that was keeping him out East. Some of his friends, such as Michael Foot, 'feared that his detention in Korea, with all the accompanying rumours about other pursuits apart from his war correspondence, might end his political career'.[50] Further cables had been sent by the Whips, commanding him – with increasing vehemence – to do his parliamentary duty. But he seemed to be in no great hurry. On his way home from Korea he visited Malaya, where he went on a jungle operation with the Scots Guards, stayed with rubber-planters living under siege conditions, attended a rubber-workers' trade union conference, went into the camps in which thousands of Malayan civilians were being concentrated, and interviewed a surrendered bandit leader.

The Labour government in Britain was hanging on by its fingers. If it lost a single division in the debate on the King's Speech – and without Tom's vote it might well do so – there would be a general election. Some ministers were already resigning themselves to their fate. On Saturday 4 November, the weekend before the crucial debates, Hugh Dalton wrote in his diary: 'I think we shall be beaten on Monday or Tuesday on the Address – most probably on the vote on the Liberal amendment on cost of living. And I'm afraid there's no doubt that in the ensuing election we shall be beaten rather badly. If we lose 50 seats we shall be in a minority of between 90 and 100. And we may lose more.'[51] The next day he felt slightly better, but was still inclined to think that the government would fall: 'We have too many sick and that bloody Driberg is still away, unpaired and unashamed.'

In the event, Labour managed to scrape through the three crucial divisions on the King's Speech, with majorities of 10, 15 and 10. The Liberals abstained on the second vote – on a cost-of-living amendment which they themselves had tabled – and the Tories had as many sick MPs as Labour. The outcome did not, after all, depend on Tom. This was just as well: he got back on the evening of Tuesday 7 November, in time for only the third of the three divisions. 'There is great indignation among our MPs against him,' Dalton wrote in his diary. 'Many think the whip should be withdrawn from him. He has certainly put the life of the government in greater danger and has been absent, money-making and having an interesting and no doubt enjoyable time, while others have been brought along on stretchers and from hospitals to vote.'[52]

Expulsion seemed probable. The Parliamentary Labour Party was, according to Michael Foot, 'in one of its most vindictive moods' when it held a special meeting to discuss the case on 15 November. But Tom's friends – few though they were – rallied round. As Foot recalled: 'We managed to secure as his chief apologist before the wretched Party inquisition the services of Jimmy Hudson, a teetotal Quaker and the most spotlessly pure member of the Parliamentary Party bar none. Jimmy saved Tom for the moment. And quickly others rushed to his aid.' A message from the General Management Committee of his local party, which was read out, paid tribute to 'his exemplary and unmatched service to the Maldon Division'. Finally, to appease his persecutors, Tom stood up and offered an abject apology, albeit in 'the iciest of tones'. The court reached its verdict: he would not be deprived of the Labour whip, but he was formally censured for 'gross neglect of his Parliamentary duties'.

It had been a humiliating ordeal – an echo of the new boys' concert at Lancing, where he had been pelted by his fellows while standing on a table and singing 'The Bay of Biscay-o'. In his younger days he would have been badly shaken. But he had learned to laugh off embarrassment. He was amused to receive a letter of condolence from a Tory-voting friend, Lionel Gough, who wrote: 'I suppose that it might harm you in the constituency, but possibly do you good in lefter circles. Anyway I should have thought that there was a lot to be said for a trained journalist to be looking into Korea rather than to be spending the time trotting into division lobbies when required.'[53] Tom assured him that 'things are not as bad as they look, and actually it seems likely to help rather than harm in the constituency.'[54]

The prediction proved accurate; even more infuriatingly for his enemies in Parliament, the Korean lapse did him no damage in the party beyond Maldon either. During his absence in the Far East, Labour's Margate conference had re-elected him to the National Executive. At Scarborough a year later, he actually increased his vote despite the opprobrium that had been heaped upon him: he and Ian Mikardo overtook Hugh Dalton in the NEC order of popularity. Dalton, who despised Tom even at the best of times, was outraged:

I'm very vexed at Driberg's and Mikardo's vote, but rather pleased at [Barbara Castle's]. Driberg wasn't exposed anywhere – though, *since last conference* he has been severely censured for neglect of duty by the

Parliamentary Party, and this was published. [Morgan] Phillips mentioned it to one or two pressmen, and [Desmond] Donnelly told me he did the same.[55]

Dalton told John Freeman that he thought 'it showed incredible levity for this large vote to be given to Driberg'. Freeman replied that Tom had a high vote because he was assiduous in addressing meetings all over the country and getting to know members of local parties. 'I suppose he keeps an address book,' Dalton harrumphed, 'and writes to them all just before Conference time.'

John Freeman was now in a difficult position. Tall, lean, handsome, he had made a dazzling entry into Parliament in 1945 as a dashing young major of extremely left-wing views ('almost Trotskyist', in Tom's opinion); in 1947 he had been appointed Parliamentary Secretary to the Ministry of Supply. He was a protégé of Dalton, who thought him 'very attractive and glamorous', but he was also Tom's closest friend on the Labour benches. Tom and Dalton fought for Freeman's hand like rival suitors. Dalton, who had been at Cambridge with Rupert Brooke, had a Hellenic fondness – chaste but unmistakably homo-erotic – for brilliant young men such as Freeman. 'My Love,' he once confided to his diary, 'is the Labour Movement and the best of the young men in it.' After Tom's Korean disgrace, Dalton made his most determined effort yet to woo Freeman away from Tom by persuading him that the association would ruin his chances of promotion. 'Freeman, I fear has had a great fall since the first wonderful summer day in the 1945 Parliament,' Dalton wrote on 4 January 1951. 'I am very grieved about this. But he's a bloody fool in his own interest, and what can he see in Driberg to justify so much public clinging?'[56] Two weeks later, Freeman was passed over in a ministerial reshuffle: his 'stock was badly down because of Driberg', Dalton claimed. At the end of January, Dalton took Freeman for a Sunday afternoon stroll in Battersea Park. 'He had been troubled,' Dalton recorded, 'by what I had told him of his backsliding in high favour because of his always being about with Driberg. He had been wondering whether this signified any doubts, at Supply of all Ministries, about his security. I said I was pretty sure it didn't. He said he would be quite willing –

and from his constituency point of view would prefer – to go back to the back-benches.'[57]

He soon did so: along with Nye Bevan and Harold Wilson, Freeman resigned from the government in April over the proposal by the new Chancellor of the Exchequer, Hugh Gaitskell, to impose charges for spectacles and false teeth in order to pay for the huge rearmament programme. Dalton begged Freeman to change his mind, promising to recommend him for a more exciting ministerial job, but to no avail. 'I said to John,' Dalton noted sadly, 'that he was a wonderful scalp for the uglies' – the uglies being Driberg and Mikardo. This was slightly unfair: Tom had also hoped the three ministers would stay in office, for fear that their departure would precipitate a general election, and 'did what little I could' to find a compromise formula. Still, once the deed was done he did not hesitate to recruit the defectors. On Thursday 26 April, three days after the resignations, Freeman, Bevan and Wilson walked into the uglies' den for the first meeting of the expanded 'Keep Left' group, in which Mikardo and Tom were two of the most prominent figures. The other MPs present were Richard Acland, Barbara Castle, Dick Crossman, Harold Davies, Hugh Delargy, Michael Foot, Will Griffiths, Leslie Hale, Jennie Lee and Kim Mackay.

'Keep Left' had started in November 1946 as a rebellion by Michael Foot and Richard Crossman against Ernie Bevin's unswervingly pro-American foreign policy. Right-wing Labour MPs had promptly denounced them as 'Communist lickspittles', but a dozen or so Members supported the Foot–Crossman amendment to a foreign affairs motion, and thereafter this little group met informally about once a week. But it was only with the resignation of Bevan that these dissidents – who in due course became better known as the 'Bevanites' – acquired a leader of stature.

'From the beginning,' Andrew Roth has written, 'this Group acted like a factional caucus, concerting its attitudes, activities and publications.'[59] Members made speeches in one another's constituencies; the Group also organised travelling 'brains trusts' which drew large audiences. It often had to fight off the accusation that it was, effectively, a party within a party – something expressly forbidden by the Labour constitution. There was certainly a collective discipline which amounted almost to an unofficial whip. Thus at that Thursday meeting the Group discussed what its four members of the National Executive Committee – Bevan, Mikardo, Castle and Tom – should do about an NEC statement that had been issued the previous day supporting Gaitskell's budget and criticising the rebels. They considered resigning from the Executive but settled for writing a joint letter of protest to Morgan Phillips, the party's general secretary.

On 10 May the Group decided that it would set out its policies in a *Tribune* pamphlet, to be published in July under the title *One Way Only*. But there was a difficulty. If all the Group's sympathisers – who by then numbered two dozen – signed the pamphlet, it would look like an alternative manifesto from a party-within-a-party, confirming all the worst fears of their critics. So it was to be presented as a work written by Bevan, Freeman and Wilson alone, explaining why they had felt obliged to resign. In fact, however, the various drafts of the pamphlet were discussed and rewritten in private conclave with other Group members, including Foot, Mikardo and Tom.

Far from shunning Tom, then, as Dalton had hoped, by the summer of 1951 John Freeman was a closer ally than ever. And on 30 June he undertook a duty beyond the call of friendship: he managed to keep a straight face while acting as best man at what the *Sunday Express* described as 'the most interesting wedding of the season' – the marriage of Mr Tom Driberg MP to Mrs Ena Mary Binfield.

CHAPTER NINE

BLACK WEDDING

'A marriage has been arranged between Thomas Edward Neil Driberg and Ena Binfield.' The brief announcement, which appeared on the Court and Social Page of *The Times* on 16 February 1951, had Tom's friends and colleagues exclaiming incredulously. '*Who?*' they asked one another. 'And *why?*'

The first question was more easily answered than the second. Tom's bride-to-be had been born Ena Lyttelton on 28 June 1902, the eldest of four children in a middle-class family of agnostic Jews in Leeds. In her teens she eloped with a man named Joe Berger, by whom she had a son, Peter. It was a joyless marriage. After leaving Joe and Peter, in 1930 she went to live with Bob Binfield in Bury St Edmunds. Although they were not married – Joe Berger was still refusing a divorce – she adopted Binfield's surname and spoke of herself as his wife. They lived together in great happiness for the next eighteen years.

With Bob's fond encouragement, Ena discovered new talents and ambitions. She joined the Labour Party in 1931, serving as vice-chairman of her local constituency party in Bury St Edmunds between 1936 and 1938. During the war she was county organiser of the West Suffolk Women's Land Army while also running five domestic science training hostels for girls. In 1946 she became the first woman to be elected as a Labour member of West Suffolk County Council. She soon made her mark as a specialist in health and public assistance: she sat on the committee of a large local mental hospital, St Audrey's; she was appointed by the government to the East Anglian Regional Health Board, which in turn appointed her a governor of Addenbrooke's Teaching Hospital, Cambridge. In 1947 and 1948 she spent much of her time travelling the country, lecturing on Aneurin Bevan's new National Health Service Act. These were pioneer days.

Her life changed abruptly after Bob Binfield's death in 1948. She could no longer afford to fill her hours with voluntary work: she had to start earning a living. There were no vacancies locally, but through connections in the health service she was offered a job the following year as Chief Administrative Officer of the Marie Curie Hospital in Hampstead. She resigned her seat on the county council and moved to London.

Ena was a gregarious, lively character, and in the capital she was swiftly taken up by several Labour MPs and Fabian intellectuals. 'Everybody loved her,' Ian Mikardo recalled. 'She was bright, jolly and witty, a tall, elegant woman.' She formed an 'intimate friendship' with John Freeman, and was a regular guest at parties given by George Strauss, the Minister of Supply, and his wife Patricia. It was while staying at the Strauss country house in Sussex one weekend in the autumn of 1949 that she met Tom, whose writing she had long admired.

And now, a year and a half later, they were engaged. What on earth was going on?

The motives of both Tom and Ena were the subject of much mystified speculation, but only a few friends actually dared ask them directly. One was John Freeman. 'Ena discussed with me at length the pros and cons of marrying such a hopeless case,' he recalled. 'I don't think she expected to reform Tom, but she probably did expect that, if she could provide him with a comfortable and stable background, his behaviour might become less promiscuous and self-destructive.'[1] According to Ena's son, Peter Berger, she knew that the union was unlikely to be consummated:

She expected, I think, to be a useful political hostess for Tom, and to enjoy some of the political excitement that seemed to surround Tom at home and abroad. She was a warm, loving person, and she had a charisma that attracted all kinds and conditions of people to her, including Tom. She also needed companionship. She hoped to get some of these things from Tom. She was well aware of his sex life; but guessed that he also needed a stable companionship. She thought they could together do a useful political job as Mr and Mrs.[2]

This was borne out by Ena herself in a number of letters to Tom over the next twenty years. 'I don't know why you married me – you never told me,' she once wrote. 'I married you because I was lonely and because I thought we had sufficient interests in common to make for a pleasant easy friendship.'[3] On another occasion she admitted: 'It *was* a marriage of convenience in that we were not to sleep together . . . I married you for a home and companionship – for a friendly relationship and because I thought we had a number of common interests – political, social and so on.'[4]

So why did Tom, as a 'confirmed bachelor' in every sense of that ambiguous phrase, marry her? There was a theory – believed to this day by some people – that it was a 'cover' for his real life. According to one rumour, Hugh Gaitskell told Tom that if he were married he would be eligible for a ministerial post, and Tom therefore took unto himself a wife. This was nonsense. It is improbable that Gaitskell would have made such a suggestion (government jobs were not his to offer, and Attlee was puritanical on questions of sex); impossible that Tom would have believed it. Certainly Tom yearned to be a Minister of the Crown, but he was not deluded enough to think that the years of lavatorial philandering – not to mention the Korean episode, and his many other transgressions – would be forgiven and forgotten if he marched up the aisle with a carnation in his button-hole. It was too late to bury the past. Besides, as John Freeman pointed out, 'if that was his motive, surely his subsequent behaviour would have been more sensible and discreet.' The reason that Tom gave Freeman seems much more plausible: that he had reached an age when he wanted to settle down and enjoy the great love of his life, Bradwell Lodge. 'He felt – or at any rate said – that for the sake of having that properly run and being able to live in it like a gentleman, he could accept the stresses of being married.' At the time, Freeman noted, Tom appeared genuinely to like Ena.

The idea of an old roué like Tom Driberg taking a bride was, unsurprisingly, more than some people could bear. Isobel Adamson, his devoutly Christian secretary at the House of Commons, immediately gave notice that she intended to quit. Tom came into his office to find a typewritten note on his desk, unsigned but obviously from her: '*Must* you do it, Mr Driberg? Is it *really* necessary – and couldn't you yourself have told me of it! Truly, I would never have thought it of you.' Tom returned the message with a pencilled scrawl protesting his innocence: 'I do not understand what all this is about. Please explain.' And explain she did: for the next couple of months the secretary waged a holy war against her employer, bombarding him with letters and religious tracts on the workings of the Holy Spirit. Sometimes her tone was piously beseeching – 'I still do honestly and absolutely believe that you're doing the wrong thing for the wrong motives' – but most of the fusillades were more straightforwardly hostile. One morning Tom found this waiting for him: 'Could you let me know when the date of your entry into unholy matrimony is to be published, or if everyone knows now, so that I may be forewarned? Not at all sorry to trouble you. Sincerely hope, for your sake, you do not marry in church, though don't put even that profanation past you.' By now Tom was losing patience. 'In view of the tone of your letter,' he replied icily, 'I take it that you will be leaving fairly soon for another job. It is now a considerable time since you gave me notice.' She held out for money, and in the end he had to pay her about £100 to go away; she left at the end of May.

Even some of Tom's oldest friends begged him to think again about the marriage, though their reasons were rather different from Isabel Adamson's. John Rayner, who was working in the Commissioner-General's Office in Singapore, wrote on 7 June that he had been 'dumbfounded by engagement (by now marriage? I hope not, I could perhaps from my experiences advise you). Had not really thought it possible that any but a dark mare would pass the post in so long a race. I can only wish you "Nox non ebria, sed soluta curis/Non tristis torus, et tamen pudicus".'

Others treated it as a huge joke. On seeing a photograph of Ena in the *Daily Herald*, Winston Churchill allegedly roared: 'Oh well, buggers can't be choosers!' A policeman at the House of Commons muttered 'Poor lady, she won't know which way to turn.' Evelyn Waugh declined Tom's invitation to the wedding, explaining that he would be abroad. 'I will think of you intently on the day,' he added, 'and pray that the church is not struck by lightning.'

Matrimony, according to the Book of Common Prayer, is a holy estate; 'and therefore not by any to be enterprised, nor taken in hand, unadvisedly, lightly, or wantonly, to satisfy men's carnal lusts and appetites, like brute beasts that have no understanding.' In his own peculiar way Tom obeyed the injunction. No one could accuse him of marrying Ena to satisfy his carnal lusts; nor was there anything light or wanton about his preparations for the great event. He wrote to the legendary Paris dressmaker Schiaparelli, whom he had met in his Hickey days, to ask if she would create a wedding outfit for Ena. 'Of course I remember you,' she replied. 'I will be delighted to do your wife dress. Just come along as quick as you can and for old friendship sake we will see that it is possible.' He immediately took Ena over to Paris to be measured – where, according to a story he often told afterwards, he had to fight her off when she tried to pounce on him in his hotel bedroom. ('And after I'd spent a fortune on her coat and hat!')

The bride's religious affiliation was the next thing to be settled. Though she was a non-practising Jew, she yielded to Tom's persuasion that she should be received into the Church of England, and on Easter Eve 1951 the Revd Jack Putterill baptised her at the church of St John the Baptist with Our Lady and St Lawrence, giving her the baptismal name Ena Mary. Putterill was the successor to Conrad Noel, the famous 'red vicar' of Thaxted, who had scandalised local Conservatives by hanging the Sinn Fein tricolour and the Red Flag in his church. Tom had first visited Thaxted church in the 1920s, during Noel's incumbency, and had been thrilled to find pamphlets urging him to 'smash the British Empire and all Empires to bits'. Noel died in 1942 but his traditions were maintained by Putterill; at the time when Ena was baptised, there was still a Red Flag hanging in a side-chapel.

There was one at their wedding, too, though it had to be smuggled in. When Tom and Ena were first planning the service, they asked the vicar if he would allow them to have 'The Red Flag' as an organ voluntary, to be played while the congregation were leaving the church. Having checked that the organist would not mind, the priest replied that they could have the socialist anthem 'so long as you wrap it up so that people who might be offended by it won't recognise it'. Hence the curious item which appeared at the foot of the service-sheet:

Organ Music
Choral Prelude on an old German folk-tune
(*'O Tannenbaum'*)   *Benjamin Frankel* (1906–   )

'*Tannenbaum*' is, of course, the tune of 'The Red Flag'. The composer Ben Frankel, a friend of Ena's, undertook the task of submerging the familiar theme in modern dissonances, but Tom thought that the strains of 'The Red Flag' still seemed 'admirably identifiable'.

The wedding was on 30 June at the church of St Mary the Virgin, Pimlico, conducted by an old Oxford friend, Cyril Eastaugh, the Bishop of Kensington. Tom awoke that day feeling 'dazed and rather unreal, as if my bones were not quite solid': in short, he had a hangover. Unable to eat any breakfast, he managed to down several large nips from a brandy bottle with his best man, John Freeman, before tottering into the sunlit morning and setting off towards Pimlico.

Across town, Ena was climbing into her Schiaparelli dress. She was to be given away by her son Peter, who was himself already married and shortly to become a father. 'TOM DRIBERG, GRAND-FATHER' was the mocking headline in the *Daily Express* when the baby was born, a week or so later.

Tom had insisted that the wedding rite, and the nuptial mass that followed, should be as outrageously ornate as possible. He was not disappointed. Kingsley Martin ('quite easily shockable in church,' according to Tom) sat through the proceedings with a look of horror fixed on his long, lean features. J. B. S. Haldane registered his disapproval by taking out his pipe and filling it during the mass. The Labour MP Hugh Delargy, who was a Roman Catholic, said the service made him feel like a non-conformist. 'I could take it all till they kissed that photograph frame,' complained one friend, referring to the osculatory tablet that Tom and Ena kissed during the canon. Nye Bevan growled that his 'Calvinistic blood was roused'. A Fleet Street editor, puzzled by the clouds of incense, asked: 'I suppose it's the bride who's a Roman Catholic?' Mary Mikardo had to leave the church because the incense was making her cough so much.

A few weeks later, meeting Ena on the terrace of the House of Commons, Mary Mikardo demanded: 'How could a good Yid-disher girl like you go through that?' Ena replied that she didn't believe in any religion and so the service had meant nothing to her; it was a 'fun thing'. For Tom, on the other hand, it was a nerve-stretching ordeal. The most tense moment was when the bishop announced 'If any man can shew any just cause, why they may not be lawfully joined together, let him now speak, or else hereafter for ever hold his peace.' But the 700-strong congregation remained silent, and Tom emitted a forceful 'Phew!' of relief that made the flames on the altar-candles flicker.

Four hundred guests were invited to the reception afterwards, on the river terrace of the House of Commons. Some had come down in coaches from the constituency; others were from rather further afield, including the West Indian athlete McDonald Bailey and the Indian politician Krishna Menon. Many of Ena's colleagues from the Marie Curie came. There were MPs galore, as well as old friends from the 1920s and 1930s such as Osbert Lancaster, John Betjeman, Osbert Sitwell and Constant Lambert; but the most gawped-at visitors were Seretse Khama and his English wife, Ruth. A year earlier the Attlee government had withheld recognition of Seretse's chieftainship of the Bamangwato tribe, in the British protectorate of Bechuanaland, for fear that the 'unity and well-being of the tribe' might be threatened by his having a white wife; he had been ordered to live outside Bechuanaland for the next five years, and was banned from visiting his country without special permission. Tom was one of only six Labour MPs who had voted against the government over this issue, and Seretse and Ruth had been his friends ever since. Their appearance at the reception was the most important story of the wedding, in Fleet Street's opinion.

The account in the next morning's *Sunday Express*, for instance, began: 'Nearly 400 guests – among them Seretse Khama and his "White Queen" Ruth – stood in the sunshine on the House of Commons terrace yesterday and drank a champagne wedding toast to Socialist MP Tom Driberg and his bride.'[5] Fortunately, no reporter overheard the gaffe committed by Kingsley Martin while he was engaging Ruth Khama in earnest conversation. 'Of course,' he told the White Queen, unthinkingly, 'you're the real nigger in this woodpile . . .'[6]

The guests were served a fragrant cup made of peach brandy, grenadine, whisky and 'champagne cider', with one glass of real champagne per person for the toasts. 'Nancy [Mitford] and I gloated over the photographs of your wedding,' Evelyn Waugh wrote to Tom a few weeks later. 'We did not like the expression: "When the champagne *ran out* . . ." in the *Sunday Express*.'[7] Tom was unashamed. 'We couldn't afford to have champagne served all the time,' he explained. 'We couldn't really afford the whole thing, anyway.' This was true enough. Tom entered the estate of holy matrimony in deep debt: his overdraft was now well over £1,000; in February 1950 the landlord of his flat in Great Ormond Street had threatened to evict him for persistent non-payment of rent; for more than a year Tom's bank manager – at the Liverpool Street Station branch of the National Provincial – had been restricting his withdrawals to £10 a week. And the bill from the House of Commons Refreshment Department for his reception, even with the minimum of champagne, came to £220.

The most considerate guests therefore gave cash as a wedding present. Tom and Ena received £100 from the Maldon Constituency Labour Party, £12 from John Freeman, £10 from Leslie Hale MP, £5 from Tom's solicitor, Peter Winckworth, another fiver from his doctor, David Cargill, five guineas from Tony Crosland and three guineas from Roy Jenkins. The list of other presents and their donors makes strange reading:

> Canon Freddy Hood (Principal of Pusey House) – cream jug.
> Lord Hailsham (Quintin Hogg) – set of Pyrex dishes.
> Naomi Mitchison – Highland rug.
> Ian and Mary Mikardo – breakfast coffee set.

Chips Channon – edition of Shelley.
J. B. S. Haldane – kitten.
Elwyn Jones – model donkey.
Tony Benn – silver card case.
Graham Sutherland – drawing (by G. Sutherland)
Ronald Searle – drawing (by R. Searle)
Evelyn Waugh – copy of *Helena* (by E. Waugh)
Nancy Mitford – copy of *The Blessing* (by N. Mitford)
Seretse and Ruth Khama – fish knives.
Ted and Barbara Castle – face towels.
Jim and Audrey Callaghan – four ashtrays (two broken).

Osbert Lancaster recorded this surreal day in his magnificent 'Ode on the Wedding of Thomas Driberg, Esq., MP':

Hark! The joyous nuptial tune
Cleaves the jocund skies of June,
Triumphant anthems rend the air
All the way to Eaton Square.
In Pimlico the strains are heard
Of Palestrina and of Byrd,
And marshalled crowds in patience wait
The due arrival of the Great.

Within the Church a tight-packed throng
Hope the Service won't be long,
A hope that I at once surmised
Unlikely to be realised;
For all experience has taught
The Very High are seldom short.
Flanked by chattering M.P.s,
BETJEMAN's down upon his knees.

Come to kindle Hymen's torch,
Yet still lingering in the porch,
Aneurin BEVAN and his wife,
Pose, with easy grace, for *Life*.
Ushers with extremist views
Show the Leftists to their pews,
But I, reactionary and grand,
Although on time, am left to stand.

Te laudamus Domine,
Chiefly in the key of A,
From CUDLIPP comes an angry belch,
For he can only sing in Welsh.
But look, they turn on every side
To see the coming of the bride,
Radiant, demure and neat,
She almost trips on BETJEMAN's feet.

But hark, the Bishop's on his toes
To ask if anybody knows
'Just impediment or cause . . .'
There follows then an awkward pause.
In every heart an anxious fear
Of what we half expect to hear.
Strike the organ! Beat the bell!
The Past is silent! All is well!

High up aloft the Happy Pair
Each seated on a golden chair
Their troth now plighted, sealed and blessed,
Are confidentially Addressed.
We cannot hear, we wish we could,
The homely words of Father HOOD
Because the choir, some thirty strong,
Are launched upon a sacred song.

Swing the censer! Wave the stole!
Let the mighty organ roll!
No length to which the priest may go
Will here be ritually *de trop*.
Counter-tenor, tenor, bass
All are purple in the face
And praise the Lord *fortissime*
As DRIBERG bears his bride away.

Friends of yours and friends of mine,
Friends who toe the party line,
Labour friends who're gratified
At being allowed to kiss the bride.
Artistic friends, a few of whom

Are rather keen to kiss the groom.
Friends from Oxford, friends from pubs
And even friends from Wormwood Scrubs.

Friends we always thought were dead
Friends we know are off their head,
Girl-friends, boy-friends, friends ambiguous
Coloured friends from the Antiguas,
Friends ordained and friends unfrocked,
Friends who leave us slightly shocked,
All determined not to miss.
So rare a spectacle as this!

There was extensive press coverage of the celebration. Ena's ankle-length gown in pure silk blue taffeta, with matching straw-hat and gloves, was much remarked upon. 'You can say it was made by Schiaparelli,' she whispered to a reporter after consulting Tom as to whether this could be disclosed. Although she was forty-nine years old, three years the senior of her husband, the newspapers unquestioningly accepted her age as forty-three (as Tom had told them). The *Essex Chronicle*, which described her as 'fresh, cool and so full of natural grace', waxed romantic:

We were come together as friends of Tom and Ena – representing hundreds of other friends whom, I know, they would have liked to ask had not numbers necessarily had to be limited – to wish them well. We drank our champagne wedding toasts with heart-deep sincerity. For this is a real love-match and they are our friends as much as they made us know we are theirs.[8]

Tom's sexual history was less well known in Essex than in London, but even so it is hard to believe that the local reporter (one Charles Douglas-Brown) was quite as innocent as his babbling about 'heart-deep sincerity' would suggest. Wedding reports do not usually stress that 'this is a real love-match': why mention it unless there is some doubt on that score?

After the reception, the newly-weds went to catch a Brighton train from Victoria station – where, rather to Tom's annoyance, they were ambushed by confetti-throwers. 'I *do* think our friends might have spared us confetti,' he tutted. 'After all, it isn't as if were a "young" couple – we are middle-aged, serious-minded, relatively staid . . . practically Darby and Joan.'[9] Punch and Judy might have been a more apt comparison (though unfair to Ena): hostilities commenced within hours of the ceremony. Tom had booked two single rooms in a Brighton hotel for their brief honeymoon, but the week before the wedding Ena – without telling him – telephoned to change the reservation to one double room. Tom exploded when he arrived at the hotel and learned that he had been billeted with his wife. For years afterwards he raged about the incident: 'She broke her marriage vows! She tried to sleep with me!'

The scene on their wedding night was repeated countless times in the next twenty years: Tom cursing at Ena, Ena begging Tom to be kind to her. Nevertheless, for the first year of marriage her un-clouded admiration for his public persona outweighed any unease she had begun to feel. She still believed that she could be his domestic helpmeet and political confidante, and she worked hard to prove her commitment. That September Tom decided that Bradwell Lodge should be opened to the public, on Wednesday and Saturday afternoons and at bank holiday weekends. Sometimes he would lead a conducted tour himself, gesturing expansively and showing off shamelessly ('That fine old tree is between 300 and 400 years old. A man from Kew estimated its age. It's an *ilex* tree . . . yes, I-L-E-X – sometimes called evergreen oak, or holm-oak, but it's not of the oak family, I believe: "ilex" is the Latin for holly . . . Now let's walk towards the house and have a look at the inside . . . These are the original beams, dating from about 1520. As you see, they're quite carefully carved, or *chamfered* . . . that's a drawing by Graham Sutherland which he gave us – one of his thorn studies . . .'); but more often it was Ena who took the visitors round, collected their 1/6d entrance fees (kept in a Victorian till in the hall), sold them postcards and cleaned their muddy footprints off the carpets. She supervised Joe and Hilda Taylor, the gardener and housekeeper, who had been at Bradwell since the war; as a result of Joe's and Ena's endeavours, the name of Tom Driberg Esquire began to appear with impressive frequency on the list of winners at the Southminster flower show. Tom seldom thanked her.

She also tried bravely to restore some order to his chaotic

finances. 'To keep such a house [as Bradwell] going at all,' Tom wrote in September 1951, 'is a constant struggle and anxiety – especially to my unfortunate wife, who tries to cope with the bills because I have always been "hopeless about money".' The self-deprecating and apparently affectionate tone was misleading; he was ungrateful for – and continually irritated by – Ena's interference. Whenever she gently pointed out that they would have to sell Bradwell Lodge unless he could reduce his debts soon, he changed the subject; often he tried to distract her attention by suggesting a game of canasta. If she persisted, he shouted at her. Occasionally this made her weep, which enraged him even more. 'Stop whimpering!' he yelled. Still she did not turn against him. 'I like you – to put it mildly,' she said – thus maddening him further. However cruelly he goaded her, in these early months her devotion was unwavering.

On 19 September 1951, the day that the doors of Bradwell Lodge were first opened to the public, Clem Attlee startled his colleagues by calling an election for 25 October. Ena immediately set to work arranging Tom's schedule. She drove him around, she cut sandwiches for him – she even addressed a few election meetings and was, according to David Cargill, 'quite a good public speaker'.

It was a busy campaign, in which both Nye Bevan and – more surprisingly – Clem Attlee came to speak for Tom. The Prime Minister packed the biggest available hall, addressing an audience largely composed of housewives and wealthy Tories at 2 o'clock on a weekday afternoon. (In case Attlee required lunch, Tom had taken the precaution of asking Mrs Attlee if there was any food her husband specially liked. After a few moments' thought she replied: 'Rice with treacle.') Bevan's visit was more difficult. Tom feared that Tory hecklers and rowdies would try to disrupt any public appearances by the left-wing bogeyman, so he ensured their silence by a technique which he commended to others in similar circumstances: a few hours before Bevan's meetings he took the loudspeaker car on a tour of the more expensive residential areas, inviting people of all views to come and observe the disgraceful behaviour of Conservatives in the audience. 'As news of these announcements got around,' Tom reported, 'there was a great toing-and-froing of young Tories, a hasty scrapping of plans to bawl and barrack. When Nye spoke, they were as still as mice.'[10] Later that night they took their revenge by sticking right-wing labels on Bevan's car and trying to put sugar in Tom's petrol tank.

These hooligans – mostly young hearties in yachting kit from Burnham-on-Crouch – were a source of embarrassment to the Conservative candidate, Aubrey Moody, who was (as Tom always said) 'a proper gentleman'. So proper, indeed, that after the 1951 campaign – his second attempt at the seat – he abandoned politics and took holy orders. Moody was a quiet, polite bachelor; at the 1950 general election, when the Liberal candidate was also un-married, some saloon-bar wits had dubbed the contest 'The Three Queers Festival'. Their hilarity rose even higher in 1951 when Lord Faringdon came to speak for Tom, for Faringdon was (to use David Cargill's delicate terminology) 'a roaring pansy'. He had once begun a speech in the Upper House with the words 'My dears' instead of 'My Lords', and on his visit to Essex he did not disappoint. He had been caught in a shower on the way up. 'Rain?' he told his audience, with a whinny of distaste. 'My dears, it *poured*.'

Tom was returned for the fourth time as Member for Maldon – but only just. His majority fell to 704, and without his local reputation he would probably have lost to Aubrey Moody: he reckoned his personal vote – those who would not vote for any other Labour candidate – at about 1,000. It is worth noting, as a historical curiosity, that the Labour vote nationally was 13,948,605, the largest figure ever achieved by any party before or since. A fat lot of good it did them: though the Conservatives were supported by a mere 13,717,538 electors they won an overall majority of 17 in the Commons, and the ailing King George VI – who had only a few months to live – asked Winston Churchill to form a government.

The right wing of the Labour Party already had a scapegoat for the defeat. At Labour's Scarborough conference in the first week of October a group of bovine but powerful trade union leaders – led by Arthur Deakin of the Transport & General and Will Lawther of the Mineworkers – had decided that the Bevanites must be crushed;

after the election the same idea occurred to many in the parliamentary party and on the National Executive. But the Left was not intimidated. Bevanites had fared slightly better than other Labour candidates at the polls, and – as Tom and his 'Keep Left' comrades delighted in pointing out – Bevanite-sounding utterances were beginning to be heard in the most unlikely quarters. In August a document published by the NEC had dutifully restated the policy that had led to the resignations of Bevan, Wilson and Freeman: 'The burden of rearmament, though heavy in its demands on raw materials and manpower, can be carried by our economy without too much strain.' Yet even before the election a retreat had begun. On a visit to Washington in September, Gaitskell had pleaded for a more modest rearmament programme 'that would avert the threat of a new financial crisis now facing Western Europe'. A *Tribune* headline asked: 'Has Gaitskell Joined the Bevanites?' A month after the election, Bevan's argument was echoed by none other than Winston Churchill, who had taken the Defence portfolio in his own government: he told the House of Commons that the defence budget he had inherited was so huge that he could not spend it all at once, and some of the rearmament programme would have to be 'rolled forward' into future years. 'The point was, I believe, made by the Rt. Hon. Gentleman for Ebbw Vale [Bevan] after his resignation,' he added teasingly.

The Bevan Group was therefore quite cheerful in the last months of 1951, in spite of the party's loss of office. To increase its effectiveness in Parliament it instituted regular weekly meetings, and on 4 December elected its first chairman – Harold Wilson. Tom's friend Lord Faringdon invited the Group to use his country house, Buscot Park, for a weekend conference on 14–15 December at which an 'alternative programme' for Labour was earnestly constructed.

Tom was not one of the crucial figures in these discussions. He had neither the oratorical flamboyance of Bevan nor the bureaucratic diligence of Harold Wilson: at the Buscot conference, for instance, Wilson produced a 3,500-word memorandum on the budget, while Bevan, who had done no homework at all, dominated the proceedings by the fertility of his ideas. Tom inclined to the

Bevan method, but lacked his rhetoric and originality. As Ian Mikardo recalled, 'he was good in policy discussions but he reacted against any form of organisation, like Nye and Curly Mallalieu and a few others. He hardly ever attended the *Tribune* Group, never did any of the bloody chores, seldom appeared on *Tribune* Brains Trusts – but he did really care.' And, unlike most of the 'Keep Left' crew, he had a place on the National Executive Committee and a weekly newspaper column; regardless of how many Brains Trusts he attended, he never lacked for a pulpit.

One week after the Buscot Park gathering, Tom was on his way to the Sudan. 'It's a bit hard to be away from home for the first Christmas since our marriage,' he wrote, 'but the chance occurred of a month in the Sudan, and the editor of *Reynolds News*, calculating that the Sudan as a subject was not of the faintest interest to eight out of ten of his readers, thought it would be a good idea if we prefaced it by the more obviously "ham" story of the troops' Christmas in the Canal Zone.' In fact Tom was much happier spending Christmas with the troops in Egypt than with poor Ena. On Christmas Eve, visiting the Parachute Regiment, he dined in the officers' mess and then made his way – via an amateur 'concert' – to the sergeants' and corporals' messes; he was still sober enough at the end of the evening to stagger into midnight mass, held in a temporary church packed with firm-jawed young National Servicemen.

Back in England, Ena refused to spend the holiday immured in lonely isolation at Bradwell. She moved into Tom's Great Ormond Street flat in London and set out to enjoy herself – and to send him daily bulletins of her revelry. On Christmas Eve she swigged several large whiskies before attending midnight mass at Margaret Street ('16 candles and all, and the procession to the crib,' she told him proudly) accompanied by her hairdresser. On Christmas Day she dined on roast chicken with John Freeman and his wife Mima ('John being fairly intolerable. He slept during the afternoon and Mima took down her back hair and I comforted'[12]). On 27 December Tony Crosland escorted her to a party at the Fitzroy Tavern, where they both got drunk on champagne. ('Tony had a wonderful time and only fell down once.') The following night

Jennie Lee and Nye Bevan took her to dinner with the Mallalieus at Hampton Court, and on New Year's Eve she went to a party at the house of Tommy Balogh, a Hungarian economist who advised the Bevan group; she and Crosland both got wildly drunk again ('*he* took down his back hair and I comforted with good advice'), and she stayed until half past four in the morning.

The first days of 1952 found Ena making drudgery divine at Great Ormond Street – staining the floors, hanging pictures and mending Tom's 'deplorable undergarments'. She told him that she was 'thriving on this curious combination'. But she quietly resolved that in the New Year she would also dip a toe into politics again. However much she enjoyed her new tasks as a housewife, she was used to more intellectual stimulation than could be had from sock-darning; since leaving her job at the Marie Curie after the wedding she had been conscious of a gap that could not be filled entirely by her adorable new husband. Besides, she felt sure that he would approve: she could be his eyes and ears in the Essex villages, in the constituency party, on the local authority. In the first week of January she accepted an offer to join the Maldon party's Central Women's Committee as a co-opted member, and later in the year she was elected to Bradwell-on-Sea Parish Council and Maldon Rural District Council.

As she was slowly learning, however, nothing she did could ever please Tom. By standing for the local council she was, implicitly, requiring him to treat her as a politically intelligent adult – and this he would not do. She strove loyally and often pathetically to establish the companionship that they had promised each other, but Tom spurned her every conciliatory gesture and called her a bitch. It was like living with Petruchio.

At first she made light of the problem. The long, affectionate letters she sent him while he was in Khartoum in January 1952 included several little jokes about his treatment of her. 'I'm a poor hand at being a bitch for very long!' she wrote in one. When she asked him to turn his attention to their money troubles, she added: 'Don't curse me in heaps!' In the second week of January, staying in Oxfordshire for a few days with her son and daughter-in-law (and the famous grandchild), she read a novel by Dane Chandos, *Abbie*, which she recommended to Tom: 'Abbie, a woman of great charm and character, but quite impossible – makes such scenes as put your acts to shame! If you haven't read it, you *must*. Her husband, oddly enough, adores her, and sits through everything quite unmoved – just like me! On second thoughts perhaps you'd better NOT read it – it might give you some ideas!'[13]

Her patient adoration and good humour merely irritated Tom still further; what Ena called 'your acts' became harder to laugh off. He never actually beat her – his terror of *any* physical contact with women guaranteed that – but the mental torture was unrelenting and unforgivable. People who knew them both were shocked by his cruelty. John Freeman said that Tom behaved 'abominably'; according to Ian Mikardo, 'He treated her like a servant' – and, as Mikardo pointed out, Tom's treatment of servants was notoriously sadistic: 'He humiliated them, and took a fiendish delight in it.' This was Ena's lot. During the week she was usually at Bradwell, looking after the house and garden while he stayed in town; at weekends she fed him and waited upon him. In return, all she asked was that he might occasionally tell her what had been happening at the House, how the Bevanite plots were progressing, who was saying what. But it was too much to ask. He snapped at her or lapsed into moody silences; to avoid talking to her he played canasta interminably; at other times he shut himself away in the belvedere or the octagonal room for hours. He insisted that they sleep at opposite ends of the house, exiling her to the gloomy Tudor wing while he occupied a small bedroom in the smarter Georgian end. Notes and postcards were often her only means of communication with him.

One anguished letter written by Ena in the summer of 1952 gives a sharp whiff of the toxic atmosphere that polluted so much of their married life at Bradwell:

I am – or was – a good tempered averagely intelligent woman, with wide interests and many friends. You are slowly turning me into a bad-tempered bitch.

I know that marriage for you must be a great strain – but you must have realised that it would need a good deal of re-adjustment – just as I did. (Though I must admit that it takes more than I bargained for.) And frankly, I don't think that you are playing fair. You said, the last time we discussed this, be specific, and it is so difficult to describe the sort of thing you do to one. But you know very well – for instance, when I sit at my desk you scowl frown and/or pout – anyway you succeed in making me feel in the way and a damn nuisance. If I – rarely – ask for a radio programme, you find fault with my choice and my arguments in favour of it – for radio read book, person, film or what have you. Anyway, you succeed in making me feel a fool. You said it was a 'dirty remark' when I said you didn't like me to talk. The times you have said you don't like conversation – the endless silent meals we sit through (I like reading at meals, but when we are three as we have been almost incessantly since the middle of summer, it is not always possible); you say one of the reasons you play canasta endlessly is so that you can avoid conversation; if the 'phone rings and occasionally it is for me – even from Peter – you fret and fume through the conversation and make one feel it is a crime to have friends . . .

I have tried to please you in every possible way; I think I cope with the constituency adequately; I do a lot of (to me) unpleasant jobs with the bank, creditors etc.; I go to church; I now do not even make up the fire. (joke!)

In return you go through the motions of being courteous – you stand up when I come in, and carry trays etc., and say caustic things in and out of season.

I know a little of what your earlier life was like, and I try to make allowances for your difficulties. But I also have a background and difficulties – we all have. But because your father was unkind to your mother (in my home it was the reverse) there is no need for you to re-enact the story. At least, I understand the reason, but am not prepared to be the victim. I respect and admire enormously your brain and your contribution to society; there are people who say that I should sacrifice myself and be content to help in any way I can so that you can go on contributing; maybe it is a fault in me that I should like to be tolerably happy as well.

Must you always be on the defensive – always hitting out at someone or something? You have so much to be proud of – you are so clever – one of the outstanding minds of the age – you have charm, wit, good looks. Oh, yes, I know the text book reasons – one of them being that you are beastly to me as a protection – well I do assure you again that you have nothing to fear from me.

So what are we going to do about it? I just don't know how to cope. You once said, after having been unusually insulting to me, 'Why don't

you fight back?' And when I do you say 'There is no need to be offensive'.
Over to you darling.

Over and out: Tom had no answer, no words of comfort or
conciliation; he could not and would not declare a ceasefire in his
guerrilla war against her. Small wonder that, before long, she was
resolving to leave him. She was dissuaded only by John Freeman,
who asked her to think of the effect the separation would have on
Tom 'professionally and socially'. In view of this, she told her
husband, 'I am willing, if you wish it, not to make a final break, but
on certain conditions.' They were as follows:

I will be with you occasionally at Bradwell – say one weekend a month,
the first Sunday if you like, so that we can go to church together.

I will, in between these weekends, and when you are abroad, go to
Bradwell and continue to look after the house, and affairs generally.

I will go with you to such functions in London and elsewhere as will
serve to keep up the façade of friendly relations between us . . .

As soon as you are in a position to do so, I would like the sum of £40
paid in to my account at Chase National Bank on a Bankers' Order each
month.

I am *very* sorry that our marriage has turned out so badly; I am sure
you know that I respected and admired you very much, but you have so
consistently undermined my self-confidence by your behaviour to me that
I cannot let it continue.[14]

But of course she did let it continue: that was the flaw in this
apparently businesslike arrangement. As long as she was his wife –
even for one weekend a month – she would be weighed down by his
insolvency, his frustration, his rage against the world. She often ran
away to stay with her aunts in Bayswater, and a couple of times she
got as far as taking a lease on a London flat, but it was hard for her to
cut loose. In 1960 she told him she was moving out:

I'm writing to you, foolishly no doubt, to try and explain to you what is
driving me away from this beautiful place, which I fell in love with nine
years ago . . . Do you think that dinner and Canasta or Scrabble, played
almost every night you have been home, for nine years, is sufficient to
keep even a semi-literate woman like me satisfied? I only wish you would
realise how sorry I am to have to take this step – sorry for both of us.[15]

She soon returned. In November 1961, once again, she promised that this time she really was leaving. 'I must ask you to make a provision for me to the extent of £750 a year (a not unreasonable figure I think) and accept the fact that I wish to separate from you completely. I have tried for ten years to make a compromise work with you in your extraordinary mode of life and now have finally given up.'[16] But Bradwell Lodge drew her back. It was only when Tom was forced to sell the house, in 1971, that she broke free. A letter she wrote to him in September 1971 could have been written at almost any moment in the previous twenty years: 'The misunderstandings between us are endless and I suppose it is useless to try to clear them up . . . I shall leave this weekend and our neighbours must think what they like . . . I have always been prepared to try and be friends but you have been unable or unwilling to respond. So there it is.'[17]

She had been achingly lonely throughout her long years at Bradwell. 'Once she happened to be on a train with me,' Ian Mikardo recalled. 'I was going to a meeting at Chelmsford or somewhere, she was going to Bradwell, and she begged me to get off the train at her stop and come home with her. She didn't mean she wanted an affair: she just wanted company.' All Tom ever offered her was canasta.

CHAPTER TEN

A MUD BATH WITH BEAVERBROOK

One Sunday in the spring of 1952, Tom had a chance encounter with the political writer Hugh Massingham after morning service at a church near Sloane Square. The two men went back to Massingham's house and drank champagne. Massingham then revealed that he was doing some occasional work as an adviser to George Weidenfeld, the publisher. Why, he wondered, didn't Tom write a book for Weidenfeld? How about a biography of Lord Beaverbrook, for instance?

Had Tom known what frustration and anguish the idea would cause, he might have left it alone. But at that moment it seemed an inspired suggestion. Obviously he could write the book only if Beaverbrook would cooperate, but he believed he could talk the old man into that. Though they had seen little of each other since the war, Tom and Beaverbrook were still friendly.

True, there had been a few squalls and thunderclaps over the years. In October 1946 Tom and Michael Foot had successfully proposed the setting up of a Royal Commission on the Press to investigate the power and influence of newspaper owners. 'I expected no better from that fellow Driberg,' Beaverbrook commented, 'but I never thought Michael Foot would do this to me.' During the debate in the Commons on their motion, Tom went out of his way to emphasise that he had no personal animus against his old proprietor: 'Personally, although I may deprecate him as a public figure, I do, and always shall, regard Lord Beaverbrook with considerable affection, with great affection and respect — personally. I have found him a very good employer to work for, and a very good employer to be sacked by.'[1] Having said which, he spent most of his speech attacking the Beaverbrook newspapers. They did not perform their proper function as organs of news, opinion and entertainment; they were 'primarily commercial properties, just as much so as a big store or a theatre or an hotel' – and, as such, were too susceptible to the influence of shareholders and advertisers. Before the war, he said, he had been standing in the office of the *Sunday Express*'s features editor one afternoon:

I was reading through the proofs of the next Sunday's page 3 and was glancing at the astrologer's contribution. I noticed that he had, as usual, played fairly safe – at that time – by announcing that there was a considerable risk in flying for the next few weeks. There was a prospect of some air crashes occurring. We were glancing at this when suddenly the advertisement manager came into the room, with a troubled face, and said: 'You know, we can't let so-and-so get away with this. We have just got a new series of advertisements from Imperial Airways.' That dilemma was solved by a simple procedure. The features editor took the astrologer's article and wrote into it the following words: 'The above remarks do not apply to British air-lines, which are astrologically lucky.'

When he was invited to give evidence to the Royal Commission, Tom regaled them with several anecdotes in the same vein. But his most damning testimony, and the most annoying to Beaverbrook, concerned the 'white list' of people whose names could not be mentioned in the *Express* newspapers and the *Evening Standard* because of their enmity – or friendship, in some cases – with the Chief Reader. The existence of this list had never been publicly revealed before, but two former editors of the *Evening Standard*, Michael Foot and Percy Cudlipp, also told the Commission of it. Tom claimed that he had been issued with one soon after joining the *Express*. The first two names were G. K. Chesterton and Hilaire Belloc. 'Chesterton was only released from the white list by death; that was the first occasion on which I had been allowed to write about him in my column,' he told the Commission. Even Stanley Baldwin had been white-listed for a short period, after his 'prerogative of the harlot' speech in March 1931 – though, since he was Prime Minister at the time, 'it was impossible to keep him permanently on the list'. The Commission was incredulous, and pressed Tom on the point: had he actually seen a list with Baldwin's name on it?

Yes. There was a standing list which was duplicated and circulated to, perhaps, 10 or 12 people in the office: in the editorial department, probably the chief sub-editor, the features editor, myself (the daily columnist), and various other people who were in a position to put things direct into print. This list would be added to or subtracted from by supplementary lists which would come round at irregular intervals: 'Please remove Mr Baldwin's name from the white list.'

Tom added that of course Baldwin was not banned altogether, for obvious reasons, but he was 'not to be publicised unduly or not to be publicised without personal reference to the editor, or something of that kind'. And for other people on the list, the prohibition was absolute. 'For instance, if I wrote a paragraph about an opera or about music and, forgetfully, mentioned Sir Thomas Beecham, that would simply be struck out of the proof.'

The Commission, whose members knew little of the newspaper industry, was sceptical. It accepted the word of the *Express*'s lawyer, Critchley, that the list was nothing more sinister than a guide to people who were litigious or otherwise troublesome, and whose names should therefore be printed only with care. Beecham, for example, had brought two libel actions against the paper. (Noel Coward, another man whose name seldom appeared in the Beaverbrook press, was in a different category: Critchley explained that 'Mr Coward himself had asked not to be mentioned in the *Daily Express*.' The Commission accepted this extraordinary revelation without so much as a raised eyebrow.) Critchley also produced figures showing that, during the period of Tom's employment with the *Daily Express*, G. K. Chesterton was mentioned 69 times and Hilaire Belloc 9 times; in the *Daily Mail* the figures were 32 and 16 times respectively. This research did not disprove Tom's contention, since the statistics failed to disclose whether most of the references to Chesterton appeared after his death in 1935. But it was enough to satisfy the Royal Commission, which concluded in its final report that 'We have not . . . found any evidence of widespread black-listing on personal or political grounds. The lists kept by the

Daily Express and the *Evening Standard* are for the most part a tangible expression of the awareness of the risks of libel actions which must be common to all editors and their legal advisers.'

The report was far less critical than the press barons had feared. In spite of the piteous ululations from Beaverbrook when the Commission was first established ('the Royal Commission on the Press . . . is one of the Government Agencies in the persecution of newspapers. Sorrow, sorrow ever more. There is nothing I can say about it except to bow my head in misery'), he had been let off. And, truth to tell, he had enjoyed it all hugely – especially his own appearance before the Commission, in March 1948, when he had deliberately shocked his audience with a mischievous admission that 'I ran the paper purely for propaganda, and with no other purpose.' Tom's 'disloyalty' was, therefore, soon forgiven. Indeed, in the very month in which Beaverbrook testified before the Commission, Tom and four other Fleet Street refugees on the Labour benches – Plummer, Foot, Mallalieu and Webb – held a 'former Beaverbrook employees dinner' and sent the Lord a telegram of greetings; Beaverbrook told Tom that the message had given him 'real pleasure'. In April the following year, Tom published a collection of his Hickey columns under the title *Colonnade*. He sent a copy to his former patron 'with my warmest regards, and in real gratitude for all your kindnesses to me'. Three weeks later Beaverbrook replied:

Dear Tom,

I have received your letter and also your book.

It is a brilliant piece of work. The introduction is a splendid essay in journalism.

You will have seen the review in the *Daily Express*.

The book is your work.

The review is my work.

Later in 1949, when Tom was elected for the first time to Labour's National Executive, Beaverbrook again sent fulsome congratulations:

I send you this message of good wishes. You have done a big job in Parliament on the wrong side of the House.

Your recognition by your party is a fine tribute to your industry and
your ability and your character and your *semi* independence.

Tom had good reason for optimism, therefore, when Massingham
suggested in 1952 that he should write a biography. He broached
the proposal with Beaverbrook and asked, with all the considerable
charm he could summon, for help. It was granted. Beaverbrook
would talk to him, and would show him correspondence and other
documents, on one condition: this assistance must remain a secret.
The book should appear to be independent and unauthorised. This
suited Tom very well: as he told A. J. P. Taylor many years later, 'I
did not want it to be thought that I was writing a "stooge" book.'
One of the first to hear of the project was Randolph Churchill, who
tried to plant an item in the *Daily Telegraph*'s Peterborough column
suggesting that it was appropriate for Lord Beaverbrook's biography to be 'written by a crypto-Communist and published by a
Socialist'.

News of the deal alarmed the long-suffering general manager of
Beaverbrook Newspapers, E. J. Robertson. No good would come of
it, he warned; Driberg was fundamentally unreliable. Beaverbrook
laughed off the cautious lieutenant's forebodings. Nevertheless, he
sent a formal letter to Tom setting out the terms of their arrangement, in the misplaced belief that this would prevent any un-
pleasantness later. Although he would answer questions and open
archives, 'I must not be put forward in any way as sponsoring the
book, giving information for it, providing access to documents, or
rendering any other assistance.' He added: 'What I do will be done
to help you personally and for that purpose only.'

If Beaverbrook was to maintain publicly that the book was
nothing to do with him, he could hardly expect any power of veto
over the contents. His letter to Tom accepted as much: 'I shall not
ask for any information as to what you write or intend to write.
That rests with you. Deal with me or my activities as you think fit.
I shall not attempt to place any limitations on what you say, or
interfere with the expression of your good or bad opinion of me.'
Perhaps Beaverbrook himself believed that at the time he wrote it.
But as Tom was to discover, it was risibly far from the truth.

Beaverbrook had for decades been a Cecil B. De Mille of politics, manipulating his actors domineeringly but invisibly from behind the camera. Both author and subject should have known that he was not about to change the habits of a lifetime.

At first, however, Beaverbrook enjoyed boasting that he was ready to take whatever his biographer wished to fling at him. As he wrote to Tom from Nassau in December 1952:

You know that I do not object to attack. I always print the evil things that men say of me. The *Express* understands my policy.

Now, the late Lord Northcliffe would not print anything in criticism of himself. He would always print the words of praise.

Even from a publicity standpoint, he was wrong.

I regret to say there is a real advantage in attack. A newspaper is helped on that account. But I must not misrepresent my own views. I am not printing attacks for the purpose of furthering the publicity of the *Express*. My attitude, briefly stated, is that I can give it and take it.

But Tom was unable to spend much time on the biography yet: in 1952 he was preoccupied with compiling a 'personal diary' to be published the following April as *The Best of Both Worlds*.[2] Much of it was warmed-up versions of his columns from *Reynolds News*, dealing with public events such as Nye Bevan's resignation from the government, the Festival of Britain and the funeral of George VI. There was also an account of his own wedding. Dick Crossman called the book 'a scissors-and-paste, pot-boiling job', but even he had to concede that the launch party at the House of Commons was 'wonderful'.[3] The guests were a typically eclectic Driberg assortment, including the former British heavyweight boxing champion Tommy Farr, the editor of the *Daily Express*, Nye Bevan, Bob Boothby, the Ambassadors of Poland and Indonesia, Stephen Potter (the inventor of gamesmanship) and the American comedian Zero Mostel. Charles Allchild, landlord of the Fitzroy Tavern, was at one end of the room; Hannen Swaffer held court at the other.

Apart from Crossman's scornful dismissal, *The Best of Both Worlds* was well-received. The editor of *Reynolds News* wrote an enthusiastic feature arguing that the book was very like its launch party – 'an astonishing range of people and experiences is packed into a small space. Tom is, in my opinion, the best reporter in Fleet Street today.'[4] Since Tom was *Reynolds News*'s star contributor this was perhaps predictable. But other papers concurred. Daniel George in *Tribune* compared the book favourably with James Agate's *Ego*: 'No fake culture here. No showing off. No false modesty either. It's a better book, I think, than it was intended to be – the unconscious self-portrait of a usefully busy man of good will, with a wide variety of interests.'[5] The one large douche of cold water came from the magazine *Truth*, which reviewed *The Best of Both Worlds* with Hugh Dalton's memoirs:

> . . . Or instead, shall I read Mr Driberg,
> Whose bright, chatty diary extends
> To back stage accounts of the Commons
> And his cultured impeccable friends?
> Shall I read of his mansion in Essex,
> Of his views on the Church (which are High)
> Will he drop me some Bevanite tit-bits
> On the personal habits of Nye?
> About half-way through in a foot-note
> I expect he will coyly confess
> In the gay unregenerate 'Thirties
> That he wrote for the *Daily Express*?
>
> Well, whom shall I go to this evening,
> To seek some enlightenment from?
> Shall I plunge into history with Hughie,
> Or go for a gossip with Tom?
> The more I consider the problem
> The more with this knowledge I'm faced –
> That the Journalist's book, and the Doctor's,
> Both fill me with equal distaste!
> Hurray then for personal freedom
> Which is still the Englishman's right!
> Away with both Driberg and Dalton –
> And would somebody turn off the light?[6]

The book sold a respectable 4,000 copies in the first four months after publication. For a while it was the second best-selling non-fiction title in Foyle's bookshop, outdone only by a biography of Rommel.

By the summer of 1953, with *The Best of Both Worlds* behind him, Tom turned his attention to Beaverbrook. 'Reports that Tom Driberg had turned to fiction writing and was completing a book dealing with the problems facing a typical family in post-war Britain came as a surprise to those who have followed his literary career,' the *Braintree & Witham Times*, his local paper, remarked in September. 'They surprised Tom Driberg more.' His next book was 'more true to form'; and the paper reported that immediately after that autumn's Labour Party conference he would travel to Canada to visit some of Beaverbrook's old haunts.

'There are, of course, other biographies of this famous Press Lord,' the newspaper added pointedly. 'Obviously Tom Driberg feels that there are facts left untold and conclusions still to be drawn.'

Beaverbrook financed Tom's trip to Canada, but because of his insistence that he could not be seen to do so the account was paid through the London Newsprint Co. – 'so as to associate this journey with you as little as possible', Beaverbrook's secretary explained to him. It is hard to see why all this capework was necessary: Beaverbrook simultaneously encouraged his staff and associates in New Brunswick to give Tom all the assistance he required, so his support for the project was unlikely to remain a secret.

Tom flew to Montreal on 10 October, and thence to Fredericton, where he stayed at the Lord Beaverbrook Hotel. He visited the University of New Brunswick (Chancellor: Lord Beaverbrook) and the St John Law School (chief benefactor: Lord Beaverbrook) as well as the public library, the ice rink, the theatre, the community centre and all the many other public monuments to Lord Beaverbrook's generosity. He and Beaverbrook walked and talked together for hours. All was serene. Beaverbrook even suggested that Tom should become a trustee of the library. And, when they were not discussing Max Beaverbrook's past, they speculated on Tom Driberg's future. Tom said that he had more or less decided to retire from active politics and resume full-time journalism 'while I am still young enough to go (like Trollope) "banging about the world" and describing strange countries and people, in the intervals of doing a regular column based on London.' He would like to return to the *Express*, as Beaverbrook had proposed more than once: 'There is an attraction in the thought of working again for a professionally run paper.' *Reynolds*, he complained, was always cutting out his best bits. But the disengagement from his present commitments would be complicated. For one thing, he was anxious not to precipitate a marginal by-election by resigning straight away; he would prefer to give public notice of his intention not to stand again at the next general election, which now looked as though it might be a couple of years away. He thought that he should, in any case, not rejoin the *Express* until the biography was published (in the spring of 1954, he still hoped). Otherwise his declarations of independence from his subject might be doubted.

Meanwhile, as he wrote to Beaverbrook after the visit to Canada, he was beset by his familiar difficulty: insolvency. The advance of £500 that Weidenfeld had paid him the previous year was long gone. He was continually having to put the book aside to earn quick money by freelance work, he grumbled.[7] 'It is difficult to concentrate on semi-long-term work when there are grocers' bills to be paid; and my income from *Reynolds News* alone (and the parliamentary salary) is, of course, inadequate.' For several months he had boosted his income by working on *Picture Post*'s Coronation issues; but that had delayed the progress of the book still further.

Beaverbrook replied on 22 November: 'I am now ready to negotiate with you on behalf of the *Daily Express* when you find it convenient.' Characteristically, he had not bothered to mention the appointment to either Arthur Christiansen, the paper's editor, or E. J. Robertson, the manager (who was a sworn enemy of Tom). But he was sure that Christiansen had always had the highest regard for Tom's ability. 'You don't need to give a thought to his attitude. He is sure to support you.' Beaverbrook was not entirely in favour of Tom's departure from the Commons – 'there is a value in that particular association' – but he agreed entirely that Tom should finish the book before coming to the *Express*. Not that Beaverbrook thought there was any danger of Fleet Street or the wider public regarding the biography as a 'stooge' work. 'On the contrary,' he wrote teasingly, 'I think I will receive some public sympathy.'

Tom accepted that there were advantages to a journalist in being an MP. But it did mean that the column became overloaded with Westminster musings, as he had found on the *Express* in 1942–3 and at *Reynolds News* since. This, he told Beaverbrook, 'is inevitable when constant attendance at the House is insisted on as it has increasingly been in these last years.' Evidently he still bore the scars inflicted after his trip to Korea three years earlier. One reason why he hoped to go back to full-time journalism while still under fifty was that he wanted to undertake other long expeditions. He had a plan to go to China, possibly by car through the Soviet Union: 'I believe I may be one of the few Western journalists who *might* be able to get the necessary permits.' But it would be out of the question while he was an MP.

In March 1954 Tom announced that he would not seek the Labour nomination for Maldon at the next election. The reasons he gave to friends were that he needed to earn some serious money, and that his demanding constituency was syphoning off too much of his time. He was also forestalling the inevitable. As his local paper pointed out, a majority of 704 would not survive another election: 'Socialists with marginal seats are as good as out.'[8] By deciding to retire from the House – rather than waiting until the electorate forcibly retired him anyway – he liberated himself from the cares of backbench life. He could afford to be slightly less assiduous in attending surgeries and village-green meetings, and could concentrate on the more gainful work of writing a life of Lord Beaverbrook.

Relations between biographer and biographee remained joshingly affectionate in the early months of 1954. Tom sent encouraging reports of the book's progress, and kept the Lord supplied with political gossip and prognostications. On 3 February he wrote to Beaverbrook in Nassau with the news that 'Bob Boothby (who writes for the *News of the World*) says there is a swing of public opinion against the fantastic and irregular methods used by the police in persecuting homosexuals.' This must have provoked a dry laugh from Beaverbrook, who well remembered how in 1935 he had saved one particular homosexual from persecution by the police and two unemployed coal-miners. The very fact that Tom was able to raise the subject suggested that he still felt confident of Beaverbrook's faith in him.

A month later Beaverbrook devised another scheme to rescue Tom, this time from his creditors. The Abbey National building society had begun to make minatory noises about foreclosing Tom's second mortgage; Mr Nichols, the manager of the Liverpool Street station branch of the National Provincial Bank, was saying that he could not honour Driberg cheques any longer. At this bleak moment the *Sunday Express* bought the serial eights to Tom's book. Or rather, as one might expect, Beaverbrook bought them for the *Sunday Express* without troubling to warn the paper. Tom would be paid £4,000 – a handsome sum in 1954 – when he delivered the first 20,000 words, which Beaverbrook understood to be already written. They would be handed over by 7 April. By 1 September the remaining 60,000 words of the manuscript would be completed. Beaverbrook arranged for the bank and the building society to be informed of their client's good fortune. '*Now* you'll have to attack me much more fiercely,' Beaverbrook told Tom with a mischievous grin.

A shrewd observer would have guessed that something must go wrong with this apparently elegant solution to Tom's difficulties; and it did. On 6 April, one day before the first deadline, Tom sent an urgent message by hand to Beaverbrook's flat off Piccadilly, requesting a meeting 'today or tomorrow'.

'There seems,' Tom scribbled, 'to be a slight misunderstanding. I explained from the first that my material for the book – totalling so far, as I guessed, 20,000 words or the equivalent thereof – was in fragmentary form; but there is quite a fair amount of actual text, not merely notes, and I can show you a sample if you wish. Only, I could not honestly sign an agreement actually to deliver, by tomorrow, precisely 20,000 words in finished form, fit for publication.' This, he continued, had created an immediate problem, since he had informed his 'principal creditors' that he could pay them on the 8th.

He concluded with a cringing apology for bothering Beaverbrook with these woes.

If Tom had hoped to melt the old man's heart, he was disappointed. He received a stern reply the same day: 'You were to deliver 20,000 words by the 7th April. You had the days before you. And you can easily write 2,000 words a day when you have your material before you.' As so often, however, Beaverbrook could not bring himself to abandon Tom to his fate. With a sigh of exasperation he agreed to pay £1,000 immediately to Tom's solicitors for the purpose of discharging the second mortgage. Another £3,000 would be paid when the 20,000 words were received, 'providing the manuscript is delivered before the 27th April, and in proper condition, suitable for publication in due course'. Thereafter Tom would have to deliver 12,000 words a month until he had yielded up the remaining 60,000 words – 'in finished form', Beaverbrook reminded him.

When Beaverbrook went to stay at his villa on Cap d'Ail later that month Tom hoped to go as well, for the purpose of 'further research'. But on 21 April Tom had a curt warning from Robertson that it would 'not be convenient' for Beaverbrook to receive him in France until the initial 20,000 words had been delivered and digested.

The new schedule meant that the whole manuscript should have been finished by 27 September 1954. There was never any likelihood of that deadline being met, but Tom did apply himself with more diligence than usual. In the middle of July he proudly informed Beaverbrook that the 'total wordage' now stood at 43,000 or so. 'I really am getting on with the job,' he promised, like a schoolboy late with his homework. Now could he come to France, please? Beaverbrook said yes. Tom had packed his bag and was about to set off for the airport when Beaverbrook suddenly withdrew the invitation. Tom was despondent. How, he asked Robertson, could he be expected to meet his deadline when the one man he depended upon – the man who was both sponsor and subject of the book – made himself unavailable?

Having missed his French leave, Tom decided that he would take three weeks in Cyprus instead, at the expense of *Reynolds News*. It was a timely moment for such a visit. Led by Archbishop Makarios, the Greek Cypriots were waging an ever more militant campaign for *Enosis*, union with Greece. The British government was intransigent. The Minister of State at the Colonial Office, an old fool called Harry Hopkinson, had rashly vowed that Britain would 'never' grant independence to Cyprus. (He was thereafter known as 'Never-Say-Never Hopkinson'.[9]) This goaded the Cypriots into huge, noisy protests. The British retaliated by threatening that anyone who argued publicly for *Enosis* would be charged with sedition. By the time Tom arrived in mid-August, the island was in a highly combustible state: the temperature was 105 degrees in the shade, and the political heat was overpowering. In Nicosia on Sunday 22 August Tom shoved his way through a 35,000-strong crowd to enter the Phaneromini church, where Makarios again defied the no-campaigning decree by calling for union with Greece. The congregation outside the building took up the illegal chant: '*Enosis* – long live *Enosis*!' In the course of his sermon Makarios also referred to the British MP who had come in friendship to hear the Cypriots' grievance; and before Tom knew what was happening he found himself carried shoulder-high down the church steps and through several streets by the cheering crowd – 'an honour kindly in intention,' he wrote, 'but somewhat exhausting not only for me but for those conferring it, since I weigh about 14 stone.'[10] One Greek newspaper reported that he shouted out 'Long live *Enosis*!', but he insisted that all he actually said was 'Thank you very much but for God's sake let me go down' – or words to that effect.

This ecstatic reception was reported widely in the British and Cypriot press. Four days later Tom's conduct was denounced in an editorial in the *Daily Express*:

He goes out to ally himself with the agitation against British policy there. He allows himself to be carried shoulder-high by Britain's enemies.

There is this to be said for Mr Driberg's activities: they can only create trouble for Britain . . . It is a shocking thing that these Socialists should go selling out their country by their foreign travels.[11]

In reply to similar criticism in the *Cyprus Mail*, an English-language newspaper, Tom sent a letter defending himself. 'I am gratified,' he wrote, 'that in your innocence you should quote the attack on me by the *Daily Express* as if it were effective and damaging. To be attacked by the *Express* is an accolade keenly sought by politicians of all parties.' Meanwhile, back in London, the *Express* continued its campaign by revealing, with many a nudge and wink, that Tom's reports from Cyprus for *Reynolds News* were being reprinted in *Neos Demokratis*, the paper of the Cypriot Communist Party. On 29 August *Reynolds News* itself joined the fray. 'What really riles the *Daily Express*,' it suggested in a leader, 'is that Tom Driberg's interpretation is likely to be rather different from the chest-beating, keep-the-natives-in-their-place idea of Europe which is favoured by that newspaper.'

There is some circumstantial evidence that the *Express*'s sallies against Tom were ordered by the proprietor himself; certainly the editorial of 26 August has his stylistic fingerprints all over it. This is no great surprise. By the time Tom flew to Cyprus in August, Beaverbrook had seen enough of the manuscript of his biography to decide that he didn't like it at all. He told E. J. Robertson that he had done his utmost for Driberg but was no longer prepared to help him.

Yet, characteristically, by the end of September he had relented, agreeing to send Tom some cuttings files for 1925 and 1926; 'and when we get those back he can get right on with the others'. Beaverbrook travelled to America, but the work-in-progress continued to reach him. Then he changed his mind yet again. On 22 November he cabled to the general manager: 'Mr Robertson. I have received this Driberg stuff. It is very wicked indeed.' Tom, undaunted, continued to post his parcels of text off to Beaverbrook at the Waldorf Towers in New York. On 1 December he transmitted the glad tidings that the book was coming along well and would be finished within a week or two, for publication in the spring.

The inevitable crisis could not be postponed for long. Beaverbrook's objections to the manuscript were too many and various to be easily accommodated: Tom's account of the 'December 1916 *coup*', led by Beaverbrook, which had toppled Asquith; Tom's version of Beaverbrook's struggles with Baldwin; a chapter dealing with his feud against Mountbatten (Tom sided with Mountbatten, and cleared this section with him); the revelation of the 'white list' of people who had incurred Beaverbook's displeasure and were therefore never mentioned in the *Daily Express*; a passage about his treatment of his first wife.

On 14 December Beaverbrook sent a long memorandum to Robertson in London, complaining that the book 'is inaccurate on many points and he has not done sufficient research to set himself straight'. Only two years earlier he had told Tom: 'You know I do not object to attack . . . I can give it and I can take it.' Now he warned: 'I am not going to let Driberg get away with the impression that he can write what he likes about me without having a considerable row.' His memo to Robertson concluded with a comically self-pitying howl of anguish which is worth quoting at some length:

Mr Robertson. I am very sorry to give you all this trouble. It is my own fault. I have made so many errors in life. I seem to be continuing them like some others I could mention. The older I grow the more frequently I blunder into mistakes.

But this fellow with cunning persuaded me by representations through other persons as well as on his own account to help him financially with this project in the belief that he was doing something that would be critical but fair, instead I find that I am subjected to accusations of a very disagreeable character. And I want to make it plain, Mr Robertson, that in order that you may form a fair judgment as far as my folly is concerned that I don't mind a bit, that I would just as soon go one way as the other. I get vexed at having fallen into a trap but that is all. I don't mind, I can scramble out all right.

No use in telling me, Mr Robertson, which several persons have a right to do, no use in telling me that I was warned, for indeed I was. Plenty and plenty of warning. But in vain – in the face of the bird is the net of the fowler displayed.

The faithful Robertson, whose apprehension about the project had now been thoroughly vindicated, decided to fire another shot across Driberg's bows. On 22 December he informed Tom that the *Express*'s syndication department had had the manuscript read by a lawyer, who 'is most definitely of the opinion that the book is defamatory of the *Daily Express*, Lord Beaverbrook, Max Aitken, as well as several other people'. None of it would be published in the newspaper until the libelled parties had given their clearance. Robertson suggested that 'either you or your publisher seek independent legal advice'.

Beaverbrook was by now wintering in the Bahamas, growling irascibly as each new set of Driberg proofs reached him. Rather than abandon Tom for good, however, he invited him to deliver the last two chapters in person, so that they could try to 'clear up matters' once and for all. The air fares would be covered, as would Tom's bills at the Royal Victoria Hotel, Nassau. (Beaverbrook's house in the Bahamas was already full of guests, including Bob Boothby.) Tom set off on Friday 7 January 1955, carrying in his luggage the final chapters of the book as well as certain essential supplies that Beaverbrook had requested – six sparklets for his lordship's soda syphon and a catalogue of the paintings in Dulwich College Gallery.

He dined at Beaverbrook's on the Saturday evening and left the new manuscript with him. After reading it overnight, the baron came down to breakfast the next morning in a fury. 'Man has been falling ever since the birth of Adam,' he told his guests. 'But never in the whole course of human history has any man fallen quite so low as that fellow Driberg.'[12]

When Tom came to the house soon after breakfast, he was given the same message *fortissimo*. Beaverbrook accused him of being driven by malice and hatred. Tom, deeply distressed, returned to his hotel and composed a long letter to Beaverbrook, which he delivered by hand later that day. 'I have no "hatred" for you: how could I have?' he asked.

On the contrary, when speaking about you (and the *Express*), even in left-wing circles, I have always stressed the contrast between my regard for you personally – with my admiration for the *Express* technically – and my political disapproval of much of what you and the *Express* stand for. You probably won't remember, but I paid a personal tribute to you in the House of Commons during the first debate on the Royal Commission.

He added that he was happy to remove passages which were genuinely unfair or offensive. Why, having asked him to come all this way, was Beaverbrook not prepared even to discuss them?

I cannot help feeling that, in reading these chapters, you have taken the favourable parts simply for granted, and have not balanced them against the less agreeable passages; just as, in the most bitter part of what you said to me this morning, you again seemed to me not to distinguish – as I say in the book that you do not distinguish sufficiently – between personal and public criticism and relations.

Tom besought Beaverbrook to get some impartial friend to read the book. As Bob Boothby was on the premises, why not ask him?

Beaverbrook was as unimpressed by this last suggestion as by the protestations of friendship and sincerity. He was not prepared to pay Tom's hotel bill for another day; nor would he welcome Tom at his dining table again. It would be best if the malicious biographer left the country at once. Tom ignored the command. He said that he would stay on until the following Friday, paying his own way. This was less easy than expected: Beaverbrook forgot to tell the hotel to cancel his original instruction that the account should be sent to him. When Tom checked out on Friday morning, the hotel flatly refused to let him pay the bill.

Beaverbrook brooded over his next move. He knew that, if pressed, Tom would change any offending passages. But this might only make matters worse. Once Tom had completed the alterations he would consider that the *Express* was morally obliged to serialise and syndicate the book. 'And I don't think,' Beaverbrook cabled to Robertson in London, 'we should do either serialisation or syndication.' But the *Express* should keep the serial rights, to ensure that no other popular paper could run extracts from the biography either.

This would prevent Tom's words from reaching the newspaper-reading multitudes. But there was still the problem of the book itself. Robertson was ordered to start intimidating the publishers, Weidenfeld. While in Nassau, Tom had let slip the fact that Weidenfeld had some sort of insurance policy with Lloyd's of London. Robertson was to ask Lloyd's whether it already had a lawyer reading Driberg's manuscript for libel; if it hadn't, it should. The lawyers for both Lloyd's and Weidenfeld were told that Lord Beaverbrook had found 'countless libels' of 'a most serious character' which would force him to sue.

'I think Mr D is much shaken by my attitude to him,' Beaver-brook wrote on 12 January. 'I imagine he thought he could make a lot of alterations in his narrative and get me to consent and go back to assure the publishers that he had my written authority to the contents of the narrative. I wouldn't be surprised if he put some things in with the intention of striking them out and thus pleasing me and making me believe in his reasonableness once more.' Beaverbrook accepted that he could probably not stop Weidenfeld from issuing the biography eventually, in expurgated form. But he consoled himself with the thought that 'I have met worse troubles than this in life.' Besides, he doubted if the book would have a very large sale.

It may be wondered why, when Beaverbrook had made his disapproval so obvious, Tom persisted in his efforts to win the old man round. Wilful blindness or stubborn resilience, perhaps; more likely, it was simply that he had not yet known his charm to fail with Beaverbrook. In the quarter-century of their acquaintance he had asked the Lord for many favours; he had never been denied. Even when he angered Beaverbrook – by his evidence to the Royal Commission on the Press, to take the most conspicuous instance – he was soon forgiven. He had no reason to suppose that Beaverbrook's latest rage would be any more enduring.

Tom thus carried on as though all was still well. He wrote a polite thank-you letter on his return, and a few weeks later felt confident enough to risk a homosexual joke when he sent Beaverbrook some photographs taken in the garden of the Nassau house. 'I thought perhaps you might like to give them to that hefty Negro gardener,' he explained in a covering note.

By now, word of the explosion in the Bahamas had reached Randolph Churchill, who again contributed a malevolent para-graph to the Peterborough column in the *Daily Telegraph*.[13] Tom protested to the paper, insisting loyally that Beaverbrook had not tried to suppress or tamper with his book. In fact, Tom himself was now tampering away like billy-o. In the first week of March he sent Lord Beaverbrook a batch of proposed emendations – 'a sincere and careful attempt to meet the objections which you detailed to me'. He had made clearer Beaverbrook's distinction between isolationism and appeasement; he had put in Beaverbrook's 'most interesting point' that Empire Free Trade might have been accepted but for the 1931 crisis; he had cut some dialogue which implied that Beaverbrook could sometimes be heartless; he had altered a reference to the Holborn by-election. There were many other modifications, which Tom hoped would prove his desire 'to write a book which, while critical in some respects, is not unfair'.

Beaverbrook took little notice. He was prepared to leave it to the lawyers, who, he trusted, would spin out the libel negotiations for as long as possible. He had also delegated to his son, Max Aitken, the task of leaning on George Weidenfeld. After several conversations with Weidenfeld, Aitken told his father on 26 March that 'he is in real difficulty. He wants to remain on the best of terms with us, because he has been having talks with Keeble on some children's books, and he considers that we are a better long-term project than any Driberg book. At the same time he has £500 invested in Driberg and is anxious to get it back.'

Aitken and Weidenfeld met again five days later, at the Reform Club. The publisher revealed that his lawyers had made many objections to the manuscript; 80 per cent of them had already been agreed by Tom, and the other 20 per cent could probably be pushed through if necessary. According to Aitken, Weidenfeld warned 'that Driberg was in a white heat of righteousness, saying that if the *Daily Express* bankrupted him he would be able to repeat all the so-called libels in court, and that if he went to prison he would become a martyr and the Oscar Wilde of Fleet Street.' Weidenfeld wanted to publish the book because he feared that Tom might otherwise sue him for breach of contract and would use the opportunity of a court hearing to repeat all his 'libels' against Beaverbrook. The publicity from such a case might actually encourage American and Canadian publishers to commission Tom to write a more hostile biography. Tom had even sent galleys to the Prime Minister, Winston Churchill, in the hope that he would say the book was not libellous.

It took almost a year before the book was sufficiently mutilated to satisfy the three sets of lawyers – Beaverbrook's, Weidenfeld's and ('most pernickety of all,'[14] according to Tom) Lloyd's. Beaverbrook had obtained an opinion from leading counsel, Helenus Milmo, that the book *as a whole* was malicious. After months of wrangling, Weidenfeld's lawyers said that if agreement could not be reached soon they would restore passages which were not libellous but had been cut in deference to Beaverbrook's feelings.

The section that caused most difficulty dealt with the *Daily Express*'s notorious vendetta against Lord Mountbatten. According to Tom, the grudge dated back to the Dieppe raid of 1942, in which more than 900 Canadian soldiers had lost their lives. Beaverbrook, he revealed, had been plunged into 'an absolute paroxysm of rage' and had directed his wrath against the man he held responsible for the raid – Mountbatten, then Chief of Combined Operations. Soon after the raid Mountbatten met Beaverbrook at dinner in Averell Harriman's London flat. Beaverbrook called him a 'murderer'. Mountbatten explained that his plan had been changed by a Canadian general, who had insisted on the disastrous frontal attack. Beaverbrook refused to listen. 'You murdered my Canadians in order to wreck my Second Front campaign,' Beaverbrook snarled. When Harriman mentioned Beaverbrook's behaviour to Churchill the next day, Churchill replied 'Don't worry, he'd probably had too much to drink' – which was true.

Mountbatten confirmed this story to Tom (as, years later, did Harriman), but it infuriated Beaverbrook. By the time it had been cleared for publication it was a shadow of its former self. Here is the final version, grubby with the marks of libel-lawyers:

When the grim toll of Canadian lives was still fresh in people's minds, Beaverbrook and Mountbatten were dinner-guests at Mr Averell Harriman's apartment in Mayfair. Beaverbrook was tired. When the conversation turned to Dieppe, there was an angry dispute, and he used language which seemed to imply that he held Mountbatten personally responsible for the heavy casualties. Harriman was shocked by this ugly scene and discussed it with Churchill the next day.[15]

Although the same anaesthetic was applied to a number of passages in the book, elsewhere Tom still managed to criticise Beaverbrook's use of power. Direct attack was replaced by irony; but the message was no less effective for that. Even after the months of snipping and

trimming, Tom's biography was still an honest and brave enter-
prise. It was to be titled *Beaverbrook: A Study in Power and
Frustration*. Weidenfeld announced that it would be published in
February 1956.

Beaverbrook had changed his mind a dozen times as to what he
should do with the serialisation. Print nothing at all? Run a short
extract tucked away in the *Sunday Express*? His sense of mischief
eventually got the better of him. Why put Tom under a bushel as
though Beaverbrook really had something to hide? No, he would
serialise the book prominently and at length – with a reply from the
injured party.[16] He prepared a series of articles defending and
explaining himself.

Then he killed them. As Arthur Christiansen noted, they 'were
alien to his technique, which is attack, always attack. That is the
Beaverbrook way when he is mauled, and the Driberg serialisation
was used for this purpose.'[17] Battle commenced in the *Daily
Express* of Saturday 11 February 1956, when the first instalment
was published. Seldom if ever has a newspaper serialised a book
so inhospitably. The extract appeared under a huge headline:
'HOSTILE BIOGRAPHY'. Another volley was fired in the
standfirst: 'To introduce you to Lord Beaverbrook as seen by
biographer Tom Driberg, former Socialist MP and ex-member of
the *Daily Express* staff, here are extracts from Chapter One. Parts
of the biography, which is hostile and frequently inaccurate, will be
serialised in the *Daily Express* next week because it is the policy of
this newspaper to suppress nothing.' The newspaper's policy, it
might have added, was to sabotage the book instead. Each extract
was gleefully undermined by footnotes which, though attributed to
the editor, were in fact written by Beaverbrook himself.

Tom had, for instance, included a story about E. R. Thompson,
the *Evening Standard* editor who in 1924 refused to obey Beaverbrook's order that he should support Churchill in his columns.
'Thompson was sent for: such mutiny could not be tolerated,' Tom
wrote. 'Fortunately the interview, though stormy, was brief: in the
course of being sacked, Thompson had a heart attack and died.' The
Express's footnote, dictated by Beaverbrook, was blunt: 'Not true.
Thompson was still editor of the *Evening Standard* in 1928, when

he was found dead in bed of a heart attack. His widow was given a pension.' Tom was particularly hurt by this refutation since the source for his original story had been none other than Beaverbrook himself.

In the absence of other factual errors, Tom was put in the stocks for his sins of omission. Beneath a paragraph about Beaverbrook's pre-war advocacy of rearmament was an *Express* footnote pointing out that 'at this time the Socialist Party, to which Mr Driberg belongs, was opposing the rearmament of Britain.' Tom had re-called that as late as August 1939 Beaverbrook refused to believe war was imminent; the *Express* reminded its readers of Tom's own prediction in his Hickey column that month: 'My tip: no war this crisis.'

Perversely, Beaverbrook's most wounding shot was provoked by a passage that was intended to show how lovable he could be. 'Often he is at his most engaging in his relations with erring employees,' Tom wrote, telling of a journalist, 'by no means senior in the firm', who had urgently needed £1,000 and requested a loan; he was handed the money as a gift instead. 'Such kindness,' Tom concluded, 'goes far beyond the shrewd self-interest which cynics detect in the largesse of rich employers.'

'Mr Driberg,' an *Express* footnote cruelly revealed, 'was the employee concerned.' Beaverbrook had wanted to add that Tom 'was at that time on trial at the Old Bailey and he asked Lord Beaverbrook for the money to provide for his defence.' Arthur Christiansen persuaded Beaverbrook that this would be improper. (It would have been untrue, too: the £1,000 gift was offered in March 1940, four and a half years after Tom's trial.)

Not that Christiansen had any sympathy for his former colum-nist. Like E. J. Robertson, he had warned from the start that Tom's purpose was to make mischief, and he believed that the final manuscript justified his apprehension: it was 'outrageous' and 'offensive'. He had no qualms about disclosing Tom's £1,000 gift. 'Old friends with left-wing views accused me of being a cad to expose Driberg,' Christiansen wrote later. 'But I had no bad consci-ence. If a man is given access to another man's private papers and accepts a large sum of money to do a job which turns out to be something of a mud bath, then that man deserves all he gets.' One left-winger who did agree was Kingsley Martin, the *New Statesman*'s editor. 'Driberg is a funny chap,' he told Christiansen. 'He honestly believes that he can bite the hand that feeds him and be thanked for it.'[18] Martin repeated the opinion to Tom himself, who affected not to understand it. 'It seems to imply that if an employer has ever paid you for working for him, he has bought also your conscience, your judgment, and your right of free expression,'[19] Tom argued – thereby missing Kingsley Martin's point. Similarly, in reply to Beaverbrook's complaint that the book had a 'Jekyll and Hyde' theme, Tom asked merely 'Isn't everybody Jekyll and Hyde?' Perhaps so; and of course Tom was entitled to award blame as well as praise. But his protestations of surprise and distress when the biographee cut up rough seem slightly disingenuous. Beaverbrook was not a modest man and, for all his insistence to the contrary, he did not suffer criticism gladly. Tom's picture of the Hyde within the Jekyll, however tactfully done, invited retaliation.

Beaverbrook's reaction may have been predictable; but it was not reasonable. No fair reader could come away from the book doubting Tom's affection for the old man. Indeed, while being flayed by the *Express* for his 'hostility' Tom was censured by Evelyn Waugh for not being hostile enough. On 23 February Waugh wrote a singularly ungracious letter of thanks for the copy of *Beaverbrook* that Tom had sent him:

I opened it with eagerness as I had seen it advertised as a 'hostile' biography. What do I find? A honeyed eulogy. You mention a few of Beaverbrook's more notorious public aberrations but you give little impression of the deep malevolence of the man . . . Was all the story of your tiff with him a 'publicity stunt' devised by the pair of you? If Beaverbrook really thinks your book hostile, he must have singularly little sense of his true position . . .

I was shocked to find you falling into the popular misuse of *expertise*. In France this word does not mean 'skill' but the judgement by an expert on the authenticity of a work of art.

All this sounds ungrateful. Please believe it is not unfriendly.[20]

Tom sent a complimentary copy to another of Beaverbrook's old foes, the former Labour Prime Minister who by now rejoiced in the title of Earl Attlee. His reply was characteristically terse:

My dear Driberg,

Thank you for sending me your book on the Beaver. I have delayed replying until I had read it. This I did with much interest. I note that in *The Times* its advertisement is next to one headed 'A bad man'. The heading might have been extended across the page.

Though reviewers of the book divided according to their opinions of Beaverbrook himself, they were unanimous in their praise for the quality of Tom's writing. A. J. P. Taylor, who himself was to write a famously hagiographical life of the Lord, found the biography 'wonderfully entertaining' but complained that it credited Beaverbrook with great power when really he had none: 'Lord Beaverbrook is in fact a victim, not a tyrant – a victim of the very illusion which he imposes on others.'[21] The *Sunday Dispatch*'s political columnist, Alastair Forbes, began encouragingly ('a first-rate book, written with all the brilliance and talent which have justified Lord Beaverbrook's long-dated and loyal patronage of this unusually cultivated journalist') but then, suddenly, turned on Tom's morals with a censorious glare:

Power, of which Lord Beaverbrook has never attained as much as he would like, is said to corrupt. It has certainly corrupted Mr Driberg, who owes whatever power he has enjoyed in his life entirely to Lord Beaverbrook.

He rather grudgingly admits his lordship has in his day done some good by stealth in mitigation of his public mischief-making. But nothing could exceed the stealth with which Mr Driberg approaches the good Lord Beaverbrook did him and the pains he took to rescue him from ill fortune.

Satan rebuking sin could scarcely make a more disagreeable impression than Mr Driberg complaining about Lord Beaverbrook's lack of 'a sense of sin', a wrong judgment surely in any case, since the son of the manse broods a great deal more about hell-fire than the regularly shriven Anglo-Catholic churchgoer.

One would respect Mr Driberg's strictures upon the 'vacuum in the soul' of Lord Beaverbrook if one did not suspect the vacuum in his own heart . . .

I hope that Lord Beaverbrook will hasten to commission Mr Osbert Lancaster to write and illustrate a biography of Mr Driberg, for which he might borrow from Stendhal the title *The Red and the Black*, in view of the main threads of his political and spiritual life.

But perhaps it would not be suitable for serialisation in the Beaverbrook Press, or even as a 'hostile biography' in *Reynolds News*.[22]

This was strong stuff. Any well-informed reader would recognise the references to Tom's promiscuity and to his prosecution in 1935. It was common knowledge in Fleet Street that Beaverbrook had kept Tom's trial out of the newspapers, and Forbes was not the only journalist to be astonished that Tom dared express even mild criticism of his patron. Hannen Swaffer was so outraged that he wrote to Beaverbrook asking for dirt on Driberg which he could work into his review of the book. Beaverbrook declined to help, but Swaffer wrote a stinging assessment anyway. Like Forbes, he all but mentioned the Old Bailey case. 'No one owes Beaverbrook more than does Driberg,' he declared with typical hyperbole. 'In the hour of his greatest need, the Beaver rushed to his aid, lavish with his influence and his money. Had I ever been a tithe as much in debt to Beaverbrook as Driberg was then, I would never have written such a "hostile" book as this.'[23]

The accusation of ingratitude wounded Tom. He wrote to Swaffer denying that he was the sort of person who 'can't forgive a kindness':

When I first joined the *Express, you* were kind to me – gave me good advice – took me to supper at the Savoy. Later, when I stood for Parliament, you helped me and spoke for me. I have always been grateful to you – and have showed my gratitude on every possible occasion, both in speech and in print.

So I do not automatically turn against my benefactors.

Beaverbrook was personally kind and generous to me on more than one occasion. I have often expressed my gratitude to him publicly (e.g., in the House of Commons) as well as privately.

But this surely does not mean that, when I undertake to write a book about him, it is to be purely a 'stooge' book (like the rubbishy books written about him many years ago)?

Swaffer sent a testy reply, repeating all his charges against Tom and adding a few new ones. He then concluded briskly: 'Anyway, do not let this affair disturb our friendship.' After this skirmish, however, Tom's gratitude for favours rendered was increasingly outweighed by his irritation at Swaffer's curmudgeonly temper and limitless egotism. Swaffer was an ardent spiritualist, and even after his death in 1962 he managed to make a nuisance of himself. In 1967, while short of cash, Tom accepted a commission to write Swaffer's biography. He regretted it almost immediately but, since he could not afford to repay the advance, he toiled miserably at the project for years. His task was made all the harder by the uncooperative attitude of Swaffer's old housekeeper and fellow-spiritualist, Rose Baston: when Tom telephoned her to arrange a meeting she said that Swaffer had 'come through' at a *séance* the previous evening and had warned her to have nothing to do with Driberg.[24]

Tom's relations with Beaverbrook were defrosted rather more successfully. For two or three years there was no sign of a thaw. But as with the departure from the *Express* in 1943, or the evidence to the Royal Commission in 1948, neither side could sustain the grudge with a straight face for long. On Beaverbrook's eightieth birthday, 25 May 1959, Tom sent a telegram: 'Warmest greetings from your unhostile biographer'. Later that year he was invited to the dinner given by Beaverbrook in honour of Arthur Christiansen, at Claridge's. Christiansen claimed in his memoirs that 'it was possibly only out of compliment to me that the Beaver buried the hatchet for that one night'. Not so; Beaverbrook confirmed the reconciliation by sending Tom a case of champagne at the same time. Tom thanked him warmly: 'It is thoughtful of you to remember that I like champagne well aged; the year is an unusual but a good one.' He then came as near as he could to contrition:

I need not, perhaps, add that I value your hospitality and your gift not only for their own sake but because they seem to me to be a token of the healing of a breach which has distressed me during the past few years. I truly regret my share in causing this breach; and I shall always think of you with affection and gratitude.

Thereafter, it was just like old times: for the rest of Beaverbrook's life he and Tom exchanged gossip and gifts, teases and flattery. When Harold Wilson was elected to lead the Labour Party, in February 1963, Tom wrote coolly: 'I think he will do.' Beaverbrook replied with greater enthusiasm: 'I think Wilson will do wonderfully.' As if to celebrate the good news, a fortnight later Beaverbrook sent Tom a cheese from his Somerset farm.

On 25 May 1964 Tom was among the guests at a magnificent dinner for Beaverbrook's eighty-fifth birthday, held at the Dorchester. He contributed a few fond reminiscences to a BBC programme which was broadcast to mark the occasion, and on 29 May Beaverbrook wrote to thank him for them. Ten days later the old man was dead. He bore no lingering ill-will to his 'hostile' biographer. A couple of years before his death, when he caught one of his secretaries surreptitiously reading Tom's *Beaverbrook*, he chuckled: 'Oh well, I expect most of the things he says about me are true.'[25]

CHAPTER ELEVEN

MOSCOW GOLD

When Tom announced in March 1954 that he would not seek the Maldon nomination again, there was some talk in the local party of adopting Ena as his successor – much of it from Ena herself. She would have made an attractive candidate, too, but the General Committee of the local Labour Party feared that this arrangement might appear ever so slightly feudal, as if the local milord from the big house were handing over the constituency as a gift to his wife. Unfair, perhaps, but there it was. The argument was academic anyway. Maldon fell to the Conservatives in the general election of May 1955, as Tom had known it would. It was a naturally Conservative seat – that was why he loved it so – and the only surprise was that the Tories had been held off for so long. Had he still been the Labour candidate he might have been hurt by the rejection; as the retiring Member he could maintain a carefree detachment. Besides, he was demob-happy. There would be no more meetings, no more interminable constituency correspondence, no speeches at Royal British Legion dinners or school prize-days. He could travel abroad for months on end; or, when the fancy took him, he could sit under the ilex tree at Bradwell composing poetry. He would miss the Commons itself, of course, but at least he would never again be pursued about the globe by urgent cables from the Labour Whips demanding his immediate return. He was fifty years old and in reasonable health: time stretched ahead of him, rich with enticement.

Or so the reverie went. What it neglected was the desperate financial abyss beneath him. The patience of his bank manager,

F. W. Nichols of the Liverpool Street station branch of the National Provincial, was almost exhausted. Nichols had threatened to take severe (but unspecified) action against his rogue customer the previous year, and had granted a stay of execution only when Tom promised to leave Parliament and earn a living. As soon as the general election was over, the man from the National Provincial began to press him again. On 5 June 1955, little more than a week after relinquishing his seat, Tom humbly submitted 'a first (interim) report on the financial prospects in my new careers':

You will appreciate that I could not really make a start on it until after the General Election campaign. This was immediately followed by the Whitsun holiday.

I therefore came to London last Tuesday – as the old saying goes – 'to seek my fortune'.

So far, I have done work or secured commissions for *immediate* execution (i.e. for payment this month) which will bring in a total of about £140.[1]

This was made up as follows: £20 from *Punch* for a review of an exhibition at Olympia; £20 from the *New Statesman* for a profile of Danny Kaye; £10 10s. from Rainbird Publishers for reading and advising on a manuscript; £31 10s. from *Reynolds News* (in addition to his regular stipend) for an article in a series he was writing about Mountbatten; £60 from *Housewife* magazine for a description of Evelyn Waugh's house. 'I think you will agree,' he told the bank manager, 'that what I have outlined is not bad going for five days in a new career.' It more than compensated for the loss of his parliamentary salary; and payments to his secretary would soon be reduced as she had already found a part-time job with a new MP. 'Meanwhile I am living as economically as possible; but of course a few current domestic and other cheques have to be paid.' He was careful not to raise Nichols's expectations too high: most of the £140, he explained, would not come in until the end of the month, and 'it is not good tactics to press too anxiously for quick payment'. No doubt Nichols had his own opinions on this point, especially after his years of having to deal with Tom.

Still, there was no denying that Tom was at last 'seeking his fortune'. On 5 June he lunched with the editor of *Picture Post*, who promised to commission some articles from him at the generous rate of 50 guineas per thousand words. A week later he dined with Malcolm Muggeridge, the editor of *Punch*, who was also in the market for Driberg products. Kingsley Martin hired him to write a weekly television review for the *New Statesman*. A producer from the Light Programme of BBC Radio asked Tom to present a report on 'events in London' every night for one week in October. *Housewife* magazine was hungry for more articles about the houses of the famous: Waugh, Constance Cummings, Randolph Churchill, the Sitwells and (inevitably) Mountbatten all found the roving reporter from *Housewife* on their doorsteps in the next few months. A publisher invited him to expand his *Reynolds News* articles on Mountbatten into a book. The fee was £500, half of it to be paid at once, but Tom was reluctant to accept since Mountbatten had told him that there was not yet enough new material to justify another biography, and he did not want to jeopardise their friendship. Meanwhile *Reynolds* had a new proposal: a series on the Duke of Edinburgh, for £150 plus a half-share in any proceeds from syndication. Tom raised it with Prince Philip the week after the election and found him 'very friendly' to the idea.

Tom had high hopes, too, that there would be lucrative employment for him in commercial television, which was due to begin in September. One of the new stations, Granada, was controlled by Sidney Bernstein, a friend from Hickey days who was now the guarantor of Tom's overdraft. Another company, ABC, had already expressed an interest in hiring Tom to present a chat-show called *Sunday Afternoon*. His television career hitherto had amounted to little more than a few appearances on the political discussion programme *In the News*; but he was convinced that he was a 'natural' for the small screen, who had been held back in the past only by his Membership of Parliament and by the BBC's political timidity.

There was some truth in this. When *In the News* began, in 1950, the regular guests had been two left-wing socialists (Michael Foot and A. J. P. Taylor), an iconoclastic Conservative (Bob Boothby) and a right-wing former Independent MP (Bill Brown). Both

Labour and Tory party bosses, abetted by the popular press, protested that these panellists were far from the 'mainstream', and eventually forced the BBC to dilute the original team. However, the 'new blood' introduced to the Labour side of the panel in 1951 was no less contaminated – Tom and Barbara Castle, both of them Bevanites. When Nye Bevan resigned from the government in April that year, loudly cheered by these two, the BBC had another purge. A few days before he was due to appear on the 4 May edition of *In the News* Tom was told that his services were no longer required, because of 'the atmosphere that has grown up around your name in the last few days'. He wrote at once to the Director of Television, George Barnes:

The fact is that I am, and expect to continue to be, a member of the Labour Party receiving the Parliamentary Party whip, and a member of the National Executive Committee of the Party; and that I am therefore as well-qualified politically as any other back-bench Labour MP to argue the Socialist or the Government case on any issue other than the particular issue that has recently been the subject of controversy within the Party – which, I take it, would in any case not be likely to be the subject of *In the News* again next Friday.

. . . Surely the BBC's main object is to see that both sides of any current topic can be presented by politicians who are also reasonably able and lively broadcasters? So long as both sides get a fair show, is it not the performance rather than the particular shade of party view that counts?[2]

In reply, Barnes murmured blandly that the BBC must be seen to be politically impartial between the government and opposition and between different factions within a party. He added: 'It did seem wrong – not to say ingenuous – that in the five remaining broadcasts following Mr Bevan's resignation there should be five appearances by acknowledged sympathisers, with no representative of the rest of the Labour Party on any of these occasions.'[3] Nothing could have better symbolised the difference between the BBC's nervous conservatism and commercial television's youthful adventurousness than the fact that, four years later, ABC hired not only Tom (as host of *Sunday Afternoon*) but also Foot, Taylor and Boothby, who re-formed their old team from *In The News* for a programme called *Free Speech*.

While accepting a job on the other channel, however, Tom was simultaneously begging for work from BBC Television. Shortly before the 1955 election he had written to Harman Grisewood, the Director of the Spoken Word at the BBC, to protest that he was being persecuted because he belonged to a minority in his party. 'At one time I used to broadcast fairly often, in overseas as well as home programmes,' he wrote. 'In the past 18 months I have been in *only one* broadcast (*Any Questions* on 10 December 1954).'[4] Now that he was leaving Parliament, could he be allowed on the air again? Grisewood tried not to be too encouraging, but he did pass on the usual platitudes about always being interested in suggestions for programmes. Unfortunately, Tom read the offer literally; before long he was pestering the Corporation with all sorts of daft proposals. At the end of July 1955 he suggested to Cecil McGivern, the Controller of Programmes (and the man who had complained of the atmosphere surrounding Tom's name), that the BBC should start a panel game called *J Is for Juggins* – to be chaired, naturally, by the popular broadcaster and former MP Tom Driberg. This was derived from the game where one player chooses a name and announces its first letter ('B', say); another player then asks some such question as 'Are you a deaf man with an ear for music?' (No, I'm not Beethoven'). McGivern passed this to his assistant, S. J. de Lotbiniere, who told Tom with feigned regret that *J Is for Juggins* was 'too rarefied' for the BBC. Not in the least deterred, Tom then asked if perhaps he could appear instead on the panel of *Who Said That?*, a quotation game. De Lotbiniere eventually had to explain that the BBC did not wish to promote Tom as a 'personality' while he was under contract to a rival channel.

Independent Television went on the air on Thursday 22 September 1955, and that weekend Tom presented the first edition of *Sunday Afternoon*. But ABC was soon having its own doubts about the wisdom of using him. There were disputes about money (he was being paid £21 per programme, which he thought rather mean) and about how opinionated he should be. By Christmas he had been dropped.

In his first year after leaving the Commons Tom earned £2,360 from his journalism, as against £1,300 in the previous twelve months; since he no longer had his parliamentary salary of £1,250, however, he was actually down on the game. The bank manager's messages became yet more menacing. Depressed and angry, Tom would cheer himself up with an expensive meal and a bottle or two of champagne of a decent vintage. In the words of an acrostic epitaph that he wrote for himself:

Things
Often
Made

Driberg
Rancorously
Irate
But
Everything
Recrystallised
Gastronomically.

He might have added that the gastronomic cure itself compounded the problem, piling yet more unpaid debts and bills on to an already intimidating ledger. But his despair was understandable. He was labouring harder than ever, turning out hack-work-to-order for anything from the *Church Times* to the *TV Times*, and where did it get him? Instead of flirting with the readers of *Housewife* magazine, he might just as well be creating something worthwhile. It was many years since Edith Sitwell had touched his shoulder and dubbed him the great hope of English verse, but he had never entirely abandoned his belief that he was meant for something grander than mere journalism. One morning in May 1952, coming across the word 'alluvial' while reading Auden's *Nones* in bed before breakfast, he had snatched up the nearest piece of paper to hand – a letter from the General Secretary of the Labour Party, as it happened – and scribbled this:

CYCLE WITH MASKS

Sovereign and sure as the alluvial downflow
   of the grand river, the loving
sprang in the swell and verve of the fevered spring.

Summer poised it glistening high-green like a salad
   for our saucy greed: oil on chin,
fleck of chive on skin or freckle on skin, fierce sun of sinning.

The swings hang still, or are strapped up for the winter.
   Wiseacres advise of a fiddle-string snapped,
of a peremptory nip in the air. Adjust your visors before leaving.

'The sixth line was rather sham-Hopkins, but I wasn't too displeased with the thing as a whole,'[5] he boldly announced. Even more bravely, he showed it to one or two colleagues at the House later that day: Nye Bevan praised the work; Tony Crosland 'roared with laughter and said it was the greatest nonsense he had ever read'; John Freeman was non-committal but thought the *New Statesman* (of which he was assistant editor) might take it for curiosity value, because of the author's identity. As Tom soon learned, the literary department of the *New Statesman* thought otherwise; so did two other editors to whom he sent it. After three rejections in quick succession he read the poem to John Betjeman, who professed to like it 'very much' and promised to put it in *Time and Tide*, whose literary pages he controlled. A few weeks later, however, Tom had a peculiar letter from the magazine's editor, Lady Rhondda:

Dear Mr Driberg,
   John Betjeman has given me your poem of which he thinks highly as also does Theodore Bosanquet to whom I showed it.
   But I am, I am afraid, a little worried. Our views – yours and *Time and Tide*'s – are so extremely widely divergent that I cannot feel it to be suitable that you should appear in its columns. It would seem to me really almost as unsuitable as if the Archbishop of Canterbury were to be printed in the *New Statesman*!
   So I am very regretfully returning it.
                     Yours sincerely,
                     Margaret Rhondda

Tom's reply to Lady Rhondda was cool but acidic. He was surprised by her reason for rejecting the poem, for I had thought that political tests were applied to non-political writings only in Soviet Russia and possibly in some quarters in the USA. However, I suppose that such literary applications of the doctrine of infection by association are but a small part of the *gleichschaltung* to which we are being subjected in the course of the Cold War; and in any case your editorial discretion is absolute.

The *New Statesman*, he pointed out, did not excommunicate literary contributors for political unorthodoxy, even in the case of extreme right-wingers such as Roy Campbell; and John Betjeman himself had reviewed books for the *Daily Herald* for some years, thought he was 'fairly obviously not in sympathy with all the political notions of the Labour Party'. Nor would Tom be troubled by the publication in the *New Statesman* of articles by the Archbishop of Canterbury. 'It may well be, of course, that periodicals of the Right have to be more scrupulously dogmatic and exclusive in this respect than periodicals of the Left.' The sarcasm was wasted. Lady Rhondda would not print his piffling poem, and nor would anyone else.

No matter. A couple of years later, after he had decided to retire from the Commons, Tom had another plunge. In June 1954 he composed a poem so bad it makes one gasp and stretch one's eyes:

A BEDLAMITE EXERCISE

(Kensington, Sunday, in the Octave
of Corpus Christi. Evening.)

The sky is blue to bursting,
The drumming of the thunder
  Disturbs the haze
  And wakes the trees
To jostle at the window.

The sun is dowsed: the brindled
And cracked chiaroscuro
  Of leaf on wall
  Deserts the sill
To fade into one shadow.

Capriciously Apollo
Ungilds and gilds the lupins
   The candles banked,
   The host distinct,
The lace a nun is primping.

The trodden herbs are pungent,
The rose-leaves in their paniers
   For Marilyn
   And little Jean
The canopy and banners

Unfurling in the vestry
Distress the vestment-sister
   She smoothes a cope
   Untangles rope
And ribbons, feels like sneezing –

Young Geoff is kindling charcoal:
The smoke drifts as he whistles,
   He shakes and blows,
   The black rings glow,
With grains of incense sizzling.

The Angelus is tolling,
The holy bustle stilling:
   Within a womb
   In dumb-struck time
The word among us dwelling.

It turns on banks and buses,
On Wallace Heaton adverts,
   On furtive eye
   And colloquy
Of cocks at Hyde Park Corner.

Anthony Hartley of the *Spectator* politely returned this small masterpiece, explaining that 'at the moment we are rather full up with poetry.' The following summer, in June 1955, Tom submitted it to John Lehmann at the *London Magazine*, who was rather more enthusiastic. He had read the poem with enjoyment, he wrote. 'There is a fresh individual voice in it which appeals to me; but all the same I don't really think you have carried it through with complete poetic success. I've thought a lot about it but I fear we shan't be able to find room for it. I'm so sorry.'

His thwarted Muse turned to other projects. Sometimes in recent years Tom had felt a faint desire to write a novel, but had been daunted by the sheer scale of the enterprise. Now the ambition stirred again. To find out whether there was any more demand for his prose fiction than for his poetry, he wrote a short story called 'Trial and Error' which he entered (under a pseudonym) in a competition run by the *Paris Review*. Its first few sentences were probably enough to persuade the *Review*'s editors that 'Mr Irving Bell' of 28 Great Ormond Street, whoever he might be, was not the new Hemingway:

Wilfred Pemberton, a business man who managed to look both dapper and stately, was meeting his wife for luncheon at one o'clock. They lived in the country, in the 'stockbrokers' paradise' of Surrey, just far enough out not to be suburban. Pemberton travelled daily to his City office. His wife came to town two or three times a month; and on these occasions, when she had done her shopping or had a few hours to wait before going to her hairdresser, she required her husband to lunch with her.

The story plods on in this fashion for sixteen pages. There is a new cigarette-girl at the restaurant. She is – horrors! – Maureen Waters, with whom Pemberton had a fling a couple of years earlier. After getting over his shock he sends her a note suggesting that they resume the affair. The note falls into the hands of a cloakroom attendant, Murphy, who – worse horrors! – is now Maureen's husband. The affronted Murphy lands a punch on Pemberton while Mrs P. is visiting the lavatory. When she returns, she asks what on earth has been happening. Pemberton extemporises some explanation about a drunken Irishman but she does not believe him. And so, not before time, the story draws to its close:

'I intend,' she said, in her most acid, measured and forbidding voice, 'I intend to come back here later today, by myself . . . I mean to get to the bottom of the whole business'; and as Pemberton followed her to the taxi, holding his handkerchief to his cheek, the officious condolences of the staff buzzing in his ears as humiliatingly as an open sneer, he felt miserably certain that she would do just what she meant to do.

The only point of interest in this otherwise negligible tale is the evident relish with which Tom describes Pemberton's dislike of his wife. As with Ena and Tom, almost everything about Mrs Pemberton arouses her husband's contempt – her clothes ('incongruously fussy femininity'), her voice ('rather too clearly edged'), her smell ('the cloying scent of his wife's face powder'), her language ('he thought it likely that his wife would leave him for a few minutes when they reached the entrance-hall, to "powder her nose" – a whimsical genteelism which always irritated him') and her 'intrinsic provincialism'. He notices her crimson nails and nicotine-stained fingers 'with an inner *moue* of distaste'. Even her way of picking up cashew nuts – 'a rapid predatory motion' – makes him wince. 'Pemberton,' Tom observed, 'would have liked to strike or to strangle this harridan to whom he was tied.' And there was no doubt that the author had every sympathy with him.

However, the editors of *Paris Review* were not reading 'Trial and Error' as a study in the misogynistic psychopathology of a British politician – not least because they did not know who 'Irving Bell' really was. The letter of rejection admonished him that 'an easy facility in marking down the foibles of people having the misfortune of belonging to a certain social class cannot substitute for a real understanding of human beings – that which makes a story worth reading.' Thus ended Tom's career as a writer of short stories.

He still yearned to prove himself as a creative artist. Since nobody wanted his poetry or fiction, the logical next step was to try his hand at drama. He had no idea how one went about writing a play, or how many pages of typescript were needed for two hours' worth of dialogue, but he was sure that Joan Littlewood, the inspirational leader of Theatre Workshop, could advise. 'Joan,' he asked her one day, 'how many columns would it be if I wrote a play?' 'Oh, quite a few columns, Tom,' she replied.

Joan Littlewood was one of Tom's very few female friends. 'He didn't like women – just one or two eccentrics like me,' she said. 'Though considering some of the women he came across, who can blame him?'[6] Her attempt to enter a plea of mitigation even on the charge of misogyny demonstrates how protective she was towards him. There were good reasons for her loyalty: Tom thought she was a genius, and since they met, shortly after the war, he had missed no opportunity to promote and assist Theatre Workshop. In January 1947, after spending some days in Middlesbrough with Littlewood and her twenty-strong company, he filled his column in *Reynolds News* with an extended advertisement for their *Lysistrata*, 'one of the most exciting theatrical experiments of our time'. Though there were many little theatre groups performing plays with socialist or humanitarian themes in England at the time, Theatre Workshop differed in one important respect: it did not apply the conventional, naturalistic technique of the modern commercial theatre. One of the original members, Howard Goorney, has described Littlewood's ideas as 'a combination of being acutely aware of the issues of the time, the development of a new language in theatre which working people could follow and appreciate, a completely modern form of movement as yet hardly used on the stage and quite simply a high degree of skill and expertise in all the theatrical disciplines'.[7] As Littlewood explained to Tom in Middlesbrough, music, dance, lights and sound were all integral to the production. 'But surely there's nothing new in that?' he said. 'Don't you get that in any Christmas pantomime?' Precisely, Littlewood replied: pantomime was now the only living relic of the traditional English theatre. In return for this *aperçu* she then demanded some advice from him: her 'modern free adaptation' of *Lysistrata* was to be set in the House of Commons and she needed to be sure that she had reproduced the rituals of Westminster procedure correctly. Tom thereupon appointed himself chief pedant to Theatre Workshop, in which capacity, over the next twenty years, he provided expert guidance and nit-picking on all sorts of subjects. According to Littlewood, 'He would always come and tear me apart if I made the slightest mistake in anything ecclesiastical – as I did in *Oh! What a Lovely War*.' At the end of that conversation in Middlesbrough Tom found that he had also been recruited to serve as prompter for the first night of *Lysistrata*.

He was so excited by the production that he stayed on for the second and third nights as well. After each performance he and the cast sat up into the small hours, drinking cocoa and singing folksongs, round a log fire in the communal house where they lived.

'I have never,' Tom told *Reynolds News* readers, 'come across any community, religious or political, or any group of stage people, so free as they are from personal pettiness or jealousy. They are completely and unselfishly single-minded. In fact, they illustrated for me the meaning of the Gospel text, "If thine eye be single, thy whole body shall be full of light."'[8]

Thereafter he was the most dedicated supporter of Joan Littlewood's troupe. He fixed visas and provided introductions when they toured Czechoslovakia in 1948; for several years in the early 1950s they accepted his invitation to camp in the grounds of Bradwell Lodge during the summer months, rehearsing in a loft above the old stables. While they were there they lived on National Assistance and whatever they could earn helping local farmers with the harvest. In the evenings, if Tom was at home, they would come into the library, talk, argue, sing and drink beer. Littlewood remembered the house being 'lit up like Versailles'.

Valued and loved as a benevolent patron, as a playwright Tom was less useful to the company. When he was out of Parliament he started writing the script of an extravaganza called *Scarborough Follies*, to be set at an imaginary Labour Party conference. 'It was great fun watching him do it,' Joan Littlewood recalled, 'but it wasn't really stageworthy.' He took the rebuff stoically. Just as Arthur Conan Doyle was continually forced by public demand to write Sherlock Holmes stories against his will, so Tom was driven back again and again into journalism. He might wish to see the works of Driberg join the canon of English literature, but the message from readers, editors and publishers – not to forget the bank manager – was that he should write more articles and fewer poems. He obeyed, and in 1956 startled them all by producing what the *Daily Mail* called 'the major news scoop of the decade', an interview with Guy Burgess in Moscow. It earned him more money than anything else he ever wrote.

Since Guy Burgess and Donald Maclean slipped out of England in May 1951, the British press had been searching for them energetically but in vain. Countless newspaper articles speculated on where and why they had fled; a Soviet defector, Vladimir Petrov, told the

People in 1954 that they had flown from Paris to Prague and then to Moscow; in January 1955 the *Sunday Pictorial* announced confidently that 'the address of Burgess and Maclean is c/o The Kremlin, Red Square, Moscow, USSR (Telephone Centre 67571)'; later that year the Foreign Office was eventually prodded into confirming that both men were long-time Soviet agents. But still there were no actual sightings.

On Saturday 11 February 1956, the Moscow correspondents of Reuter and the *Sunday Times*, together with Soviet journalists from Tass and *Pravda*, were invited at short notice to Room 101 of the capital's National Hotel, where, to their astonishment, they found Guy Burgess and Donald Maclean waiting for them. A statement was handed out in which the two 'former members of the British Foreign Office' (as they chose to describe themselves) sought to explain their behaviour. They admitted to having been Communists at Cambridge, but denied ever having been Soviet agents. They had emigrated to Moscow merely because they were alarmed that Anglo-American foreign policy was entirely dictated by a crude and dangerous anti-Communism. 'We both of us came to the Soviet Union to work for the aim of better understanding between the Soviet Union and the West, having both of us become convinced from official knowledge in our possession that neither the British nor, still more, the American government was at that time seriously working for this aim. We had in the positions we occupied every reason to believe that such an understanding was essential if peace was to be safe.' After distributing the statement Burgess and Maclean withdrew from the room, declining to answer questions.

Tom had followed the saga of Burgess and Maclean with close attention, not only as a thriller-like tale of pursuit and escape but also for what he perceived as its deeper significance: 'it illustrated vividly, in the personal dilemma of two intelligent and gifted men, the plight of a whole generation caught in the confusions and contradictions of mid-century Britain.' One phrase that lingered in his mind from the millions of words written about Burgess and Maclean, was the oft-repeated accusation that they were 'split men', leading double lives. It was intended as a term of reproach, and he wondered why:

In a split world, does not a humanist – a humanist in the broad sense of the word, a man concerned with the well-being of all his fellow-men – necessarily feel conflicting impulses and doubts within him? Does any thoughtful man now believe that an international issue – and particularly the greatest issue of our times, the relations between East and West – can be discussed adequately in cold-war propaganda terms, as if it were a matter of absolute blacks and whites, a contest between devils and angels?

Of course, there is always a balancing of rights and wrongs, but this judicial process should always be accompanied by a constant effort to better the atmosphere in which a wrong, real or imaginary, can be magnified into an ideological *casus belli*. Every man in the Western world is, more or less, a split man: it is enlightened self-interest as well as good-neighbourliness to try to unite divided humanity and, in doing so, to ease private tensions and achieve personal integration.[9]

Such generous reflections were rare at the time. As far as Fleet Street and most MPs were concerned, Burgess and Maclean were traitors, *tout simple*, who probably ought to be hanged for treason if ever they were foolish enough to set foot in England again, and whose actions proved just how devilish the Red menace was. The *Daily Express*, in particular, had had a riotous time in the five years since the diplomats' disappearance, with Chapman Pincher spotting 'cleverly organised Communist plots' all over the place. Surprisingly, one of the few voices of caution had been that of the Conservative peer Lord Hailsham, who warned of 'a very real danger that the natural anger fired by the affair may degenerate into a witch-hunt'. The point was put more boldly by Tom in a *Reynolds News* column in October 1955:

The Burgess-Maclean witch-hunt is now being transformed into a Morrison-Macmillan witch-hunt.

I say it is better that there should be a few Burgess-Maclean cases than that our public services, and our nation, should be like a McCarthyite police state, with elaborate checks on people's movements and associations and with power for security officers to detain and question suspects – which is what the uproar by the sensational press would really require.

In my view the matter is still open: the value of any secrets that Burgess and Maclean may have conveyed to Russia may well have been exaggerated: it is not proved, indeed, that they did pass on any secrets, and, if it be true that they have been advising the Kremlin on relations with the West, and are so to some extent responsible for the easing of East-West tension, they may yet be hailed as benefactors of the human race.

This provocative dissidence caused outrage. 'Since when was it a witch-hunt to seal the gaps in national security?' snorted the *Daily Express*. There was no question of smearing character in McCarthy fashion, it insisted. 'The missing diplomats are established traitors. The weaknesses exposed by their defection must be put right . . . That is not McCarthyism — it is plain prudence.' The left-wing *Daily Herald* attacked Tom almost as vehemently.

The public reappearance of Burgess and Maclean in February 1956 set off yet again the old chants about Communists and treachery. Even the more erudite commentators, such as Cyril Connolly and Rebecca West, seemed to Tom unable to grasp the true meaning of the story (they were disabled, he suggested, by their personal fears and prejudices — 'Mr Connolly's fear of the real world around him, Miss West's deeply-rooted anti-Soviet prejudice and her antipathy to the irrelevant phenomenon of homosexuality'). A few days after the Moscow press conference, noticing that some newspapers had been able to contact Burgess simply by writing to him at the National Hotel, Tom decided to try it for himself: he sent a letter asking if he could come and talk to Burgess in Moscow. Though his expectations of success were low, he did have several advantages over the other journalists who were pleading for an 'exclusive interview'. Not only had he spoken up for the defectors; he also happened to be, in a small way, a friend of Guy Burgess.

They had come to know each other during the war, when Burgess was producing a weekly BBC programme which Tom sometimes presented, *The Week in Westminster*; their homosexuality formed an immediate bond between them. Fragments of correspondence in the BBC Archives give a flavour of the relaxed, gossipy (though chaste) relations that quickly developed. In April 1944 Tom informed Burgess that fourteen MPs had spoken to him about his last *Week in Westminster* broadcast, all of whom were congratulatory 'except Granville who said it was too slow, and Lady Astor, who said that I had no right to boost that terrible woman Horsbrugh.' Burgess replied that he was 'glad we annoyed Granville and Lady Astor – I rather wish we had done so more.' He went on to praise Tom's speech in a debate on Poland, and suggested meeting for a drink the following week.

Healthy appetites for alcohol and young men were two of the many tastes they had in common. They shared a contempt for the *bourgeoisie*, and a romantic fondness for the aristocracy and the working class. They were both congenitally and self-destructively indiscreet, yet agile at eluding the retribution which their indiscretion seemed certain to provoke: Burgess had glided effortlessly through the Foreign Office and the secret service even though he seldom bothered to conceal his political sympathies, just as Tom's sexual adventures, of which he boasted so recklessly, never led to the nemesis that colleagues feared and predicted. Tom's curiosity about Guy Burgess thus had a personal motive at least as strong as that which he condemned in Cyril Connolly or Rebecca West. It is not fanciful to imagine that, in his quest to understand Burgess, he hoped that he might come to understand himself.

On 15 March 1956 Tom received a telegram at the Great Ormond Steet flat:

MANY APOLOGIES DELAY ANSWERING STOP LETTER CUTTING AND SUGGESTION RECEIVED STOP AM GRATEFUL ATTITUDE AND INTERESTED SUGGESTION STOP AM SUPPORTING YOUR PLAN WITH MENTAL RESERVATION ABOUT UTILITY OF CONTINUING PERSONAL CONTROVERSY JUST NOW STOP [. . .] IN PRINCIPLE AGREE YOUR PLAN STOP MORE DETAILS BY LETTER POSTED TODAY STOP PLEASE ACKNOWLEDGE THIS WIRE AND ALSO LETTER WHEN RECEIVED IN CASE ACCIDENT STOP POSSIBLE OBSTRUCTION YOUR END ONLY STOP WARM GREETINGS GUY MY ADDRESS POSTE RESTANTE CENTRAL TELEGRAPH OFFICE MOSCOW USSR

Tom wired an acknowledgement the same afternoon, and, feeling rather pleased with himself, settled back to wait for the promised letter.

It arrived a week later. Burgess was 'touched and grateful' for

Tom's remarks in *Reynolds News* and exasperated by most of the other press coverage, though 'I don't want to go here into a long screed about not having been an agent. There is no evidence that I was: in fact I wasn't, and that's that.' As for the proposal that Tom should come to Moscow,

Speaking for myself I am very much in favour of your idea and should welcome it. There is nothing I have to fear from any questions even if put by such a shrewd person as yourself. And I know you well enough to be certain that unlike some people who disgrace Fleet Street I should get fair and objective reporting from you.

So I am supporting your plan. Of course if what I thought important was to clear my name as a Red Herring (not to speak of a Scarlet Woman) I'd tell you to come tomorrow and try and insist on it. If I did I think it could be arranged at once.

My reason for not pressing the matter too hard however is that as I said in my 'Statement' the only thing I am interested in is (not my personal case but) Anglo-Soviet relations and their possible improvement. Would these causes be helped in any way by renewed controversy about my case? . . .

However since I am sure we agree about this and might find a way of doing so if we met, I am supporting your plan . . . I should like to go round Moscow with an English Socialist. You remember of course what Lincoln Steffens said after his visit to the very young Soviet Republic: 'I've seen the future and it works.' It still does – and it's the present now.

Tom replied immediately. He agreed that the story of Guy Burgess was secondary to the theme of Anglo-Soviet relations and their improvement, but argued that one was necessary to the other, 'as many who would merely skip an article devoted only to the main theme might well be led to think seriously about it by the reading of the personal story'. One morning soon afterwards, while Tom was working at his London flat, the telephone rang. After the operator had checked that he was prepared to take a personal call from Moscow, a familiar voice broke in: 'Hello Tom. . . . This is Guy.' They talked for ten minutes. Further letters were exchanged, and in July Tom stumped up £290 for a first-class return ticket to Moscow on Air France plus fourteen days' 'luxe-class Intourist all-inclusive vouchers'. On the evening of 10 August he arrived in the Soviet Union.

When Burgess was not at the airport as he had promised, Tom did not worry unduly: he booked into the National Hotel, dined on caviar and bortsch and went to bed. By lunchtime the next day, however, there was still no sign of the fugitive and Tom was beginning to feel rather gloomy about the whole enterprise. Then the *maître d'hôtel* summoned him to the telephone: it was Guy Burgess calling from his suite in the Moskva Hotel, just fifty yards away across the square, suggesting that they meet outside the Moskva's entrance. As they shook hands a few minutes later, Tom felt rather like Stanley greeting Livingstone; their first words were certainly as banal as Stanley's. 'I'm afraid,' Burgess sighed, 'we've both got rather fatter since we last saw each other.'

In the following weeks they spent many hours together. Burgess spoke eloquently and with conviction about his political motivation, but revealed that he was wretchedly lonely in Moscow – 'starved not only of congenial non-political company but of sex'. Because of his official position he could not easily go out cruising as he had in London; in any case, he knew of nowhere to go. Here was Tom's opportunity to do his old friend a good turn. When it came to 'cottages' he had the directional sense of a homing pigeon, and within days of arriving he had achieved what Burgess had failed to do in almost five years, locating the one gents' lavatory in central Moscow where pick-ups could be had. It was a large underground urinal behind the Metropole Hotel, open all night, and, according to Tom, 'frequented by hundreds of questing Slav homosexuals – standing there in rigid exhibitionist rows, motionless save for the hasty grope and the anxious or beckoning glance over the shoulder'. Burgess decided to risk a visit, which was more successful than he had dared hope: among the Slavs in the stalls he found a young electrician named Tolya, who moved in with him shortly afterwards and cured him of his loneliness. Burgess could never thank Tom enough for this service. 'I continue to be very happy with [Tolya],' he wrote in a letter several years later. 'I don't know what saint in your calendar to thank. Perhaps only Greek Church, or Armenian, has such a saint. I *do* wish you were similarly suited. It's the best thing.'

After interviewing Burgess intensively for many hours, Tom came back to London at the end of August to turn his notes into a book for Weidenfeld & Nicolson – who, in spite of their protracted difficulties with him over the Beaverbrook biography, were smart enough to recognise a hot property when they saw one. This time there would be no delays: Tom had a scoop on his hands, and his eagerness to have it printed as soon as possible was redoubled when his literary agent, Jean LeRoy of Pearn Pollinger & Higham Ltd, sold the serial rights to the *Daily Mail* for the astonishing sum of £5,000, to be paid on publication. Tom wrote *Guy Burgess: A Portrait with Background* in less than a month, at a rate of two chapters a week, and then flew to Moscow to go through the proofs with Burgess. It was too late to make any substantial changes, but fortunately the subject of this biography had no Beaverbrookian tantrums: he found the tone admirably 'objective' (i.e. sympathetic). Having finished with the proofs the two men went off together for the weekend to Burgess's *dacha*, where, sozzled on Georgian white wine, the Old Etonian spy would sit down at a decrepit upright piano every evening and pick out with two fingers the hymns he had known at school, tears rolling down his cheeks.

Burgess's drunkenness, more apparent than on Tom's previous visit, was sometimes a nuisance. Weidenfeld had asked for some pictures to illustrate the book and Burgess had promised to bring a photographer to Tom's hotel one afternoon. 'They were late for the appointment,' Tom recalled, 'but, opening my door impatiently, I saw them coming along the corridor – Guy as drunk, one may say, as a commissar, reeling and chortling idiotically and then, when the photographer tried to do his job, making silly faces at the camera.'[10] Tom irritably told Guy and the photographer to come back the next day, this time in a sober condition. At 8 am the following morning Burgess rang to say that he would be late: 'I've been "sent for" about yesterday afternoon.' When he arrived some hours later, Tom asked what being 'sent for' involved. Burgess explained that his Soviet boss had given him 'a bit of a talking-to', but had been 'extremely nice' about it – 'exactly like the best type of English public-school housemaster'.

In all the many days that Tom spent with Guy Burgess while he was preparing the book, he did not meet the other 'missing diplomat' once: Maclean had refused to have anything to do with the project. Although the duo had become as inseparable in the public mind as Waring and Gillow or Flanagan and Allen, they were not, in fact, particularly close. When Goronwy Rees sold his reminiscences of the Cambridge spies to the *People*, what most upset Burgess was the claim that he and Maclean had been brought together through some kind of homosexual association. 'The *idea* of going to bed with Donald!' he told Tom. 'It would be like going to bed with a great white *woman*!' Maclean nursed his suspicion of Tom unforgivingly. Some years later Ian Mikardo was visiting Moscow on business and found himself at a dinner table with Melinda and Donald Maclean. 'Tom's name came up and Donald immediately froze,' Mikardo recalled. 'There was an obvious dislike.'

Guy Burgess, on the other hand, was delighted by Tom's work — so much so that he used his influence to secure an introduction for Tom to Nikita Khrushchev. The interview, which appeared in *Reynolds News*, was notable mainly for the General Secretary's disclosure that he had been impressed by parliamentary question-time when he was in London. 'I like it,' he told Tom. 'It *is* a democratic feature of your Parliament. To some extent it raises the blood-pressure of the ministers. It is democratic and interesting. Probably we ought to find some way of introducing a similar procedure in the Supreme Soviet.' Tom's earnest reporting of this remark ('Mr Khrushchev himself told me that there was a possibility that the Supreme Soviet might experiment with something on the lines of the question-time in the House of Commons') might seem risible with hindsight, but it should be remembered that the interview was conducted not long after Khrushchev's famous speech to the Twentieth Congress of the CPSU, in which he had criticised Stalinism: for a brief moment, the unthinkable was possible.

With the proofs of the book corrected and despatched to the printers, Tom returned to London in the second week of October to await publication. Ever since the *Daily Mail* had announced its purchase of the book the previous month, letters to the editor had been seething with indignation. 'Sir,' fulminated a reader from Alperton, 'Why all this publicity for Guy Burgess? He chose Russia

– let him stop there, and let the British press stop making heroes out of such men. Mr Tom Driberg must be easily fooled. Such information as he obtained could only be by Russian sanction. We certainly do not want either Burgess or Maclean here – unless to stand trial.' Major-General G. G. Waterhouse, of London w8, was 'astounded at your proposal to print the story about Burgess. Why should any reliance be placed on the statements of either of the two people concerned?' These reactions were understandable: the politics of the *Daily Mail* had never strayed outside the narrow spectrum between right-wing Conservatism and outright fascism, so why should the newspaper now print an apologia on behalf of one Bolshie scrimshanker by another? As early as 21 September – a month before it published the extracts from Tom's book – the *Mail* felt obliged to carry an official statement emphasising that 'the *Daily Mail* was the most severe critic of the actions of Burgess and Maclean when they fled the country.' Because the circumstances of their disappearance had been a mystery for five years, Burgess's version of the affair was 'news which any responsible newspaper would publish'. But there had been no slackening of the sinews: 'Its appearance in the *Daily Mail* does not mean that this newspaper's view of the whole shocking episode has altered in the slightest degree.'[11]

The series was due to run in the *Mail* throughout the week beginning Monday 22 October 1956, and for days beforehand it was advertised at every opportunity. On Friday 19 October the London *Evening News* – which, like the *Daily Mail*, was owned by Lord Rothermere – splashed a gigantic headline advertising its sister paper's forthcoming revelations: 'WORLD NEWS – SCOOP FROM MOSCOW! GUY BURGESS: How I Got Away'. The story was 'diplomatic dynamite!', it promised. 'Controversial and alarming? Yes. But it's news – news that even M I 5 could not get! It starts Monday 22 October. Only in the *Daily Mail*.' The story was given an even more effective promotion on television that night, when the ITV programme *This Week* showed a film of Tom and Burgess visiting the Lenin/Stalin tomb in Moscow. 'Thousands of televiewers throughout Britain saw for the first time last night a special newsreel of Tom Driberg and Guy Burgess in Moscow,' the

Mail yelled on Saturday morning. 'But ITV didn't hear the full story. That begins in the *Daily Mail* on Monday.'[12]

On the Monday morning, one must assume, *Daily Mail* readers were leaping out of their beds at dawn and scampering down to the newsagents in a fever of anticipation. Nor would they have been disappointed: Burgess's racy account of his escape from Britain was spread over two pages inside and, for the benefit of anyone with a short attention-span, was pithily summarised in the news report which led the front page under the headline 'GUY BURGESS TELLS ALL'. Once again, however, the newspaper had to distance itself from the man to whom Burgess had chosen to talk. In a peculiar little box marked 'About Driberg', the following disclaimer appeared:

Tom Driberg has been a journalist and Socialist all his adult years. From 1942 to 1955 he was MP for Maldon, Essex. He is a member of the National Executive Committee of the Labour Party – is now Vice-Chairman.

Now 51, he is author of a controversial biography of Lord Beaver-brook – was formerly William Hickey of the *Daily Express*.

His Burgess story is a frankly partisan work. With many of his opinions the *Daily Mail* disagrees . . . but prints it none-the-less un-censored. Differing opinions cannot obscure the fact that it is the major news scoop of the decade.[13]

Thus, for the second time in a year, Tom found himself publicly disowned by a newspaper that was about to serialise one of his books.

He was handsomely compensated, however: on 13 November Associated Newspapers sent him the promised cheque for £5,000.

The uncensorious tone in which Tom wrote about Burgess was calculated to shock, and he was duly denounced in some quarters as a dupe of Moscow. He had expected no less. But it has since been suggested that there was more – much more – to Tom's 'scoop' than that. The claim, which comes from our old friend Chapman Pincher, is that Tom wrote the book as a favour to both MI5 and the KGB and, even more fantastically, that each side knew and accepted that he was simultaneously working for the other.

According to Pincher's imaginative theory, MI5 ordered the 'dispatch of Driberg to Moscow' as part of an exercise 'to prevent the embarrassing return of Burgess to Britain'. The embarrassment was that the security service did not have enough hard evidence to bring spying charges against the defector if he tried to re-enter the country; in order to keep him away, therefore, someone would have to trick him into committing an offence. And so (the theory continues), at MI5's behest, Tom cajoled Burgess into vouchsafing a few details about his work for the wartime Special Operations Executive, which he included in the manuscript of the book. At last MI5 had what it wanted: it announced that Burgess had broken the Official Secrets Act by revealing confidential information and would be arrested if he came to Britain. Having served its purpose, the paragraph was then removed before publication. Pincher reports that almost everyone was happy:

Driberg's book contained enough lies and slanders against MI5 and the political system of the West for the KGB to be pleased with it, while MI5 regarded these as a worthwhile trade-off to prevent the return of Burgess. Driberg made money out of it while being paid by both the KGB and MI5. So all the participants, save for Burgess himself, who died aged 52, lonely and sick in Moscow in 1963, were well satisfied.[14]

MI5 feared that Burgess might be able to visit Britain with impunity: that much is true. The trouble with the rest of the story, as so often in Pincher's work, is that it is unsupported by proof, logic or common sense. Here is what actually happened. Admiral Thomson, the jovial secretary of the D-Notice Committee who acted as liaison man between Fleet Street and MI5, demanded to see Tom's manuscript (as is the D-Notice Committee's habit with such books). He insisted on one deletion – not of the wartime SOE reference (which survived intact) but of a paragraph about a botched post-war attempt by the secret service to overthrow the government of Albania. Tom pointed out that his source for this was Burgess, who had cleared every chapter in the book with his superiors in Moscow; it was therefore reasonable to assume that the Russians already knew of the Albanian fiasco. 'Good heavens old boy,' the Admiral replied with a laugh. 'It isn't the Russians we worry about. It's *the British public* we don't want to know about it!' Tom protested, but the *Daily Mail* and Weidenfeld & Nicolson obeyed Thomson's instruction.

Although the offending paragraph contravened the Official Secrets Act, there is no evidence that it was written in order to make trouble for Burgess: indeed the idea is self-evidently ridiculous, since Burgess read Tom's entire text in proof and had a power of veto over it. Ironically enough, the person who definitely *was* working for MI5 during this episode, and who *did* allow himself to be used by the security services in order to keep Burgess from returning to London, was not Tom but his accuser – Chapman Pincher himself. MI5 saw in the Albanian disclosure an opportunity to frighten Burgess off by threatening him with prosecution; and the man chosen to transmit this message was Pincher, in his familiar role as the official urinal at which senior spooks and mandarins leak in the national interest. A few days before Tom's book was due to appear, Pincher was telephoned at the *Daily Express* by Admiral Thomson, who said he was speaking on behalf of the head of MI5, Sir Roger Hollis. 'We lunched together,' Pincher admits, 'and the admiral then told me that MI5 would be grateful if I reported, with prominence, that it now had evidence that could lead to the arrest and prosecution of Guy Burgess should he ever return to Britain.' The admiral explained that 'through stupidity on the part of Burgess and Driberg, the former had committed technical breaches of the Official Secrets Act.' The *Express* reporter obediently did as he was told. 'At that stage,' he adds, 'I had no knowledge of Driberg's connivance in this operation against his old friend.'

If we are to believe Pincher, Tom's study of Burgess was a dishonest exercise from the beginning, and the sentimental optimism of its conclusions – preaching peace and understanding between nations – was breathtakingly, almost blasphemously, disingenuous. But Pincher is hardly the best judge: as urinal to the men of MI5 and MI6 he cannot rid himself of the stench imparted by his patrons' acrid piss. His is a mind in which 'left-wing' and 'sinister' are still synonyms rather than etymological cousins many times removed; nor does it occur to him that some people are less awestruck than he by the giggling pantomime that dignifies itself with the title of Security and Intelligence.

Tom could never bring himself to regard the spying business as anything more than a game. He enjoyed games, of course – from canasta to croquet – and he therefore enjoyed flirting with the secret world, as in those gossipy lunches with Max Knight in the 1930s. But he knew that there was life beyond games. Inconceivable though it may be to Pincher, perhaps things really were as they seemed: Tom wrote to Burgess as an old acquaintance; he was invited to Moscow; he then composed a book that tried, however naively, to explain the yearnings of a conscientious objector in the Cold War. The advantage of this theory is that, unlike Pincher's, it goes with the grain of the known facts. Far from being dictated by MI5 and the KGB as part of some devious plot, *Guy Burgess: A Portrait with Background* reflected Tom's genuine preoccupations; its language, with a Christian emphasis on words such as 'humility' and 'penitence', was entirely consistent with his other utterances of the time. Dribergian socialism had always had a distinctly religious flavour, but in the 1950s this became more pronounced. As Richard Crossman had noted after a National Executive Committee weekend conference in December 1952:

Tom Driberg . . . relapsed into a bronchial gloom, which increased as we discussed exports, nationalisation, etc. These are things which he cannot think of without nausea and, after an hour or so, he interrupted to plead for an ethical approach to the problem. His is really an aesthetic kind of socialism, which has nothing to do with planning or nationalisation or housing but with getting justice for coloured peoples and, though I don't understand quite how, trying to get a Christian social ethic in this country.[15]

On the last page of his Burgess book, Tom quoted some lines of Shelley:

> Oh, cease! must hate and death return?
>   Cease! Must men kill and die?
> Cease! Drain not to its dregs the urn
>   Of bitter prophecy.
> The world is weary of the past,
> Oh, might it die or rest at last!

Tom proposed the verse as 'an apt epitaph on the Cold War and all the other wars of our time'. Was this a pose adopted on the instructions of a spymaster, or was it sincere? Undoubtedly the latter. The Cold War and the nuclear arms race had touched Tom's aesthetic and religious sensibilities as powerfully as colonialism or colour prejudice, and in his last few months in the Commons he had been horrified by the government's plans to develop a British H-bomb. He was disgusted, too, by the mealy-mouthed reaction from his own party: the Labour front-bench's amendment to the defence estimates in March 1955 accepted that 'it is necessary as a deterrent to aggression to rely on the threat of using thermo-nuclear weapons.' Aneurin Bevan urged the Left to abstain, but Tom, thinking this an inadequate protest, placed an unequivocal amendment of his own on the order paper:

This House regrets the decision of Her Majesty's Government to proceed with the manufacture of the hydrogen bomb without full consideration by Parliament and the nation of the ethical aspects of its use; questions the practical value of the security likely to be provided thereby; refuses to assent to the development of a weapon, of immense and indiscriminate destructive power, whose effect on the life and civilisation of mankind may be disastrous; and calls on Her Majesty's Government to regain for Great Britain the moral leadership of the world by taking an initiative, at the present disarmament conference or on other appropriate early occasions, that may lead to the general outlawing of this and other thermo-nuclear weapons.[16]

This was the first time any MP had attempted to advocate unilateral nuclear disarmament (a Labour motion on the subject of the H-bomb the previous year had merely called for a top-level disarmament conference), and Tom recognised that the party whip might be withdrawn from him in consequence. He set out his reasons in a letter to Attlee:

I do not presume to pass judgment on the decision reached, somewhat perfunctorily, at a party meeting last week or to claim with any certainty that the view expressed in this amendment is correct. The individual conscience is no more infallible than a collective sense of expediency; but in the absence of authoritative guidance from theologians and scientists, I do not see what else one can go by in a matter of fundamental importance to the future of mankind; and I find it impossible, on this issue, merely to abstain from voting for the official Opposition amendment.

That amendment, indeed, contains criticisms, with which I agree, of the government's incompetence in handling Defence; but it also commits us to support of the government's decision to go ahead with the production of all kinds of thermo-nuclear weapons. This is what I cannot bring myself to let pass without expressing in some positive way a sense of horror which is, I believe, widely felt in the Labour movement and in the country generally.[17]

In the event Tom's amendment was not called. He had to content himself with abstaining on the Labour resolution, along with Nye Bevan and fifty-five others; and even this mild protest nearly had Bevan expelled from the party.

Tom returned to the subject often during his years out of the House, both in his *Reynolds News* column and at the National Executive Committee. He also did something to remedy the lack of 'guidance from the theologians' to which he had alluded in his letter by convening a group of Socialist Christians, including two MPs (Hugh Delargy and Fred Willey) and a dozen clergymen (among them Donald Soper, Mervyn Stockwood, Canon John Collins and Jack Putterill, Conrad Noel's successor at Thaxted), who between 1956 and 1959 met every few weeks in an upstairs room at the Lamb, a pub near his Bloomsbury flat. Tom served as minute-taker to these colloquia and in 1959 published a pamphlet summarising their deliberations, *Papers From the Lamb*.[18] It led to the creation of the Christian Socialist Movement in 1960.

Papers From the Lamb is as near as Tom ever came to publishing his personal credo. There is nothing very startling or complex in it, but then that was how Tom's political opinions — as against his character — tended to be: the pamphlet confirms that Dick Crossman was right to interpret Tom's socialism as a simple desire for justice and a 'Christian social ethic'. Common ownership was desirable because it was a form of *koinonia*, or fellowship; Christianity should renounce imperialism because the domination of one people over another was 'intrinsically evil'; the immigration of coloured people into Great Britain presented Christians with 'an opportunity to practise fellowship and social equality'; nuclear weapons were 'blasphemies against the creative principle'; and so on.[19] The pamphlet's warnings of the dangerous consequences of East–West misunderstanding in the nuclear age echoed the conclusion of *Guy Burgess: A Portrait with Background*, and it is surprising that Chapman Pincher has never detected the hand of MI5 or the KGB – or both – in the work of Tom's congeries of clerics.

The comradeship of these discussions in the upstairs room of a London pub contrasted sharply with the arguments on the same questions that were conducted in the statelier surroundings of Transport House, on the fourth Wednesday of every month, at the Labour Party's National Executive Committee. NEC meetings in the mid-1950s, Ian Mikardo wrote, 'provided us Bevanites with a short cine-trailer of the horrors of Hades'. The Right used its majority 'as a cudgel to beat us over the head . . . They were never interested in arguing with us, only in voting us down: in every discussion one of them would move at the earliest practical moment that the questions be now put, and the monolithic majority would faithfully raise their hands.' According to Mikardo, Tom used to emerge from these sessions 'worn out like a dishrag'. This was a time of great rancour on the National Executive (Mikardo describes some of the right-wing members as 'dedicated haters in the gold medal class') and what made it especially agonising for Tom was the fact that his fiercest tormentors – Edith Summerskill, Alice Bacon, Bessie Braddock, Alice Horan, Jean Mann – were women. 'He would sit there and agonise,' Mikardo recalled. 'He felt himself to be a victim.' More excruciating still was the annual ritual of linking hands and singing 'Auld Lang Syne' at the end of party conference, for as a member of the National Executive, with a place on the platform, Tom often found himself next to one of the fearsome females. 'Ugh!' he used to exclaim afterwards. 'That awful Alice Bacon with her clammy hands!' (Small wonder he so enjoyed his evenings with the Christian Socialists: the group that produced *Papers From the Lamb* had twenty-three members, not one of whom was a woman.) However, there were men on the NEC whom he thought almost as repulsive, such as the right-wing union nominees – 'the TUC dummies' – whose clod-hopping crudity provoked countless *cris de coeur* from Tom to Mikardo after Executive meetings. 'I can't bear the *vulgarity* of those people,' he wailed. (And, Mikardo agreed, 'he was right'.)

There was another reason for his fear and loathing of the TUC men. Although the chairmanship of the Labour Party is a position of no great importance, the title has a certain ring to it and most party time-servers look forward to their year in the job, which is passed on annually by the sophisticated electoral system known as Buggins's Turn. Having become deputy chairman in October 1956, Tom was due to be promoted to chairman automatically a year later; but by the summer of 1957 he was convinced that the union dummies would try to thwart his elevation because of their puritanical antipathy to homosexuality. On the train to the party conference in Brighton that year he told Dick Crossman of his anxiety. Crossman assured him that trade union leaders were 'men of protocol' and, if they had wanted to stop him being chairman, they would have done so when he was elected vice-chairman the previous year. Later that day, during a promenade along the Brighton front with Harold Wilson, Crossman laughingly mentioned Tom's suspicions of the trade union bosses. Wilson cut in sharply: 'Oh, but he's quite right. Some of them are going to make an effort before this Conference is out.'

They failed. The challenge had been left too late, and could not now be pressed without making more trouble and scandal for the Labour Party than one year of Tom's chairmanship was likely to cause. Besides, there was already more than enough controversy at Brighton in 1957: this was the conference at which Bevan left his followers aghast by arguing that, if Britain renounced nuclear weapons, 'you will send a Foreign Secretary, whoever he may be, naked into the conference chamber.' Any intended plot against Tom was abandoned. The former sacristan of Lancing Chapel, former acolyte of Aleister Crowley and former Dragoman was elected Chairman of the Labour Party, at the age of fifty-two.

He now began to contemplate a return to the Commons. As his ex-secretary Rosemary Say observed, 'He was tremendously tied up with the House and its procedures. The House of Commons to him was like the Catholic Church to Evelyn Waugh – sometimes a joke, but underneath serious and worthy of reverence.' He missed the confraternity of Westminster, its masculine aroma of old socks, its reassuringly irrational codes of behaviour and quasi-liturgical ritual. (Tom could find religious echoes in the unlikeliest places. Soon after his first election to Parliament he had noticed that the Speaker's announcement at the end of Questions, 'The Clerk will now proceed to read the Orders of the Day', fitted the tune of 'Mine eyes have seen the glory of the coming of the Lord' – which he hummed thereafter whenever the Speaker uttered the sentence.) The looming insolvency that had forced him to leave the House two years earlier had receded since his lucrative collaboration with Guy Burgess; there was no longer any reason to stay away. When a by-election was called in the safe Labour seat of St Helen's in the spring of 1958 and a couple of organisations affiliated to the local party asked Tom if they might nominate him, he accepted happily.

But the 'union dummies' were ready to humiliate him. The Lancashire miners' leader, Edwin Hall, said on 19 April that he 'couldn't see Mr Driberg being nominated for a seat which trade unionists had built up'. In 1945 those same trade unionists had been bullied by the national party bosses into adopting the barrister Hartley Shawcross, and it had rankled ever since; they were not going to have another celebrity from London foisted on them. Two days after Hall's speech the general management committee of the local party drew up a short-list of six, which included four candidates sponsored by big unions (the miners, railwaymen, engineers and distributive workers) as well as two unsponsored candidates – but not Tom. As *The Times*'s political correspondent commented, it was 'somewhat ignominious' for the Chairman of the Labour Party to be excluded thus.

There was further ignominy to come. Under the Labour Party constitution, Transport House had the right to nominate candidates for by-election short-lists, and a National Executive sub-committee consisting of the chairmen of other sub-committees now took it into its head to add Tom's name to the list in St Helen's. This infuriated both the St Helen's party and the trade unionists on the National Executive, who expressed their 'strong resentment'. To save himself more embarrassment, Tom told the NEC meeting on Wednesday 23 April that he didn't want to be nominated after all. *The Times*'s political correspondent again made the most of his misfortune:

If any more proof were needed that the trade unionists mean earnest business when they say they are not going to play second fiddle to the political ambitions of television performers, popular journalists or professional men just back from some private Damascus, the stinging snub given to Mr Tom Driberg, the Chairman of the Labour Party, should provide it. In the St Helen's candidature affair they hit hard and hit high, with calculation. They are well pleased . . .

The *Times* man went on to imply that it was bad form to desert a marginal like Maldon and then jump into a safe seat like St Helen's at the next opportunity. Revealing that the Labour candidacy in Maldon was vacant again, he concluded mockingly: 'At any rate, if Mr Driberg still searches for a seat, Maldon is there for the asking. Moreover, no trade union yet wants it for its own.'[20]

Tom replied to this taunt in a long letter which *The Times* printed three days later. He insisted that it 'would not have occurred to me to attempt to stand in St Helen's' if he hadn't received pressing local invitations, but that in any case it was unfair to expect him to stick with Maldon come what may. A marginal rural seat that included dozens of scattered villages 'must involve an amount of constituency work greater than we can all afford the time for, especially if we attend diligently at the House of Commons', whereas a compact urban constituency 'can be served just as faithfully and adequately as a seat like Maldon in one tenth of the time'. This was a case he had argued before, even while he was the Member for Maldon, but he was evidently hoping that *Times* readers would not remember the plea in mitigation which he used to add. As he had written in 1952:

So the rural MP sometimes wonders if he shouldn't, like a footballer, get a transfer . . . But then he goes to speak for a friend in Birmingham or Bradford, and his spirit is weighed down by the sheer ugliness of wet Sunday slate roofs and Victorian Gothic town halls and pretentious super-cinemas and the rest of the paraphernalia of private greed rampant; and he returns with relief to his serene market towns, his villages huddled about their great churches, his Dickensian rustic inns, his rolling farms, and his old fishermen sunning themselves on jetties.[21]

Now, it seemed, the Dickensian scene had lost its charm; besides, as his friend Betjeman was continually pointing out, Victorian Gothic was not so bad – rather splendid, in fact. Even though it 'would not have occurred' to Tom to apply to St Helen's, there was no doubt that he would have snatched the nomination gratefully if it had been offered. So why had he been rejected? In his letter to *The Times* he argued that it was an over-simplification to attribute the composition of the short-list solely to the unions' mistrust of 'luminaries', for the newspaper had neglected to mention 'one significant fact: of six names on the short-list, at least four, and probably five, are the names of Roman Catholics. So great a preponderance in favour of one denomination can hardly be due to pure coincidence.'[22]

This was a sensational new twist. A Conservative MP, Peter Rawlinson, accused Tom of stirring up hatred against Catholics, but the vicar of the largest parish in St Helen's, V. L. Tucker Harvey, came to Tom's defence with the assertion that 'it is widely accepted in this constituency that the selection of a short-list of candidates for nomination in the forthcoming by-election by his party is the culmination of a "catholic action" campaign.' A local newspaper detected 'a small but highly organised clique, operating under the cloak of a particular religious belief', which had been seeking to control the St Helen's Labour Party. And on the eve of the selection conference at which a candidate would be chosen from the six finalists, Alderman J. E. Hughes noisily resigned from his posts as secretary of the St Helen's Trades and Labour Council and political agent to the local party. Hughes, who was also the leader of the town council, had been Tom's strongest local supporter; in his resignation speech to the executive committee he condemned the 'religious discrimination' apparent in the short-list.

Tom had exacted a satisfying revenge by revealing the Popish plot. Reporters were already investigating the story, and now it was the turn of the St Helen's apparatchiks to wish they could retreat into the shadows. At the selection conference on May Day they took the only way out by choosing as their candidate Leslie Spriggs, the one person on the short-list who was a member of the Church of England.

In most years, the Chairman of the Labour Party is hardly noticed in the press except during conference week. But Tom was an unusually eye-catching figurehead: his comings and goings during his term – especially his overseas wanderings – were carefully logged in the newspapers, usually in tones of mild derision at the very idea of Tom Driberg holding office of any sort. If he went abroad in his official capacity – as a fraternal observer at some social democratic conference, say – this would be written up in absurdly inflated language, as if he were the UN Secretary-General setting off on a dangerous mission on which the peace of the world depended. When he travelled merely on behalf of *Reynolds News*, there would be sniggering hints that he was actually undertaking some sensitive 'undercover' task for the Labour Party. A fair sample of what was to come appeared only a fortnight after his election as Chairman, in the *News Chronicle*:

Where was Tom Driberg, chairman of the Labour Party? That was the mystery puzzling party supporters at Ipswich last night.

He was expected to speak in support of their by-election candidate, Mr Dingle Foot. But he did not turn up.

Mrs Driberg said at her Essex home: 'I don't know where my husband is. I expect him back at the week-end.'

Mr Driberg was on the way to MOSCOW.

Mr Morgan Phillips, Labour Party secretary, had one word for Ipswich rumours of a party mission to Moscow – 'Nonsense.'[23]

The same word might have been applied to the *News Chronicle*'s bizarre and confusing story. There was no great mystery: the Soviet Union had just launched the first sputnik into space, and Tom had been sent to Moscow by the *Sunday Dispatch* – for a fee of £1,050 – to see if he could track down the space scientists and interview them. The newspaper had contacted him on Wednesday 16 October and he had rushed through a visa application on Thursday, planning to fly that afternoon. But the flight was delayed. He did not arrive in Moscow until Friday evening, which left only one day in which to find the elusive scientists and transmit his article. His contact, a colleague of Guy Burgess whom Tom called 'Nick', promised to do what he could and told Tom to remain in the hotel. At 11.30 on Saturday morning, as Tom sat in his suite wondering what excuse might placate the *Sunday Dispatch*, the telephone rang. It was Nick. He revealed that Tom could interview the sputnik scientists in their laboratory at midday; as a special treat, at 2.45 pm he would be taken for a late lunch in the Kremlin with 'an interesting person'.

The interviews at the lab were over quite quickly, and Tom was back at his hotel by 2 o'clock. But he had not managed to finish his report or phone it to London by the time the huge Zil limousine arrived to transport him to the Kremlin's 'interesting person' – who, as he had guessed, turned out to be Khrushchev again. Comrade Nikita was in a genial mood – rather too genial for Tom, who had a tea-time deadline to meet – and he began with a pleasant, unhurried, off-the-record talk about the distinctions between the British Conservative and Labour parties. Tom takes up the story:

It was now four o'clock: I had been asked to lunch at three. I still had an afternoon of urgent work ahead of me. No book of etiquette known to me contains advice on how to say to the ruler of one of the two most powerful nations in the world: 'Sorry – we must stop talking now. It's time to eat.' But Mikhailov the interpreter somehow conveyed this tactfully to my host – who was in any case pleased that I should be writing about a triumph of Soviet technology.

He jumped up from his desk at once and led the way, his stubby figure waddling briskly, along a short passage into a fine oval room, of the eighteenth century, in which three places were laid at a large table: Khrushchev sat at one side of it, Mikhailov and I at the other. There were the customary courtesies in vodka – a brown-coloured vodka, made with pepper, he said, very good for colds – but again, appreciating that I had work to do, he was sensible enough not to press me to go on drinking: none of the rumbustious bibulousness of the legend. It was a fairly long luncheon – small helpings, but many courses. Both of us were so busy talking that we kept poor Mikhailov even busier – course after course, his plate was swept away with the food untouched. At last, I said to him: 'Please tell Comrade Khrushchev that he and I must stop talking for five minutes, to let you eat some lunch.' Mikhailov whispered back: 'It is all right. I knew that this would happen, so I had my lunch beforehand.'[24]

Rather to his surprise, Tom was able to finish his report and dictate it to the copy-takers at the *Sunday Dispatch* in London, as well as wiring a photograph of the scientists, before the deadline expired. He then went to dinner with Guy Burgess and Tolya.

Tom travelled widely during his year as Chairman of the Labour Party – Russia, Germany, Israel, Egypt, Lebanon, Jordan, Cyprus, Greece – and, though most of these trips were undertaken for *Reynolds News*, the impressive title guaranteed him VIP status wherever he went. 'Even before he held this post, whose nature often misleads foreign observers,' Alan Watkins has written, 'Driberg was assumed by several Russian politicians to be leader of the Labour Party. This was on account partly of his grave, episcopal manner, and partly of his ability to get on well with Russians.' No doubt Guy Burgess should take some credit, too; he seems to have given his bosses in Moscow a rather exaggerated impression of Tom's seniority and influence in British politics. It was probably at Burgess's prompting that the Soviet government invited Tom and Hugh Gaitskell, with their wives, to take a holiday in the Black Sea resort of Sochi in the summer of 1958. Burgess hoped to join them, though he accepted that that would depend on the attitude of 'Hugh Gaiters', as he called the Labour leader. 'I have met him once before and got drunk with him in the house of a great mutual friend,' he wrote to Tom in June. 'So I think *personally* Gaiters might not object . . . to meeting. But *politically* it might be quite impossible – *unless* he believes (what is true) that I can be trusted on *important* matters *only* not to let anything leak.'[25] The supposition that a meeting between the Communist defector and the leader of the Labour Party 'might' be impossible was something of an understatement; Burgess did not realise, apparently, that most public figures in Britain would no sooner be seen with him than share a bath with an alligator. Many of his proposals at this time had a similar barmy optimism. 'Would it help or harm *Reynolds*, such a good paper, only one except *Daily Worker* in fact now, if I suggested being in some way their Moscow correspondent?' he casually inquired in a letter to Tom. 'I am *not* a journalist – but I do know more than many journalists do and certainly more than Embassy.' *Reynolds News* declined the offer.

In the event Tom also had to turn down the invitation to Sochi, because of Ena's poor health. 'Uxorious' was one of his favourite epithets, which he had many times hurled at friends who would rather go home to their wives than sit up drinking with him all evening; but now, though still several furlongs short of uxoriousness, his behaviour towards Ena was – for the first and only time in their marriage – quite considerate. She had been taken ill in the spring with TB and pneumonia; in June, while she was still in hospital recovering, a doctor recommended that she should have a benign but sizeable tumour removed from her right lung. She was eventually spared the operation – a surgeon said there was no need for it yet – but Tom seems to have been genuinely moved by her suffering. While he was in the Middle East in June and July he sent her friendly letters and telegrams, and consoling bouquets of flowers. At the end of July, on her return to Bradwell, she decided to book herself a long, slow cruise through the Mediterranean; in the meantime she spent most of her days resting. Yet even now Tom did not rage or stamp his feet, though Ena's convalescence deprived him of his holiday in Sochi by trapping him at Bradwell Lodge for the summer. 'The house is open to visitors two days a week until late September,' he wrote to Guy Burgess's mother, explaining why he could not carry a message to her son, 'and we are rather short of help to shepherd them and show them round.'

The Labour Party conference, with Tom enthroned in the chair, opened in Scarborough at the end of September. He had prepared for the great event with some care. Weeks beforehand he had written to the manager of the conference hotel, the Grand, demanding an assurance that there would be no sauce bottles or other vulgar condiments on the dining tables during his stay. He had drafted and redrafted the speech that he was to deliver on the first day. And he had promised himself that, if he couldn't actually remain chaste during his week at the seaside, he would try to be rather more discreet than usual.

This was no small sacrifice, for his sexual rapacity and recklessness at party conferences were legendary. At the last Labour gathering in Scarborough, four years earlier, the *Daily Mirror* journalist Terence Lancaster had been drinking with Tom and Ena and a couple of left-wing MPs one evening, when he noticed an attractive youth entering the pub; Tom strode across, introduced himself to the boy, and within ten minutes had disappeared with him – leaving poor Ena, as Lancaster recalled, 'high and dry'. Some time later one of the MPs, Stephen Swingler, proposed reserving a table for dinner somewhere. 'What about Tom?' asked Lancaster innocently. 'Don't bother about Tom,' Swingler replied, with the weary air of one who had been through this all too often. 'He'll not be back.' And he wasn't.[26]

Another of Tom's pick-ups at that same Scarborough conference was witnessed by Henry Fairlie of *The Times* and George Gale of the *Manchester Guardian* when they turned into a café on the lower promenade, at the bottom of the cliffs, for a cup of coffee. It was a cheap sort of place, and the two journalists were surprised to see there 'a familiar, large, soft-bodied, middle-aged and upper middle-class figure . . . consorting in an amatory fashion with a couple of rough yobs he had obviously just picked up'. There was nothing surprising about Tom seducing young roughs, of course; what startled Gale was the time and the place. 'When he was in a town crawling with delegates, reporters and photographers, he risked his own career, the success of his cause and the welfare of his party all for the sake of a snatched few seconds of mutual masturbation.'[27]

At Scarborough in 1958 he risked all these things again, but by his words rather than actions. In the 3,000 copies of his chairman's speech to conference that were circulated in advance to delegates and the press, he argued that Tory philosophy was 'not essentially different from the *Herrenvolk* philosophy of the Nazis'. When he actually came to deliver the speech, on 29 September, he left out the phrase 'of the Nazis'; but what remained was quite enough to ignite fire-crackers of indignation from the Conservatives and Fleet Street. The Tories, he said, 'sincerely believe that they are a master race called to rule the "lesser breeds" whose mineral wealth and sweated labour have been so profitable to them. This is why the welfare of the Colonial people must be on all our consciences. The Tories, though they cannot undo the advances initiated by Labour, still treat the people of overseas territories as they treated

British workers a century ago. The trade unions put a stop to that.'

Once again he had set out to *épater* the Tory *bourgeois*, and he had been entirely successful. Whether it would do the Labour Party much good was another matter. A year earlier, in September 1957, opinion polls had shown Labour to have a remarkable 13 per cent lead over the Conservatives; now, according to Gallup, the Tories were ahead for the first time since 1955. 'Mr Driberg's *Herrenvolk* sneer,' T. F. Thompson of the *Daily Mail* opined, 'may prove to be the most costly political blunder since Mr Bevan described Tory supporters as "lower than vermin".' Thompson reported that Conservative Central Office was 'amazed last night that, at a time when Socialist fortunes are so low, the Party chairman could make such a major miscalculation.'[28] Another right-wing newspaper, the *Daily Telegraph*, chastised Tom in a gleefully admonitory editorial:

When Mr Driberg, chairman of the Labour Party, says that the Tory philosophy is 'essentially a *Herrenvolk* philosophy', he subordinates history to his own shrill hysteria. Nobody with the possible exception of a handful of lunatics could possibly believe it – and the Socialists will not be voted back into power by a handful of lunatics. The phrase is absurd, but it will be remembered and quoted, as was Mr Bevan's sudden descent into the mud with the word 'vermin'. Indeed, the British electorate, which prefers its politics hard, dry and clean, may well apply the lines of Mr Belloc's cautionary tale:

> Take that, abandoned boy,
>   For playing with disgusting mud
> As if it were a toy.

One of the first lessons which infants have to learn in the nursery is how to keep their pinafores clean.[29]

Discernible in this picture of him as a mud-bathing mucky-pup was a faint outline, presumably intentional, of the rough-trading cottage-cruiser, a man overwhelmed by uncontrollable *nostalgie de la boue*.

After Tom's belligerent speech on the opening day, the rest of the conference was subdued. Perhaps some of the fizz had gone out of the delegates since Harold Macmillan's announcement, a fortnight earlier, that he would not call a General Election that winter; perhaps the Left was still too grief-stricken at Nye Bevan's desertion the previous year. The new alliance of Gaitskell and Bevan carried the day without difficulty. As Dick Crossman remarked, 'day by day the morale went up as the delegates were agreeably surprised to find their leaders weren't so bad and their policies made sense.'

At the end of the week Barbara Castle was elected Chairman, and Tom returned to his previous, unofficial title of chief sub-editor to the Labour Party, the man who (in Ian Mikardo's words) translated party documents 'from Transport House Chinese into the well of English, pure and undefiled'. He shared this drudgery with Dick Crossman, but although they had done much useful work together – at the 1951 and 1955 elections, for instance, they had rewritten the Labour manifesto in plain English – their stylistic differences, magnified by Tom's pedantry, often made it an uneasy partnership. They were, after all, rival newspaper columnists, Crossman of the *Mirror* and Driberg of *Reynolds News*, seeking applause from their audience with the nervy, smiling competitiveness of finalists in a talent contest. Tom had encomiasts on both wings of the party. Michael Foot, in a typically extravagant tribute, commended the 'special precision and purity' of Tom's style, his 'nose for every form of falsity, bombast and misleading rhetoric', his ability to 'detect cant or humbug in an unwanted adjective or a misplaced comma'.[30] But even George Brown, no great crony of Tom, saluted his 'quite unrivalled sub-editing and rewriting gifts', which were 'of a much superior order to those of Dick Crossman'.[31]

Comparisons of this kind were odious to Crossman, who always had the immodesty of a true Wykehamist. When the National Executive authorised him to produce a pamphlet setting out Labour's policies in simple language, immediately after the Scarborough conference in 1958, he announced that Tom's assistance would not be required this time; he intended to collaborate with Hugh Cudlipp and Sydney Jacobson from the *Daily Mirror* instead. It was a foolish hope. Having almost completed the document, Crossman invited Peter Shore (from the party's research department) and Hugh Gaitskell to come and inspect it one Sunday afternoon. As he recorded in his diary:

Peter Shore came in at three o'clock and so did Tom Driberg, who had insisted, against my will, on studying the draft. He's the greatest verbal snob in the world and I knew we were in for trouble. This wasn't rendered any easier by his conviction that the stinking cold he was suffering had been caught from me at the Executive. So I put him grilling over a fire in the drawing room and sent Peter Shore downstairs to the study, with Gaitskell, when he turned up.

. . . After [Gaitskell] had read it for an hour he said, 'This shouldn't take me long, I've only got three or four points.' At this point I made the fatal mistake of saying, 'Let's go upstairs and do them with Tom Driberg.' Forty minutes later we were still drooling over the first page, of which practically every sentence had been almost rewritten, including Driberg's semi-colons and Gaitskell's policy haverings, which always recur when he has time to rethink.[32]

Tom liked Hugh Gaitskell. Years later, he complained that he had failed to achieve even the most junior ministerial office because 'both the Labour Prime Ministers with whom I served, Attlee and Wilson, knew of my reputation as a homosexual and both were deeply prejudiced puritans'. Gaitskell was altogether more civilised. He had had homosexual stirrings himself (the famous crush on John Betjeman at Oxford), and in the late Twenties he had sometimes drunk with Tom at 'the most bohemian pub in London', the Fitzroy Tavern in Windmill Street. The Driberg *demi-monde* did not shock him.

Tom began to think that if he could haul himself back into the Commons – and if Labour could win a majority – Gaitskell might actually give him a job. He was too diffident to ask directly; but Gore Vidal, at Tom's request, sounded out the Labour leader over dinner at A. J. Ayer's house one night. 'How *can* we?' Gaitskell replied with an incredulous laugh. Vidal suggested Archbishop of Canterbury as a suitable appointment: this would both please Tom and extinguish Christianity in England, he pointed out. Gaitskell, an enlightened atheist, was delighted by the idea. Then he said, seriously: 'I suppose we could make him Minister of Works. The old thing would love that, mucking about with curtains for embassies.' Tom was thrilled to hear of this.[33]

He renewed his search for a constituency, and in the New Year of

1959 he found one at Barking, part of the dreary metropolitan backyard between London and Essex. The sitting Member since 1945, Somerville Hastings, was retiring at the next election, bequeathing a Labour majority of more than 15,000; on 5 February Tom was chosen as the prospective parliamentary candidate. Unlike the elders of St Helen's, Barking Constituency Labour Party had no prejudice against celebrities, journalists or southerners. Quite the reverse: according to Jo Richardson (who succeeded Tom as MP for Barking fifteen years later), 'they were thrilled that they were going to be represented by such a famous person. Barking is on the edge of London, and many there think of it as being out of London. They still say "Have you come down from London this morning?" They were slightly in awe of him, I think, of this sophisticated London world he moved in.'[34] The Times remarked pointedly that Barking 'is considered to be one of the safest and most convenient constituencies for a Labour Member in the London area' – no doubt remembering the lament of the former MP for Maldon that he could not be bothered with rural marginals any longer. 'Tom said that the Barking people would only expect him to come to one meeting a year,' David Cargill recalled. 'The constituency didn't need nursing. He told me that being MP for Barking was a piece of cake.' One meeting a year was an underestimate, which did not take into account his 'surgeries' in Barking town hall between 6.30 and 8 pm on the first and third Fridays of every month. But it indicated his determination not to visit the place more than he had to. Even Jo Richardson, who insists (with the respect due to an ancestor) that Tom was 'a very dedicated MP in Barking', will allow that 'he wasn't one who'd go to everything in the constituency'. She elaborates:

I'm not saying he neglected it, but he tended to go to as few events as possible. He wasn't an unsocial animal but he didn't particularly enjoy the kind of jolly dances they have in Barking. They're big on dances in Barking – kind of knees-uppy dances. Tom didn't enjoy that at all, he got bored and irritated by it. He preferred quieter contact.

Even his 'quieter contact' was limited, however. He never arrived at his surgery a minute before the chime of 6.30 struck. (Today Jo

Richardson comes at 4.30 or so, 'because the queue starts then'.)
And, as Richardson admits, he was ill-equipped to deal with 'the
personal and intimate problems' – families disintegrating, homeless
women weeping, parents losing custody of their children. He often
gave the impression that every moment spent in the constituency
was an excruciating ordeal for him. On the rare occasions when he
did go to a knees-up in Barking he stood about with a forbidding
scowl on his face, complaining furiously if he was brought any drink
other than Bell's whisky with ice; after half-an-hour he would then
say 'I've had enough' and demand to be driven back to London. He
had an agreement with the Labour MP for the neighbouring seat of
Dagenham, John Parker, that when the two of them were invited to
an official function locally (a mayoral reception, say) they would
'both go or neither go – and on the whole go to as few as possible'.
Another old colleague, Ian Mikardo, is less reticent than Jo
Richardson in his verdict on Tom's record in Barking. 'He was a
very, very bad constituency MP,' Mikardo says. 'He despised his
constituency party. It was an absolute *mésalliance*, the Barking
Labour Party and Tom – it was like Zsa Zsa Gabor marrying
Freddie Ayer.'

Nevertheless, it served its purpose. At the general election of
October 1959 Tom was returned to the House of Commons as the
Member for Barking. His majority over the Conservative candidate
was precisely 12,000.

He was back in Parliament. Any dreams of fame and glory at the
Ministry of Works, however, would have to be postponed for
several years, since the Conservative Party had increased its majority in the Commons to 100 seats and Harold Macmillan was again
Prime Minister.

Most commentators blamed the scale of the defeat on some
careless comments by Hugh Gaitskell about income tax, but the
Labour leader and his coterie had other scapegoats in mind. On the
Sunday after the election, a gamy ragout of trusties – Woodrow
Wyatt, Douglas Jay, Patrick Gordon Walker, Roy Jenkins, Anthony
Crosland – met at Gaitskell's house in Frognal Gardens, Hamp-
stead, and persuaded one another that the Left was to blame: that

the election had been lost because voters still thought of Labour as a working-class party committed to socialism. Never mind that the Labour manifesto, *Britain Belongs to You* (another Crossman and Driberg co-production), had been a document of exemplary moderation and timidity. What must be done, the Frognal chorus chanted, was to transform the Labour Party into something more like the Democratic Party in America – malleable, featureless, classless, blank. Labour must publicly dissociate itself from such unpopular ideas as public ownership of the means of production, distribution and exchange; Clause IV of the Party's Constitution, where these heretical notions still lingered, must be erased; indeed, why not abolish the Labour Party's name itself – so evocative of clogs and cloth-caps, so insulting (suggested Douglas Jay, a Wyke-hamist) to those affluent working-class voters who liked to think that they were superior to mere labourers?

Thus began the attempt – repeated cyclically ever since – to detach Labour from socialism. Old-fashioned talk of institutional change or moral imperatives was to be shushed, brutally if necessary. The party now promised merely to manage the existing system better than the Conservatives. 'Modernise', 'purposive', 'efficiency' – this was the language that would reassure nervous electors. Tom, who abhorred moderation, was deeply depressed by it all. What had hitherto made the Party habitable for him was its susceptibility, however slight, to extremism – to the unqualified Christian moral-ity of Sir Stafford Cripps and Sir Richard Acland, or the emotional Celtic quasi-Marxism of Aneurin Bevan. Now the misgivings he had felt about Labour when he was a youth came rushing back. Gaitskell was determined to impose a 'middle-stump' orthodoxy, banishing smells and bells from the supposedly 'broad church' of the Labour Party. The death of Aneurin Bevan in July 1960, after a six-month struggle with cancer, seemed to Tom to mark the death of passion also.

Of course the reinvention of Labour as a movement fit for technocrats did not go unresisted, and Tom played his part in that resistance – particularly on the question of nuclear disarmanent. At Scarborough in October 1960, with the aid of Frank Cousins's block vote from the Transport and General Workers' Union, the party conference passed two unilateralist motions, provoking Gaitskell's pledge to 'fight and fight and fight again' to overturn the policy; a month later, when the Prime Minister announced that a base for the Polaris missile-firing submarines was to be established at Holy Loch, Gaitskell chose not to move an amendment condemning the proposal. With the party leader so at odds with his own members, the National Executive decided to set up a tripartite 'Committee of Twelve' – four from the NEC, four from the Parliamentary Labour Party, four from the Trades Union Congress – to draft a new policy on defence. Rather to his surprise, Tom found himself elected as one of the NEC's quartet: Gaitskell had wanted to pack the committee with his own supporters, but Crossman had insisted that it was important to have 'a balanced team, which showed some respect for the Scarborough decisions'.

The committee was nevertheless heavily weighted against the unilateralists. At the first meeting George Brown arrived drunk and started berating Frank Cousins; when Tom tried to intervene, Brown shouted 'Shut up! You haven't got the votes!' It was impolite but true. There was no support for a draft submitted by Cousins and Tom which rejected 'the threat to use nuclear weapons'; a compromise motion from Crossman, opposing the *first* use of nuclear weapons, was also voted down. Gaitskell's lieutenants on the committee, George Brown and Denis Healey, forced through a straightforward right-wing policy – pro-Bomb, pro-NATO – which was then adopted by both the Executive and the Parliamentary Party, in defiance of the Scarborough decision. In a letter to a friend, Gaitskell wrote that everyone 'is behaving pretty much as expected – Mr Cousins impossible – Mr Crossman petulant and treacherous – Mr Driberg like a tired snake. On . . . our side [there] has been more loyalty and firmness and successful planning than for a long time.'[35] But Tom was not too tired to repeat his ethical point once again. 'Tom Driberg said that we had to refuse all nuclear weapons equally, since all are equally evil,' was how Crossman recorded Tom's contribution to a meeting of the International Sub-Committee in April 1961. It made no difference. Thanks to some spirited lobbying of the more backward trade unions by Gaitskell's head gofer, William Rodgers of the Campaign for Democratic

Socialism, at that October's conference, the unilateralist policy which had been adopted only one year earlier was abruptly dumped.

Tom and his fellow-disarmers on the Labour benches fought and fought and fought again, though to little effect. They demanded that Labour condemn the resumption of nuclear testing by Britain and America in the spring of 1962, but Gaitskell chose to believe a private assurance he had been given by President Kennedy that the tests were strictly necessary. In a speech in the House on 23 July Tom pointed out that this had been contradicted by Kennedy's own Defence Secretary, Robert McNamara, who had told a congressional committee that nuclear testing was not necessary but merely 'desirable'. That, Tom said, disposed of Gaitskell's excuse, 'which, on the testimony of the American Secretary of Defence himself, is seen to be a phoney argument'.

In the same speech, he asked about the biological effects of the Christmas Island tests:

The Prime Minister told us when he announced the resumption of testing that all the pros and cons of it had been weighed very carefully before it was decided to take this grievous decision and go ahead with the tests. I maintain that he had no right to take that decision and go ahead with the tests unless in that balance sheet of pros and cons he had at any rate some approximate figure of the biological damage – if he did not know roughly how many new cases of bone cancer and leukemia would be likely to be caused by the series of tests, how many cases of genetic damage, and so on. Yet at question time he has repeatedly dodged answering questions on this point.

Yesterday afternoon at question time Hon Members were rightly concerned and indignant because a number of babies have been born, and are being born, deformed as a result of the marketing of a drug that had not been adequately tested in advance. Yet this, deplorable as it is, was at least accidental. Many more thousands of babies are going to be born deformed or idiot as a result of the deliberate decision of the British and American governments. The Prime Minister and the President have agreed that it is in the public interest that x hundred thousand people – innocent people who have not been consulted about it – should die agonisingly of bone cancer or leukemia. This is surely an extreme example of the doctrine that the end justifies the means.

The former Minister of Defence wrote me a letter – I was exchanging some correspondence with him about the matter – saying that, regrettable as all this human suffering is, it is part of the price that we have to pay to secure the defence of the free world.

Everyone will agree that a good and desirable end justifies the use of some means, perhaps means unpleasant or violent. The classic doctrine of the just war is a case in point. But can any end, however good, justify this peculiarly horrible and indiscriminate form of genocide? This, the consequences of the testing alone, quite apart from the use, is what makes nuclear weapons utterly different in kind, not only in degree, from all other weapons and makes some of us say that, whatever other nations may do, these are weapons that it is absolutely impermissible for us to have, to test, or to threaten to use.[36]

He was here restating an argument that he had first put in *Papers From The Lamb*. Hardly anyone had listened then, and even fewer listened now – not least because his speech was delivered at about four o'clock in the morning, during an all-night sitting. He might as well have been whistling in the dark in any case. Gaitskell had smacked and wheedled the Labour Party into accepting the Bomb and all its accoutrements, and the question was now closed. Dissent was either ignored (as in Tom's case) or punished (as when Michael Foot and four other back-benchers had had the Labour whip withdrawn in 1961 for voting against the Government's defence estimates).

What deepened Tom's estrangement was the lack of an alternative helmsman for the party. Some of the old Bevanites, such as Michael Foot and Barbara Castle, were seduced by the Yorkshire cadences of Gaitskell's most prominent rival, Harold Wilson, who liked to suggest that he had inherited the mantle of Nye and that the Left should therefore pledge allegiance to him. Tom had always suspected Wilson of being a shifty old fraud, however, and he saw no reason to revise that opinion now. True, Gaitskell was right-wing whereas Wilson was (or so he claimed) a man of the left. But at least Gaitskell was honest in his convictions; who could say what Harold Wilson *really* believed? Besides, Wilson was prudish about sex. One evening Wilson tried to recruit Dick Crossman, Tony Greenwood and Tom to his supporters' club, but after he had left the room the three left-wingers 'revealed to each other that we would all prefer to keep Gaitskell rather than work for Harold Wilson'.[37] After Gaitskell's sudden death in January 1963, Labour MPs had an unenviable choice between Harold Wilson, George Brown and Jim Callaghan for the leadership. Tom voted for Wilson, but without enthusiasm. 'I think he will do,' he wrote coolly to Lord Beaverbrook. Any hope of appointment to the curtain-ordering department of the Ministry of Works, or the Archbishopric of Canterbury for that matter, was now finally abandoned.

Political disappointment was not the only reason for his increasing detachment from the affairs of the Parliamentary Labour Party. He was preoccupied by another, sadly familiar distraction.

In a letter to Beaverbrook just over a year earlier, in December 1961, Tom had boasted that 'one of *my* compensations for growing old is that publishers now pay much more handsome advances on royalties than they used to. One of them is sending me to America this Christmas to do research for a book ...' True, he had just signed a contract with Secker & Warburg to write *The Mystery of Moral Re-armament*, and the payment did indeed seem generous in view of the limited audience for such a book: a £2,000 advance on royalties, plus £400 expenses to cover a research trip to America and £100 for travel in Europe. As so often happens with book advances, however, the money seemed to shrink while in transit between the publisher's bank account and the author's. Under the terms of the contract, signed in December 1961, £750 would be paid to Tom at the end of 1962, and another £1,000 was due on delivery of the manuscript, sometime in 1963. Only £250 would be handed over straight away – and £25 of that went to his literary agent in commission. Of the 'handsome' £2,000, in other words, he had made a mere £225 to finance him during his first year's work on the book.

It was also in 1961 that one of his most dependable sources of income since the mid-1950s, his *New Statesman* television column, was axed by the new editor, John Freeman, who apparently felt unrestrained by the ties of old friendship. Freeman's behaviour was perfectly reasonable, in fact: the column had been appearing for five years and Tom had long since run out of anything new or entertaining to say about television; most of his reviews were downright dull. But the job had earned Tom twenty guineas a week. Being sacked was 'a severe blow', he told Freeman in a pained letter, 'and it is hard, at my time of life, to face a further contraction of my exiguous income; but I shall have to make the best of it, remember Peter ii, 20, and scrape together what little I can by writing as many articles as can be accommodated.'[38] He wrote of 'the agony and humiliation of this profoundly and protractedly traumatic experience'. Freeman said that he would welcome other features from Tom, but could no longer buy them at the specially high rate of fifty guineas a page that Kingsley Martin had established. The most Tom could expect in future was thirty guineas a page – 'if you hold out for more than that,' the editor warned, 'you inevitably price yourself out of the market.'[39] A rather over-zealous manager at the *New Statesman* then wrote to demand the immediate return of Tom's television set, for which the magazine had been paying the rent.

By the autumn of 1961, in spite of his brave words to Beaverbrook, Tom was plummeting ever deeper in the financial abysm, his fall broken only occasionally by loans from friends such as John Betjeman, Sidney Bernstein and Canon Freddy Hood. On 9 November the new manager of the Liverpool Street branch of the National Provincial, Mr B. Bluck, delivered a message which was, in the circumstances, surprisingly irenic:

Can I remind you that the borrowing on your account is creeping ever upwards, and that the overdraft is now about £600 higher than a year ago?

This is not merely a question of credit squeeze or of absence of security – this borrowing is costing you something like £150 per annum in interest. Is it possible to re-budget and to reverse the trend?

This quiet suggestion elicited another of Tom's self-pitying howls of woe, in the form of a sixteen-page letter to Bluck on 14 November. It was one of his best ever excursions into the *genre*:

Thank you for your warning, and for the gentle tone in which you write.

Only yesterday, as it happens, I paid a few bills – all overdue and absolute 'musts': the rent of my flat, due at Michaelmas (£30), my

London 'phone-bill (£25), an agency commission (£9), and £50 on account to Thomas Cook (the House of Commons Transport Office), who were pressing for payment of £60-odd owing for air fares.

But I had, at least, waited to send these cheques until I knew that you had lately received two payments from Higham's, and that the *Reynolds News* monthly payments should have come in.

The general position is, I agree, pretty bad, and I am sorry that the overdraft has increased so steeply – though I admit I had not realised how much I am paying in interest. The increase in the overdraft is partly due to inevitable increased expenditure by my wife, who has had to spend a lot of time in the past year looking after her aged parents (her mother died of cancer a few weeks ago, and her father is aged 88 and needs constant attendance); and partly to a decline in my earnings from the *New Statesman*, for which I no longer write as frequently as I did . . .

My agent (Miss Leroy, of Higham's) has been making strenuous efforts to find me more work. By her arrangement, I lunched last week with the editor of the *Daily Herald*, and am lunching this week with the editor of the *Evening Standard*; both of these discussions should bear fruit – the latter a possible series of articles on television for which Miss Leroy hopes to get, perhaps, £200–£250.

This all helps, but does not, of course, do more than just keep one's head above water; and it means a fearful struggle, and constant anxiety and overwork, on top of all one's political duties . . .

The general situation, I am afraid, is even worse than you can realise. I was adding up fairly urgent outstanding debts yesterday, and they totalled (including the sums which I have mentioned as having now been paid) nearly £1400. This includes the following really urgent items:

(1) Balance of money owing to Baker's of Danbury (who have been paid *thousands* in the past year or two for major repairs to Bradwell Lodge): £250.

(2) Balance due *now* (just confirmed by surveyors) on installation of septic tank: £204.

(3) Income-tax (Schedule D) and surtax for 1958/59 (both now threatening): £530.

The trouble about the fairly hopeful, but not certain, prospective extra earnings from the *Herald*, *Standard* etc is that they won't come through quickly enough to enable me to meet these pressing claims at once; and, as an MP, I can't risk being bankrupted.

Not since Job had any man been so vexed and persecuted: his

lamentations went on and on. The Georgian part of Bradwell Lodge had already been made good, at huge expense, but now the walls of the Tudor end had started caving in; several hundred pounds would have to be spent damp-proofing the house for the coming winter. The whole exterior, which had not been redecorated for eight or nine years, needed to be painted before Bradwell reopened to the public at Easter. The boiler, put in just before the Second World War, hardly worked any more; he had been quoted a fee of £2,000 for installing new central heating. Clearing the dry rot, wood beetle and other infestations would cost another £4,000. On the recommendation of the Historic Buildings Council, his beloved Ministry of Works had agreed to award him a grant, but that would cover only half the expense. The 'most maddening thing' was that the builders, Baker's, were refusing to mend any more holes in the roof until he had paid the £250 already owed to them. 'Do you know,' he asked the bank manager, 'how one approaches one of those big trusts which are always giving away money – Gulbenkian or Nuffield or the Pilgrim Trust? I suppose it's just possible that some of them might be interested.' He also wondered if Bluck could speak to 'any City magnate you know' who might be interested in sponsoring Tom.

Almost all his difficulties would disappear, of course, if he sold Bradwell. 'But I don't know,' he submitted, 'that this would *really* be so sensible.' He had spent thousands of pounds saving the house from decay, 'and whatever price one got for it would presumably not fully cover all that has been put into it. It might thus be a fearful waste of all our efforts.' The market for a house of that character on the Essex coast was limited. Some executive from the nearby nuclear power station might buy or rent it, perhaps; or it might stand empty for years and sink rapidly into ruin; or, since more and more tourists were coming to the east coast, it might be 'turned into a motel or something like that – which would be almost worse than its destruction'.

For some years Tom's preferred solution had been to give the house to the National Trust, on the understanding that he would be allowed to live in it rent-free for the rest of his life. The Trust would take responsibility for repairs; he would be a mere 'curator'. As long ago as 1953 the secretary of the National Trust's Historic Buildings Committee, Robin Romilly Fedden, had come to Bradwell at Tom's invitation and reported himself 'enchanted' by it – 'a perfect and most interesting example of the "rural villa" of the late eighteenth century, so many of which have disappeared.'[40] But Fedden had explained that 'however much the Trust might wish to accept Bradwell, it could not afford to do so if the house were to be a financial liability'; the property must be unencumbered by mortgage and endowed with a fund of £14,000 to cover the cost of future maintenance. Tom's reply to Fedden, which was a forebear of his long jeremiad to Mr Bluck of the National Provincial Bank almost a decade later, revealed his 'outstanding anxiety' that if he couldn't afford to live in Bradwell Lodge 'it might fall into the hands of someone without any taste, who might turn it into a hideous road-house.' There was also the same blithe fantasy that money could be raised through begging letters: 'Did you notice that last week's big pools winner, Mr C. Coulton, Tregarvon Road, Battersea, said in an interview that he simply did not know what to do with his £190,000? It is, of course, a very long shot, but it might conceivably amuse such a man to become a public benefactor.'[41] This desperate hopefulness was understandable. Without the assistance of a rich man, Tom would never raise enough money to satisfy the National Trust.

Or so he thought until he had his own small pools win – the Guy Burgess scoop of 1956. He used his £5,000 fee from the *Daily Mail* to pay off the mortgage on Bradwell, and created the Bradwell Trust (trustees: John Freeman and Canon Freddy Hood) to receive other income from his Moscow enterprise. This would form the endowment on which the National Trust had insisted. Money cascaded into the fund from foreign serialisation of his book and articles; a couple of photographs of Guy Burgess that he had taken in Moscow earned him hundreds of pounds in syndication fees.

By 1961, however, the Bradwell Trust still had only £4,000 in its account, as against the £14,000 which the National Trust required before it would accept Bradwell Lodge. Meanwhile Tom had borrowed £5,000 on the security of the house, plunging himself as deeply into hock as he had been before clearing the mortgage five years earlier. 'To free the house of debt and hand it over,' he told the bank manager in his letter of 14 November 1961, 'one needs about £15,000.' This was a trivial sum to Gulbenkian or Nuffield, he noted, 'but unattainably vast, at the moment, to me'. To get completely straight – overdraft, income tax and all – Tom would need several thousand pounds more, but even he conceded that 'I can hardly expect a Trust grant for that'.

Tom's frankness with Bluck suggests that he had taken rather too literally the exhortations, often repeated in advertisements at this time, to treat one's bank manager as a father-confessor and friend. 'Your suggestion that we might be able to "re-budget" is a kindly euphemism,' he wrote, 'but too optimistic: as my wife and my accountant long ago discovered, I am what is called "hopeless about money". I have always lived from hand to mouth, and can never keep accounts or even fill in cheque counterfoils.' This was not a message likely to reassure the bank that its prodigal client could be trusted to mend his ways. In reply to the sixteen-page plea *de profundis*, Mr Bluck of the National Provincial sent a brief and formal note informing Tom that 'the borrowing has now reached the stage at which I want to ask the advice and guidance of my head office'.

Ena was no more impressed than Bluck. Since her mother's death a few weeks earlier, she had been staying with her father in his flat at Forset Court, a large block behind Marble Arch which had become a family nest for the Lytteltons in recent years: Ena's unmarried sister, Phyllis Lyttelton, shared her father's flat; an aunt lived a few doors away; two more aunts occupied another flat in the block; yet another flat housed an uncle. Ena had often taken refuge there, sometimes for weeks at a time. Now, after reading a copy of the letter to the bank manager, she told Tom on 25 November that she was leaving him for good:

When you come to a decision about your financial affairs I must ask you to make provision for me to the extent of £750 a year (a not unreasonable figure I think) and accept the fact that I wish to separate from you completely.

I have tried for ten years to make a compromise with you in your extraordinary mode of life and have now finally given up.[42]

She would probably have spent much of her winter in Forset Court anyway, as both her father and her sister were ill and she found Bradwell all but uninhabitable in cold weather. But the idea of a formal separation disturbed Tom. How could he avoid scandal in the village? Who would supervise the gardener and the house-keeper, who would show round the visitors when they turned up and paid their half-crowns? He sent her a rancorous letter mocking her prim, 'bourgeois' financial sobriety, and implying that she had deserted him in his hour of need. Unsurprisingly, this rough wooing technique did nothing to win her back. Quite the opposite, in fact. A week later she sat down in Forset Court and wrote one more farewell note:

Your last letter simply confirms what was already indicated in your letter to the bank – that you are unable to take a realistic view of your serious situation. Your arguments are those of a child not wishing to face up to the realities of life, and the bank's reply was exactly what could have been foreseen, not only by me, but by any realistic thinking adult.

My dissatisfaction with our present situation can be simply stated.

1. I can no longer tolerate being associated with anyone whose whole way of life is based on dishonesty. Poverty is no disgrace, but to carry on deliberately a way of life that you cannot afford, and to owe money in all directions, is immoral and dishonest, especially when you earn the money, but prefer to maintain a fable rather than pay the debts you have incurred.

2. Apart from the above, I can no longer stand the strain of never knowing that the cheques I write will be honoured. Of knowing that when I meet people in Bradwell or elsewhere we owe them money for which they have waited a long time and will have to continue to wait.

My 'bourgeois middle-class' mentality gave me a belief that one should pay for what one had, and the strain of living a completely dishonest life has become more than I can bear.

Just to forestall the cliché about rats and sinking ships, if you were able to pay all your debts tomorrow it would make no difference to my decision, as it would only be a matter of time before you were in the same position again, and this distressing cycle would repeat itself.[43]

As a parting shot, she revealed what the psychiatrist Dr Anthony Storr had told her – that Tom was 'incapable of having an adult relationship with anyone'. She did not mention, because she did not know it, another of his assessments: after a career in which he had encountered most forms of human folly and perversity, Storr believed that Tom was the one person he had met who could justifiably be described as evil.

Ena was back at Bradwell within a year. She stayed there for another decade.

CHAPTER TWELVE

STREET-FIGHTING MAN

Sexual intercourse, as every reader of Philip Larkin knows, began in 1963, between the end of the Chatterley ban and the Beatles' first LP. For Tom, as for Larkin, this was rather late (especially as male homosexuals had to wait another four years before their couplings were legalised, and then only between consenting adults over twenty-one in private). But better late than never: it was the decade for which Tom had been waiting all his adult life, and he dived into it with as much vigour as his ageing body and enfeebled bank account would permit. 'There has always been a war between age and youth,' he had said on 30 October 1959, almost the very eve of the 1960s, in his maiden speech after being elected for Barking. 'It is the one war in which, as I think Cyril Connolly said, every one changes sides.' He himself was the exception to Connolly's rule, as he made clear in the same speech. Drawing attention to 'the widening gap between contemporary youth and the adult community', he argued that 'when we in this House are talking about youth . . . we are talking about millions of people large numbers of whom regard us as practically senile and hopelessly "square".' But daddy-o Driberg was no square. He complained that, from the enormous publicity given in the press to juvenile delinquency, 'one might imagine that all or the majority of teen-agers were delinquents or hooligans', whereas in fact – 'as we all know' – it was 'quite a small minority'. He detected a different problem in Britain's youth, one of torpid *ennui*:

There is a rather disquietingly large number of young people, mostly teen-agers, who seem to drift through life in a bored and sullen apathy –

that urban and subtopian *malaise* which is perhaps the twentieth-century equivalent of the medieval sin of acedia.[1]

By the time sexual intercourse began in 1963, however, the listlessness had vanished. It was the year when *Time* magazine revealed to the world the existence of 'Swinging London', the year of Profumo and, yes, the Beatles' first LP. Young people were everywhere: they edited magazines, they lampooned cabinet ministers on satirical television programmes; by the spring of 1964 they were even running their own radio station, with a regular audience of seven million listeners, from a boat moored ten miles off the Suffolk coast. 'I have enjoyed the new amenity of Radio Caroline – which, living near the east coast we get clearly at 199m. (MW),' Tom boasted in a newspaper article after its first week on the air. 'From 6 to 6 daily, this brain-liberating opiate has been as nearly continuous as possible: a pretty good selection of pops, jazz, folk and standards, with minimal announcements and time-checks (and no ghastly "light" music or organ syrup).'[2] He had just entered his sixtieth year.

The forces of Age were not slow to fight back. In 1964 a magistrate, Dr George Simpson, described Mods as 'these longhaired, mentally unstable, petty little hoodlums, these sawdust Caesars'; taking their cue from him, newspapers denounced the youngsters as 'wild morons', 'human wolves', 'dumb brutes' and 'vermin'. But the exuberance and assertiveness of teenagers, so frightening to killjoy magistrates and journalists, excited Tom. So did the irruption of working-class actors and singers and gangsters, the collapse of censorship, the permissive society, the sex and drugs and rock'n'roll. For the rest of the decade his constituency was not so much Barking as Youth, and he became an indefatigable defender of Youth's right to read dirty books or listen to dirty music. When the scabrous American comedian Lenny Bruce was banned from entering Britain to fulfil an engagement at the Establishment Club in Soho, it was Tom who protested in Parliament; he did so again when two Conservative backbenchers launched a private prosecution of *Last Exit to Brooklyn* for obscenity. If an underground newspaper was in trouble, he would send it a fiver. If a petition was raised in support of cannabis or pop festivals, his name was sure to be on it. He became a friend to many of the famous and infamous of 'Swinging London', from Ronnie and Reggie Kray to Mick Jagger and Marianne Faithfull.

He met the Kray brothers at a night-club they owned, the Kentucky in the Commercial Road, to which Joan Littlewood took him for a drink one evening in the spring of 1963. The twins chatted politely to Tom (he remembered Reggie as being 'particularly agreeable'), quizzing him about his powers as an MP and leading him on by expressing their doubt that he, as a mere backbencher, could or would ever achieve anything for his constituents. No, no, Tom assured them, he often managed to help people in one way or another. Reggie then baited the trap: he had a friend, he said, who was desperate to move from Dartmoor to a London prison because of ill health. If Mr Driberg were as conscientious and as interested in prison conditions as he suggested, perhaps he could take up the case? Tom readily agreed. He wrote to the Home Office, and soon afterwards the prisoner was transferred.

The twins were impressed. As their biographer John Pearson wrote, 'it opened up an avenue of possibilities. Politicians had their uses which could be exploited; the twins were good at using human frailty to make men do as they were told. Quite suddenly they saw what could be done with a discreet gangsters' lobby of carefully fixed members in either House.'[3] Parliament was the one place where the criminal's two main enemies – the police and the prison service – were, however slightly, accountable. Who could say what might not be achieved by a quiet word with a Home Office minister or civil servant? Having originally underestimated Tom's influence on the executive, they were now exaggerating it; and the human frailty which they exploited was his appetite for young men, preferably aged eighteen or so. Since Ronnie Kray himself was a homosexual of similar tastes, he already had an established network which kept him supplied with youths and could easily procure a few extra for the Member for Barking. Tom became a regular attender at parties in Ronnie's flat in Cedra Court, where rough but compliant East End lads were served like so many canapés.

With his customary skill at eluding Nemesis, Tom managed to avoid any unpleasant publicity for his friendship with the Krays, even after they had been convicted of murder and sentenced to life imprisonment in 1969. He did not desert them: he lobbied the Home Office tirelessly, urging that the twins should be in the same prison or should at least be allowed frequent reunions, and complaining at the restrictions on their visitors and correspondence. He also visited them in Parkhurst at least once. But he was not entirely honest in declaring his interest: he told a Home Office minister in 1970 that he had had only 'a very slight acquaintance'[4] with the Krays, whereas in fact, as Reggie has said, Tom 'was a regular customer at many of our clubs'.[5]

His friend Lord Boothby was rather less lucky. On 12 July 1964 a huge headline was splashed across the front page of the *Sunday Mirror*: 'PEER AND A GANGSTER: YARD INQUIRY'. The story alleged that an unnamed peer was being investigated by Scotland Yard for his homosexual relationship with a leading thug (also unnamed) from the London underworld. They had been to 'Mayfair parties' together; there was talk of blackmail. Four days later the *Daily Mirror* claimed that it had a photograph, which it could not use, showing 'a well-known member of the House of Lords seated on a sofa with a gangster who leads the biggest protection racket London has ever known'. The same day Boothby returned from France to find London 'seething with rumours' about himself; he rang Tom immediately for advice. Later that week the German magazine *Stern* named the pair in the *Mirror* report as Lord Boothby and Ronnie Kray. Boothby, having retained the services of two leading lawyers, Arnold Goodman and Gerald Gardiner QC, wrote a letter to *The Times* which identified himself as the subject of the *Mirror* articles and denied all the allegations against him. He said he had been photographed with Ron Kray only once, 'in my flat (which is also my office)', when the supposed gangster had come with two friends 'to ask me to take an active part in a business venture which seemed to me of interest and importance'. He had later turned the proposal down. Boothby continued:

I am not a homosexual. I have not been to a Mayfair party of any kind for more than twenty years. I have met the man alleged to be the 'King of the Underworld' only three times, on business matters; and then by appointment in my flat, at his request, and in the company of other people . . . In short, the whole affair is a tissue of atrocious lies.[6]

Five days after his *Times* letter the *Mirror* offered Boothby an unqualified apology and £40,000 in compensation, plus costs. In fact, however, the lies were not as atrocious as all that. The rumour that he, like Tom, was supplied with sexual playmates has been unusually persistent, though never proved. Certainly he knew the twins quite well and was willing to make himself useful to them, in spite of his protestations to the contrary. When Ronnie was charged with obtaining money with menaces from a West End club owner, for instance, Boothby put down a question in the House of Lords demanding to know why Mr Kray had been held in custody for five weeks.

Boothby later told Susan Crosland that he had given away his £40,000: 'The whole of it. I regret it bitterly now. But I felt I couldn't live with it. I hadn't earned it.' Sometimes he spun the same yarn to Tom; but on other occasions he hinted that he had used the money to buy a country house which he had always wanted. 'Either way,' Tom said, 'he was wise to say that the money was entirely gone. Otherwise I might have tapped him.'[7]

The war between age and youth was fought out at the General Election of October 1964. That, at least, was what Harold Wilson told the electorate: Labour was forward-looking, 'modern', led by a youngish man whose head was full of exciting ideas which had something to do with computers and white-hot technology; the Tories were effete after thirteen long years in office, led by a 14th Earl who looked older than his years and whose head was disconcertingly skull-like – the Yorick of Downing Street. Wilson consciously (and comically) tried to liken himself to John F. Kennedy, the youthful American President who had been assassinated a year earlier; he spoke of the need for 'a programme of 100 days of dynamic action'. And it worked. The voters' verdict – which gave Labour an overall majority of just four seats – may not have been a resounding mandate but it was enough to carry Harold and Mary Wilson to 10 Downing Street.

As a senior member of the National Executive Committee, Tom

had played his part in the Labour campaign by rewriting documents and advising on election broadcasts. Christopher Mayhew, Tony Wedgwood Benn and Tom were regarded as the party's 'television experts' on the grounds that they had presented programmes themselves, or had at least seen the inside of a studio from time to time. One note from Tom to Wilson after a party political broadcast gives a flavour of the advice that was offered: 'Last one a great improvement on previous one: far more assured and calm, no sign of your eyes following teleprompter. When you glanced down at your notes, it might have been better to let the paper be seen (it wasn't, on my screen); otherwise this perfectly natural and accept-able gesture may look slightly furtive . . .' Wilson said that he was 'most grateful' for these comments. Tom's dealings with the new Prime Minister were almost always civil. But he expected nothing from the Wilson government, and he was not disappointed.

What disturbed him was the ecstatic optimism of some old confederates from the Left. Michael Foot was moved to produce *Harold Wilson: A Pictorial Biography*, an embarrassingly reveren-tial doxology composed entirely of such sentences as this: 'Harold Wilson, then, is a *dedicated* person, dedicated to politics, to the Labour Party, to his own interpretation of Socialism which he believes can contribute so much to the well-being of the British people.'[8] Other old Bevanites, such as Richard Crossman and Barbara Castle, were invited to join the Cabinet. Tom remained on the backbenches, disagreeing with the government on almost every issue of consequence: Rhodesia, Vietnam, the Common Market, economic policy, industrial policy and immigration (on which Wilson's capitulation to the racialists culminated in the 1968 Commonwealth Immigrants Bill, described by *The Times* as 'prob-ably the most shameful measure that Labour members have ever been asked by their whips to support'). He and Ian Mikardo and their lonely band of dissenters formed a new faction, the *Tribune* Group. As Mikardo wrote:

In our Group, as in the Party outside Parliament and in the trade unions, disillusion with the government grew apace. We worked hard and fought hard to get the government to change some of its policies, and if they didn't we would oppose them. But in the last resort our opposition was constricted by the straitjacket that we always had to stop short of a vote that would bring down the government and let in a Tory administration that would be far worse.[9]

Alienated though he was, Tom had enough loyalty to the old party to hesitate before attacking Labour directly. Even on Vietnam, where Wilson's support for American policy disgusted him, he could not quite bring himself to admit the logic of his own argument. In a debate in April 1965 he had to be continually heckled by Tory MPs before he would admit that his objection to the Pentagon's use of napalm and gas in Vietnam was also an implicit criticism of the British government, which had pointedly refused to condemn the napalming of Vietnamese villages. In the private conclaves of the National Executive and the Parliamentary Party he could speak with some openness, but in the House itself, as in public speeches elsewhere, he had to walk on tiptoe for fear of disturbing the precarious balance of power. Rebellion became rather easier after the General Election of March 1966, at which Labour won another forty-six seats; but it was commensurately less effective. Cushioned by his comfortable majority on the floor of the House, Wilson could afford to ignore the malcontents. When Ian Mikardo and Tom abstained in October 1966 on the government's proposal for a wages freeze, the *Daily Express* remarked scornfully that 'their protest had all the impact of a piece of wet cod dropping in a snowdrift.'

On subjects which would never topple a government, however, Tom took full advantage of his pulpit at Westminster to infuriate both Conservatives and conservatives. In June 1965, hearing that a Scottish stipendiary magistrate had described the Rolling Stones as 'complete morons who wear their hair down to the shoulders and wear filthy clothes', Tom retaliated with a motion deploring 'the action of a Glasgow magistrate, James Langmuir, in using his privileged position to make irrelevant, snobbish and insulting personal comments on the appearance and performance of a "pop" group, the Rolling Stones, who are making a substantial contribution to public entertainment and the export drive'. This brought forth an especially rich crop of hate mail, which pleased Tom enormously since it confirmed that he was *épatant les bourgeois* as intended. One correspondent ('former Labour, but *now* no longer') wrote: 'Dear Sir, You need your brains tested to back up the "Rolling Stones". We lived near one of them in Cheltenham, and *know their background* and *former* activities!' Another vilified Tom as a 'certifiable lunatic' and 'Bloody Fool'. Better still was a thoughtful letter from Blackheath addressed to 'Mr Tom Driberg MP MBE' (a reference to the MBEs awarded to all four Beatles in the last honours list):

Dear Sir,
  So you don't like magistrates using their privileged position to scurrilise riff-raff.
  But you have NO objection to your friends in the House scurrilising people – with no fear of libel actions. Mr Langmuir was quite right. The Rolling Stones behave exactly as they look – vicious ruffians of the first water. There is a case pending against three of them at the moment. The three marked X [on an attached press photograph] are the ones – and I ask you have you ever seen more vile physiogs.
  You are like Wilson MBE, the stupid Clitheroe kid – you'd consider hanging your mother if you thought it would ensure one more vote for the Labour Party.
  Don't be too hasty about closing the House and going away on vacation. Britain is at death's door mate – and there will be nowhere to start when you all return from the Riviera.
  Tell Wilson MBE not to forget Tommy Steele, the Rolling Stones, the Train Robbers, the rail vandals, the TUC bosses, the London airport strikers, the Jaguar strikers, the PO go-slowers, the ambulance men and all your fraternity who put you where you are – when he is dishing out MBEs in future. What do you or he know about the British Empire – except that you threw it away 1945–50.
  Excuse me while I vomit.

Tom had not met the Rolling Stones, in spite of the fact that his god-daughter Cleo Sylvestre had been Mick Jagger's girlfriend in the early 1960s, but in the London of the time it was inevitable that someone would bring Tom and Jagger together sooner or later.
  The man who performed this useful service was Allen Ginsberg. He was introduced to Tom in 1965 at a dinner given by a wealthy American hostess, Panna Grady, a patron and friend of William

Burroughs and other survivors of the Beat Generation. The burly, balding homosexual poet and the burly, balding homosexual MP took to each other at once. 'He said he'd been a student of Aleister Crowley,' Ginsberg recalled. 'I was really amazed because I'd never met a public affairs man who was so sophisticated and literate, and had such an exquisite, hermetic background. I thought it was remarkable for Driberg to have survived that youthful experience. He was gay, and we talked a little bit about that. He'd read Burroughs and admired him and I thought that was very sophisticated in a politician.'[10] Ginsberg also thought it might please his friend Mick Jagger to meet such a man. When he was next staying in London, in the spring of 1967, he took Tom round to Jagger's flat in Marylebone Road, where the three of them spent all afternoon and evening sitting side by side on a sofa, talking about art, politics and the ills of the world. As Ginsberg began to expound his idea of using William Blake's poems as lyrics for rock music, Tom's glance wandered to a large, brightly-painted sculpture of a phallus on the chimneypiece, and thence, by logical progression, to the bulging trousers of the pop star beside him. 'Oh my, Mick,' Tom finally blurted out, gazing hungrily at the topography of his crotch, '*what* a big basket you have!' Jagger blushed like a little boy.

'I was slightly embarrassed, as Driberg was my guest,' Ginsberg says. 'I was also astounded at his boldness. I had eyes for Jagger myself, but I was very circumspect about Jagger's body. Yet here was Driberg coming on crude. There was a kind of zen directness about it that was interesting: I suddenly realised that with directness like that you could score many times.' Tom did not score with Jagger, however. Or with Ginsberg, come to that: a few years later, after dinner one evening, Tom begged the poet to stay the night, but the invitation was refused. 'I was scared and embarrassed,' Ginsberg says. 'It hadn't occurred to me that he fancied me; I didn't think of myself as a handsome sex object, but I guess he had a catholic appetite. I just left. He was a little disappointed.'

Tom and Mick Jagger became good friends in spite of that guileless pass on the sofa. Like Ronnie Kray, Jagger saw the advantage in having an unofficial advocate at Westminster; and in the spring of 1967 he needed all the advocates he could find, since he and his fellow-Stone Keith Richard were awaiting trial on drugs charges arising from a raid on Richard's Sussex house in February. The gravamen of the case was unbelievably trifling: Jagger, for instance, had been found in possession of precisely four pep pills which were freely and legally available on prescription. (They belonged, anyway, to his girlfriend Marianne Faithfull, but he had gallantly insisted on taking the blame.) Yet the police, the courts and the press insisted on treating the defendants as if they were suspected of murder or worse. After the committal proceedings, which were held in Chichester on 10 May, Tom complained that the reporting of the case was creating prejudice against the accused before they had a chance to defend themselves. During the trial itself, at West Sussex quarter sessions in the last week of June, Jagger was led in handcuffed to a prison officer; Tom again asked questions in the House.

He could lobby ministers, but he could not sway the jury. On 29 June 1967 Mick Jagger was found guilty of possessing a potentially harmful drug – his four pep pills. Before sentence was passed, Michael Havers QC pointed out on Jagger's behalf that 150 million tablets identical to these were prescribed every year on the National Health Service. The judge, an addle-brained local landowner with the apt surname of Block, was unimpressed: he sentenced the offender to three months in prison. Keith Richard was given one year in jail for allowing his house to be used for the smoking of cannabis. Tom, once again, protested in Parliament.

Other voices in the Establishment now spoke up for the Rolling Stones: even *The Times* condemned Jagger's excessive punishment, in an editorial headed 'Who Breaks a Butterfly on a Wheel?' (a phrase from Pope's *Epistle to Dr Arbuthnot*). The day after the conviction, Jagger was released on bail pending an appeal. Meanwhile an American doctoral student from Oxford who had attended the trial, Steve Abrams, brought forward a plan he had had for some time – to take an advertisement in *The Times* calling for more liberal treatment of cannabis users. It appeared on 24 July:

The signatories to this petition suggest to the Home Secretary that he implement a five-point programme of cannabis law reform.

1. The government should permit and encourage research into all aspects of cannabis use, including its medical applications.

2. Allowing the smoking of cannabis on private premises should no longer constitute an offence.

3. Cannabis should be taken off the dangerous drugs list and controlled, rather than prohibited, by a new ad hoc instrument.

4. Possession of cannabis should either be legally permitted or at most considered a misdemeanour punishable by a fine of not more than £10 for a first offence and not more than £25 for any subsequent offence.

5. All persons now imprisoned for possession of cannabis or for allowing cannabis to be smoked on private premises should have their sentences commuted.

Signatories included the Beatles (who had paid for the space), David Bailey, David Dimbleby, Jonathan Miller, Kenneth Tynan, David Hockney and just two MPs – Brian Walden and Tom. 'Signing it,' Tom wrote later, 'was the only thing I did which provoked overt hostility among some of my political supporters in Barking.'

Four days after the advertisement appeared, he returned to the subject in a parliamentary debate. This time he had a trick up his sleeve. In the House of Commons library he had looked up, at Allen Ginsberg's request, the proceedings of the East India Hemp Commission from the 1890s, and had found to his astonishment that his own father, J. J. S. Driberg, had testified on the harmlessness of ganja. Support for cannabis now became 'almost an act of filial piety'. In his speech on 28 July, after arguing that 'it is very easy to blame drugs for outbreaks of violence, or various other evils in society, the real root causes of which have not been sufficiently analysed or determined,'[11] Tom revealed with a flourish that this was not merely the view of the notoriously modish Member for Barking but also the considered opinion of John James Street Driberg, the severely respectable colonial servant. Mr Driberg had told the Hemp Commission that when violently insane people in Assam were sent to the police, a form had to be filled in giving the cause of their condition: 'The safest thing to say is "ganja". The police know that no further inquiry will be made, so they stick it down.'

Replying to the debate on behalf of the government, the Home Office minister Alice Bacon maintained that cannabis was 'harmful to society' and that 'it would be entirely mad for the government to relax the laws.' Tom, who loathed Alice Bacon even at the best of times, heckled and barracked throughout the speech. When she claimed that 97 per cent of heroin addicts known to the Home Office had a previous history of cannabis-taking, he added 'And of alcohol'; when she condemned Paul McCartney for taking LSD, Tom praised him as 'a very good man'; when she asked 'What sort of society will we create if everyone wants to escape from reality?', she was interrupted once more by the familiar voice from behind. 'They want,' Tom shouted, 'to escape from this horrible society we have created.'

Three days later Mick Jagger's jail sentence was quashed by the Appeal Court and replaced with a one-year conditional discharge. 'That means,' he was warned by the Lord Chief Justice, Lord Parker, 'you will have to be of good behaviour for twelve months.' As Jagger bowed his head in acknowledgement, Lord Parker continued: 'You are, whether you like it or not, the idol of a large number of the young in this country. Being in that position you have very grave responsibilities.'[12]

Jagger himself was beginning to be conscious of his influence and the uses to which it might be put. Unlike Keith Richard, he was not content with a jejune life of indolence and narcotics. His political opinions might be a rather confused salad of anarcho-socialistic mumblings, but he was willing to learn. After the successful appeal he and Marianne Faithfull often invited Tom to dinner at their elegant new house in Cheyne Walk, where they would question him earnestly about the workings of Parliament. Why were governments so slow to react to people's wishes? What could a backbencher do? During one of their conversations, Tom asked: 'Why don't you try politics, Mick?'

Jagger was curious. 'If a man with anarchistic feelings did go into politics, where would he fit?' he wondered. 'The Labour Party, of course,' Tom replied briskly. He was suddenly captivated by the idea of getting Mick Jagger into Parliament. It would entice hundreds of thousands of young voters to vote Labour; it would rejuvenate the Left in Parliament; it would rattle Wilson and his gang. 'Labour is the only hope,' he repeated.

Warming to his theme, Tom added that in a few years, what with labour unrest and general dissatisfaction, Britain would be in a revolutionary situation. 'I know that's the view of some of the Trotskyites, that it is all breaking up and loosening up. And the Labour Party is where a young man should be when it happens.' What, Jagger asked, were the chances of a revolution occurring – 'not necessarily fighting in the streets, mind you, but a revolutionary change?' 'The Trotskyites may be right,' Tom murmured dramatically, 'it may be starting at this moment.' He was rather surprised to hear himself saying this, since he didn't believe a word of it. 'One begins,' he later explained to an interviewer, 'to share that revolutionary hope when one is in the company of someone like Mick.' He was so excited by Jagger's youth, his beauty, his intelligence, that he had been 'carried along with him'.[13]

While Tom tried to lure Mick Jagger to Parliament, his own attachment to the place was looser than ever. Outside Westminster his boredom and despair at the Wilson government were widely shared: at the 1967 Labour conference, for instance, Ian Mikardo and Tom came first and second in the poll for the constituency section of the National Executive. But in the House itself he was less popular. In the spring of 1967, after sixty-eight Labour MPs abstained on the Defence White Paper, Harold Wilson told his backbenchers that every dog was allowed one bite, but if the biting became habitual its owner might not renew the dog licence – a clear threat to withdraw the whip from incorrigible dissidents.

Nor could Tom simply cease attending the House. As he had learned after his Korean trip in 1950, reckless absenteeism was as serious an offence against party discipline as calculated abstention. What he needed was official permission to stay away from Westminster, allowing him the clear conscience of an abstainer without any of the accompanying punishments or privations. The only excuse for absence usually accepted by the whips' office is a life-threatening illness; so this was what Tom acquired, thanks to the connivance of David Cargill, his GP in Maldon. In November 1967 Cargill wrote a letter which was ostensibly addressed to Tom but was, as Cargill later admitted, 'intended for other eyes' – those of John Silkin, Labour's Chief Whip. It was a bravura performance. The doctor wrote that Tom had 'bloody well got to give up Parliament and all that goes with it' straight away; never mind if the time was inauspicious for a by-election, he must leave the Commons at once and 'get out of the country, at least for a few months'. He should do nothing more strenuous than a little 'gentle literary work, with no deadlines'. His blood pressure was now 240/160, and rising fast. 'You are taking too many sedatives and drinking much too much. You are, in fact, a straightforward battle casualty of parliamentary life and *at the present rate of going* your outlook for five years of survival approximates to that of a snowball in hell. What *is* the good of asking a doctor's advice if you pay no attention to it?' Even Tom, who had put Cargill up to it, was slightly shaken by the message of doom. 'Sorry my last letter was "threatening",' Cargill wrote a few weeks later. 'It was meant to frighten whoever you showed it to.' In this it succeeded. Silkin asked Tom not to force a by-election, promising that he could convalesce for as long as he wanted without harassment from the whips.

The doctor's note could hardly have been more disingenuous. Tom was indeed 'taking too many sedatives and drinking much too much', but in these vices he had for many years been aided and abetted by Cargill himself. Since the early 1950s Cargill had prescribed a generous quantity of stimulants and sleeping pills – 'buckyou-uppers and slowyoudowners' or 'passports to Nirvana', as he liked to call them – which, he advised Tom, would be all the more effective if swallowed with beer or claret. Except in the letter that was written for Silkin's benefit, Cargill never suggested that his patient was overdoing the sedatives or the booze. Quite the opposite. 'I think we all have too much to worry about without worrying as to whether comparatively harmless drugs are habit-forming,' he reassured Tom. 'As Churchill said, "I have taken more out of alcohol than alcohol has taken out of me", and if drink did kill him at 90-plus, what the hell? So if drinamyl suits you, I should take it.' It suited Tom very well, especially when boosted with paracetamol. So lavish was Cargill's generosity that in December 1966 he had been visited by an investigator from the Department of Health who wanted to know why he had given Tom no fewer than 500 drinamyl capsules – three or four months' supply – on a single prescription. Tom was alarmed when he heard of the inquiry, but Cargill himself was typically nonchalant. He invited the man from the Elephant and Castle ('the Elephant's Arsehole', in Cargillese) to issue him with a written directive forbidding him to prescribe 500 tablets at a time; the Elephant man said he had no power to do so. Cargill then sent him packing, claiming (as a parting shot) that the investigation was some sort of official retaliation for Tom's refusal to support the government's prices and incomes policy. Less than a year later, Cargill had the nerve to chide Tom for excessive pill-popping.

The letter of November 1967 was a charade for the benefit of the Labour Whips, of course; nevertheless, its diagnosis was more accurate than either doctor or patient may perhaps have realised. Tom was young in spirit, but his sixty-two-year-old body was beginning to rebel against the years of self-indulgence. In January 1968, while on a lengthy tour of Cyprus to observe the Presidential election in his capacity as chairman of the PLP's Commonwealth Group, he had a slight heart attack and was laid up for several weeks in the British military hospital at Dhekelia. His stay there was enlivened by the presence of two Barking constituents, Signalmen Len Morgan and Peter Coleing, who insisted on serenading their MP with guitars. Better still, there were plenty of local youths; ignoring a warning that the coronary might have been caused by 'overdoing it' sexually, Tom invited several of them to clamber on to his sickbed. 'He had a great time in the military hospital with his Cypriot boys,' Rosemary Say recalled. On his return to Britain, Tom jokingly told the press that his doctor had advised him to 'avoid crowds and occasions of violent controversy'.

The doctor also recommended that Tom should not give up his seat. 'No need to resign until the next Parliament, is there?' Cargill wrote. 'You can draw the money and attend when you feel fit enough.' The parliamentary salary should be treated 'as a pension', Cargill explained: 'I think it's a case of "Carry on Barking". Surely the thing to do is to live until you die and use your ill-health as an excuse for long vacations when necessary.'

In fact Tom had only one vacation that year, and even that was more work than play: in July, at very short notice, he was invited by the Archbishop of Canterbury to attend the Assembly of the World Council of Churches in Uppsala, Sweden, as an Anglican delegate. These meetings took place once every seven years, and were attended by more than 2,000 people. 'It was,' Tom said in a BBC radio talk on his return, 'a very *big* affair.' Malcolm Muggeridge, who was in Uppsala to make a television documentary, decried it as 'the largest ever gathering of the legatees of a bankrupt Christendom'. Tom replied that 'the Assembly as a whole was indeed *involved* in the world, thus exciting the displeasure of those spiritual twins Peter Simple of the *Daily Telegraph* and the chief contemporary spokesman for the Manichean heresy, Mr Malcolm Muggeridge.'[14] He pointed out that Muggeridge had stayed in Sweden for only two days before returning to the UK to make his programme and pen a magnificently scornful 'Uppsala Diary' in the *New Statesman*. Muggeridge had once liked Tom: in the 1950s, as editor of *Punch*, he had commissioned occasional reviews and features from him. But their characters and tastes were ultimately incompatible. Tom adored youth, and acted as if he were still a careless teenager himself; Muggeridge, by contrast, though he was Tom's senior by only two years, gave a convincing impersonation of the Oldest Man in the World, a modern Methuselah who grumbled about the creaking of his ancient bones and yearned for death. The causes that Tom championed so energetically in the Sixties – pop music, cannabis, sexual permissiveness, free expression – were to St Mugg the final spasms of a godless Gomorrah; and the subjects that occupied most discussion at the WCC Assembly – apartheid, and the napalming of Vietnamese villages – proved to Muggeridge that the churches, in their 'final decrepitude', were ignoring all their 'spiritual responsibilities'.

The two men glimpsed each other a few times in Uppsala. Muggeridge thought the setting 'exactly right' for Tom – 'Scandinavian ultra-permissiveness providing the background to a meandering discussion in which expressions like "life-style", "identity" and "third world" occurred with great profusion.'[15] In his *New Statesman* article, Muggeridge lampooned the delegates' eager ecumenicalism:

They were able to agree about almost anything because they believed almost nothing. They reminded me of a pub turn-out in my youth, with ten or a dozen drunks holding on to one another, swaying to and fro, but managing to remain upright. Alone, they would infallibly have fallen into the gutter. It was all tremendously reminiscent of the United Nations, that tragically absurd assembly — stony faces between earphones, paper circulating in prodigious quantities (the Swedish government allotted ten tons, which got used up in the first two days), oratory to match, interminable discussions about the precise wording of statements of belief and purpose which few would read and none heed, a well-equipped but little-used press room, documents of no conceivable importance or interest to anyone urgently rushed out to choke the pigeon-holes of absent journalists. If ever in human history there was a non-event, this was it.[16]

The ecumenical *mélange* was precisely what appealed to Tom in the event. He was billeted in the university students' quarters, and shared a table at breakfast with a Russian (who wore, for some reason, a Japanese kimono), an African, a German and a Dane. Pete Seeger performed songs denouncing the Vietnam War. Guest speakers included Barbara Ward and James Baldwin. Tom was appointed to a committee that was composing a resolution on Vietnam; its other members were an American Lutheran and a Russian orthodox delegate. Though Tom's draft was rejected by his two colleagues, because he laid the main responsibility for the war on the United States, he did at least try to see that the English version of the motion they eventually produced 'was tolerably readable', with the requisite semi-colons all present and correct. In the report of another working group Tom was horrified to notice the phrase 'ongoing structures', and when he found a passage claiming that discrimination against women was a 'pervasive impediment to community development', he emitted a loud yelp of disgust. On this, if nothing else, he and Muggeridge would probably have agreed.

*

On the morning of 9 August, a week after returning from Sweden, Tom woke to find the vision in his left eye slightly blurred. He assumed it would pass. By the following week it still hadn't. He went to a specialist, who dilated the pupil, shone a bright light into the eye and gazed. The verdict: a detached retina. He was immediately taken into St Bartholomew's Hospital in Smithfield.

'Mr Driberg has had a run of misfortunes recently,' the London *Evening Standard* reported, recalling his heart attack in Cyprus earlier in the year. 'He remains cheerful, however, and the political significance of the fact that it is his left eye which is damaged has not escaped him.'[17] While waiting for the extremely delicate operation to re-attach the retina he spent six days lying immobile with his head flat on the pillow, since any movement might pull the displaced membrane down further; afterwards, he had to stay in bed for several more days with both eyes bandaged, frustratingly unable to read or write. By then he was feeling rather less cheerful.

Still, the operation seemed to have been a success. At the beginning of September he was allowed out to convalesce at Bradwell, with strict warnings against jerking his head, stooping to pick things up or even, if possible, sneezing. He managed pretty well, except for a bad jolt in a taxi that braked sharply. Two weeks after his release from hospital he went back for an examination. 'Sorry,' he was told, 'it's gone again.' He was readmitted to Bart's in the middle of September, with the prospect of another operation and three or four weeks lying flat on his back in a hospital bed. He was now decidedly less cheerful. He would not be able to attend the Labour Party conference at Blackpool.[18] Worse, as he wrote to Allen Ginsberg, 'I am missing all sorts of interesting things, such as the London opening of *Hair* on the day after the Lord Chamberlain's censorship of the theatre has been abolished.'[19]

Ginsberg, on the other hand, had been missing nothing. He sent Tom a vivid account of the Democratic convention in Chicago — 'like a mafia-style police state' — at which Mayor Daley's uniformed goons had beaten up anti-war protesters. 'I wandered around with Jean Genet,' he revealed. 'Wound up necking in bed with him — and Wm Burroughs, all week listening to them and teargassed thrice in their company.'[20]

No doubt with the best of intentions, Ginsberg decided to instruct the International Society for Krishna Consciousness to call on Tom in hospital. These jangling, shaven-headed zealots, mostly Americans, had lately arrived in London with the purpose of creating an ashram but had run into trouble with the immigration authorities. Ginsberg was convinced that Tom, even from his sick-bed, could help them 'contribute a stable, cheerful and potentially very strong mantric experience to the scene' by badgering the Home Office on their behalf. If only he would attend one of their *pujas* – services at which the devotees chanted the words 'Hare Rama, Hare Krishna' for two hours – 'you would immediately see where they were at'. At the beginning of October, soon after Tom's second operation, a party of Krishna followers turned up at his bedside to give him a taste of their hypnotically dreary chanting; they also brought with them a large plate of vegetarian food, which slightly distressed the nurses since it seemed to imply that he was not being fed adequately. They left halva and flowers, as well as a card printed with the Krishna mantra which they said would send him to sleep. When they paid another call, a week later, he assured them that it had helped, though honesty compelled him to add that it had been fortified by a hefty dose of Nembutal. On this second occasion, the Krishnas arrived in strength – four men and one woman – while Tom was being visited by an extremely conventional friend from the Foreign Office. The poor FO man was lectured at great length by the Krishna woman on how to elevate his spiritual consciousness, much to Tom's amusement. 'I find them completely charming in their innocence,' he wrote to Ginsberg – though he emphasised that he could not be a financial guarantor of their temple 'because I am too heavily overdrawn at the bank'. Excited by Tom's apparent enthusiasm for the saffron-robed fakirs, and remembering his connection with Aleister Crowley, Ginsberg sent him a note revealing confidentially that 'Dread Apocalypse is finally on the planet.' What was needed was 'some form of cosmic vibration ... to channel the energy and make it impressive in a non-verbal way', he wrote. 'I keep thinking – the present world politics scene seems more and more like Magic, and there should be a breakthrough of White Magic, exorcism ceremonies etc as street theater ...'[21]

All this helped to take Tom's mind off his disturbingly slow recovery from the second operation. It was a welcome distraction, too, from the ceaseless noise of the hospital – the pneumatic drill in the street outside, the Smithfield market traffic, the gurgling sinks, the squalling three-year-old boy in a neighbouring ward. (Tom later discovered the reason for the infant's screams: he had just had his one remaining eye removed.) The patient in the bed next to Tom was a garrulous old bore, given to making extraordinary general observations such as 'I'm afraid I take rather a poor view of archaeology.' Joan Leigh Fermor (the former Joan Rayner) sent caviare and champagne, which Tom shared with a couple of 'the nicer and more permissive night nurses' after the stern night-sister had done her rounds. 'All our intake and output of liquid is strictly measured,' he wrote to Joan Leigh Fermor, 'but as they do not know about the midnight champagne, the statistics will not be very accurate.' An even more thoughtful present came from Gore Vidal in Italy, who had known Tom since the 1950s and had been encouraging him for some time to write a scandalous volume of memoirs. Hearing that his friend was laid up with his eyes in bandages, Vidal sent him a tape recorder into which the great work could be dictated. Unfortunately Vidal did not know about the presence in the next bed of the anti-archaeologist, whose attentive ears inhibited Tom from making much progress on the book.

The surgeon was unhappy with Tom's condition. He called in another consultant – 'a friend whose hobby is retinas' – who said that a third operation was advisable. Since the cause of the unsatisfactory symptom was not visible they would have to work 'empirically', poking about and seeing what they could find. The operation was performed on 23 October. Unlike the others, it was followed by considerable pain for a week or so – not surprisingly, since the eye had now been subjected to 'three severe surgical insults' (as the consultant put it). 'I have been having some rather bad nights and days,' Tom wrote to his agent, Jean LeRoy, on 30 October.

On 6 November he was finally released, this time after six and a half weeks in hospital, again with orders to convalesce quietly in the country. But his left eye grew dimmer still. Further medical checks showed that it was 'indolent'. On 12 December he lost the sight of it altogether. To be strictly accurate, he had perhaps two per cent vision – if he held a sheet of white paper beneath it and looked down he could discern the whiteness. Otherwise, as he wrote in an article for the *People* soon afterwards, 'I "see" only a fantastic and often picturesque pageant of moving, silver-bright shapes – stars, Alpine scenery, snow-clad boughs, flying saucers . . .'[22] He had to adjust to the different focus of looking through one eye only, as he learned when he poured whisky down the outside of a glass. Steps and staircases were difficult, if they were toplit and not distinguishable by shadow or conspicuous edging; sometimes, too, he bumped into people standing on his blind side. John Betjeman sent him a touching letter of condolence:

My dear Thomas,

  I am very sad to read you have lost the sight of an eye. For us aesthetes this is a serious loss. The lady who makes my breakfast in the mornings told me that she had not been able to see out of one eye for over a year and that she would always be blind in it. I asked her if it made much difference. She said not at all except for getting up and down stairs. She needed to hold on to baluster rails sometimes. I hope you are not ruined financially by it. Let me know how things are. I shall think of you over Christmas. Love to Ena. Bung ho, old man.[23]

Betjeman's housekeeper was right: on the whole, Tom was surprised by how small the handicap was. He could still watch films and plays; he could read and write as before. He joked about the one-eyed man being king in the country of the blind, and told friends proudly that the detached retina, like his heart trouble, had probably been caused by too much sex. He began the New Year of 1969 in a surprisingly cheerful mood.

His political seduction of Mick Jagger could now be resumed. Between the heart attack in January and the onset of eye trouble in August the two men had met once a month or so, sometimes over lunch *à deux* at the Gay Hussar in Greek Street (where Tom happily defied medical opinion by downing many glasses of Hungarian red wine), and sometimes for long afternoons or evenings at Cheyne Walk. Jagger was maddeningly pusillanimous. Often, after Tom left, he would tell Marianne Faithfull: 'I'm going into politics.' Then he would change his mind in the morning. Faithfull doubted that Jagger had any serious political ambition; he was merely troubled by being 'too rich'. But Tom listened to him with respect – so much so that before long the roles of teacher and pupil (or wooer and wooed) were swapped. Instead of Tom winning Jagger for the Labour Party, Jagger was arguing Tom out of it. The MP had originally insisted that only through Labour in Parliament could change be effected, while the idol of youth dreamily envisaged burning barricades and crowds in the streets. During 1968 the Wilson government seemed bent on confirming Jagger's mistrust of Westminster by supporting Nigeria in the Biafran war and America in Vietnam, as well as forcing through its odious Commonwealth Immigrants Bill; meanwhile students occupied the LSE (Jagger's old college) and anti-war demonstrators, including Jagger, laid siege to the American Embassy in Grosvenor Square. The anthem of the summer was the Rolling Stones' song 'Street Fighting Man'. Tom had followed much of this from his hospital bed, and the more he saw of young people's alienation from conventional politics the more alienated he became himself. Perhaps the Labour Party was not 'the only hope'; it might, indeed, be the problem rather than the solution.

A new movement was needed to represent this idealistic multitude – something along the lines of Sir Richard Acland's wartime Common Wealth party, Tom thought. Acland had been living quietly in Devon for years, working at a college in Exeter. On 5 February 1969 he received a letter from Tom out of the blue:

My dear Richard,

Are you likely to be in London again 'in the foreseeable future'?

As you know, there will be *six million* new voters at the next election – an average of 10,000 a constituency! Anything could happen: not that they are all likely to vote the same way.

I have been discussing the electoral possibilities, and the problems of revolution (and the difficulty of founding a new party) with two people, friends of mine, who could have some influence among the young: Mick Jagger and his lady, Marianne Faithfull – both more intelligent than you might suppose from their public *personae*. They would like to meet you. Would you?[24]

Acland was ecstatic. 'What an extraordinary coincidence,' he replied. 'You write to me on the one subject that has been occupying my thoughts almost to the exclusion (I am ashamed to say) of the work that the college pays me to do.' It had always been his view that no new party could be launched unless two conditions were met: '(a) there was a clear cause to be promoted; and (b) it was obvious that the cause could not be promoted by any existing party, *nor by any wing of any existing party*. It is in respect of these last eight words that (in my judgment) a suddenly new situation confronts us.' He continued:

It is not simply that the battle between official Labour and official Conservative has ceased to be a battle between making, and not making, profound change in the structure of society; this has been clear for quite a long time past. The new factor is that, in this situation, the left wing of the Labour Party has demonstrated itself powerless to raise any new enthusiasm.[25]

Acland enclosed a twenty-four-page synopsis of a book he proposed to write, restating the old Christian Socialist ideals of Common Wealth 'in the light of a further quarter century of social experience'. Its title was *Left Auxiliary*.

Now it was Tom's turn to be pleasantly surprised. 'I think you have got *the* idea,' he wrote back at once. 'Perhaps Common Wealth was a not-quite-right rehearsal?'[26] His only reservation was that 'there is very little or nothing in your synopsis about "permissiveness" — sex, drugs etc — though *some* recruits, carefully screened, would presumably be drawn from among the permissives? Their "vices" are often simply, for them, the handiest expression of revolt against the present order.' Take Mick and Marianne, for instance: in the public imagination they might be drug-racked, sex-gorged diabolists, but in real life, as Tom could testify, they were models of quiet domesticity: 'When they are free from show-biz work, they hate going out — stay at home playing records and cooking dinner.' Tom confessed that, since his discussions with Mick Jagger and his long period in hospital, Parliament seemed 'increasingly dusty and boring to me'; he was now persuaded that a new party was required. He would like it to be called Logos, but he accepted that this would need constant re-explaining and might seem too religious. 'Left Auxiliary' would serve as a working title. He and Acland must arrange a meeting with Jagger and Faithfull 'within the next few weeks'; Tom proposed also to invite the *Private Eye* journalist Paul Foot, whom he liked and respected – 'if he gave an absolute promise of secrecy for the time being'.

Did Tom really believe that a revolutionary new political force could be brought into the world by this incongruous quintet of midwives – Driberg, Acland, Jagger, Faithfull, Foot? Apparently so. The correspondence that shuttlecocked back and forth between Tom and Acland in February and March 1969 shows that both men were perfectly serious. They argued the pros and cons of allowing Labour MPs to defect to the new party ('I think there might be a few,' Tom predicted); Acland reported excitedly that he had received 'a very encouraging letter from the headmistress of a mixed comprehensive school saying she is quite sure that thousands of young people would respond to this kind of thing'.[27] Alas, the oft-promised meeting in London had to be continually postponed because of the elusiveness of the two members of the party's Cheyne Walk branch, who decided that they were under quite enough strain without the added responsibility of saving Britain. One evening Tom turned up at 48 Cheyne Walk to try to rekindle their interest. Marianne Faithfull said she was expecting a few people for dinner, a special occasion for which Mick had promised to be home early; but while Tom was there, Jagger rang to say that he was working in the studio and would not be back until very late. Bursting into tears as she replaced the receiver, Faithfull implored Tom to stay for dinner as her escort. He was flattered but had to attend a political dinner which couldn't be missed. She said she understood, and then asked, sobbing loudly: 'Will you please go down to the pub and buy me a few bottles of wine? I have no money.' It was a pitiable spectacle. Tom was fond of Marianne Faithfull, and kept in touch with her after she left Jagger in 1970. A couple of years later he invited her to a dinner he gave for W. H. Auden at the Gay Hussar, 'to diversify the company'. This she certainly did: as they took their seats, Auden leant over and asked Faithfull, in his hazy semi-American accent, 'When you're smuggling drugs, d'you pack them up your arse?'

The three remaining founders of Logos, or Left Auxiliary or whatever it was to be called, finally came together in London in April 1969. Tom had been bullying Paul Foot for weeks to come and meet Sir Richard Acland, but Foot still had no idea what the purpose of the gathering was when they arrived for dinner at the inevitable Gay Hussar. As Tom and Acland chatted animatedly over the wild cherry soup, Foot realised that they wanted to create a new version of the Common Wealth party. As politely as he could, he explained that he thought their notions were rather nostalgic and sentimental, and that anyway he was a member of a revolutionary organisation – the International Socialists – which had rather different ambitions than producing left-wing Members of Parliament. 'It was all rather stilted, though perfectly jolly,' Foot recalled, 'and I remember particularly that after the dinner was over and I was anxious to get home, Tom rebuked me for "uxoriousness" – which was singularly inappropriate since I had just left my wife.' Tom then all but forced his two companions to go to 'some ghastly gay bar in one of those shady streets in Soho, where he flirted in a quite appalling manner with the waiters'.[28] Foot made an excuse and left as soon as possible.

Thus ended the Left Auxiliary, the group that was to inspire the nation's youth and set Westminster ablaze with radicalism. One dinner in the Gay Hussar, one foray into a gay club, and nothing more was ever heard of it.

Many of his schemes and dreams had perished in Soho. It was while he was living in the fat ladies' brothel forty years earlier that Edith Sitwell had shoved him into Fleet Street and – as he believed – ended his hope of poetic glory. He had often returned to those streets, to their restaurants and drinking clubs, as if to reassure himself that he was still the same old Bohemian. Now, as other helpers failed and comforts fled, the area became a second home to him.

Where else could he go while he was in London? The House of Commons, which he had so revered, no longer enticed him as a place in which to spend his afternoons and evenings. He had been forced to give up his beloved flat in Great Ormond Street when the new owner of the freehold, the Hospital for Sick Children, demolished the terrace to make way for nurses' accommodation. For a time he rented a flat in Upper Wimpole Street, but he hated 'the smug, bourgeois character of the neighbourhood, the distance from the H of C, and above all the stair-climb through that filthy dentists' smell'. It was much more expensive than Great Ormond Street, too, and when the landlord announced his intention of raising the rent still higher, early in 1969, Tom moved out. He took refuge in the vicarage of St Matthew's, Westminster, where his friend the Revd Gerard Irvine had recently been installed as prebendary. Irvine offered Tom a couple of upstairs rooms almost rent-free in return for a promise to have them decorated. This was preferable to Upper Wimpole Street – and only a few minutes' walk from the Commons – but it was still not exactly homely, especially as there were other lodgers on the premises. Tom also conceived a fierce dislike of Irvine's housekeeper, a German woman who had appeared in the celebrated 1931 lesbian movie *Maedchen in Uniform*. She brought out the most pathological side of his misogyny: he refused to drink out of any cup or eat off any plate that she might ever have used, no matter how many times it had been washed.

He was thus drawn back continually to Soho, lunching at the Gay Hussar in Greek Street, dining at the Hostaria Romana in Dean Street; in between he might amble towards Bloomsbury on a tour of his favourite cottages, or drop in at a homosexual club, before heading for the Colony Room in Dean Street, an afternoon drinking den run by the notoriously cantankerous but sentimental Muriel Belcher. While there he might telephone an item of gossip through to the 'Londoner's Diary' on the *Evening Standard*. Alan Watkins remembered Tom appearing at Muriel's with 'a succession of young men – usually in their early twenties, though it was difficult to tell – whom he would invariably introduce individually to the assembled company as "one of my constituents". He would then provide the young man of the afternoon with a handful of loose change, and direct him to the fruit machine in the corner to divert himself, while Driberg gossiped with his cronies.'[29] Another journalist, Russell Miller, interviewed Tom for the *Sunday Times* during one of those lost afternoons.

There were only a few people in the club when I arrived [Miller wrote] – Muriel, a couple of faded actresses, a tanned barman with his shirt open to the navel, a couple of young men and Tom Driberg, sitting contentedly at the bar with a vodka and tomato juice. In spite of the sober dark blue suit, collar and tie he was wearing, his familiarity with the surroundings made it obvious he was a regular part of the scene . . .

The somnolent atmosphere was disrupted soon afterwards by the arrival of a well-oiled advertising man, who was determined to brighten the two actresses with a stream of dirty jokes which made him laugh a lot and them even sadder. After ignoring this disturbance for some time, Tom suddenly broke off what he was saying and loudly interjected: 'What a fool that man over there is!'

As they left the club at the end of the afternoon, picking their way down the narrow stairs, Tom and his interviewer literally bumped into Francis Bacon, another habitué of Muriel's, who greeted Tom effusively. The *Sunday Times* man thought he detected a twinge of regret in the MP's face as he embraced the artist:

He would have been happy as a poet and has always enjoyed Bohemian company, finding many friends among the strange community who have made their spiritual home in Soho. Instead, journalism and politics imposed on him the need to preserve some vestige of respectability and it is a mantle which has always been uncomfortable round his shoulders.
When we were walking away from the Colony Room late that sunny afternoon, our brief encounter with Francis Bacon obviously triggered off a familiar sequence of thoughts in Driberg's mind because he was silent for some time, then, looking around at the flickering neon signs of the strip clubs and restaurants and pubs and delicatessens, he said, quite softly, as if to himself: 'You know, I've always wished in a way that I could have lived this kind of life.'[30]

He did live it, or something very like it, in the late 1960s. Ian Mikardo recalled a long lunch at the Gay Hussar after which, just as he was preparing to hasten back to Westminster, Tom said: 'Fancy another drink? I'll take you to a place.' A reluctant Mikardo was dragged off to a bar in an alley between Dean Street and Frith Street. 'As far as I was concerned,' Mikardo says, 'it was an out-of-hours drinking club, but in fact it was a gay club, and he was obviously a long-standing member. They all knew him.'

Other regular ports of call were the *Private Eye* office in Greek Street and the Coach and Horses pub just down the road, where Tom turned up to the fortnightly *Private Eye* lunch regardless of whether he had been invited or not. His arrival at the private dining room on the first floor of the Coach and Horses was often conducted in an absurd cloak-and-dagger fashion. He scuttled into the room introducing himself as 'Mr Richmond' (even though most guests knew perfectly well who he was) and then peered suspiciously from behind the pub's moth-eaten curtains at the street outside – where, he claimed, agents of Harold Wilson's chief snoop, George Wigg, were sitting in a car spying on him. In fact, the main reason for his regular attendance at the lunches was a passionate craving he had conceived for Patrick Marnham, one of the magazine's reporters; Marnham did not reciprocate. Another unwilling prey was the *Private Eye* typesetter Steve Mann. Tom would deliberately scribble his contributions illegibly so that he had to come and dictate them to Mann in the office, where he gazed with sheep's eyes at the lean young fingers nimbly racing over the IBM keyboard. 'Oh, Steve!' he would murmur with a heavy sigh.

When they first met Tom, in the mid-Sixties, the young but gerontophilic satirists at the *Eye* were flattered by his interest and enthusiasm. The editor, Richard Ingrams, was a man who adopted elderly iconoclasts and anarchists – Malcolm Muggeridge, Claud Cockburn – and in spite of his well-known antipathy to homosexuals he was prepared to add Tom to the list. In June 1966 Ingrams started paying Tom a retainer of £10 per issue in return for scuttlebut from the Commons, but since Tom attended Parliament so seldom himself he did not provide much useful information. Besides, when he did acquire some savoury titbit he usually sold it to the *Evening Standard*, which paid better. As Alan Watkins noted, Tom's principal activity at the *Eye* lunches was to point out or engage in solecisms, whether syntactical, ecclesiastical or social, as in: 'My dear Richard, I am astonished that you don't appear to know the correct way to refer to the younger daughter of a Marquess.' By the end of 1968 the retainer had been phased out, though he was still given an occasional fiver for specific items of gossip. He then proposed that he should compose a regular prize crossword whose main characteristics would be extreme difficulty and moderate obscenity. Ingrams liked the idea, and the first *Private Eye* crossword appeared on 28 February 1969; the solutions included ERECTION ('Stiff enough to transmit electricity! (8)') and PROSTITUTE, as well as references to an Australian penis (PERCY), a fart (WIND) and a hashish-smoker (POTTER). This was par for the course thenceforward. Perhaps his finest moment was Crossword 98, in 1972, which had such clues as 'Seamen mop up anal infusions (6)' (ENEMAS) and 'Sounds as if you must look behind for this personal lubricant (5)' (SEBUM) The winner of the £2 prize for that particular puzzle was a Mrs Rosalind Runcie, the wife of the then Bishop of St Albans.

Tom kept his identity as compiler of the crossword a secret. Originally he was described merely as 'a distinguished academic churchman'; he wrote a booklet for *Private Eye* on the language of crossword clues under the name 'Old Palindrome'; from 1972 onwards he used the pseudonym 'Tiresias', after the blind, transsexual Theban of legend, described in Eliot's *Waste Land* as 'an old man with wrinkled dugs' who had 'walked among the lowest of the dead'. According to Tennyson's rendering of the story, the gods had told Tiresias: 'Henceforth be blind for thou hast seen too much.' It was an apt choice.

He had seen too much, and one day he would tell what he had seen. Since Gore Vidal sent him that tape recorder he had often ruminated on the idea of writing a confessional volume of memoirs. It would (so a psychiatrist told him) be a therapeutic exercise. It would make his fortune, too – a shield against penurious old age. On the other hand, it would also oblige him to leave the country.

He could not afford to write it for a year or two anyway. His income was now lower than at any time for twenty years; apart from his parliamentary salary and tip-fees from *Private Eye* and the *Evening Standard*, he was kept afloat only by book-reviews for a Sunday newspaper, the *People*, at £75 each. In 1967, in a moment of madness, he had signed a contract to write a biography of

Hannen Swaffer for an advance of £1,000 immediately and £1,000 on publication. As ever, he was attracted by the ready cash, but once that had been spent he was still left with the tiresome chore of actually writing the book. Eventually he hired his old secretary Rosemary Say to do most of the research. She in turn had to be paid; and so the overdraft worsened. By 1969, with his account more than £10,000 in the red, the National Provincial had had enough: he was ordered to sell Bradwell Lodge.

Enemies and creditors – there were plenty of each – seemed to pounce from every direction. In March 1969 the *Barking and Dagenham Express*, a paper he despised, printed a front-page story headed 'PARTY BID TO AXE DRIBERG', which claimed that several leading figures in Barking Labour Party no longer wanted him as their candidate even though he had already been automatically nominated to stand at the next general election. One unnamed member of the general management committee told the newspaper: 'There is a lot of ill feeling about the way Mr Driberg has treated his constituents. Many of us feel he is ignoring us. It seems that he has forgotten the people who got him to Parliament.' Another committee member, also anonymous, said: 'He has had all the time in the world to prove himself as far as we are concerned. Reconciliation is quite out of the question.'[31] There were reported to be up to twenty people on the general management committee who would support a motion to have his selection rescinded.

The story was largely true; but the local paper had not paused to consider whether its nameless sources would be ready to stand up if Tom should sue for libel. However much his critics in Barking might resent him, their loyalty to the party would surely inhibit them from giving evidence in court against their own MP. As an old newspaperman himself, Tom was quick to spot this weakness – especially as he had had an almost identical experience nine years earlier. In November 1960, a year after his first election victory at Barking, the *Ilford Recorder* had alleged that Tom was being 'sharply criticised because so far he has not considered it necessary to visit the borough to explain his attitude towards existing disagreements on important policies.' He was 'seldom seen in Barking', and some members of the local party were 'openly criticising their member's interpretation of his duties as an MP to the constituency he represents'. Not all that openly: the quotes in the *Ilford Recorder* came from somebody identified merely as 'one party member' or 'the *Recorder* informant', who told the newspaper, 'Nobody could accuse Mr Driberg of coddling his constituents. We know he is a busy man and much in demand but we should like to see him more often, and to have the benefit of his advice and guidance.'[32] As soon as a writ was threatened, the *Recorder* discovered that its informant had gone to ground. It had to print a humble apology to Tom 'for any erroneous impression of his constituency activities caused by the article'.[33]

When the *Barking and Dagenham Express* fell into the same trap nine years later, Tom saw the chance of easy money. Barrack-room lawyers at the Commons assured him that he could expect £15,000 damages in court or £8,000 as a settlement out of court, and for a delirious day or two it seemed that he might not have to sell Bradwell Lodge after all. His libel solicitor, Michael Rubinstein, soon punctured this swelling hope. Such figures were 'completely unrealistic by reference to libel damages these days', Rubinstein advised him. 'You must forget about those tempting thousands of pounds.'[34] Two months later he accepted an offer of £1,000 and a statement in open court.

He expected the bank to be pleased with his windfall; perhaps he would even be left in peace for a few weeks. Not a bit of it. No sooner had he paid in his cheque for £1,000 than he received another peremptory letter demanding to know why it was taking so long to sell Bradwell. He was furious. 'I may in passing mention (though not to excite any further comment from you),' he wrote tetchily to the manager, M. E. Roberts, 'that this is the only letter or message that I have had concerning the libel action that contained no word of appreciation or congratulation on its satisfactory settlement. £800 or £1,000 does not contribute much to the reduction of my overdraft and other debts; but I thought it better than nothing.' Nor was he pleased to find himself still chivvied and harassed by the National Provincial on the subject of Bradwell Lodge. The asking price was £35,000 but, as he had already told the bank, every local estate agent agreed that there was little demand for houses worth more than £20,000 on the east coast at the moment. 'It is not my fault (nor, I suppose, the agents') that Bradwell has not been sold yet,' he snapped at Roberts, 'and, having agreed, under pressure from you, to sell it, I accept no blame for this. As the agents have said, it often takes some time to find the right buyer for a house of this character ... I am doing everything I possibly can (including the sale of more chattels) to reduce the overdraft; and there is really no point in your sending me censorious letters which take no account at all of my efforts and merely serve as nerve-racking irritants rather than corrective stimulants.'[35]

His temper was not improved by the Swaffer book. 'Why did he write so much?' Tom would groan as he pored over another huge wad of old press clippings. He longed to abandon the whole project, but since he couldn't afford to repay the advance there was no choice but to struggle on. While researching Swaffer's spiritualist beliefs, he went with Rosemary Say to see a medium in Muswell Hill. 'Tom wanted to find out about the mechanics,' Say recalled. 'The medium said: "I can tell a great deal about you, Mr Driberg, and I can tell your sister is very worried about you." Crash! Tom got up and said "Come on Rosemary, we're going." '[36] Say often collected Tom from his Westminster vicarage on Saturday morning and drove him to Bradwell for a weekend's work on Swaffer. But there were countless interruptions and distractions: on the journey up, in between studying the *Times* crossword, Tom would insist on stopping at antique shops, churches and pubs; they arrived just in time for him to show round visitors between 2 and 4 pm; after that he settled up the takings from postcard sales and admission fees, and by then it was almost time for dinner. Sometimes they travelled up on Friday evening instead, but this was no more conducive to literary collaboration. According to Rosemary Say,

Car journeys in the pitch dark of Essex winter nights with Tom singing pre-Wesleyan hymns or talking of his coming death, of his mother, of his failed marriage ('I gave her everything I could manage') often ended in the Bradwell kitchen with Tom reading poetry as he scooped baked beans from the tin. He would cry with the words, and so would I because we were both pissed out of our minds, had barely escaped death on the road, and the poetry was superb.[37]

They drank a lot. 'Tom had worked out that I could have three double Scotches but no more because it would not be safe driving.'

More assistance was needed. In September 1969 Say brought an acquaintance of hers called Michael Jackson to Essex for the weekend, since he had told her that he had plenty of spare time and was willing to help with the Swaffer book. Soon afterwards he was temporarily paralysed after an accident; Tom invited him to recuperate at Bradwell and, as Jackson says, 'I ended up running the place.' Though he bridles at the suggestion that he became Tom's housekeeper, he was at least an endlessly useful all-purpose assistant, a valet and cook and secretary, a gentleman's gentleman. But he was never formally employed by Tom.

Jackson and Say competed jealously for the master's attention. They had (and have) an amusing, bickering rivalry. 'Tom never made a pass at Michael Jackson,' Say reveals slyly. 'Michael wasn't pretty enough.' Jackson in turn recalls that 'Tom would ring me up and complain that Rosemary was infuriating him.' They squabbled endlessly over who should be allowed to have the one bedroom with a private bathroom. (Jackson won.)

Poor Ena was not consulted about these additions to the ménage, and was none too pleased by them; fortunately she had recently bought – with money inherited from her father – a cottage of her own at Chorleywood, Hertfordshire, to which she could retreat. She did not give up entirely, however: during 1969 and 1970 she often returned to Bradwell at weekends, and Jackson particularly remembers one Saturday in the spring of 1970 when 'Ena came down, cooked us all a grand supper and made a real effort'. All to no avail. Jackson's diary entry for the following day read simply: 'Not very good Sunday at Bradwell. Ena vs. Tom.'

There were many fraught weekends in the early months of 1970, and none more so than that of 7–8 February, when the usual household of Tom, Rosemary Say and Michael Jackson was joined by a twenty-four-year-old criminal whom Tom had befriended, Steve Raymond, and his Australian girlfriend Mardy Kros. Raymond had been in prison until the previous August, serving a sentence for armed robbery, and had a string of other convictions.

Neither Say nor Jackson was fully aware of his record but they knew enough to be slightly uneasy. 'Steve and Mardy slept in my room, Rosemary had the other big bedroom and I went to Ena's old room in the Tudor wing,' Jackson recalled. 'An hour or so after going to bed Rosemary came down and asked to swap – she said she didn't like sleeping next door to a murderer.'[38]

Murder was one crime that Raymond hadn't yet committed, in fact; but Rosemary Say's jitters were understandable. Though Steve Raymond was intelligent, attractive and capable of enormous charm, he could also be a deeply menacing and unnerving presence. Between 1967 and 1968 he had been held for a year in Grendon Underwood, Britain's only psychiatric prison, where he had been classified as a psychopath. A report by his psychiatric social worker there, Mrs E. M. Miller-Smith, described him thus:

At Grendon we see many men who can only be regarded as psychopathic and I think we have come to recognise a syndrome of recurrent imprisonment resulting from chronic conflict with the law (with or without violence), high intelligence and charm, fascination for the opposite sex, the inability to form mature relationships and perhaps most significant characteristic of all, the callously manipulative and destructive exploitation of others and readiness to bite the hand that feeds them. In particular I'm afraid I personally think that Steve qualifies only too well for the designation.[39]

Raymond had grown up among the street gangs of North London, a brilliant child who always came top of the class in spite of missing almost all his lessons. He was eventually expelled from school for unruly behaviour. In April 1959, at the age of fourteen, he was placed on probation for housebreaking and larceny, and from then on he was constantly in trouble – burgling, forging cheques, stealing cars, taking drugs. He was sent to remand homes and detention centres, from which he invariably absconded. In 1963 he did a stretch in Borstal. Then came his first serious crime: in October 1964 the nineteen-year-old Raymond took part in an armed robbery at the house of the actress Florence Desmond. He was sent to prison for six years.

It was in May 1965 that he first contacted his MP, Tom Driberg.

The letter he wrote from Aylesbury jail was perfectly civil, but already there were hints that he might be an embittered and demanding customer if he did not get his way. He wanted a transfer; he wanted to know why he had been deprived of his long-term prisoner's privileges; he wanted to be allowed to visit his ill father. Over the next few months he sent many more demands, all of which Tom passed on to the Home Office. Like the Krays before him, Raymond soon realised that Tom was a soft touch and didn't hesitate to take advantage of it. By July he was writing: 'Anyway Tom, I hope you don't mind me calling you that, only Mr Driberg seems so remote . . .' He added: 'Just let me know when I become too much of a nuisance.' The letters were signed: 'Take care and be lucky. Steve.'

When he took up the complaints with the Home Office Tom found to his embarrassment that many of the details in Raymond's letters were untrue. The Minister of State, Alice Bacon, told Tom in September that Raymond had 'a completely selfish, antagonistic attitude to life' and had been mixing with the 'worst elements' among the other long-term prisoners: 'Until he changes he is a potentially dangerous and quite unscrupulous person.' Tom passed the letter on to Raymond, who was incensed. 'Antagonistic?' he spat back. 'I wonder how Miss Bacon would feel if she was snubbed or insulted . . . Mixed with the worst elements? I had George Blake teach me German (the famous spy), a solicitor book-keeping and another prisoner bee-keeping. Hardly the worst elements.' Tom gave him the benefit of the doubt, and in return Raymond let him down: in October 1965 he tried to escape from Wandsworth jail. 'If you've stuck your neck out on my behalf,' he wrote to Tom, 'I hope this won't be any embarrassment to you.'

Still Tom continued to meet every demand. Whenever a book was requested, he sent it (including one of his valuable Aleister Crowley editions which Raymond subsequently claimed to have lost). Raymond developed a passion for literature and began to write verse – 'quite the equal of Bunting and others, I'm sure,' he boasted. One of his poems included the lines 'Do I turn in my rage and frustration, on the very devils that are tormenting me so?/Do I in turn plunder, torment, rage and ravage and become a devil king in my fight?' In 1967 the Home Office decided that he was betraying signs of 'instability' and transferred him to Grendon Underwood. It was later suggested that he had faked the symptoms to get himself moved to the comparative comfort and liberality of the psychiatric prison.

In his letters to Tom, Steve Raymond presented himself as a misunderstood kid who sincerely wanted to educate and rehabilitate himself. He gave a very different – and more honest – impression to Tony Parker, who was interviewing inmates of Grendon at this time for his book *The Frying Pan*.[40] Appearing in the book as 'Archie', Raymond shamelessly explained how he manipulated the system:

For a start you begin by telling everybody you haven't the remotest intention of changing . . . then signs of progress should start slipping out. You mustn't overdo it, of course. They like to feel they're having a battle; you've got to strike just the right balance so they can persuade themselves they've got a hope of winning in the end.

This was the technique he used on Tom.

There is no doubt that some of the appeal of Steve Raymond, as of the Krays, was sexual. He was working-class, good-looking, lean, intelligent but rough – precisely Tom's type. If he had been a toothless, paunchy old villain (or, worse still, a woman) it's unlikely that Tom would have spent so much time and sympathy on him. Nevertheless, the interest was not wholly sexual. Tom thought that Raymond's problems were caused by his frustration at being a highly intelligent youth living in no-hope circumstances; if he could only put that brain and those skills to more constructive use . . . Tom could not believe that anyone was beyond redemption. There was a touch of the Professor Higgins in his determination to make Raymond conform to his fantasy, but it was a noble enough project.

At the end of 1968 Raymond was moved from Grendon to Chelmsford prison; the following August he was released on licence. He worked briefly as assistant manager at a hotel, where he met and fell in love with Mardy Kros, an attractive though rather puritanical Australian who allowed him to sleep with her only if he kept his clothes on and stayed outside the covers. Tom hoped that she might alleviate Steve's psychopathic condition. He tried hard to help Steve himself, urging him to go to university, paying him for odd jobs sorting out Tom's files and papers at the vicarage in Westminster, and inviting Steve and Mardy up to Bradwell for that first weekend in February 1970.

Steve Raymond repaid Tom's generosity by betraying him once again. While sorting the papers at the vicarage in London he found a proof of *The Times*'s obituary of Harold Wilson, which the newspaper had asked Tom to update a couple of years earlier. Raymond sold it to *Private Eye* for £10 – a fair price for such a scoop, since no *Times* obituary had ever leaked while its subject was still alive. Richard Ingrams had no idea that it had been stolen from the magazine's own crossword-setter: the wily Raymond had snipped Tom's name off the covering letter from *The Times*'s obituaries editor, and when he turned up at the office he refused to say who he was or where he had found the documents. But as soon as the obituary appeared in *Private Eye* – less than a fortnight after Steve and Mardy had enjoyed Tom's hospitality at Bradwell – *The Times* was on to Tom at once. 'You may have seen,' William Rees-Mogg wrote coldly on 24 February, 'a reference to a now obsolete draft of *The Times* obituary on Mr Harold Wilson in *Private Eye*. The *Private Eye* article contains an accurate quotation from a letter written to you in September 1967 by the head of our Obituary Department. Obviously from our point of view this is a distressing and regrettable leak. I should be very grateful if you could let me have any information which would shed light on the situation.' Tom sent long letters to both Rees-Mogg and Harold Wilson relating the sad saga of the ex-con whom he had employed to tidy his desk, a man who had come out of prison six months ago 'and was making a difficult, but apparently genuine, effort to go straight'. In view of this, he wrote,

it seemed not too risky to employ him for this task for a few hours at a time, on days when I was in the flat myself; and he worked intelligently and well. Fortunately or unfortunately, I do not know where he now is. It is arguable that I ought to get the police to look for him; but I should, even after this very bad let-down, be reluctant to have him sent to prison again, possibly for some years.[41]

The Prime Minister and the editor of *The Times* were most under-standing of his predicament. 'I think we all very much sympathise with each other's position,' Rees-Mogg replied. 'These things are distressing and I am afraid increasingly frequent in modern journalism.' He added, characteristically: 'I don't so much mind the standards of *Private Eye* in *Private Eye*. What I do find worrying is the way in which unchecked and sometimes damaging assertions appear in more serious publications or on television.'[42]

It was not true to say that Tom was ignorant of Raymond's whereabouts: he was lounging in the flat at the vicarage, affecting surprise at the embarrassment and inconvenience he had caused. 'Oh yes, I thought that was rather a useless cutting and you didn't need it,' he replied sweetly when Tom asked him why he had stolen it. 'I tried to control my anger,' Tom said later. 'But that was when I began to lose confidence in his rehabilitation.'

Even so, he was still reluctant to excise Steve Raymond from his life altogether. In the evening of 25 March 1970, just as Tom was leaving the House of Commons to meet Michael Foot and Dingle Foot for dinner at the Gay Hussar, Steve rang to say that he and Mardy were having dinner at the Mirabelle in Curzon Street to celebrate their engagement and would love Tom to join them. Tom explained about his prior commitment to the Foot brothers but suggested that the young couple should come to the Gay Hussar for coffee and liqueurs after dinner. At about ten o'clock Steve and Mardy duly arrived in Greek Street, where Dingle Foot, as a former solicitor-general, was thrilled to meet a real live crook who was apparently articulate and thoughtful. They chatted animatedly about penal reform until well after midnight.

This, though Tom didn't know it at the time, was Raymond's alibi. While they were all sipping their Tokai in the convivial surroundings of the Gay Hussar, in the back room of a Tottenham shop a gangland leader called Eddie Coleman was being bludg-eoned and shot to death by Norman Parker, a friend of Steve's. Parker and an accomplice, David Woods, packed the body into a trunk that Raymond had bought the previous day and buried it in shallow earth in the New Forest. They then went to stay at

Raymond's flat in Highbury; a few days later he drove them to a remote corner of Scotland and hid them there.

While Parker and Woods were lying low, Raymond seemed to go out of his way to draw attention to himself in spite of being wanted by the police. Soon after returning to London he scarpered to Scotland again, taking with him a fistful of loot that included Tom's Diners' Club credit card and a wad of the special vouchers used by MPs for travelling by rail to and from their constituencies. With one of the vouchers he managed to persuade a railway ticket clerk to give him a first-class return ticket to Oban; he also managed to con a free meal in the dining car by posing as an MP, complaining loudly about the food and threatening to telephone the head of British Rail. (A pretty accurate impersonation of Tom, by the sound of it.) On reaching Scotland he went on a spending spree with the credit card, which ended only when a suspicious shop manager in Glasgow doubted that this twenty-four-year-old could really be the veteran MP Tom Driberg. He was fined £25 at Glasgow Sheriff Court on 13 April. The following day the police began to interrogate him about the Coleman murder, and he immediately told them where Parker and Woods were hiding. 'They would have been caught anyway,' he said to Tom afterwards.

At his Old Bailey trial later in the year he was acquitted of murder because of his alibi ('Trunk Case Defendant Says He Was With MPs'). He was sentenced to three years for impeding Parker's arrest; Parker himself got life. The case ended Steve's engagement to Mardy, who returned to Australia on the edge of a nervous breakdown; but Tom could still not cut loose. He helped Steve get a transfer from Wandsworth to Dartmoor, he sent him books, he smuggled money in to the jail so that Steve could buy tobacco; he even wrote to Norman Parker in the hope of convincing him that Steve hadn't grassed on him. 'You wouldn't believe how much I know I owe you – and how I appreciate it!!' Steve wrote. 'I am so sorry to ask you to do so much but you really are the only one I can trust to do things properly *and* with discretion. I owe you plenty – and, like God, pay debts in other coins but money.' But his gratitude needed constant fuelling. When he thought Tom was not pursuing one of his complaints with enough vigour, he wrote sarcastically: 'Perhaps silence is a parliamentary privilege.'

Thanks to Tom's endeavours Raymond was allowed a weekend's home leave in March 1972, a few months before the end of his sentence. On the following Monday Dartmoor prison rang Tom to say that he hadn't returned. Minutes later Tom had another call, asking him to ring Steve on a Dublin number. 'I was amazed and furious because he was implicating me,' Tom told the *Sunday Times*. 'I gave the police the number.' Steve managed to get as far as Australia – where he hoped to find Mardy – before the police caught up with him. He served the rest of his sentence in Wandsworth and Pentonville, and was released in July 1973.

After the many betrayals and abuses Tom had suffered at the hands of this seductive psychopath, the final break was provoked by a comparative trifle, when Steve invited him to a 'thank-you' dinner at a West End club in 1974. Towards the end of the meal Tom overheard him conning a free meal out of the manager by telling him that his famous guest, Tom Driberg, often wrote anonymously for Egon Ronay's restaurant guide. It was one liberty too many. Tom's lifelong belief that no one was immune to rehabilitation had to be abandoned. 'I'm afraid,' he said, 'I learned by experience that this optimistic maxim doesn't apply to a psychopath.' He told Steve that he would never help him again.

But Steve Raymond could not be rinsed out of one's life as easily as that. In 1975, back inside for using false documents to drive a car, he bombarded his old patron with letters. 'Although you're a mistrustful, prickly old bastard at times, I'll always be grateful to you for what you've done,' he wrote. He came out of Pentonville at the end of April 1976 and within a fortnight had found work with a security firm at Heathrow Airport, Purolator Services Ltd. His mother, though thrilled that her rogue son had respectable employment at last, was surprised that the company didn't check his record. She doubted he would hold on to the job for long. A month later, on Saturday 26 June, two million pounds in foreign currency disappeared from Heathrow. Two men had signed for and collected the money from cargo centres at the airport; they had produced the necessary documents, police revealed, and one had been in the uniform of Purolator Services. Scotland Yard named Stephen Patrick Raymond as one of the suspects for whom it was searching.

Years later, long after Raymond had been found and convicted, the Tory MP Nicholas Winterton alleged that Tom himself had been involved in the heist and had been paid a cut of £25,000 from the proceeds. This seems to be another sublime example of the posthumous mythologising of the rackety and intriguing Driberg reputation: as with Chapman Pincher's efforts in the *genre*, no proof was offered or needed; as with the vast sums in Moscow gold that Tom supposedly earned from the KGB, there was no explanation of how he disposed of this swag. And what was Tom paid for? Why would the Heathrow gang spend all that money to retain the services of an elderly and infirm MP who had no skills that would be useful in the planning or executing of such a raid?

It is true, however, that Tom profited from the crime: the *Sunday Times* paid him £1,250 for the long extracts from his ten-year correspondence with the 'psychopath' that were printed in a full-page article headed 'How Stephen Raymond Took Everyone In'. It was fair compensation for the depredations he had endured, and it certainly trumped the £10 Steve had extracted from *Private Eye* six years earlier.

Of all the many embarrassments that Steve Raymond inflicted on Tom the publication of Harold Wilson's obituary in the spring of 1970 was probably the worst, if only because of the exquisite timing; for it occurred just as Tom was, for once in his life, striving to ingratiate himself with Wilson. With Tom's sixty-fifth birthday looming in May 1970, and a general election certain in the next twelve months, the Member for Barking had lately been considering his future. Opinion polls showed the Conservatives 5 or 6 per cent ahead of Labour. Did he really want another term at Westminster? He began to dream fondly of a salaried sinecure elsewhere. Though Gore Vidal's suggestion of installing him at Lambeth Palace would never be taken up, there was another post, also in the Prime Minister's gift, which Tom thought he would fill admirably. Early in 1970 he proposed, quite seriously, that Harold Wilson should appoint him British ambassador to the Vatican.

'I am, of course, aware of the objections that would be raised to my appointment,' he wrote in one of his letters to the Prime Minister on the subject. Presumably the Foreign Office would be unhappy to see the job given to an outsider, but 'the Legation to the Holy See is very much a special case, and a post which not every diplomat nearing ambassadorial rank would wish or be qualified to fill'. Tom, by contrast, was unimprovably well qualified: 'I have for some time had good relations with people of influence both in Geneva and Rome: the Archbishop of Canterbury nominated me as a delegate to the WCC Assembly at Uppsala in 1968, and I have had private audiences with the present Pope and (for 40 minutes) with one of his predecessors.' In the 'steadily improving ecumenical climate' he believed that he could make 'a major contribution to ultimate Christian unity' as Minister to the Holy See; 'and this might provide an agreeable final chapter in my memoirs, on which I shall shortly be embarking.'

Wilson was unmoved. He pointed out that, in any case, the retirement age for senior officers of the Diplomatic Service was sixty, and 'in these circumstances I fear that it would not be possible to consider appointing to a post of this kind someone from outside the Service who is over that age'.

'I hope,' he added, 'this will not be too great a disappointment to you.' But of course it was. Tom had told Wilson that this was 'clearly the last possible moment for a change in my working life' and that 'I would, frankly, welcome a change'. Too poor to retire, he now had no choice but to stay at Westminster and use his parliamentary salary 'as a pension', as his doctor had recommended. In June 1970, with a sigh, he presented himself to the electorate of Barking once more. He was now sixty-five years old; the 1960s were dead. His spirit still sided with Youth but his heart was weary and aged. He was, in Larkin's phrase, crouching below Extinction's alp.

CHAPTER THIRTEEN

THE FIRST AND LAST
LORD BRADWELL

Britain went to the polls on Thursday 18 June 1970, and by the following evening furniture vans were pulling up at the back of 10 Downing Street to remove Harold Wilson's belongings while Ted Heath, grinning hugely, entered through the front door. Outside Transport House, the Labour Party's headquarters, members of the Cabinet and the National Executive stood on the pavement of Smith Square to cheer the defeated Prime Minister as he arrived – all except Tom, who scowled furiously at Wilson. 'That man misled us all and picked the wrong date,' he complained to Tony Benn. 'Why should I cheer for him?' It was, Benn thought, 'a very sour comment'.[1] But then Tom was an embittered man, even though his own majority in Barking had not been too badly dented by the Tories. At a joint meeting of the Cabinet and National Executive shortly before the campaign, he had argued that proposals for nationalising pharmaceutical companies and part of the aircraft industry should be included in the manifesto; this was 'contemptuously brushed aside' by the majority. A few months later he told the annual conference of Labour students that it was 'to Labour's disgrace' that the 1970 manifesto was the first not to include any plans for public ownership. The party, he said, 'deserved to lose the election'.[2]

Detached though he was, in the years of the Heath government he proved that he had lost none of his talent for controversy. He tabled a motion describing the Department of the Environment's new office block in Marsham Street as 'the grossest architectural affront to the London environment since the erection of the Shell building on the South Bank and Bucklersbury House in the City'. In another motion he condemned the 'poverty-stricken' facilities available for Members and their guests on the 'sordid' House of Commons terrace, which resembled 'a bad four-ale bar in Glasgow at closing time on a Saturday night'. He spoke alongside Bernadette Devlin at a rally in Northern Ireland, where he told civil rights demonstrators: 'I don't think the British Army will be here much longer . . . The real terrorists are in Stormont and Westminster.' When 130 MPs of all parties signed a motion welcoming the arrival in Britain of Cardinal Mindszenty, the exiled primate of Hungary, who was saluted as 'one of the foremost champions of democracy and freedom in Europe', Tom promptly put down an amendment which 'recognises [Mindszenty's] courageous tenacity but is aware that he has been for many years a symbol of the old feudal Hungarian régime which was by no means a model of democracy and freedom.' He was disappointed not to be jailed ('a modest spell in prison would be usefully educative for any MP') after refusing to fill in his 1971 census form because he found the questions 'far too intrusive'; since the Registrar-General had said that all census-dodgers would be prosecuted except for the very old and the mentally retarded, Tom demanded to know 'which category I am in'.

The Sixties might be over, but there were a few dying kicks. In March 1971, during a Commons debate on a bill introduced by a Conservative backbencher to stop the Isle of Wight pop festival, Tom goaded the Tories by calling them 'haters of youth'. When the three editors of *Oz* were jailed in August for producing an 'obscene' School Kids' Issue, he condemned the sentences as contrary to British justice; three months later, after the trio had been released on appeal, Tom spoke of 'training needed by some judges in both impartiality and ordinary common sense – such as the judge in the *Oz* case'. (The Attorney-General, Sir Peter Rawlinson, replied that 'not many people would agree with Mr Driberg.') The year ended with Tom trying to attend a Communion service at St Paul's Cathedral to celebrate the third anniversary of the musical *Hair*, only to find his path blocked by 2,000 torch-bearing religious protesters who were shouting 'Sodom and Gomorra had nothing on *Hair*' and 'Come back Judas, all is forgiven'. Unable to force his way through, he stood on the steps of St Paul's berating the crowd as 'hypocritical sanctimonious unChristian fascist swine' who ought to be 'on their knees in confession'. He had seen *Hair* four times, he boasted, and it was 'a marvellous show'; as a regular Church of England communicant he was 'eager to see it associated with the Eucharist'. Meanwhile, inside the Cathedral, the Dean was earnestly telling the cast of *Hair* that 'you have come near to God's meaning with your musical.' Hit songs from the show were then performed.

The next morning Tom tabled one of his most magnificently provocative Early Day motions:

That this House congratulates the Dean and Chapter of St Paul's on their enlightened action in encouraging the participation of the cast of *Hair* in a service of Holy Communion, thus reviving in modern form the medieval tradition of the morality plays; deplores the illiterate fanaticism of some demonstrators outside the Cathedral who sought to obstruct and intimidate those wishing to attend this act of worship; notes without surprise that the well-meaning, if misguided, Evangelical demonstrators were joined by members of the National Front and other fascist and racialist groups; regrets that because of the presence of these brawlers it was thought necessary to shut the Cathedral doors and to instruct the police falsely to inform those seeking admission that the Cathedral was already full; and recognises that the attack on St Paul's Cathedral, like other manifestations of the Puritan backlash, represents an attitude, based on hatred, fear and prejudice, identical with that of the Pharisees who were the principal enemies of Jesus Christ.

He was immediately submerged beneath a predictable avalanche of enraged hate-mail: all over suburbia, members of the God-bothering class scrawled notes of varying literacy and legibility informing Tom that they were not fascist swine; he, rather, was a Communist degenerate, an agent of Satan, a senile maniac. He loved every word of it.

On occasion, then, he could still throw the *bourgeois* into a tizzy of irritation. But he was too preoccupied to do it as often as he would have liked. The familiar and banal horsemen of his personal apocalypse – bank managers, unpaid tradesmen – were galloping at his heels, threatening pestilence and war. By the time of the 1970 election his overdraft had risen to an astounding £15,000, and the bank was harassing him ceaselessly over the lack of a purchaser for Bradwell. His total income from journalism in 1970 was a mere £1,382.

The elusive house-buyers were sighted at last in March 1971: Jimmy and Betty Mann, a cheerfully vulgar couple of Londoners who had made a few bob out of Jimmy's large grocery business in the East End and now wanted a house to match their new status. Jimmy Mann was a body-builder of the Charles Atlas school who had once won the title 'Mr Barking' – a coincidence that pleased Tom. 'You and I, Jimmy,' he would say gravely, 'have both had the good fortune to represent the borough of Barking.' Betty was the more sensitive partner, and it was she who was adamant that they should live at Bradwell Lodge. When they offered £26,000 for it, Tom had no choice but to accept.

The Manns were embarrassingly reverential to their eminent vendor. They said that they would be honoured to buy any furniture or paintings which Tom was prepared to leave behind; they intended to hang his portrait in the hall; he would have a standing invitation to spend weekends there as often as he liked; Betty even proposed that after the sale 'you and your wife might like to have a few rooms set aside for your occupation'.

In fact Tom's wife was poised for flight. For twenty years she had laboured at the impossible job of being Mrs Tom Driberg, and though she had often sought sanctuary with her father or aunts or sister or son for weeks at a time, she had always returned to Bradwell in the end. Now there was to be no more Bradwell. It was inconceivable that she and Tom might buy a house or flat together; this was the natural moment for her to move permanently to her cottage at Chorleywood. She had bad arthritis in her feet – she had to attend hospital three times a week in the summer of 1971 – and a final separation could only be therapeutic. 'If in your plans for the future you could "include me out",' she wrote when he first put Bradwell up for sale, 'I think it would be better for both of us.' But even as they packed their cases and prepared to say farewell the squabbling continued, more by biological instinct than reason, like the cheeps and chirps of baby pigeons. At dinner one Saturday,

Rosemary Say observed that Dr David Cargill had a happy and well-organised life. 'I'm glad somebody has,' Ena murmured wistfully. Tom later accused her of making 'constant side-digs'. She in turn complained of his 'extremely glacial' demeanour. He retorted that, since she had promised to 'be off' as soon as the sale was completed, 'I have taken you at your word, and see no need to pretend to feel any friendliness, at any rate in private (though I see no reason, either, to bother or distress our neighbours at Bradwell by airing disagreements to them).'[3] On 8 September, three weeks before the Manns were due to take over, she told Tom: 'I shall leave this weekend and our neighbours must think what they like'; he could always say that she had an appointment with a specialist. She added that since she had for years been left to cope with the housework almost alone, and since they had never discussed what she should do when the house was sold, 'you surely are not surprised that I have felt hurt, angry and humiliated. Very foolish of me no doubt, after years of similar treatment.' She had 'always been prepared to try and be friends' but he had been 'unable or unwilling to respond'.[4]

Tom's reply seethed and bubbled with rancour. 'You were always (no doubt, in one sense, rightly) urging economy; and it was you, long before the bank manager got around to it, who kept on saying, year after year, that I ought to sell Bradwell,' he wrote. 'Now that you and he have had your way, I might be spared lamentations about your hardships.' As for his unwillingness to behave civilly to her: 'I do not see how you can "be friends" with someone to whom you have given notice that you are quitting. As Nye Bevan used to say, a certain amount of social hypocrisy is necessary in political and public life. There seems to be no reason to extend this to private life.'[5] And so it died as it had lived, this cancerous marriage, in spluttering recrimination and unremitting cruelty. On 12 September 1971 Ena walked out of Bradwell for the last time.

While she retreated to Hertfordshire, Tom abandoned country life for London. On being thrown out of his Great Ormond Street flat in the mid-1960s he had, on the advice of a vicar in Cornhill, added his name to the waiting list for flats in the new, high-rise Barbican development in the City of London. Now, conveniently, his number had come up. He was offered a sixth-floor flat in a block with the splendid name of Mountjoy House, for a rent of £950 a year on a five-year lease. He told the Manns that he would evacuate Bradwell at the end of September.

There were a few 'famous last weekends', like those on the eve of the Second World War. Guests that summer included John Rayner and his new wife, Miranda; Neil Levis, a reporter on a local paper; Richard Leask, a bookseller from Carlisle; the Revd Gerard Irvine, his landlord at the Westminster vicarage; and, most often, Joan Littlewood and her lover Gerry Raffles, swerving along the winding Essex lanes in Raffles's big blue American car which was equipped with a fridge in the back because he was diabetic.

Joan and Gerry were at Bradwell for Tom's penultimate weekend, on Saturday 18 September. On the Sunday night Jimmy and Betty Mann entertained Tom and Michael Jackson to dinner. The next morning – *post hoc* but not, of course, *propter* – Tom had a minor stroke. In spite of doctors' warnings, he insisted on going to London for an unmissable engagement at the Gay Hussar that very evening, so, after he had rested for a few hours, Michael Jackson and a villager drove him from Bradwell to Soho. They dined downstairs, he upstairs. A week later, after he had stripped Bradwell Lodge of all that he needed, Tom wrote his last entry in the visitors' book that John and Joan Rayner had presented to him thirty years before: 'Peed under the ilex tree and tried to feed the ducks, but it was too late. It was dark.' On Tuesday 28 September the removal men from Bishop and Sons began packing Tom's cargo for the journey to the Barbican: two sofas, two chests of drawers, one wardrobe, three single beds, dozens of paintings and 4,000 books. He was too upset to stay and watch. It was like 'the bustle in a house / The morning after death', in the words of an Emily Dickinson poem that he recalled. Joan Littlewood and Gerry Raffles turned up again and took him out for a meal in London to distract him.

Tom was bereft, and not only from natural grief at losing the house he loved. In his last year or two at Bradwell he had become besotted with a lad called John Struth, the son of the landlord of the Cricketers' Arms. The fact that his ardour was not returned did nothing to dim it: he sat for hours in the pub gazing adoringly at this unprepossessing youth, whose ambition in life was to paint pub-signs, and whose dull sketches of packhorses or kings' heads would excite cries of exaggerated praise from his elderly admirer. Struth tolerated Tom's fawning, spaniel-eyed attentions in the hope that this well-connected old lecher could – as he promised – advance his career. He was well rewarded: a year after leaving Bradwell Tom wrote a new will in which he left one fifth of his residuary estate to John Struth – 'the pot-boy from the Essex marshes', as Rosemary Say contemptuously labelled him. What Tom did not know, for he hadn't seen Struth since moving to London, was that in the mean-time the pot-boy had married.

A few months after his departure, Tom succumbed to the Manns' continual entreaties that he should come and stay for the weekend. It was a disaster. Betty Mann unwittingly gave him the bedroom in the Tudor wing that Ena used to occupy ('Ugh! I had to sleep in the same room as That Woman!' he told a friend); more horrifying still, Jimmy Mann had been making some 'improvements' to the décor of the Georgian end. In Tom's old bathroom the fittings had been ripped out and replaced with a dazzling modern 'suite' – black bath and basin, gold taps, black and gilt mirrored tiles on the walls, floor and ceiling. The weekend was purgatory: enough of his possessions were there for the house still to feel as if it were his – the Georgian dining-room furniture, for instance, and many of the oil paintings – but this made the desecration all the more unbearable. He never went back to Bradwell Lodge again.

During October and November 1971 Tom was busy moving into the Barbican. His was the first flat in Mountjoy House to be occupied, and the surrounding area was a wasteland of earth and builders' rubble, empty concrete flower boxes and raised walkways; to reach the makeshift entrance of his block Tom had to yomp through a muddy car-park. None of this was likely to raise the spirits of a man who was keenly conscious of his surroundings and loathed most modern architecture. 'He liked to think he was an innovator, in a way,' was Michael Jackson's explanation for Tom's otherwise inexplicable decision to live in a tower in this soulless *arrondissement.* (He was also slightly cheered to learn that, centuries earlier, the land on which Mountjoy House stood had been known as Sodomites' Walk.) 'It will be interesting,' the *Daily Mail* commented, 'to see how the gentle Driberg reacts to his new concrete-and-steel existence.'[6]

Far from all his old haunts at Soho and Westminster – far from everywhere, in fact – the Barbican, on the edge of the City, was an area that effectively closed for the evening at 5 pm when the office workers went home. There was little or no night-life; at weekends the streets were dead. He told his god-daughter Cleo Sylvestre of his fear of being mugged as he walked back along the walkway late at night – 'though that was always said with a little gleam in his eyes,' she added, 'as though he'd rather like some young bloke to come up and wrestle him to the ground'.[7] Alone in his 'concrete prison', eating out of tins, Tom began to yearn for a permanent mate. 'He was looking for a lover and companion, someone who could share his books and paintings,' one friend said.[8] But while his sexual taste was for rough trade, his preferred social companions were aesthetes and aristocrats. How was he to find anyone who would satisfy both requirements?

His solution was to take a rent-boy and try to civilise him. The first guinea-pig was Cliff, a working-class Cockney in his early twenties who had done time in Wormwood Scrubs for robbery. He was, in the words of a prison visitor who knew him, the Revd William Hurdman, 'a fairly inadequate sort of bloke', and not even very skilful as a thief – 'When he went out to do a robbery he always made a mess of it.' He had an explosive temper, but was also 'attractive, generous, kind and loving, a fairly physical sort of chap who'd made a lot of money from selling his body'. The money had all been spent as fast as earned, and when Tom asked him to move into Mountjoy House at Christmas 1971 he happily did so.

Tom told visitors that Cliff was there to paint the bookshelves 'and generally helping to tidy the place up' – which indeed he did. But of course there were sexual duties too. 'At one level Tom got what he wanted,' William Hurdman agreed, 'but at another level Tom was genuinely trying to help him out. I think Tom was quite fond of Cliff, or he wouldn't have had him living in his flat. After all, he had plenty of one-night stands from the East End, but he never asked them to move in.'[9] Tom's own version, given in a letter to Hurdman at the time, was that 'I didn't particularly like him – though I was sorry for him in his obvious fecklessness – and sometimes, as he put it, "snapped at" him.'[10] The animosity simmered through January, heated by Cliff's lack of money: Tom had given him £20 at Christmas and thereafter only an occasional fiver, 'as needed'.

In February Tom was invited by the Northern Ireland Civil Rights Association to speak at a demonstration in Newry, in protest at the 'Bloody Sunday' massacre by the British Army in Derry. As he prepared to set off, he was astonished to hear Cliff say that he too was flying to Northern Ireland that afternoon. How, Tom asked suspiciously, had he raised the fare? Cliff said it was a loan from Hurdman – a claim which Tom quickly disproved by one telephone call. There was then a screaming row: Cliff had a bad hangover and was, according to Tom, 'quite hysterical'.

When he returned to the flat a couple of days later, Tom found a note scribbled on the back of a large House of Commons envelope:

My Dear Tom,

Well, it's hapened at last your trust in me has been broken. I don't fit in your world no more than you do mine. The urge to go to London Derry and on to Newry is with me and I no you can't take me along so I've sold *your* coins for the cash to go.

But not only that I need the money. If there is a god (thoe I suspect not) may he forgive *us*.

You have every right to go to the police and absolutely nothing to fear. You haven't done anything shamefull other than give me a job and your kindness is probly the finest I have ever now.

But your horid temper and the way in which so many things you have supresed my mind, actions views to the extent that this is a direct result of your making me feel inferior. I thank you for everything and at this moment I am trully sorry and sad for what I've done but I've no intention of revoking my 'scarey' adventure.

Cliff

As a PS he added that he had given Tom love but had been repaid with hate ('something I'm incapable of ').

The coins that Cliff had snatched were an 1887 Jubilee set, given to Tom's parents as a wedding present by a friend who was an official of the Royal Mint, and housed in a leather case engraved with the couple's initials and wedding date (20 June 1887). Tom said the coins were, 'for personal and sentimental reasons, by far the most treasured of the relatively few things that I inherited from my parents'. His rage and distress at the loss overflowed into a letter he wrote to Hurdman:

Coming on top of other acute current worries, this has been a most dramatic shock – both the loss and the betrayal. I wake in the night worrying, and feel filled with hatred for the vicious little rat – though I realise that he is probably schizophrenic, and that one ought to pity him. I could certainly never again leave him alone in my flat: another crazy impulse like his visit to Belfast might come over him.

To get the thing out of my system, I asked a priest (not Gerard), whom I had heard preaching about love and being let down by those whom we'd helped, if in such a case it was best simply to forgive, forget and write it off. He said, 'No, there must be restitution.'

Cliff sold the coins for £190 to a dealer in Chelsea, who had sent them on to Germany by the time Tom traced him. But Tom did retrieve the case, and from the same dealer he bought an identical set for £250. Six weeks after the Northern Irish trip Cliff rang, breathless with excitement, to say that his parents would compensate Tom to the full value of the coins. He immediately added: 'Can I have my job back?' Four days later he telephoned again, admitting that the last story was an invention: he had told his parents nothing, and he had no intention of paying. He disappeared from Tom's life with a giggle to continue his career of petty theft and prostitution elsewhere. Eight years later he killed himself.

There was no shortage of rent-boys willing to take advantage of Tom's vulnerability: only a few months after the rupture with Cliff, the replacement set of coins was stolen from the flat by another young rough he had picked up. This time Tom consulted not a vicar but an off-duty City of London policeman, Donald Rumbelow, with whom he had become friendly. 'He told me he knew who had taken them,' Rumbelow recalled, 'and he wanted me to go round and kick his door down and "sort him out" and get the coins back. I said "You can't do that!" He was very upset.'

The libidinal drive might be expected to slacken a bit as one approaches the age of seventy, but not in Tom's case. 'He really was in a highly advanced sexual state in the last years of his life,' Rosemary Say recalled. He believed that frequent consumption of semen kept one young, and had even persuaded himself that the age of the donor made a difference – an eighteen-year-old's was far more rejuvenating than, say, a twenty-eight-year-old's. Hence he recruited a number of eighteen-year-olds from the East End who agreed to be 'on call' for the spermophagous pensioner and pop round to the Barbican whenever he was feeling depleted; he paid them ten pounds a time for their trouble. One of these boys, Michael Duffy, got into the game through his uncle, a strange character called Ivor Powell who had once been an adviser to President Nasser but now lived at the Barbican and earned his living as a Tarot-reader and clairvoyant in West End clubs. 'Ivor basically never touched a woman in his life – he was well gay,' Duffy says. 'He said to me that Tom liked sucking boys' dicks because the chemical content would extend his life, and would I mind? I was on the fence of sexuality in those days, but I wasn't averse to earning a tenner through lying down on the chaise longue and having my dick sucked. Ten quid was a lot of money in those days.'[11]

The *Tribune* Group of MPs threw a party at St Stephen's Tavern on 6 July 1972 to celebrate – a week late – the thirtieth anniversary of Tom's election to Parliament, generously overlooking the fact that the Labour Party had officially condemned his candidacy at the 1942 by-election. Called upon to say a few words, he told his colleagues that he would not be standing again. The next day's *Evening Standard* reported that *Tribune* MPs 'were clearly surprised by the news', though this seems hard to believe: he had taken his decision shortly after the 1970 election and since then had never troubled to hide his demob wish. Tom revealed to the *Standard* that when he retired he would start on his memoirs, 'something you can't do until you are out of Parliament – and preferably out of the country'. His disengagement went one stage further at the party conference that autumn when he lost his seat on the National Executive Committee after twenty-three years of service. Three recounts eventually established that Tom had been narrowly squeezed into eighth place in the ballot for the seven-member constituency section, 3,000 votes behind Denis Healey; but the cause of his downfall was Michael Foot, who had decided to stand for the NEC after a twenty-year absence and came top of the poll. 'Tom Driberg will be missed,' the *Daily Mirror* commented. 'His crisp phraseology was responsible for livening many an executive statement.'[12] Tom himself was understandably cheerful in defeat. 'I've got some regrets about it, but in some ways it's a relief,' he told reporters. 'One of the great reliefs is that I shall never in my whole life have to come to Blackpool again.'[13]

The new Labour candidate chosen for Barking was Jo Richardson, Ian Mikardo's old secretary, who during 1973 'shadowed' Tom at constituency surgeries and – most usefully for him, as a veteran cadger of lifts – ferried him back and forth between London and Barking in her car. She soon learned that the lot of a Driberg chauffeuse was unenviable. One evening, while she was driving a typically grumpy Tom home after an official reception in Barking, he insisted that they should stop for a 'real drink' (Bell's whisky) at a pub called Charlie Brown's in the West India Dock Road, which turned out to be almost empty but for a couple of women sitting at the bar. When two Swedish sailors came in shortly afterwards – it was a mariners' pub, being in the docks – Tom raced over to chat them up, returning after a minute or two to tell Jo Richardson that he was 'just going outside for a moment'. He then disappeared with the sailors. As the 'moment' grew into a quarter of an hour or more, Richardson fell into conversation with the women at the bar – who turned out to be transvestites, eager to swap opinions with her on the best types of mascara and eye-shadow. Tom eventually returned after half an hour, beaming from ear to ear, and announced that he was now feeling 'much better'. Of the sailors there was no sign.

On another journey from Barking he suddenly turned to Jo Richardson with a look of fearful desolation. 'I do regret going,' he murmured. 'I don't know if I've done the right thing. What am I going to live on?'[14]

It was a fair question. Though the proceeds from the sale of Bradwell had cleared his debts (and enabled him jubilantly to close his account at the hated Liverpool Street branch of the National Provincial Bank, by now calling itself the National Westminster), he would still need to support himself after the crutch of his parliamentary salary had been kicked away at the next election. In 1973, having completed the Hannen Swaffer biography – which appeared the following year to unenthusiastic notices – he resolved to devote himself to the lubricious, lucrative memoirs. But he was hampered by failing health. On 2 August 1973, while lunching at the Gay Hussar, he had another heart attack and had to be carried down the restaurant's narrow staircase on a stretcher. (He apologised to other diners for the interruption of their meal.) For the next week he was kept in the Middlesex Hospital for observation, where he was advised that in view of his high blood pressure he should consume no more than 1,000 calories a day. This, the *Evening Standard* noted, 'is a big blow for a man of his disposition and build, accustomed to an intake of up to 2,500 calories'.[15] After convalescing with friends in the West Country for a couple of weeks he flew to Italy to stay with Gore Vidal. There, egged on by the novelist's exhortations to 'tell everything', and revivified by the plentiful supply of local rent-boys, he finally started to compose the autobiography in earnest. He wrote it as a sequence of anecdotes, each entered on a small card. The working title was *Not Waving But Drowning*.

Parliament was dissolved early in February 1974, as Ted Heath – petulant after a winter of power cuts, three-day weeks and a miners' strike – went to the country with the question: 'Who governs Britain?' By the end of the month he had his answer. Labour won four more seats than the Tories, and though neither side had an outright majority Harold Wilson eventually winkled Heath and his grand piano out of Downing Street.

'Driberg is 68 now,' the *Evening Standard* had reported on the last day of the old Parliament, 'and like some of his colleagues who decided not to stand at the next election feels slightly robbed by Mr Heath's precipitate decision one and a half years before his full five-year gamut.'[16] He changed his mind when he saw the result. 'For the nation,' he wrote in the New Statesman a month later, 'premature and unnecessary as the election was, it is a good thing that Heath, Carrington and Tory Central Office made the mistake of precipitating it.'[17] He was glad to see that his successor, Jo Richardson, had already been branded by the press as an 'extremist'. She in turn paid handsome tribute to her predecessor in her maiden speech ('Somebody said to me I went over the top,' she recalls). On a valedictory visit to Barking, Tom was presented by the local Labour Party with an illuminated scroll that recorded its 'sincere appreciation of the great service rendered to the Nation, the National Labour Party and the Barking Constituency Labour Party by Tom Driberg . . . who unstintingly devoted himself to the public interest and to the service of his constituents, with great ability, efficiency and ardour'.[18] It was a generous but not entirely undeserved tribute. He had always tried whenever possible to skip the ceremonial drudgery – mayoral lunches, Royal British Legion dinners and the like – but he had never turned away any constituent who was suffering from genuine hardship or injustice. And, as a friend said, although it obviously helped if the constituent in question was young and male and rugged, it wasn't obligatory. One of his most dogged letter-writing campaigns was on behalf of Marie Meter, a working-class widow with an autistic son.

Now that he was out of Parliament, Tom was invited by the editor of the New Statesman, Anthony Howard, to write the magazine's 'London Diary' regularly. The Statesman was not a lavish payer – certainly not by the standards of a man who had been employed by the Express in its days of Beaverbrookian extravagance – but he was grateful for the work; his only other recurring journalistic commission at the time was the fortnightly Private Eye crossword, for which the fee was now £20. Besides, he enjoyed visiting the New Statesman office at Great Turnstile to cast his eye over the pert and playful young writers on the staff: Christopher Hitchens, a dark, witty heartbreaker with a hint of the young Guy Burgess in him; Martin Amis, a young novelist with a pouting sneer as irresistible as Mick Jagger's. He also took a great fancy to a friend of Christopher Hitchens called Martin Walker, who wrote the

'Open File' column in the *Guardian*. Hitchens and Walker enjoyed flirting with Tom. 'I once told him,' Hitchens recalled, 'that he had no chance with Martin Amis. "You never know," he said. "If there's even five per cent in there one can usually count on *something*."' One night at Mountjoy House he made a desperate lunge at Amis and proved himself wrong.

He was not living off cheques from *Private Eye* and the *New Statesman* alone, of course. A month after his retirement from the House he signed a contract with Jonathan Cape which guaranteed him an advance of £8,000 for *Not Waving But Drowning* (whose title he changed, later that year, to *Ruling Passions*): £2,000 straight away, another £1,000 in the autumn, £2,000 in April 1975, £2,000 on delivery (May 1976) and £1,000 on publication. It was not in the same class as his Guy Burgess interviews, but quite a *coup* nevertheless. During 1974 and 1975 he spent many weeks labouring on the book at Gore Vidal's villa in Italy – the only place where he could write it, so he claimed. 'He worried a lot about Jennie Lee's reaction to the fact that he had blown Nye,' Vidal says. 'He decided not to include the interlude. I said he should write *everything*, suppress certain things for publication, then when all were dead the ur-memoir would be made available.' Tom agonised endlessly over the story of the Bevan blow-job. He told Christopher Hitchens that he was 'definitely going to put it in', but was worried not so much about the feelings of Jennie Lee as about the sensibilities of working-class Labour voters. Another person he consulted was Donald Rumbelow, his friend from the City police:

In one way [according to Rumbelow] he was quite pleased by what he was saying, with Gore Vidal urging him on; but he did also get quite distressed by it. He mentioned two elderly women in the constituency who would be shocked and upset. And he didn't know what to write about his wife. 'What am I going to say about that bitch?' he used to ask.

Then there was a chapter called 'Loving Kevin', a minutely detailed account of how he had seduced a Young Socialist while the pair of them were travelling across Europe by train on their way to an international conference. Gore Vidal pointed to an omission in the otherwise exhaustive description: 'You've made no reference at all to his scrotum.' Tom agreed; perhaps he should get in touch with 'Kevin' and ask for a repeat performance to refresh his memory, he suggested. Eventually he did show the narrative to 'Kevin', who was now a married man – and who unsurprisingly forbade Tom to use it. In spite of the pseudonym, he said, his wife would recognise him instantly.

Tom did write some of the book at Mountjoy House, gulping down a daily tonic of seminal fluid to boost his energy, but it was a struggle. He was continually lapsing into melancholy – or, some suspected, striking melancholic poses. Stewart Trotter, a friend of Cleo Sylvestre, called at the Barbican flat one afternoon and found him watching television. Suddenly Tom let out a heart-rending groan: 'I'm so old and lonely.' 'Are you?' Trotter asked in alarm. 'No,' Tom replied, laughing. 'That was just a pathetic ploy to try to get you into bed.'

Stewart Trotter and Cleo Sylvestre helped the trusty Michael Jackson to organise a party given for Tom at 601 Mountjoy House on 21 May 1975, the eve of his seventieth birthday. While they were moving furniture and laying out glasses beforehand, Tom did another of his comically self-pitying turns. 'I wish,' he suddenly said, 'that I was sixteen again.' Then a pause. 'No I don't. I wish I were dead.' Before Sylvestre or Trotter had time to protest, he broke into a sly smile. For that evening, at least, his anxieties about health and cash and death were completely anaesthetised as he surveyed with pleasure the dozens of old friends who squeezed themselves into the flat to honour him. His birthday presents from Cleo Sylvestre were a hard-core gay porn magazine and magnifying glass, which she hid under his pillow. ('Most interesting reading,' he said a few days later when he rang to thank her. 'I have passed it on to a bishop of my acquaintance.') John Betjeman recited a poem he had written for the occasion:

Nothing can hide the pleasure that I feel
Who here salute you, Thomas Edward Neil,
On this your seventieth birthday. Can it be
That of the sons of Lancing you are he
Who Roxburgh's standard into Fleet Street bore
Further than Fulford, Molson, Evelyn Waugh,

Dudley Carew and others? Yes it can
Guilielmus Hickeyus né Dragoman,
Christ Church and Church of England, who would guess
That you would ever write for the *Express*,
A Presbyterian journal with a tone
More puritan and moral than your own?
Testy at breakfast, difficult at tea
But in the evening oh how free, how free!
True poet, honest aesthete, loyal friend
Kindly be with me till my sticky end.[19]

Tom was happy as a king. Half-way through the party he sidled over to Michael Jackson in the kitchen and boasted: 'One duke, two dukes' daughters, sundry lords, a bishop, a poet laureate – not bad for an old left-wing MP, eh?' The senior peer was the Duke of Grafton, who had met Tom through a shared interest in historic houses, and had once accompanied him on a tour of Castle Howard; the dukes' daughters were Lady Elizabeth Cavendish (who came with Betjeman) and Lady Diana Cooper. Other guests included Lord Bernstein, Lord Kinross, Patrick and Joan Leigh Fermor, John and Miranda Rayner, Michael Foot and Jill Craigie. The bishop, Mervyn Stockwood, togged himself out in full episcopal purple and was exceeded in sartorial garishness only by Don Rumbelow, the policeman, who wore a frilled shirt and velvet jacket. Tom spent much of the evening gazing admiringly at Christopher Hitchens ('the prettiest person in the room,' he sighed) and Martin Walker. For once, there was not a 'lad' in sight.

Tom may have felt slightly wistful as he pointed out the lords and ladies at his birthday party. After almost half a century of journalistic eminence and public service, he was still plain Mr Driberg. Why? This had first been aired publicly by the *Sunday Express* in November 1974, when reporting that Tom had already written half of his 120,000-word memoirs.

But some of his political friends are wondering [it continued] why he is not more gainfully employed – in the House of Lords.

They envisage Mr Driberg, who was the *Daily Express*'s first William

Hickey, as Baron Driberg of Bradwell – Bradwell was the name of the beautiful eighteenth-century house he sold last year.

Will it ever be so?[20]

Several of Tom's old colleagues on the Labour benches asked Harold Wilson the same question, only to be turned down flat. In the summer of 1975 the *Sunday Express* returned to the subject, with more mischievous speculation:

The question of why the former Labour MP Tom Driberg, 70, has not received a peerage has been raised again. MPs have conflicting ideas of why the 32-year Commons career of Mr Driberg did not end on the red leather benches of the House of Lords.

It is known that friends of Mr Driberg like Michael Foot suggested him for a peerage to Harold Wilson. But it is said that Mr Wilson rejected the idea.

So it is assumed that Mr Wilson simply does not like Tom Driberg. Why should this be so?[21]

The newspaper then revealed for the first time that Tom had unwittingly been the source of the leaked obituary of Harold Wilson that had appeared in *Private Eye* in 1970. It added (wrongly) that Tom was also the author of the obituary, which had been none too flattering. Wilson, it deduced, must have borne a grudge ever since.

This was too much for Tom. He missed Westminster more than he had expected, and was indeed quietly hoping for a peerage: he knew, too, that the Labour Party's general secretary, Ron Hayward, as well as Michael Foot and others, had been prodding the Prime Minister on his behalf. The last thing he wanted now was for Wilson to be reminded of the wretched affair of the stolen *Times* proof. Tom wrote to 10 Downing Street expressing his shock at the 'garbled and obviously malicious report' in the *Sunday Express*. 'Among the inaccuracies in it the most serious is the statement that I had "prepared" the obituary . . . Almost exactly the opposite is true. *The Times* had asked me to revise the obituary (which they realised was too hostile in tone) and to make it more objective and sympathetic.'[22] In the draft of his letter to Wilson he added: 'I hope I may assume that the main point of the *Express* story is equally untrue and that you would not allow your natural indignation at this regrettable episode to influence your judgment on the peerage question.' But he then thought better of it and struck the sentence out.

The PM's reply was typically wily. He wrote merely that he 'was not aware – even if it is true – that you had written an obituary for *The Times*. I need hardly add that I do not believe all that I see in *Private Eye*, still less in the *Sunday Express*.'[23]

When Tom had called in at Downing Street briefly the previous year to suggest names for a number of ecclesiastical appointments, Wilson had told him that he was 'on the list' of potential peers. But in truth Wilson had no desire to let Tom make trouble and scandal in the Upper House, especially while Labour was in office. His resolve failed only after the further intercession of Michael Foot, who, as Secretary of State for Employment, was now a figure of some influence in the Prime Minister's counsels. Tom was sad and ill, he said; it would freshen his spirits no end to potter about in the ornate retirement home that is the House of Lords – and he would not live for long enough to embarrass the government. On this understanding, Wilson relented.

Tom almost died too soon. On 22 November, hours after arriving in Kenya to attend a World Council of Churches assembly, he had another heart attack. A few days earlier he had told a friend that the high altitude of Nairobi 'could prove fatal'; he had been unable to have a check-up before his departure because of a dispute in the National Health Service. 'If I die,' he declared, 'please say it was because of the doctors' strike.' But he recovered quickly and left hospital on 8 December feeling 'much better', though he was advised to make the return journey by sea. The next day there was a summons from the British High Commissioner in Nairobi, Stanley Fingland, who revealed that the Prime Minister 'had it in mind' to recommend Tom for a peerage. His acceptance was then relayed back to London as a diplomatic telegram. Just over a week later, while he was convalescing on Kenya's Indian Ocean coast, the name of Tom Driberg appeared on a 'surprise pre-Christmas list' of nine new peers announced by Harold Wilson. 'With a humble sense of pride,' the *Daily Express*'s latest William Hickey wrote the following morning, 'I salute today the man who founded this column in the *Daily Express* more than 40 years ago.'[24] The 1975 Hickey guessed that his forebear would probably take the title of Baron Driberg of Bradwell – 'but watch him prove me wrong!' Tom duly did. After returning to London in the New Year, he chose to gazette himself by the name, style and title of Baron Bradwell of Bradwell juxta Mare in the County of Essex. He took his seat on Wednesday 28 January 1976, introduced by Lord Pitt, the only black peer, and the venerable eighty-seven-year-old Lord Brockway; before the ceremony he hosted a lunch at the House of Lords for a few friends, including Osbert Lancaster, Michael Jackson and John Betjeman – who had just composed a postscript to his seventieth birthday verse:

> The first and last Lord Bradwell is to me
> The norm of socialist integrity:
> He makes no secret of his taste in sex,
> Preferring the lower to the upper decks.[25]

Kitted out in his borrowed robes, Tom looked more gravely distinguished than ever – alarmingly so. Irresponsibility had always been his saving grace; his pompous and pedantic excesses were mitigated by the wild Bohemian glee he took in shocking complacent old fools. Would that now cease? He would not have been the first firebrand to fizzle out damply in the humid, passion-killing smugness of their lordships' chamber. It is a commonplace of political correspondents that the Upper House has 'a much higher standard of debate' than the Commons, but it is poppycock. The exaggerated cross-party civilities, the lack of voices raised in anger – these are the features of an institution so self-satisfied that it suffocates almost all who enter it.

And yet, miraculously, the first and last Lord Bradwell was not overwhelmed: he defied the cloying politeness of the place almost at once. In a debate on press freedom, a month after his introduction, he claimed that if the *Daily Telegraph*'s editor wanted to publish an article objectionable to his proprietor, Lord Hartwell – or to Lady Hartwell, for that matter – 'he would not get away with it'. The House tut-tutted at Tom's breach of etiquette in criticising a fellow peer, and Hartwell himself angrily complained of 'a most offensive innuendo about myself and my wife'. Lady Hartwell – better known as Pamela Berry – was a lively London hostess whose hospitality Tom had often enjoyed; she now wrote to inform him icily that he would never again be welcome in her house.

After this promising start Tom was regrettably *hors de combat* during most of March and the first week of April, incarcerated in the men's public ward at Guy's Hospital for cardiac treatment. Christopher Hitchens, on a visit, found his newly-ennobled friend 'in the public ward democratically helping the nurse push the tea-trolley around'; Tom was known to the old basket-cases around him as 'Mr Bradwell', which amused him. He was, however, depressed. 'Look at this,' he sighed, showing Hitchens a letter from Mervyn Stockwood, the Bishop of Southwark.

Tom had sent the half-finished MS of *Ruling Passions* to Stockwood in February, asking for his comments and explaining that 'the main theme, which I hope to bring out in an introduction, is (a) that it is possible for a practising homosexual to lead a reasonably useful public life, but (b) that there are still many obstacles set up by prejudice and ignorance.' On 19 March Stockwood replied. 'I enjoyed not only the book,' he wrote, 'but it's [sic] style, and, above all, it's [sic] use of words . . . It is a joy to rediscover the loveliness of English.' But whatever his personal reactions might be, he added, 'I think it would be impossible for you to remain happily in the country if the manuscript were published in its present form . . . I suspect that the general reaction would lead to ostracism. And there would be much hurt all round.' Tom, already vulnerable and expecting another heart attack soon, was deeply injured by the suggestion that he would be short of friends if he published the book. 'Do *you* think people would abandon me?' he asked Christopher Hitchens beseechingly. A furious Hitchens shopped the bishop to *Private Eye*.

There was another anxiety. From his hospital bed Tom had secured a debate in the Lords about Northern Ireland, a debate which the Labour government was desperate not to have. Several old comrades on the Labour front-bench, he told Hitchens, had been leaning on him to drop the matter and 'not embarrass the government at this stage'. Afraid that the old boy's nerve might be failing, Hitchens shopped the Labour trimmers to the *Guardian*; the following diary paragraphs appeared on 7 April, two days after Tom left hospital and one week before the debate was due:

One of the great undebated issues of the decade (in Parliament, that is) is whether British troops should be withdrawn from Northern Ireland. Of course it comes up from time to time and of course Dick Crossman made much of the idea during his period editing the *New Statesman*. But a full-scale debate on the subject is something else.

Lord Bradwell (Tom Driberg as was) has now seized the nettle. Lord Bradwell recently won a place in the Lords ballot for private members' bills. He has put down a motion, due for debate on 15 April, calling for withdrawal. He is apparently under considerable pressure from Labour whips to withdraw the motion in favour of something a little less controversial. In the interests of open government, as the Prime Minister might say, he should stand his ground.[26]

Detecting the source of the story, Tom rang Hitchens. 'There was no need for that,' he told him. 'I had already decided to go ahead with the motion.'[27]

In the event, the debate was rather an anti-climax. Tom's motion asked merely that the government should 'start to consider and discuss' the withdrawal of British troops and the ultimate severance of the British connection with Northern Ireland; of the fifteen peers that spoke, only one – Lord Soper – supported even this modest request. As is the way of the Lords, however, the other speakers were wearyingly civil. No sparks were struck.

It was his last notable performance in the House. Now that Mervyn Stockwood's discouragement had been over-ridden by the reassurance of Christopher Hitchens, Gore Vidal and other friends, Tom returned to his memoirs. In August he would fly to Italy for another writing holiday at Vidal's house in Ravello; in the meantime he retired to Oxford, working during the day at a desk in the Christ Church deanery, spending his evenings with John Sparrow, the warden of All Souls, who had for years shared with him the task of proof-reading John Betjeman's poems for errors of syntax and scansion. He told his agent that the manuscript would be ready by Christmas.

The reason for urgency was that Tom guessed his next heart attack would be his last. He spoke often about his anticipation of death, unnerving some friends by the calmness with which he faced it: he would discuss his funeral, for instance, as if he were no more than an amused observer. Years ago a radio interviewer had asked Tom whether he feared dying. 'I'm interested in death,' he replied. 'I'm a coward about physical pain, but I haven't any fear of death in itself. Apart from trying to be a Christian I take the Socratic view that death will be either complete obliteration, just like a deep and dreamless sleep, or else it will be an opportunity of meeting all the great men of the past. And that would be very interesting indeed.' He had always kept as a *memento mori* a pair of bier stools on which his mother's coffin had rested. 'I like very much,' he explained, 'this interweaving and interpenetration of life and death into part of the whole enormous dialectic of the Universe.'[28]

On the morning of Thursday 12 August 1976, a few days before his intended departure for Italy, Tom came to London to collect his mail and pack his bags. Arriving at Paddington, he hailed a cab for the Barbican. Ten minutes later he was dead.

The Times's obituary, which filled almost two columns, noted in its final sentence that 'he married, in 1951, Mrs Ena Mary Binfield'. A couple of other newspapers fleetingly mentioned the marriage, but only one reporter – Barry Powell of the *News of the World* – thought to seek out the widow. He called at her cottage in Hertfordshire five days after Tom's demise.

Now seventy-four years old and crippled by arthritis, Ena was still a commanding figure. 'Don't you dare refer to me as Lady Bradwell,' she warned. 'I never took the title because I've always disapproved of the House of Lords. The Lords should be abolished and a Senate instituted in its place.' Promising to respect her wishes, the reporter was invited in.

It was an unusual interview. 'If only I could die this week, it would make a nice tidy end for the Dribergs,' she told a startled Powell. 'I only look pretty fit and remain upright because I'm living on a drug. Without it I'd be dead in a flash, and eventually it will kill me anyway. I've really come to the end of a useful life – and Tom's finished his.' What seemed to upset her most was that he had died in a taxi: 'How demeaning . . . But then I don't suppose it matters where or when you go.' She added, with more fidelity to her late husband than to truth, that though they had lived apart since 1971 they had parted 'without rancour': there had never been 'any real animosity or bitterness' between them. 'We had twenty years of marriage. I won't say what they were like, that would be disloyal. I always admired and had a huge respect for Tom's journalistic skills, political power and championship of the underdog. If that admiration didn't extend to our personal life, well, that's a purely private matter.'

As ever, she was poorly repaid for her devotion. Tom left her £500 in his will, as against £1,000 to Michael Jackson and generous bequests – one fifth of his residuary estate each – to the Rector of St Thomas, Bradwell-juxta-Mare, for 'parochial purposes'; the Dean Simpson Memorial and Choral Endowment Appeal at Christ Church, Oxford; the National Council for Civil Liberties; John Struth, the pot-boy at the Cricketers' Arms in Bradwell; and, most extraordinarily of all, the Friends of Lancing Chapel. Any future royalties from his books or articles were to be divided between Ena, John Rayner and the Anti-Apartheid Movement. More than a dozen friends – including John Betjeman, Joan Littlewood, Michael Foot, Joan Leigh-Fermor and Gerard Irvine – were given £50, two pictures and twelve books each.

Most of Tom's circle had apparently forgotten that Ena existed, but Foot and Betjeman both sent touching letters of condolence and offered to visit her. Betjeman was particularly attentive. 'Life must have been very difficult for you up there in Essex,' he wrote just after Tom's death.

The old thing was so crotchety just as his father must have been whose false eye used to fall into his soup but what was so marvellous about Thomas was what you yourself told me about him and that was that he took a great deal of trouble over unimportant people. He took a great deal of trouble over my poetry punctuating it clarifying vagueness and listening for rhythm.[29] I shall miss him for that help more than I can say. But most I shall miss him as a friend for he never changed. He said exactly what he meant and he had a firm faith which I have not. He had no doubts and stepping out of the train at Paddington last week, getting a taxi and sitting down in it and seeing God must have been all that happened to the old thing . . . Thomas was born to be a cockpit of the fight between good and evil and I think life was very difficult for him and for you. I was very very fond of him and miss him terribly.[30]

Betjeman continued his correspondence with Ena, and that autumn he made the journey out to Chorleywood to see her. (He knew the way without directions: the row of cottages in which she lived had appeared in Betjeman's television programme *Metroland*.) A few days before his visit he wrote: 'I can quite understand how you miss Thomas Edward Neil. I find myself constantly thinking of the old thing, and his crotchetiness and his tremendous integrity and humility and, lucky old thing, faith. I think Faith is rather like an ear for music, a gift kindly supplied by the Management. Mine is very weak and I only hope I shall be able to face the advance of old age with the courage and goodness you show. Arthritis is a fearful thing and doctors are very poor about dealing with pain.'[31] Ena eventually died, of coronary and rheumatoid arthritis, on 1 October 1977.

Though she wouldn't and couldn't attend Tom's funeral, Ena had some say in how it was ordered. She told Tom's solicitor, John Underwood, that she 'didn't believe in funerals', but if one had to be held there ought to be a red flag on the coffin: this would be appropriate, she suggested, since the tune of 'The Red Flag' had been played at their wedding. The Labour Party was contacted and Transport House was searched, but no red flag could be found. Eventually one had to be run up overnight by a London company.

The service was held at St Matthew's, Westminster, on the swelteringly hot morning of Thursday 19 August, exactly a week after Tom's death. It was, in the words of the Revd Gerard Irvine, 'a typical mixture of friends from all walks of life sitting hugger-mugger mixed up altogether'. This was partly the responsibility of one of the ushers, Brian Bell, who kept 'camping up the way the seating was arranged': a Third Secretary from the Soviet Embassy was sent to the back by Bell on the grounds that 'I don't like Russians, dear'; an alcoholic defrocked clergyman who lived in a Salvation Army hostel down the road and had never actually met the deceased was directed to sit in the front row. Meanwhile, Osbert Lancaster stood up in his pew and announced in a loud voice: 'I will not sit next to Joan Littlewood, because she smells.'

Mervyn Stockwood gave the address, describing Tom as 'a gadfly, a searcher for truth' who 'liked to sting, to annoy, especially the pompous'; he was a non-conformist, but 'of his loyalty to the socialist cause there was no question'. John Betjeman read the lesson.

Although the troublesome red flag was draped over Tom's coffin, in deference to the rubric it was covered by a pall – purple velvet and designed by Comper, very much to Tom's taste. At the end of the Mass the pall was removed and the red-flagged coffin was loaded into a hearse for the journey to Essex. The cortège had to pause outside Barking town hall for a civic reception organised by Jo Richardson and the mayor, before proceeding to Tom's final resting place in the overflow cemetery at Bradwell, a short stroll down the road from St Thomas's. 'The little ceremony at Bradwell was very moving,' Gerard Irvine reported to Ena. 'There was a good turn out from the village. Many of them sprinkled the coffin with holy water. One woman dropped a rose and sprinkled, and as she did so she said "Carry on the work, Tom."'[32] Tony Benn stood by the graveside taking photographs.

After the interment, Jimmy and Betty Mann invited the mourners to tea and sandwiches at Bradwell Lodge. Most of the party then returned to Gerard Irvine's clergy house in Westminster, where they found that both the cook and the housekeeper were blind drunk and uproarious. It was a fitting end to the day.

In a memorandum attached to his will Tom had asked that some time after his funeral there should be a solemn requiem mass, at St Mary the Virgin in Graham Terrace, to be conducted 'in accordance with a customary Western rite, and, at least for the Introit, Dies Irae, Sanctus, Agnus Dei etc., in the Latin tongue'. It would be 'an act of charity' if the Bishop of Stepney, Trevor Huddleston, or the Bishop of Southwark, Mervyn Stockwood, were willing to assist pontifically at the service. He added:

In place of the panegyric commonly delivered at other Catholic obsequies, the Reverend Gerard Irvine or some other discreet, learned and

Godly clerk of my acquaintance should be invited to preach an anti-panegyric on this occasion. In default of such, Mr Michael Foot, MP, should be invited to deliver an address.

The service should be advertised in *The Times* as a 'memorial requiem'. In addition, its time and place should be publicised in advance by courtesy of the editors and columnists of newspapers, such as the *Daily Mirror*, read by the generality of my friends.

The funeral expenses referred to in my Will are to be interpreted as including provision for ample refreshments.

It was entirely characteristic – the insistence on plenty of food and drink, the affected belief that the 'generality' of his friends (John Betjeman? Gore Vidal? Lady Diana Cooper?) subscribed to the *Daily Mirror*, and, above all, the self-loathing implicit in his request for an 'anti-panegyric' excoriating his vices.

Though the Latin Mass was 'too difficult' to arrange, most of Tom's wishes were respected. The requiem was sung at lunchtime on Tuesday 7 December, to a traditional chant and polyphony by Casciolini, after which Gerard Irvine delivered his 'anti-panegyric'; later that afternoon Jo Richardson hosted a party in a House of Commons dining room at which champagne and tears flowed. She had a budget of £100. 'It was a lovely do,' she said. 'Everyone got quite drunk.'

Gerard Irvine's address at the memorial service was the most thoughtful of all the many assessments of Tom, printed or spoken, that had appeared since his death. He argued that to know one's own evil, as Tom did, is the wisdom of a saint; but Tom was not a saint, for he was ambivalent about his faults. 'He hated them, but he fostered them; while despising himself for them, he would boast about them.' His self-hatred was so pronounced that it was almost a death wish: 'This was his greatest vice.'

To meet Tom's wish for a catalogue of his vices, Irvine then gave a 'Tom-rating' on each of the seven sins that traditional morality numbers as deadly:

GLUTTONY. Certainly, no question about it. In the literal sense of gluttony he would eat and drink to excess, and was intolerably exigent about the standards of food and drink. But it was always social feasting in the company of friends. And there was another side. Often, returning home late from his MP surgery at Barking, he would content himself with a glass of milk and – of all horrors – spoonfuls of unheated tinned soup, rather than put the household where he lodged [Irvine's own Clergy House, in fact] to the inconvenience of keeping a meal warm.

In an analogical sense he was a glutton too. He was greedy for experience, the more bizarre the better. Partly this was a journalist's instinct; but not wholly. It had to be not just experience or knowledge as such, but *his* experience and *his* knowledge. He was tolerant and sympathetic to human perversity; a tolerance which made him a first-class journalist and constituency MP. Had he been more discreet in the use he made of such knowledge, he would have been also a first-class confidant. This, regrettably, he was not.

SLOTH. Not at all. Few men less guilty. To the day of his death he crammed more, and more varied, activities into a day than most men into a month. Nor was he intellectually slothful. Though not an academic, he had a wide learning and was a self-confessed pedant, particularly in matters of language, as many a public figure who was rash enough to utter clichés in his hearing learnt to his cost. When he was young, Edith Sitwell hailed him as the hope of English poetry. Though doubtless she was wrong, he was a better poet than given credit for. He had a poet's sense of verbal craftsmanship, and better poets than he took serious note of his judgment.

There is also a state of spiritual sloth, which theologians call 'accidia', that paralysis of the will in literature typified by Hamlet. Tom was 'not Lord Hamlet nor was meant to be'. On the contrary he knew what he wanted for himself, his friends and (typically) those he believed to be victims of injustice. For them he would set about getting what he wanted without scruple and using every resource of official contact and old boy network.

Of the unattractive vice of ENVY he was also reasonably free. He was indeed ambitious, and used to quote with pretended approval the cynical maxim of a clever friend [Gore Vidal]: 'It is not enough to succeed. Others must fail.' But I doubt if in fact he ever cared if others succeeded or failed more than he did. In either case, he was loyal to his friends; he never trimmed his sails to success; nor avoided unpopular persons or opinions. When he joined issue with others, whether he won or lost, he was magnanimous towards them. In this, as in other matters, his *animus* was magnified beyond the usual.

LUST. Of course. He made no secret of it, nor of the directions it led him. The erotic chase provided him with a lifetime's amusement and excitement, and took up far too much of his time and energy to the detriment of his career. The tragedy is that it never made him happy.

Doubtless psychoanalysts can find a cause in childhood relationships with an elderly and unsympathetic father (born in 1842) and a doting mother, for a psychic adolescence prolonged through life. He was always something of a greedy boy. His sexual activities suggest gluttony – the demand for immediate gratification – rather than of the real, cold lechery.

What about AVARICE? He loved beautiful possessions, pictures, books and above all his house at Bradwell, and he took responsible care of them. But so far as money goes, he had no sense at all. He needed money to keep up the way of life he demanded. He earned much and spent much – he was extremely, if erratically, generous – and was always more or less broke. Nevertheless he demanded the privileges riches can confer: good meals, first-class accommodation, luxury travel – and usually got them at the expense of others richer than he. His socialism was of a sybaritic kind, as far removed from the austerity of Sir Stafford Cripps as from the plebeian *bonhomie* of some of his trade union colleagues. But how many of us, if we had the choice, would opt for the more ascetic way?

WRATH. Guilty here. He was undeniably testy and irascible; even cantankerous. A minor example known to many of his friends: those appalling rows with waiters about food or service which could make restaurant meals in his company so hideously embarrassing. He was quick to anger, and clever at eliciting it. He loved a fight, and the more paradoxical the cause he had to maintain the better he liked it. He sincerely believed that the less socially acceptable a cause was, the more likely it was to be true. [. . .]

The last and worst of the deadly sins is PRIDE. He certainly had his share of this vice. But pride has the characteristic of being able to co-exist with its contrary virtue of humility. Thus a man can be proud of being humble, and humble about his pride. Tom was not in the least proud of his humility. He didn't think he had any. He was, however, humble about the pride that he knew he had. And if one can take it as a rule of thumb that acceptance of jokes against oneself is a sign of humility, Tom was humble. For he loved all jokes, and this included jokes against himself. Many will recall how when the joke was on him he would wrinkle with laughter and raise his right hand to the side of his mouth, in a gesture I am told he inherited from his mother. A man with humour cannot be far from the kingdom which the Beatitude tells us is the portion of the humble.

This score-card for the seven sins was probably more generous than Tom would have liked. He wanted his sins exposed, not a rehearsal of his virtues: why else had he begged for the scourge of an anti-panegyric? No doubt, Irvine suggested, it was partly a characteristic send-up of the canons of traditional good taste; but it was also in accordance with the Christian doctrine which holds that humans are all sinners by nature, saved only by grace. 'Tom knew he was a sinner and in need of grace; he also knew how to avail himself of it,' Irvine said.

So his asking for an anti-panegyric was not only a Dribergian tease, it was also, you might say, a Dostoevskian insight.

For there was something Dostoevskian about him in that he was a man of heights and depths. Whether a great man, I cannot say, but certainly an outsize one. Everything about him was a little larger than life: his physique, his virtues and vices, his adventures, his journalism . . . A wise priest (Canon Freddy Hood) who knew him for most of his life and loved him dearly, used to say that he was capable of greater good and greater evil than most of us. Tom's soul was a cockpit, a Belgium of the spirit.

Here, perhaps, was an explanation of why agents of God and the Devil had both taken him to be one of their own. Aleister Crowley hoped Tom would succeed him as the wickedest man in the world; the wildly religious Hollywood film star Jane Russell, whom Tom first met while he was Hickey, believed he was divine. She once wrote in great excitement to tell Tom that 'Our Lord' had spoken to her about him: 'It was quite wonderful. He said he had placed you in a highly strategic place and he was using you and would continue to use you.'[33] Nor was it only raisin-brained fruitcakes in whom he aroused such extreme and opposing reactions. The psychiatrist Anthony Storr, a famously mild and measured man who had studied some of the most gruesome criminals of modern times without flinching, thought Tom was simply 'evil'. (Evelyn Waugh, perhaps rather less seriously, often described Tom as 'satanic'.) Yet A. J. P. Taylor wrote: 'Now I come to think of it, if I were asked if I had ever known a good man, I should reply: "Yes, Tom Driberg was a good man."'[34]

In his anti-panegyric Gerard Irvine quoted this last judgment, with the comment that 'Mr Taylor is surely right.' But he swiftly repeated that of course Tom was not a saint. He lacked the integration of mind and heart that the Gospel calls the 'single eye', which is the criterion of sanctity. There was a discrepancy between his elitist social attitudes and his political beliefs. There was, too, that divorce within the personality, not uncommon among religious people, between certain areas of conduct and his professed faith. 'With him this divorce was so marked that sometimes people were deceived into thinking that his religion was nothing more than the indulgence of an ecclesiastical hobby. To think this would be a mistake. Tom had a genuine and deep religion.' This is a claim that some have found it hard to believe. Surely, they say, his religion must have been nothing more than an affectation? How could a promiscuous homosexual be a sincere Christian?

Affectations, however, are seldom maintained so unwaveringly for so long, from early schooldays until death. Besides, Tom belonged to a well-established tradition. There had been a recognisable male homosexual subculture in the Anglo-Catholic movement since the late nineteenth century. A Wesleyan writer in the 1890s described the Tractarians (who founded Lancing) as 'characteristically feminine',[35] and in *Brideshead Revisited* young Charles Ryder is warned at Oxford (in what may even have been a deliberate dig by Waugh at Tom): 'Beware of the Anglo-Catholics – they're all sodomites with unpleasant accents.' A recent academic paper on the subject by David Hilliard suggested that for homosexual men Anglo-Catholicism 'provided a set of institutions and religious practices through which they could express their sense of difference in an oblique and symbolic way.'[36] Tom's sense of difference was compounded by his estrangement from the politics of his class. Here, too, the Church gave him succour. As Gerard Irvine pointed out in his anti-panegyric, Tom's political vision was of the Social Gospel propounded in the Magnificat: 'He hath put down the mighty from their seat, and hath exalted the humble and meek. / He hath filled the hungry with good things, and the rich he hath sent empty away.'

After reciting the Virgin Mary's inspiring message, which echoed around the walls of the Bourne Street church that bore her name, Irvine concluded with a blessing of his own:

In this Mass we commend him through the prayers of the authoress of the Magnificat to a judgment at once more searching and compassionate than any we can make. Exasperating and lovable, kind and unreliable, sometimes seeming almost satanic, at others nearly a saint, he was at once greedy for inferior satisfactions, and hungered and thirsted after righteousness. We cannot doubt but that he will be, and progressively more and more, filled with the joy which, despite the fun he gave and received, was something elusive to him in his life.

So, Thomas Edward Neil Driberg, Lord Bradwell – if you are still Lord Bradwell, for neither the Godhead nor the College of Arms has told us if life peerages are valid for the next life as well as this one – we bid you farewell, in sure and certain hope of resurrection.

SOURCES

Introduction

1. *Colonnade* by Tom Driberg (The Pilot Press, London, 1949), p. 8.
2. Reviewing *Ruling Passions* in *The Times*, 23 June 1977.
3. The previous working title had been *Not Waving But Drowning*.
4. Letter from John Freeman to the author, 26 October 1987.
5. *Summer Lightning* by P. G. Wodehouse (Herbert Jenkins, London, 1929).
6. *Financial Times*, 1 July 1977.
7. *Inside Story* by Chapman Pincher (Sidgwick & Jackson, London, 1978; revised paperback edition, 1979), p. 27 of 1979 edition.
8. Conversation between Pincher and the author, 1985.
9. *Daily Telegraph*, 26 March 1981.
10. *ibid.* See also *The Times* Diary, 26 March 1981.
11. *The Swimming-Pool Library* by Alan Hollinghurst (Chatto & Windus, London, 1988), p. 224.
12. Letter to the author, 21 April 1988.

Chapter 1: A Boy's Own Story

1. *High Windows* by Philip Larkin (Faber & Faber, London, 1974), p. 30.
2. *Ruling Passions*, p. 7.
3. *ibid.*, p. 9.
4. Letter from Polly Binder to the author, August 1988.
5. *Sunday Telegraph*, 16 December 1962.
6. Untransmitted interview for pilot programme of BBC series of interviews, provisionally titled *Who's Who*, recorded on Saturday 26 April 1952.
7. *Ruling Passions*, pp. 27–8.
8. *King*, December 1966, p. 48.
9. Rice is the name Tom gave him in *Ruling Passions*. In another account of this teacher, printed in the *New Statesman* in 1960, Tom called him Graves. Since The Grange has disappeared, and its records with it, there is no simple way of checking which is correct. But it is possible that he used a false name in the *New Statesman*

piece in case Rice was still alive. The choice of pseudonym may well have been a joke at the expense of Robert Graves, who had a ridiculous but long-standing grudge against Tom.

10. *New Statesman*, 22 October 1960, p. 602.

11. *Ruling Passions*, p. 12.

12. *The Grange Magazine*, December 1914, p. 12.

13. *New Statesman, op. cit.*

14. *A Fragment of Friendship. A Memory of Evelyn Waugh When Young* by Dudley Carew (Everest Books, London, 1974), p. 38.

15. *A Little Learning* by Evelyn Waugh (Chapman & Hall, London, 1964; reissued by Methuen, London, 1983), p. 106 in Methuen edition.

16. *ibid.*, pp. 102–3.

17. *The Diaries of Evelyn Waugh*, edited by Michael Davie (Weidenfeld & Nicolson, London, 1976), p. 27.

18. *Ruling Passions*, p. 52.

19. These were for short sight. By the time he went up to Oxford he had dispensed with them.

20. *A Little Learning*, p. 128.

21. From Fulford's essay 'At Lancing', in *Evelyn Waugh and His World*, edited by David Pryce-Jones (Weidenfeld & Nicolson, London, 1973), p. 19.

22. *Lancing College Magazine*, November 1919.

23. *Ruling Passions*, p. 4.

24. *The Letters of Evelyn Waugh*, edited by Mark Amory (Weidenfeld & Nicolson, London, 1980), p. 343.

25. *Ruling Passions*, p. 49.

26. *The Diaries of Evelyn Waugh*, p. 20.

27. *New Statesman*, 3 October 1975, p. 410.

28. *A Fragment of Friendship*, p. 20.

29. *A Little Learning*, pp. 143–4.

30. *Ruling Passions*, p. 49. See also *Evelyn Waugh: A Biography* by Christopher Sykes (Collins, London, 1975; revised edition published by Penguin, Harmondsworth, 1977), p. 57 of Penguin edition.

31. *Ruling Passions*, p. 55.

32 Conversation between TD and John Betjeman, *King*, December 1966, p. 48.

33. *Ruling Passions*, p. 50.

34. *ibid.*

35. *ibid.*, p. 47.

36. *ibid.*, p. 51.

37. Letter from Henry Bowlby to the Dean of Christ Church, 5 April 1924.

Chapter 2: Oxford Red

1. Constable, London, 1977.

2. Conversation between TD and John Betjeman, *King*, December 1966, pp. 46–9.

3. *T. S. Eliot* by Peter Ackroyd (Hamish Hamilton, London, 1984; Abacus, London, 1985), p. 128 of Abacus edition.

4. *Sunday Times*, 10 January 1965.

5. *Ruling Passions*, p. 58.

6. *ibid.*, p. 79.

7. *Harper's* magazine, June 1973.

8. *English History 1914–1945* (Oxford University Press, Oxford, 1965), p. 260.

9. 'Still, That Is What Tom Liked' by A. J. P. Taylor, *New Statesman*, 24 June 1977, p. 857.

10. *A Personal History* by A. J. P. Taylor (Hamish Hamilton, London, 1983), p. 68.

11. 'Class War: 1926' by A. J. P. Taylor, *New Statesman*, 30 April 1976, p. 572.

12. *Ruling Passions*, p. 71.

13. *Young Betjeman* by Bevis Hillier (John Murray, London, 1988), p. 154.

14. *Sunday Worker*, 3 April 1927.

15. I am grateful to June Wells, the Christ Church archivist, for tracing this letter for me.

16. 'The Soul of Indiscretion', *Sunday Times* Magazine, 25 August 1974, pp. 8–18. In the same interview, Tom exaggerated his success slightly, boasting to Russell Miller that 'when I ran for the presidency of the Union I got a third of the votes.'

17. *George: An Early Autobiography* by Emlyn Williams (Hamish Hamilton, London, 1961; new edition Penguin, Harmondsworth, 1988), p. 400 of Penguin edition.

18. *Cherwell*, 28 May 1927.

19. *Summoned by Bells* by John Betjeman (John Murray, London, 1960), p. 106.

20. *Isis*, 1 June 1927.

21. Michael Dugdale was a raffish aesthete from Balliol whose tastes – modernist and homosexual – were naturally in sympathy with Tom anyway.

22. Quoted in *Ruling Passions*, p. 69.

23. *Sunday Times*, 29 May 1927.

24. *The Magic of Aleister Crowley* by John Symonds (Frederick Muller, London), p. 41.

25. *Modern Printed Books and Manuscripts which will be sold at auction by Christie, Manson & Woods, Wednesday 4 April 1973*, p. 70. Jeremy Rex-Parkes, the archivist at Christie's, kindly provided me with a copy of this catalogue.

26. *The Crest on the Silver* by Geoffrey Grigson (The Cresset Press, London, 1950), pp. 114–15.

27. *Sunday Times* Magazine, 25 August 1974, p. 13.

Chapter 3: Tarts and Debs

1. *Ruling Passions*, p. 87.

2. *ibid.*, p. 88.

3. *ibid.*, p. 91.

4. 'Edith Sitwell At Home. A Partial Recall – By Tom Driberg', *Encounter*, May 1966, pp. 51–5.

5. *The Times*, 10 December 1964.

6. In his *Encounter* article of May 1966 Tom wrote: 'Eventually her brother Osbert persuaded the managing editor of the *Daily Express*, Beverley Baxter, to see me – which he did after a good deal of the preliminary stalling inevitable (as I now realise) in such cases.' But in *Ruling Passions* (p. 94), ten years later, he contradicted his previous account: 'I had to telephone Baxter's secretary several times before an interview was fixed, and then it was not with him but with the Features Editor, Reginald Pound . . .' This tallied with the version he gave to Russell Miller of the *Sunday Times* Magazine in 1974: 'I had to keep ringing the *Express* – Baxter naturally didn't particularly want to see me – and eventually I got an interview with a very nice man called Reginald Pound, who was then the features editor.'

7. Quoted in *Beaverbook* by A. J. P. Taylor (Hamish Hamilton, London, 1972), p. 264.

8. *Ruling Passions*, p. 94.

9. Quoted in *Frank Buchman: A Life* by Garth Lean (Constable, London, 1985), p. 136.

10. *The Mystery of Moral Re-Armament* by Tom Driberg (Secker & Warburg, London, 1964), p. 61.

11. *The Open Secret of MRA: An Examination of Mr Driberg's 'Critical Examination' of Moral Re-Armament* by J. P. Thornton-Duesbery (Blandford Press, London, 1964), pp. 13–14.

12. *The Mystery of Moral Re-Armament*, p. 16.

13. *Ruling Passions*, p. 95.

14. *Brian Howard: Portrait of a Failure* edited by Marie-Jaqueline Lancaster (Anthony Blond Ltd, London, 1968), p. 229.

15. *ibid.*, p. 230.

16. *Daily Express*, 18 October 1930.

17. *Daily Express*, 16 October 1930.

18. *Daily Express*, 12 July 1928.

19. *Daily Express*, 8 October 1930.

20. *Evelyn Waugh: A Biography*, p. 128 of Penguin edition.

21. *ibid.*, p. 157 of Penguin edition.

22. *Daily Express*, 1 October 1930.

23. *Daily Express*, 11 September 1932.

24. *The Letters of Evelyn Waugh*, p. 108.

25. *ibid.*, p. 112.

26. *Ruling Passions*, p. 102.

27. *Vile Bodies* by Evelyn Waugh (Chapman & Hall, London, 1930).

28. *Ruling Passions*, p. 102.

29. *Daily Express*, 7 October 1930.

30. *The Diaries of Sir Robert Bruce Lockhart: Volume One, 1915–1938*, edited by Kenneth Young (Macmillan, London, 1973), p. 214.

31. *Daily Express*, 12 May 1933.

Chapter 4: Darling Bill Hickey

1. *Sunday Times* Magazine, 25 August 1974, p. 15.
2. *Daily Express*, 25 August 1937.
3. *Colonnade* by Tom Driberg (The Pilot Press, London, 1949), p. 10.
4. *Colonnade*, p. 11.
5. *Daily Express*, 11 August 1937:

> 'The thing to do,' said Canon Sehoza, 'is to lie flat on your back with your feet together, arms to your sides, head well down.
>
> 'The python will then try to push its head under you, experimenting at every possible point.
>
> 'Keep calm: one wriggle and he will get under you, wrap his coils round you, crush you to death. If you remain plastered to the ground, he has no power in his head alone to raise you.
>
> 'After a time the python will get tired of this, and will probably decide to swallow you whole without the usual preliminaries. He will very likely begin with one of your feet. Keep calm . . .
>
> 'You must let him swallow your foot. It is quite painless and will take a long time.
>
> 'If you lose your head and struggle, he will quickly whip his coils around you. If you keep calm and still he will go on swallowing.
>
> 'Wait patiently till he has swallowed up to about your knee. Then, carefully, take out your knife and insert it into the distended side of his mouth. Then with a quick rip slit him up.'

6. *ibid.*, 21 July 1937.
7. *ibid.*, 18 November 1937.
8. *ibid.*, 5 May 1938.
9. *ibid.*, 29 March 1939.
10. *ibid.*, 30 March 1939.
11. Letter from TD to Maurice Webb, Minister of Food, 8 May 1950. Tom himself might have made a rather good Minister of Food. As a backbencher in the years of rationing he certainly kept the department on its toes, pestering it with queries great and small. In January 1948, for instance, he wrote to the Ministry to inquire whether spaghetti could be served at a meal if there were also *hors d'oeuvre* and a main course. 'In our opinion,' Edith Summerskill replied with due solemnity, 'this combination of dishes in one meal would not be contrary to the law. The only qualification I must make is that if the *hors d'oeuvre* contained more than 25 per cent of meat or of certain fish specified in the Meals in Establishments Order (such as salmon or processed herring), it would become a main dish and no other main dish could be served at the same meal.'
12. Quoted in *A. J. A. Symons: His Life and Speculations* by Julian Symons (Eyre & Spottiswoode, London, 1950; reissued, with a new afterword, as an Oxford University Press paperback, 1986), p. 143 of OUP edition.
13. *ibid.*, p. 206.

14. *Ruling Passions*, pp. 195 and 81; see also p. 70 of *The Best of Both Worlds: A Personal Diary* by Tom Driberg (Phoenix House, London, 1953).

15. *A. J. A. Symons: His Life and Speculations*, p. 174.

16. *Evening Standard*, 19 May 1938.

17. *Forget Me Not* by Margaret, Duchess of Argyll (W. H. Allen, London, 1975), p. 49.

18. *Headlines All My Life* by Arthur Christiansen (Heinemann, London, 1961), p. 137.

19. Letter from John Freeman to the author, 26 October 1987.

20. John Rayner, interview with the author, 1988.

21. *Beaverbrook: A Study in Power and Frustration* by Tom Driberg (Weidenfeld & Nicolson, London, 1956), p. 306.

22. *Ruling Passions*, p. 132.

23. *The Diaries of Sir Robert Bruce Lockhart: Volume Two, 1939–1965*, edited by Kenneth Young (Macmillan, London, 1980), p. 245.

24. *ibid.*, pp. 462–3.

25. *Daily Express*, 4 November 1937.

Chapter 5: No War This Crisis

1. *Collected Shorter Poems of W. H. Auden* (Faber & Faber, London, 1976). When Tom issued some of his *Express* and *Reynolds News* columns between hard covers (*Colonnade, op. cit.*), he titled the Thirties chapter 'That Valley Is Fatal'.

2. *Daily Express*, 5 October 1937.

3. *Trail Sinister* by Sefton Delmer (Secker & Warburg, London, 1961), p. 284.

4. *Daily Express*, 6 October 1937.

5. See TD's article on Spain in *Left* (newspaper of Labour Party Young Socialists), October 1972.

6. *Daily Express*, 6 October 1937.

7. *ibid.*, 8 October 1937.

8. *Colonnade*, p. 10.

9. *Headlines All My Life*, p. 143.

10. *Daily Express*, 17 March 1939.

11. *ibid.*, 10 July 1939.

12. *ibid.*, 16 January 1939.

13. *ibid.*, 24 August 1938.

14. *The Origins of the Second World War* by A. J. P. Taylor (Hamish Hamilton, London, 1961; Penguin, Harmondsworth, 1964), p. 210 of Penguin edition.

15. *Daily Express*, 25 August 1938.

16. *ibid.*, 27 August 1938.

17. *ibid.*, 22 April 1939.

18. *ibid.*, 23 May 1938.

19. *ibid.*, 30 September 1938.

20. *ibid.*, 1 October 1938.

21. *ibid.*, 18 October 1938.

22. *Colonnade*, p. 106.

23. W. H. Auden celebrated by sending Tom from Brussels an *Ode to the New Year (1939)* in which many of their mutual friends – Brian Howard, Stephen Spender, William Coldstream – were gently teased. It ended with this unsettling stanza:

> Now before the party is over,
> I must mention the haters of Man,
> The passport officials at Dover,
> The military chiefs in Japan;
> To those who sold us at München,
> To those who betrayed us in Spain,
> And to all the dictators wir wünschen
> The paralysis of the Insane;
> To Fascists, Policemen, and Women,
> Long nights on the glaciers of fear,
> And a lake of brimstone to swim in;
> And a BLOODY NASTY NEW YEAR.

24. *Ruling Passions*, p. 116.

25. *Daily Express*, 4 February 1939.

26. *ibid.*, 6 February 1939.

27. *ibid.*, 31 March 1939.

28. *ibid.*, 17 February 1939.

29. *Roman Fountain* by Hugh Walpole (Macmillan, London, 1940), pp. 286, 288–9.

30. *Daily Express*, 13 March 1939.

31. *ibid.*, 17 May 1939.

32. *ibid.*, 5 May 1939.

Chapter 6: Famous Last Weekends

1. *The Best of Both Worlds: A Personal Diary* by Tom Driberg (Phoenix House Ltd, London, 1953), p. 74.

2. *ibid.*, p. 76.

3. 'A House For Posterity' by Tom Driberg, *Ideal Home*, April 1966.

4. *Ruling Passions*, p. 41.

5. *ibid.*, p. 29.

6. *The Times*, 6 February 1946.

7. *Ruling Passions*, p. 31.

8. *The Best of Both Worlds*, p. 106.

9. *New Statesman & Nation*, 16 February 1946.

10. *Ruling Passions*, p. 34.

11. Major Humphrey Butler, the man in question, was actually equerry to the Duke of Kent, the Prince of Wales's brother. He had met Buchman the previous

Christmas, when the Prince and the Duke travelled to South America on the same ship as Buchman.

12. Manuscript belonging to Alan Thornhill, quoted in *Frank Buchman: A Life* by Garth Lean (Constable, London, 1985), p. 149.

13. Quoted in *Frank Buchman: A Life*, p. 150.

14. Quoted in *Ruling Passions*, p. 36.

15. *Ideal Home*, op. cit.

16. Quoted in *The Lamberts: George, Constant and Kit* by Andrew Motion (Chatto & Windus, London, 1986; Hogarth Press, London, 1987), p. 245 of Hogarth Press edition.

17. Letter from Julian Symons to the author, 24 October 1987. Julian Symons also tells the story in *A. J. A. Symons: His Life and Speculations* (Eyre & Spottiswoode, 1950), in which Tom is identified merely as 'X', and 'a well-known writer on a daily newspaper'.

18. *Ideal Home*, op. cit.

19. In the first draft there is an extra line after 'The stroking of muscles . . . of passion', which runs: 'Want a wash? How you fixed? Flat? A few bob, no matter which way.' This is omitted from his fair copy of the manuscript (dated 14/4/42).

20. Letter to TD from Wilfred Beard, December 1953.

21. *The Collected Essays, Journalism and Letters of George Orwell. Volume II – My Country Right or Left 1940–1943* (Secker & Warburg, London, 1968; Penguin, Harmondsworth, 1970), pp. 99 and 107 of Penguin edition.

22. Hannen Swaffer of the *Daily Herald* and William Connor ('Cassandra') of the *Daily Mirror*. Both were noisy, combative curmudgeons. Connor wrote of his first meeting with Swaffer: 'Being fairly handy in the verbal business myself, I thought I could get a word in edgeways. It was like trying to hammer butter into marble. So I said to him, "Shut up, you old goat, and listen to me!" The hurricane of words roared louder and faster, and my thin piping was swept away in the gale.' In 1974 Tom wrote Swaffer's biography.

23. E. J. Robertson, general manager of Express Newspapers.

24. *Daily Express*, 10 January 1941.

25. *ibid.*, 9 April 1941.

26. *ibid.*, 15 April 1941.

27. *ibid.*, 22 April 1941.

28. *ibid.*, 17 March 1941.

29. *ibid.*, 18 March 1941.

30. *ibid.*, 18 April 1941.

31. *ibid.*, 13 October 1941.

32. *ibid.*, 1 November 1941.

33. *Ruling Passions*, p. 168.

34. *Daily Express*, 9 December 1941.

35. *ibid.*, 15 June 1942. (Tom had, of course, been back in Britain for some time by then; he was prompted to write about Parker by the release of *Saboteur* in Britain.)

36. *ibid.*, 8 January 1942.
37. *Ruling Passions*, p. 174.

Chapter 7: Honourable Members

1. He introduced this swipe at Kensington quite gratuitously in his Hickey column on 20 October 1937.
2. *Ruling Passions*, p. 150.
3. *MI5: British Security Service Operations 1909–1945* by Nigel West (Bodley Head, London, 1981; Triad/Panther, London, 1983), p. 427 of Triad/Panther edition.
4. *Their Trade is Treachery* by Chapman Pincher (Sidgwick & Jackson, London, 1981; revised paperback edition, 1982), p. 116 of 1982 edition.
5. *The Man Who Was M: The Life of Maxwell Knight* by Anthony Masters (Basil Blackwell, Oxford, 1984; Grafton, London, 1986), p. 213 of Grafton edition.
6. *Mask of Treachery* by John Costello (Collins, London, 1988), p. 413.
7. Letter from TD to A. J. P. Taylor, 13 November 1970.
8. *The Man Who Was M*, p. 226.
9. *The Time Has Come . . .: The Memoirs of Dennis Wheatley. Drink and Ink, 1919–1977* (Hutchinson, London, 1979), pp. 131–2.
10. *The Man Who Was M*, p. 90.
11. *The Time Has Come . . .*, p. 120.
12. *One Girl's War: Personal Exploits in MI5's Most Secret Station* by Joan Miller (Brandon Book Publishers, Dingle, County Kerry, 1986), pp. 66–7. Absurdly, the British government prevented this charmingly innocent book of wartime memoirs from being published in the United Kingdom.
13. *ibid.*, p. 93.
14. *ibid.*, pp. 111–12.
15. Interview with Barrie Penrose of the *Sunday Times*, quoted in *Conspiracy of Silence: The Secret Life of Anthony Blunt* by Barrie Penrose and Simon Freeman (Grafton Books, London, 1986; revised edition, Grafton Books, 1987), p. 285.
16. *The Man Who Was M*, p. 235.
17. *Their Trade is Treachery*, p. 245.
18. 'The Judas Syndrome' by Leo Abse, *Spectator*, 20 March 1982.
19. From the 'Anti-panegyric' preached by Irvine at Tom's requiem, 8 December 1976, and an interview with Irvine by the author, 1988.
20. Interview with Barrie Penrose and Simon Freeman, quoted in *Conspiracy of Silence*, p. 333. It should be said that not everyone accepts Harbinson as a reliable witness. Jack Hewit, who was a lover of both Blunt and Burgess, told me in 1988 that Blunt seldom went cottaging.
21. *Daily Express*, 1 May 1942.
22. *Birmingham Gazette*, 8 June 1942.
23. *Daily Express*, 8 June 1942.
24. *Essex Chronicle*, 19 June 1942.
25. *Essex Weekly News*, 5 June 1942. Also *Essex Chronicle* of same date.

26. *Barking Advertiser*, 20 June 1942.

27. Letter from Sir Richard Acland to the author, October 1987.

28. *Ruling Passions*, p. 183.

29. *Essex Weekly News*, 19 June 1942. Also *Essex Chronicle* of same date.

30. *The Second World War. Volume IV: The Hinge of Fate* by Winston S. Churchill (Cassell & Co, London, 1951), p. 350.

31. *The Diaries of Evelyn Waugh*, p. 523.

32. *Daily Express*, 27 June 1942.

33. ibid., 1 July 1942.

34. *'Swaff': The Life and Times of Hannen Swaffer* by Tom Driberg (Macdonald & Jane's, London, 1974), p. 214.

35. Quoted in *The Second World War. Volume IV: The Hinge of Fate*, p. 354.

36. *Hansard*, 7 July 1942, cols. 687–91.

37. ibid., 4 August 1942, cols. 833–4.

38. ibid., 29 September 1942, col. 670.

39. ibid., 11 September 1942, cols. 628–30.

40. ibid., 10 November 1942, cols. 2246–7.

41. ibid., 20 April 1943, cols. 1646–7.

42. ibid., 28 July 1942, cols. 403–4.

43. *Daily Express*, 6 July 1942.

44. Dr David Cargill, interview with the author, 1989.

45. *The Best of Both Worlds*, pp. 188–9.

46. Tom Wintringham is a forgotten figure today. This is a shame: until his early death in 1949, his was one of the most original and effective brains on the British Left. A founder member of the Communist Party in 1920, a founder of the *Morning Star*, a founder of the International Brigade – he was a great one for starting things. He also made things work. In a pamphlet called *How to Reform the Army* he applied the lessons he had learnt while fighting in Spain to Britain's struggle against Hitler. His message, which he repeated continually in columns in *Picture Post* and the *Daily Mirror*, and in several Penguin Specials, was that a truly democratic resistance was required, for which the most promising vehicle was the Home Guard. This may sound faintly ridiculous to anyone who knows the Home Guard only through *Dad's Army*, but Wintringham detected parallels between these 'local defence volunteers' and the republican army in Spain. Edward Hulton, the proprietor of *Picture Post*, was so impressed by the argument that he provided the money and premises for Wintringham to start an unofficial Home Guard Training School at Osterley Park, staffed mainly by fellow veterans of the International Brigade. Having failed to close the place down, the War Office was eventually forced to take it over, with Wintringham still in charge.

Tom had met him through the CP in the 1920s. Too restless and anarchic a character to tolerate Moscow-line orthodoxy indefinitely, Wintringham resigned from the Party in 1937; but their friendship survived, with Tom regarding him 'as a kind of *guru*'. The populist ideas promoted by Wintringham in the early years of the war were taken up, in necessarily more coded and moderate language, in the William Hickey column.

The only recent attempt to rescue Wintringham from oblivion, as far as I know, was David Fernbach's brilliant article in the *New Statesman* of 24 October 1980, to which I am indebted for much of the above information.

47. *Ruling Passions*, p. 144.
48. *Thin Ice* by Compton Mackenzie (Chatto & Windus, London, 1956), p. 197.
49. *Ruling Passions*, p. 187.
50. *Sunday Times*, 26 June 1977.
51. Letter from John Freeman to the author, October 1987.
52. *Tony Crosland* by Susan Crosland (Jonathan Cape, London, 1982), pp. 53–4.
53. *Headlines All My Life*, p. 250.
54. *Beaverbrook* by A. J. P. Taylor (Hamish Hamilton, London, 1972), p. 550.
55. *Spectator*, 9 July 1943.
56. Letter from W. R. Richardson to TD, 6 October 1943.
57. *The Leader*, 30 October 1943.
58. *Daily Mirror*, 23 October 1943.

Chapter 8: Distant Trousers

1. *Reynolds News*, 27 August 1944.
2. *ibid.*, 10 September 1944.
3. *ibid.*, 17 September 1944.
4. *ibid.*, 10 September 1944.
5. *ibid.*, 17 October 1943.
6. *ibid.*, 24 September 1944.
7. *Ruling Passions*, pp. 209–10.
8. Quoted in *Winston S. Churchill. Volume VII: Road to Victory 1941–1945* by Martin Gilbert (Heinemann, London, 1986), p. 1305.
9. *Buchenwald Camp: The Report of a Parliamentary Delegation* (HMSO, London, 1945, Cmd. 6626).
10. *Reynolds News*, 29 April 1945.
11. Interview with the author, January 1988.
12. *Reynolds News*, 17 June 1945.
13. *Swaff: The Life and Times of Hannen Swaffer*, pp. 222–3.
14. Interview with the author, April 1988.
15. Letter to TD from Mountbatten, 14 August 1946.
16. Letter to TD from Mountbatten, 28 July 1947.
17. Letter to Mountbatten from TD, 11 May 1948.
18. Letter to TD from Mountbatten, 22 October 1945.
19. *The War Against Japan. Volume V: The Surrender of Japan* by Major-General S. Woodburn Kirby CB CMG CIE OBE MC (HMSO, London, 1969), p. 254.
20. *Ruling Passions*, p. 215.
21. *The Best of Both Worlds: A Personal Diary*, pp. 66–7.
22. *Reynolds News*, 30 September 1945.
23. *New Statesman*, 11 April 1975.
24. Letter to TD from Mountbatten, 4 October 1945.

25. Letter to Mountbatten from TD, 11 May 1948.
26. *Ruling Passions*, p. 38.
27. *Ideal Home*, April 1966.
28. *Reynolds News*, 10 February 1946.
29. *Ruling Passions*, p. 32.
30. Dr David Cargill, interview with the author, March 1989.
31. *Ruling Passions*, p. 40.
32. *Frank Buchman: A Life* by Garth Lean (Constable, London, 1985), p. 151.
33. *The Times*, 27 July 1946.
34. *Hansard*, 5 July 1946, cols. 2562–82.
35. *The Times*, 3 August 1946.
36. Letter from John Freeman to the author, October 1987.
37. Interview with the author, April 1988.
38. Letter to Mr L. A. Butcher of Braintree, 21 December 1950.
39. From an untransmitted interview with the BBC, 26 April 1952.
40. *Reynolds News*, 10 September 1950.
41. Untransmitted BBC interview, 26 April 1952.
42. Interview with TD by Stephen Black for *Personal Call*, transmitted in the BBC's 'London Calling Asia' programme, 14 August 1953.
43. Interview with the author, May 1989.
44. *Reynolds News*, 1 October 1950.
45. *The Listener*, 28 December 1950.
46. Interview with the author, June 1989.
47. Interview with the author, June 1989.
48. Untransmitted BBC interview, 26 April 1952.
49. *Reynolds News*, 22 October 1950.
50. Postscript by Michael Foot to *Ruling Passions*, p. 252.
51. *The Political Diary of Hugh Dalton 1918–40, 1945–60*, edited by Ben Pimlott (Jonathan Cape with the London School of Economics and Political Science, 1986), p. 492.
52. *ibid.*, p. 493.
53. Letter to TD from Lionel Gough, 16 November 1950.
54. Letter to Lionel Gough from TD, 20 November 1950.
55. *The Political Diary of Hugh Dalton 1918–40, 1945–60*, p. 558.
56. *ibid.*, p. 497.
57. *ibid.*, p. 499.
58. *Sir Harold Wilson: Yorkshire Walter Mitty* by Andrew Roth (Macdonald & Jane's, London, 1977), p. 140.

Chapter 9: Black Wedding

1. Letter to the author from John Freeman, October 1987.
2. Letter to the author from Peter Berger, November 1987.
3. Undated letter to TD from Ena.
4. Letter to TD from Ena, 19 February 1960.

5. *Sunday Express*, 1 July 1951.

6. *The Best of Both Worlds: A Personal Diary*, p. 57.

7. *The Letters of Evelyn Waugh*, p. 352.

8. *Essex Chronicle*, 6 July 1951.

9. *The Best of Both Worlds*, p. 58.

10. *ibid.*, p. 81.

11. *ibid.*, p. 90.

12. Letter to TD from Ena, 3 January 1952.

13. Letter to TD from Ena, 10 January 1952.

14. Letter to TD from Ena, 13 September 1954.

15. Letter to TD from Ena, 19 February 1960.

16. Letter to TD from Ena, 25 November 1961.

17. Letter to TD from Ena, 8 September 1971.

Chapter 10: A Mud Bath with Beaverbrook

1. *Hansard*, 29 October 1946, cols. 495–504.

2. *The Best of Both Worlds* by Tom Driberg (Phoenix House, London, 1953).

3. *The Backbench Diaries of Richard Crossman* edited by Janet Morgan (Hamish Hamilton and Jonathan Cape, London, 1981), p. 222.

4. *Reynolds News*, 26 April 1953.

5. *Tribune*, 8 May 1953.

6. *Truth*, 8 May 1953.

7. He is by no means the only biographer to have experienced this problem.

8. *Recorder*, 23 March 1954.

9. He ascended to the Upper House as Lord Colyton in 1955. A few years later he was introduced to the journalist Paul Johnson at a party. 'Colyton?' Johnson frowned, trying to place the face. 'Oh – didn't you used to be Never-Say-Never Hopkinson?' Colyton winced. 'I wish people wouldn't always remember me for that one remark,' he said sadly. 'My dear chap!' Johnson roared. 'If it wasn't for that remark no one would remember you at all!'

10. *Reynolds News*, 29 August 1954.

11. *Daily Express*, 26 August 1954.

12. *G – For God Almighty: A Personal Memoir of Lord Beaverbrook* by David Farrer (Weidenfeld & Nicolson, London, 1969), p. 168.

13. *Daily Telegraph*, 22 February 1955.

14. Letter from TD to A. J. P. Taylor, 17 May 1971.

15. *Beaverbrook: A Study in Power and Frustration* by Tom Driberg (Weidenfeld & Nicolson, London, 1956), p. 290.

16. A. J. P. Taylor has an alternative explanation for Beaverbrook's decision, attributing it to weariness rather than mischief: 'In the end Beaverbrook got bored with the controversy as he often did and allowed the book to appear' (*Beaverbrook* by A. J. P. Taylor, Hamish Hamilton, London, 1972, p. 618).

17. *Headlines All My Life* by Arthur Christiansen (William Heinemann, London, 1961), p. 253.

18. *ibid.*
19. Letter to A. J. P. Taylor, 17 May 1971.
20. *The Letters of Evelyn Waugh*, p. 467.
21. *Observer*, 26 February 1956.
22. *Sunday Dispatch*, 26 February 1956.
23. *World's Press News*, 24 February 1956.
24. *'Swaff': The Life and Times of Hannen Swaffer* by Tom Driberg (Macdonald & Jane's, London, 1974).
25. *A Little Nut-Brown Man: My Three Years With Lord Beaverbrook* by C. M. Vines (Leslie Frewin, London, 1968), p. 22.

Chapter 11: Moscow Gold

1. Letter to F. W. Nichols from TD, 5 June 1955.
2. Letter to George Barnes from TD, 29 April 1951 (BBC Written Archive).
3. Letter to TD from George Barnes, 1 May 1951 (BBC Written Archive).
4. Letter to Harman Grisewood from TD, 18 April 1955 (BBC Written Archive).
5. *The Best of Both Worlds*, p. 101.
6. Interview with the author, August 1988.
7. *The Theatre Workshop Story* by Howard Goorney (Methuen, London, 1981).
8. *Reynolds News*, 12 January 1947.
9. *Guy Burgess: A Portrait with Background* by Tom Driberg (Weidenfeld & Nicholson, London, 1956), p. 2.
10. *Ruling Passions*, p. 236.
11. *Daily Mail*, 21 September 1956.
12. *ibid.*, 20 October 1956.
13. *ibid.*, 22 October 1956.
14. *Their Trade is Treachery*, p. 243.
15. *The Backbench Diaries of Richard Crossman*, p. 188.
16. House of Commons Order Paper, 2 March 1955, p. 1284.
17. Letter to Clement Attlee from TD, 28 February 1955.
18. *Papers From The Lamb* (Malvern Press Ltd, London, first published May Day 1959, second impression January 1960).
19. *The Times*, 24 April 1958.
20. *ibid.*, 28 April 1958.
21. *The Best of Both Worlds*, p. 189.
22. *The Times*, 1 May 1958.
23. *News Chronicle*, 18 October 1957.
24. *Ruling Passions*, p. 248.
25. Letter to TD from Guy Burgess, 11 June 1958.
26. *Daily Mirror*, 23 June 1977; and interview by Terence Lancaster with the author, June 1989.
27. *Daily Express*, 23 June 1977.
28. *Daily Mail*, 30 September 1958.
29. *Daily Telegraph*, 30 September 1958.

30. Postscript to *Ruling Passions*, p. 253.

31. London *Evening News*, 22 June 1977.

32. *The Backbench Diaries of Richard Crossman*, p. 717.

33. Letter to the author from Gore Vidal, August 1988.

34. Interview with the author, December 1988.

35. *Hugh Gaitskell: A Political Biography* by Philip M. Williams (Jonathan Cape, London, 1979), p. 635.

36. *Hansard*, 23 July 1962, cols. 1192–1202.

37. *The Backbench Diaries of Richard Crossman*, p. 829.

38. Letter to John Freeman from TD, 17 May 1961.

39. Letter to TD from John Freeman, 16 May 1961.

40. Letter to TD from R. Romilly Fedden, 21 January 1953.

41. Letter to R. Romilly Fedden from TD, 24 February 1953.

42. Letter to TD from Ena, 25 November 1961.

43. Letter to TD from Ena, 4 December 1961.

Chapter 12: Street-Fighting Man

1. *Hansard*, 30 October 1959, cols. 608–14.

2. *Sunday Citizen*, 5 April 1964.

3. *The Profession of Violence: The Rise and Fall of the Kray Twins* by John Pearson (Weidenfeld & Nicolson, London, 1972; Panther Books, London, 1973), p. 157 of Panther edition.

4. Letter to Mark Carlisle MP from TD, 13 November 1970.

5. *Our Story* by Reg and Ron Kray with Fred Dinenage (Sidgwick & Jackson, London, 1988), p. 60.

6. *The Times*, 2 August 1964.

7. Susan Crosland's interviews with TD and Lord Boothby, December 1970.

8. *Harold Wilson: A Pictorial Biography* by Michael Foot (Pergamon Press, Oxford, 1964), p. 11.

9. *Back-Bencher* by Ian Mikardo (Weidenfeld & Nicolson, London, 1988), p. 175.

10. Interview with the author, May 1989.

11. *Hansard*, 28 July 1967, cols. 1155–7.

12. Quoted in *The Stones* by Philip Norman (Elm Tree Books, London, 1984), p. 211.

13. TD interviewed by Anthony Scaduto, author of *Mick Jagger* (W. H. Allen, London, 1974). The quotations from the conversation with Jagger are also based on Tom's recollections, as told to Scaduto.

14. *Ecumenical Paperchase*, talk broadcast on Radio 3, 11 August 1968.

15. *Observer*, 26 June 1977.

16. *New Statesman*, 26 July 1968.

17. *Evening Standard*, 15 August 1968.

18. His absence made quite a difference. On the Sunday before conference the NEC agreed to support the government's prices and incomes policy, but only by

the casting vote of that year's chairman, Jennie Lee. 'It was maddening to be stuck here during Blackpool,' Tom wrote to Hugh Cudlipp on 9 October. 'I don't think the political correspondents noted that the government was saved from embarrassment on that first Sunday, not primarily by Jennie's casting vote but by the second detachment of my left retina.'

19. Letter to Allen Ginsberg from TD, 27 September 1968.
20. Letter to TD from Allen Ginsberg, 23 September 1968.
21. Letter to TD from Allen Ginsberg, 7 October 1968.
22. *People*, 12 January 1969.
23. Letter to TD from John Betjeman, 20 December 1968.
24. Letter to Sir Richard Acland from TD, 4 February 1969.
25. Letter to TD from Sir Richard Acland, 5 February 1969.
26. Letter to Sir Richard Acland from TD, 9 February 1969.
27. Letter to TD from Sir Richard Acland, 27 March 1969.
28. Letter to the author from Paul Foot, 22 January 1988.
29. *Brief Lives* by Alan Watkins (Hamish Hamilton, London, 1982), p. 24.
30. *Sunday Times Magazine*, 25 August 1974.
31. *Barking and Dagenham Express*, 7 March 1969.
32. *Ilford Recorder*, 17 November 1960.
33. *ibid.*, 1 December 1960.
34. Letter to TD from Michael Rubinstein, 3 April 1969.
35. Letter to M. E. Roberts from TD, 14 July 1969.
36. Interview with the author, November 1987.
37. Letter to Christopher Hitchens from Rosemary Say, 15 August 1977.
38. Interview with the author, May 1988.
39. Quoted in James Fox's full-page article, 'How Stephen Raymond Took Everyone In' (*Sunday Times*, 4 July 1976), an invaluable account of Raymond's dealings with Tom.
40. *The Frying Pan* by Tony Parker (Hutchinson, London, 1970).
41. Letter to Harold Wilson from TD, 27 February 1970.
42. Letter to TD from William Rees-Mogg, 4 March 1970.

Chapter 13: The First and Last Lord Bradwell

1. *Office Without Power: Diaries 1968–72* by Tony Benn (Hutchinson, London, 1988), p. 296.
2. *Morning Star*, 20 December 1970.
3. Letter to Ena from TD, 27 August 1971.
4. Letter to TD from Ena, 8 September 1971.
5. Letter to Ena from TD, 11 September 1971.
6. *Daily Mail*, 2 November 1971.
7. Interview with Cleo Sylvestre by the author, August 1988.
8. Interview with Donald Rumbelow by the author, May 1989.
9. Interview with Revd William Hurdman by the author, July 1989.
10. Letter to Revd William Hurdman from TD, 6 April 1972.

11. Interview with Michael Duffy by the author, July 1988.

12. *Daily Mirror*, 4 October 1972.

13. London *Evening Standard*, 3 October 1972.

14. Interview with Jo Richardson by the author, December 1988.

15. London *Evening Standard*, 9 August 1973.

16. *ibid.*, 8 February 1974.

17. *New Statesman*, 5 April 1974.

18. The scroll still hangs at Bradwell Lodge: the house's present owner, Mary Martin, is a left-wing journalist from Turkey who feels a certain kinship with Tom and cherishes the few possessions of his that remain at the Lodge. She has also vowed to remove the hideous black-and-gilt bathroom installed by the Manns. She is, in short, a good egg.

19. I am most grateful to Michael Jackson for finding what may be the only surviving copy of this poem for me.

20. *Sunday Express*, 24 November 1974.

21. *ibid.*, 17 August 1975.

22. Letter to Harold Wilson from TD, August 1975.

23. Letter to TD from Harold Wilson, 10 October 1975.

24. *Daily Express*, 18 December 1975.

25. My thanks to Gerard Irvine for reciting these lines to me.

26. *Guardian*, 7 April 1976.

27. 'Tomboys' by Christopher Hitchens (*New Review*, August 1977).

28. Interviewed by Stephen Black on *Personal Call*, broadcast in the BBC's 'London Calling Asia', Friday 14 August 1953.

29. This letter well illustrates why Betjeman needed all the help he could get with punctuation.

30. Letter to Ena from Sir John Betjeman, 14 August 1976.

31. Letter to Ena from Sir John Betjeman, 1 October 1976.

32. Letter to Ena from Revd Gerard Irvine, 21 August 1976.

33. Letter to TD from Jane Russell, 25 November 1949.

34. *New Statesman*, 20 August 1976.

35. I am indebted to the Revd Kenneth Leech for sending me his essay 'Beyond Gin and Lace: Homosexuality and the Anglo-Catholic subculture', which appeared in a Jubilee Group pamphlet on gay Anglicans in 1988.

36. 'UnEnglish and unmanly: Anglo-Catholicism and homosexuality', by David Hilliard, in *Victorian Studies* (Winter 1982, pp. 181–210); quoted by Kenneth Leech in 'Beyond Gin and Lace'.

INDEX

All Pan books are available at your local bookshop or newsagent, or can be ordered direct from the publisher. Indicate the number of copies required and fill in the form below.

Send to: **CS Department, Pan Books Ltd., P.O. Box 40, Basingstoke, Hants.   RG21 2YT.**

or phone: 0256 469551 (Ansaphone), quoting title, author and Credit Card number.

Please enclose a remittance* to the value of the cover price plus: 60p for the first book plus 30p per copy for each additional book ordered to a maximum charge of £2.40 to cover postage and packing.

*Payment may be made in sterling by UK personal cheque, postal order, sterling draft or international money order, made payable to Pan Books Ltd.

Alternatively by Barclaycard/Access:

Card No.

Signature:

Applicable only in the UK and Republic of Ireland.

While every effort is made to keep prices low, it is sometimes necessary to increase prices at short notice. Pan Books reserve the right to show on covers and charge new retail prices which may differ from those advertised in the text or elsewhere.

NAME AND ADDRESS IN BLOCK LETTERS PLEASE:

Name————————————————————————

Address————————————————————————

3/87